North Woods, Great Lakes

An Introduction to the Natural History of Minnesota's Coniferous Forests

Minnesota Master Naturalist

www.minnesotamasternaturalist.org

Acknowledgments

This book is the result of innumerable contributions from dozens of individuals, and we wish to thank them all. Everyone has been exceptionally generous with time, photographs, ideas, and solutions. If there are inaccuracies please let us know. We understand that no matter how careful we have been, we can always improve on our efforts and accuracy. Now, head outside and Explore, Teach, and Conserve!

The Minnesota Master Naturalist Team

Project Manager

Dawn Atwell Flinn

Editors

Rob B. Blair, University of Minnesota Extension
Dawn A. Flinn, Minnesota Department of Natural Resources (DNR)
Amy R. B. Rager, University of Minnesota Extension
Andrea Lorek Strauss, University of Minnesota Extension

Contributing Authors

Marilyn K. Andersen, Minnesota Master Naturalist Volunteer
Rob B. Blair, University of Minnesota Extension
Stephan P. Carlson, University of Minnesota Extension
Laura Duffey, Minnesota DNR
Don Elsenheimer, Minnesota DNR
Dawn A. Flinn, Minnesota DNR
Joan M. Gilmore, Minnesota Master Naturalist Volunteer & Instructor
Danielle M. Hefferan, Wolf Ridge Environmental Learning Center
Sarah L. Keefer, Minnesota Master Naturalist Volunteer & Instructor
Barb W. Liukkonen, Retired, University of Minnesota
Nathan J. Meyer, University of Minnesota Extension
Karen S. Oberhauser, University of Minnesota Extension

Amy R. B. Rager, University of Minnesota Extension
Tommy Rodengen, Minnesota Master Naturalist Volunteer & Instructor
Andrea Lorek Strauss, University of Minnesota Extension
Joe Walewski, Wolf Ridge Environmental Learning Center

Technical Reviewers

Oakley Biesanz, Maplewood Nature Center
Kacie Carlson, Minnesota DNR
Britt Forsberg, University of Minnesota Extension
Katie Fritz, Minnesota DNR
Michelle Haggerty, Texas Parks & Wildlife
Cindy Hagley, University of Minnesota – Sea Grant
Diane Hedin, Minnesota DNR
Jodie Hirsch, Minnesota DNR
Carrie Jennings, Minnesota DNR
Janine Kohn, Minnesota DNR
John Kohlstedt, Wolf Ridge Environmental Learning Center
John Loegering, University of Minnesota Extension
Nadine Meyer, Minnesota DNR
Eli Sagor, University of Minnesota
Pete Smerud, Wolf Ridge Environmental Learning Center
Rubin Stenseng, Minnesota Master Naturalist Volunteer
Larry Weber, Naturalist, Minnesota Master Naturalist Volunteer & Instructor

Species Spotlight Reviewers

Norm Aaseng, Minnesota DNR
Kevin Kenow, U.S. Geological Survey
Craig Prudhomme, Retired, Audubon Center of the North Woods
Heidi Rantala, Minnesota DNR
Al G. Stevens, Minnesota DNR

Scientific Name Researchers

Melanie Countryman, Bridget Doyle, Joan Lund, Minnesota Master Naturalist Volunteers

URL Reviewers

Joseph Alexander, Nicole Anderson, Ulrike Axen, Joan Lund, Jane Stevens, Todd Stevens, Minnesota Master Naturalist Volunteers

Technical Assistance

Lynette Lothert, University of Minnesota Extension
Christian Wood, University of Minnesota Extension

Assistant Editors

Judson Haverkamp, Minnesota Master Naturalist
    Volunteer
Mary Hoff

Designer

Mark Ohm

Cover Photos

Benjamin Olson, Professional Photographer benjamin-olson.com (front cover, birch trees), Dawn A. Flinn (white pine needles), Carrol Henderson, Minnesota DNR Nongame Wildlife Program (loon), Dave Pauly (moose), Deb Rose, Minnesota DNR (mine pit lake), Brett Whaley (lady's-slipper)

Funding Statement

This material is based upon work supported by the National Science Foundation under Grant No. 0540358. Any opinions, findings, and conclusions or recommendations expressed in this material are those of the authors and do not necessarily reflect the views of the National Science Foundation.

Suggested Citation

Blair, R. B., Flinn, D. A., Rager, A. B., & Strauss, A. L. (Eds.). (2017). *North Woods, Great Lakes: An introduction to the natural history of Minnesota's coniferous forests.* Saint Paul, MN: Regents of the University of Minnesota.

Contact Information

Discover more about the Minnesota Master Naturalist Program at www.minnesotamasternaturalist.org or call (888) 241-4532.

Book Availability

This book is available only to those individuals who have taken the North Woods, Great Lakes Minnesota Master Naturalist course. Sign up for a course now at www.minnesotamasternaturalist.org so you can obtain your own copy! If you are from a library, institution, or out-of-state program and are interested in purchasing copies, please contact us at info@ minnesotamasternaturalist.org or call (888) 241-4532.

UNIVERSITY OF MINNESOTA | EXTENSION
Driven to Discover℠

Contents

What Is This All About?

An Introduction to the Minnesota Master Naturalist Program & Minnesota's Biomes

Rob B. Blair and Dawn A. Flinn

Goal

Understand the Minnesota Master Naturalist Program structure and the role of a naturalist.

Objectives

1. Define three characteristics that make a good naturalist.

2. Describe the scope and intent of the Minnesota Master Naturalist Program.

3. Describe ways in which Minnesota Master Naturalist Volunteers can help protect and promote Minnesota's natural environment.

Introduction

So you want to be a Minnesota Master Naturalist Volunteer? Welcome! We're happy you've decided to join this group of "volunteers for nature." Throughout this course, you'll have fun, learn a lot, and gain the expertise you need to provide Minnesotans with increased opportunities to experience and study the natural environment of our great state. When the course is over, you'll be part of what we hope is a long-term partnership with the Minnesota Master Naturalist Program. You'll have frequent opportunities for service projects, advanced training, and networking with fellow Minnesota Master Naturalist Volunteers and staff.

During this 40-hour course, we'll look closely at Minnesota's ecology—focusing on the geology of the land, the organisms and natural communities found throughout the state (particularly in the Coniferous Forest biome), and the ways in which humans and the environment affect each other.

*Definitions of most italicized words throughout the book are found in the glossary.

Being a Naturalist

What is a naturalist? The answer to this question is not as simple as it would seem. The term *naturalist** has multiple meanings. The simplest definition of a naturalist is "one who is a student of natural history."

Figure 1. John James Audubon was one of America's premier naturalists. However, methods of studying nature have changed since the 1800s. Audubon shot birds, then posed them in lifelike situations so he could paint their portraits.

Figure 2. Rachel Carson, a 20th century naturalist and activist, alerted the American public to the hazards of DDT and other pesticides.

This definition brings up images of 19th century adventurer-biologists such as John James Audubon (Figure 1), Charles Darwin, John Muir, and Henry Thoreau, who all had a fascination with the natural world. The image changed during the 20th century when biologists such as Aldo Leopold, Sigurd Olson, and Rachel Carson (Figure 2) became activists promoting conservation of natural resources.

In the 21st century, a naturalist is more likely to be someone like Connie Cox (Figure 3), who works for the Minnesota Department of Natural Resources (DNR) at Itasca State Park and conducts natural, cultural, and recreational programs and activities. By participating in the Minnesota Master Naturalist Program, you will have the opportunity to experiment with all of these roles, along with others you may invent.

Figure 3. DNR naturalist Connie Cox helps young visitors at Itasca State Park understand how to identify birds using an audio device.

As a Minnesota Master Naturalist Volunteer, you will gain opportunities to **explore** the natural world, **teach** others about your passion, and **conserve** our natural resources. Consequently, the official slogan of the Minnesota Master Naturalist Program is "Explore! Teach! Conserve!"

Natural History and Ecology

Now that a definition of a naturalist is crystal clear in your mind, you may be wondering about the term *natural history*. Natural history is the scientific study of the natural world using a variety of disciplines, including botany, zoology, ecology, paleontology, astronomy, and even meteorology. The term traces back to the late 18th and early 19th centuries, when academic study typically fell into three disciplines: natural history, political history, and ecclesiastical history. It is still used today, enshrined in the names of many museums, including the Smithsonian Institution's National Museum of Natural History,

New York City's American Museum of Natural History, and the University of Minnesota's Bell Museum of Natural History (Figure 4).

Another way to think of natural history is the ability to "put things in order" when you wander in the woods or visit your favorite lake. Once you become familiar with a natural area, you have expectations of what you will and won't see. You don't expect to see a loon playing in a puddle on a road, or a red oak in the middle of a bog. You do expect to see a red squirrel chattering from an evergreen and a cardinal perched on a bird feeder. Knowing which organisms can be found where, and why, is the science of ecology. More formally, *ecology* is the study of the distribution and abundance of organisms and their relationship to each other and their environment.

The Minnesota Master Naturalist Program emphasizes the biological facets of natural history, in particular, ecology. By starting with the basics of ecology, we will be able to build the story of why Minnesota, and the North Woods, Great Lakes region in particular, is such a marvelous place. Of course, it would be impossible to provide a comprehensive guide to the natural history of the region in such a small amount of time and space. Rather, our goal is provide snapshots that will start you on a lifetime of learning. We hope you'll find that the information presented here provides a valuable taste of a big topic, whets your appetite to explore more—and provides the resources you need to do so.

Figure 4. This diorama, one of dozens created for the Bell Museum of Natural History in the Twin Cities, portrays Minnesota's coniferous forest. It depicts Cascade River on the North Shore. The background was designed and painted by Minnesota native Francis Lee Jaques.

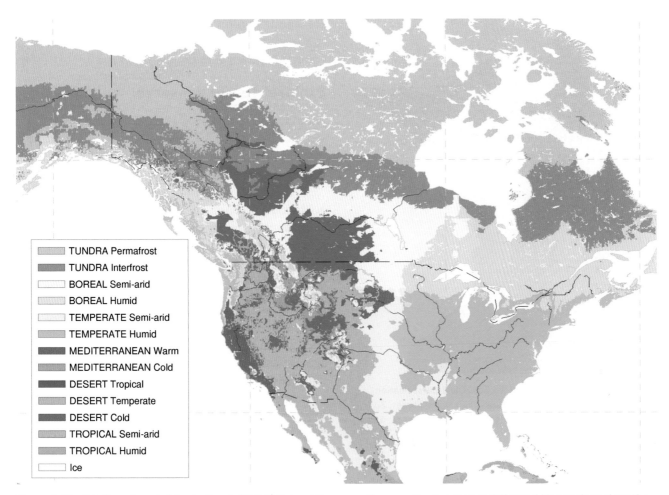

	TUNDRA Permafrost
	TUNDRA Interfrost
	BOREAL Semi-arid
	BOREAL Humid
	TEMPERATE Semi-arid
	TEMPERATE Humid
	MEDITERRANEAN Warm
	MEDITERRANEAN Cold
	DESERT Tropical
	DESERT Temperate
	DESERT Cold
	TROPICAL Semi-arid
	TROPICAL Humid
	Ice

Figure 5. The U.S. Department of Agriculture's (USDA) Natural Resources Conservation Service has delineated biomes throughout the world. This map depicts the delineation for North America.

Minnesota's Biomes

Ever notice how natural areas seem to cluster into categories—forests, grasslands, and so on? Ecologists refer to the various categories as *biomes* (Figure 5). This North Woods, Great Lakes course focuses on one of the four biomes in Minnesota: the large Coniferous Forest biome (also called Boreal or Eastern Broadleaf Forest) that covers the northeastern third of the state. This biome contains large stands of pine and is dotted with thousands of lakes. We've included Lake Superior as a bonus—after all, Minnesota is as much about our water as our land.

Minnesota has three other biomes: the Deciduous Forest biome, running in a band from southeast Minnesota to the northwest; the Tallgrass Aspen Parklands at the top of this band; and the Prairie

Grassland biome, which once covered southwest and western Minnesota. Our Big Woods, Big Rivers course covers the Deciduous Forest and the Tallgrass Aspen Parklands biomes. Our Prairies and Potholes course covers the Prairie Grassland biome and the small lakes, called potholes, that dot the landscape.

This isn't the only way to classify ecological landscapes, however. The U.S. Environmental Protection Agency calls major landscapes *ecoregions*, and World Wildlife Fund uses the term *major habitat types*. The U.S. Forest Service (USFS) and the Minnesota DNR use the term *provinces* for units of land defined by major climate zones and native vegetation. These two agencies also have developed an Ecological Classification System (ECS) for mapping and classifying landscapes (Figure 6).

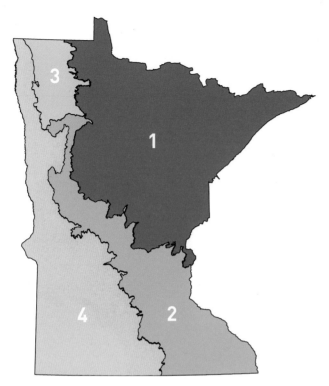

Figure 6. The four provinces of the Ecological Classification System in Minnesota are the 1) Laurentian Mixed Forest, 2) Eastern Broadleaf Forest, 3) Tallgrass Aspen Parklands, and 4) Prairie Parkland.

They use sophisticated mapping programs to help define these units. The system uses associations of biological and environmental factors, including climate, geology, topography, soils, hydrology, and vegetation, to identify, describe, and map progressively smaller areas of land with increasingly uniform ecological features. ECS mapping helps resource managers to identify areas with similar management opportunities or constraints and customize their work for areas as large as North America or as small as a single timber stand.

The Minnesota DNR's ECS classifies Minnesota into four provinces that, not coincidentally, have very similar names to the biomes we introduced earlier: the Laurentian Mixed Forest, Eastern Broadleaf Forest, Tallgrass Aspen Parklands, and Prairie Parkland. These provinces are further divided into sections and subsections. So, for example, a person from Virginia, Minnesota, lives in the relatively small Nashwauk Uplands subsection of the medium-size Northern Superior Uplands section of the large Laurentian Mixed Forest province.

It's unusual for four biomes to converge in one state without mountains, and this is one reason for Minnesota's abundant biological diversity.

Explore! Teach! Conserve!

Each chapter of this book is divided into three sections. The first—the one you just finished reading—provides an overview of the content that typically will be covered in the corresponding Master Naturalist class. It outlines the learning goals and objectives to guide you in both the recommended reading and the activities that will take place during the class. Note that some chapters may be covered in a different order in your course than they are in the book.

The second section, titled Master Naturalist Toolbox, includes recommendations on places to visit in Minnesota so you can experience outdoors what you learned in class (Explore!). It also includes two activities designed to help you share your newfound knowledge with your friends and the public (Teach!). And it lists groups that conduct restoration, stewardship, and management activities in Minnesota, along with information on how you can volunteer (Conserve!). Last, we provide resources for further exploration: a journaling exercise, two to three books, two websites, and two to three organizations or groups you should get to know. This final section is called "Expand!"

This introduction has only condensed versions of these sections. You will find more fully developed Master Naturalist Toolbox sections in later chapters.

In addition you will receive a Linnaeus List, a miniature field guide for your biome. It contains drawings and descriptions of approximately 100 plants, animals, *macroinvertebrates*, and rocks found throughout the biome that will help you recognize and learn about the flora and fauna of the region.

Explore

The "Explore!" section of each chapter highlights locations of great examples of topics covered in the chapter. Each listing includes a brief description of the locale's features along with contact information.

The following places offer great opportunities for learning about various parts of the North Woods, Great Lakes region through interpretive programs. Please check them out online, then head out to discover them in real life!

Superior National Forest

WHAT Managed for multiple use by the USFS, the Superior National Forest is a 695-square-mile property known for its boreal forest ecosystem, numerous clean lakes, and colorful cultural history. The million-acre Boundary Waters Canoe Area Wilderness (BWCAW) lies within its borders. Popular recreational activities include fishing, hunting, camping, canoeing, swimming, hiking, snowmobiling, and skiing.

WHEN Open year-round.

WHERE Head to the northeastern corner of Minnesota.

WHO Superior National Forest, 8901 Grand Ave. Place, Duluth, MN 55808, (218) 626-4300.

FOR MORE INFORMATION www.fs.usda.gov/superior/

Big Bog State Recreation Area – Waskish, Minnesota

WHAT Big Bog State Recreation Area offers an outdoor experience like nothing else. Overlying the ancient Glacial Lake Agassiz, the recreation area is home to a 500-square-mile peat bog, the largest in the contiguous United States. Visitors can get up close to a peatland ecosystem and its unusual and often rare or endangered vegetation by hiking Big Bog's one-mile boardwalk, said to be the longest in the United States. Enjoy a naturalist-led program in summer or winter, or set out on your own to look for moose, black bears, bobcats, great gray owls, snapping turtles, and lots more.

WHEN The visitor center is open Monday–Saturday 9 a.m.–4 p.m.

WHERE Follow State Highway 72 north nine miles from Waskish.

WHO Big Bog State Recreation Area, P.O. Box 428, Waskish, MN 56685, (218) 647-8592, bigbog.statepark@state.mn.us

FOR MORE INFORMATION www.mndnr.gov/state_parks/big_bog/index.html

Gooseberry Falls State Park – Two Harbors, Minnesota

WHAT Visitors come to Gooseberry Falls State Park for a view of its five spectacular waterfalls and end up captivated by the hiking, wildlife watching, and opportunity to spend time on the shore of the world's greatest lake. Wildlife species found here include wolves, pine marten, and an abundance of migratory birds that use the Lake Superior flyway in spring and fall. You can also view the rocky remnants of ancient lava flows along the river and lakeshore. The visitor center offers interpretive displays, a video introduction to the natural history of the area, and a welcoming gateway to the park's 20 miles of hiking trails, 15 miles of paved bike trails, and 12 miles of cross country ski trails.

WHEN The park is open daily 8 a.m.–10 p.m. (as are all state parks). Visitor center hours vary.

WHERE From Two Harbors, follow State Highway 61 northeast 13 miles to the park.

WHO Gooseberry Falls State Park, 3206 Highway 61 East, Two Harbors, MN 55616, (218) 834-3855

FOR MORE INFORMATION www.mndnr.gov/state_parks/gooseberry_falls/index.html

MASTER
NATURALIST
TOOLBOX

Teach

The "Teach" section of each chapter typically includes two lesson plans for activities that will reinforce the content of the chapter. You may experience some of these activities as a student in your Master Naturalist class. You are welcome to use these lessons with other audiences if you find yourself in the role of "natural history interpreter" as a Minnesota Master Naturalist Volunteer. The activities have been chosen for their adaptability to a wide range of ages and settings.

LESSON 1

Keeping Track of Nature: Making Journals

Objective

Participants will create a journal to use in class and to record observations throughout the course.

Audience Type

Teen/Adult

Supplies

☐ Paper cut to 6" x 6" (or other size),
  20 sheets per journal
☐ Two cover sheets per journal cut slightly larger
☐ One rubber band per journal
☐ One stick for binding (approximately 5")
☐ Paper punch
☐ Paper clip

Background

The first European explorers who came to the United States used journals (Figure 7) to help them create maps and report information back to the government officials who sent them on their journeys. In their historic journals, Lewis and Clark described new lands, people, plants, and animals they encountered all along their voyage of discovery.

Journals, logs, diaries—whatever you choose to call them—are a written, drawn, or otherwise illustrated record of your experiences. They can be as simple as a small notebook kept in your pocket to list the birds you see in a particular location, or as elaborate as a collection of color photographs of plants and birds you encounter. How you keep a nature log can vary, too. Some people choose to keep their logs or journals on their computer; some prefer beautiful, leather-covered books; some create homemade journals or calendars; and some make simple notebooks. The form doesn't matter—just use what works for you!

Figure 7. This nature journal uses rings to hold it together so more pages can be added later. You may choose to go more natural and use a twig for the spine and a rubber band to secure the pages.

There are many types of journals. Biologists around the world use Grinnell journals. These are made up of two parts: a daily account of observations in a specific place, and a running record of individual plant or animal species. Phenology journals are seasonal accounts of the plants and animals in a specific location. You can keep this type of journal simply by recording events on a calendar, such as the first robin of spring or the first snowfall. Location journals are used to keep informal records of a specific place such as a park or a backyard. This type of journal can be used to record plant and animal sightings and the impact of humans. Whichever you choose, it's a good idea to include the date, time, location, and weather for each entry. This will help in later years when you reflect on the information you recorded.

Activity

1. Assemble the pages of the journal with a cover page on the top and bottom.
2. Use the punch to create a hole one inch from the top and one inch from the bottom along the left edge of the papers.
3. Thread one loop end of the rubber band through the top hole and attach to the stick.
4. Straighten out a paper clip on one end to use as a hook to go through the bottom hole of the paper. Grab the rubber band with the hook end of the paper clip, and pull through the bottom hole of the paper. Attach the rubber band to the bottom of the stick.
5. Decorate the cover as you wish.
6. Begin your journaling experience!

Note: You can easily disassemble your journal to add more paper as needed. You may wish to make front and back covers or add other decorative features to make your journal special.

OPTION FOR YOUNGER GROUPS To do this activity with younger learners (ages 5–7), first preassemble journals (steps 1–4). Do this activity outside, or go for an outside hike and collect samples of items to write about (take pictures, collect leaves, birch bark, etc.) and bring them indoors. Ask the children what kind of words, drawings, and stories they might want to include in their journals. List their words on a large piece of paper or white board for all to see. Use simple words and drawings, such as rain, ladybug, snow, worm, acorn, and leaf. Provide crayons, pencils, and colored pencils. Avoid using abstract words (for example, use "rain," not "weather," and "squirrels," not "mammals").

Older youth (grades 3–6) can record weather observations, read rain gauges and measure snow depth, and write paragraphs and stories.

Resources

You may want to read the journals of some famous naturalists. Below are four well-known naturalists and their best known works.

Darwin, C. (1839). *The voyage of the Beagle: journal of researches into the natural history and geology of the countries visited during the voyage of H.M.S. Beagle.* New York: Modern Library Classics. Available at www.gutenberg.org/ebooks/3704. This is the log of Darwin's trip to the Galapagos, which planted the seeds for his thoughts on evolution.

Leopold, A. (1949). *A Sand County almanac: and sketches here and there.* London: Oxford University Press. The first part of this book is a literary gem of a nature journal. The second part calls for action by establishing a "Land Ethic."

Lewis, M., and & Clark, W. (1806). *The journals of the Lewis and Clark expedition.* Available at lewisandclarkjournals.unl.edu/index.html. These journals detail the amazing journey of Lewis and Clark as they explored the West.

Fabre, J. H. (1921). *Fabre's book of insects,* retold from Alexander Teixeira de Mattos' translation of Fabre's Souvenirs entomologiques. New York: Dodd, Mead and Co. Available at www.archive.org/details/fabresbookofinse00fabriala. J. Henri Fabre was a French entomologist in the 1800s. His books offer amazing descriptions of insects and the natural world.

LESSON 2

What Is a Naturalist?

Objective

Participants will understand the many definitions of the term naturalist and how the term has changed over time.

Audience Type

Teen/Adult

Supplies

- ☐ 3″ x 5″ card
- ☐ Pen

Background

The term *naturalist* is not easily defined. A recent Google search returned the following definitions:

- an advocate of the doctrine that the world can be understood in scientific terms

- a biologist knowledgeable about natural history (especially botany and zoology)

- a person who studies nature (including plants and animals) and natural history (how plants and animals evolve)

- an expert in natural history

- a person, often a scientist or a writer, who studies and promotes nature

- a specialist who studies and/or teaches about nature

- a scientist who studies plants and animals from the natural world

- a person who studies nature

- a style of art made by artists who, longing for pre-industrial life, sought out healthy, untouched rural subjects. Observing nature firsthand was important.

As you can see, the word evokes different meanings for different groups of people.

The term *naturalist* has shifted from the 19th century term for a field biologist to the professional interpretive naturalist we know today. Interpretation is the bridge that connects the two. The Minnesota Master Naturalist Program defines a naturalist as an individual who studies nature and natural history. This program will give you a basic knowledge about the ecology of Minnesota and the ability to go out and share it with others.

Now that we know what a naturalist is, let's look at why naturalists are needed. Minnesotans are amazingly dedicated to the outdoors and education. In August 2004, Hamline University and the Minnesota Office of Environmental Assistance issued The Second Report Card on Environmental Literacy, which showed that residents of Minnesota value the environment. Ninety-five percent of the women and 87 percent of the men who responded said that environmental education should be provided in schools. Minnesotans also demonstrated their ability to move attitude to action, with 87 percent of respondents reporting they frequently conserve energy and 51 percent reporting they frequently conserve water. The Minnesota Master Naturalist Program helps support these interests and actions by promoting

MASTER
NATURALIST
TOOLBOX

environmental literacy for Minnesota citizens and providing opportunities for individuals to learn and teach others about the natural history of our state.

Pioneer naturalists played an important role in shaping the United States as we know it today. Two naturalists who played an important role in shaping our thoughts and leading preservation efforts in the Upper Midwest, in addition to their naturalist roles as observers and interpreters of nature, were Sigurd Olson (Figure 8) and Aldo Leopold (Figure 9).

Activity

1. Read a short story or show a video about a naturalist to familiarize participants with the concept.

2. Think of a naturalist you admire. What are the qualities that make this person a good naturalist? Which of these qualities do you have? Which would you like to acquire? Write them down on a 3"x 5" card and keep it in your Minnesota Master Naturalist book. At the end of the course, take it out and see if you feel that you have gained these skills. If not, how can you make a plan to seek them out?

3. Find an interpretive naturalist at a nature facility near you. Interview him or her about what the job entails and how he or she came to this career.

4. Learn more about professional organizations that support naturalists in Minnesota from the Minnesota Naturalists' Association (www.mnnaturalists.org), Minnesota Association for Environmental Education (www.minnesotaee.org), National Association for Interpretation (www.interpnet.com), and National Association for Environmental Education (www.naaee.org).

MASTER
NATURALIST
TOOLBOX

Sigurd F. Olson

Sigurd Ferdinand Olson (April 4, 1899–January 13, 1982), writer and conservationist, was born in Chicago, Ill., the son of Lawrence J. Olson, a Swedish Baptist minister, and Ida May Cederholm. He spent most of his childhood in northern Wisconsin, where he formed his lifelong attachment to nature and outdoor recreation.

Olson earned a bachelor of science degree from the University of Wisconsin in 1920. He returned briefly in 1922 for graduate work in geology, and earned a master's degree in animal ecology from the University of Illinois in 1932. Meanwhile, in 1921 he married Elizabeth Dorothy Uhrenholdt; they had two sons.

From 1923 to 1936, Olson taught at a high school and then at a junior college at Ely, in northeastern Minnesota. In 1936, he became dean of the Ely Junior College, a position he held until he resigned in 1947 to become a full-time writer and professional conservationist.

Figure 8. Minnesota naturalist and environmental activist Sigurd Olson enjoyed exploring the wilderness by canoe.

Ely remained Olson's home for the rest of his life. An iron mining town on the Vermilion Range, it was located at the edge of several million acres of lake-dominated wilderness in the United States and Canada known as the Quetico-Superior. Olson traveled and guided there for many years, and grew convinced that wilderness provided spiritual experiences vital to modern civilization. This conviction formed the basis of both his conservation and his writing careers.

Olson became an active conservationist in the 1920s, fighting to keep roads and then dams out of the Quetico-Superior. In the 1940s he spearheaded a precedent-setting fight to ban airplanes from flying into the area; the conflict propelled him to the front ranks of conservation. Olson served as wilderness ecologist for the Izaak Walton League of America from 1948 until his death, as vice-president and then president of the National Parks Association from 1951 to 1959, as vice-president and then president of the Wilderness Society from 1963 to 1971, and as an advisor to the National Park Service and to the secretary of the interior from 1959 to the early 1970s. He helped draft the Wilderness Act, which became law in 1964 and established the U.S. wilderness preservation system. He played a role in the establishment of Alaska's Arctic Wildlife Refuge and helped to identify and recommend other Alaskan lands ultimately preserved in the Alaska National Interest Lands Conservation Act of 1980. Among his many other activities, he played key roles in the establishment of Point Reyes National Seashore in California and Voyageurs National Park in Minnesota. In recognition, four of the five largest U.S. conservation organizations—the Sierra Club, the Wilderness Society, the National Wildlife Federation, and the Izaak Walton League—each gave Olson their highest award.

Often pictured with a pipe in his hand and a warm yet reflective expression on his weathered face, Olson became a living icon to many environmentalists, "the personification of the wilderness defender," according to former Sierra Club president Edgar Wayburn. He was

MASTER NATURALIST TOOLBOX

trusting and sentimental, but also a strong leader who could bring together warring factions of environmentalists. "I think he always kept his eye on the star, and he didn't get down here where we more common folks deal more with personalities," said former Wilderness Society president Ted Swem. "He made wilderness and life sing," said George Marshall, a former president of both the Sierra Club and the Wilderness Society. And yet in Olson's home town of Ely, where many blamed wilderness regulations for the poor local economy, he was jeered and hanged in effigy. And, until he left the junior college in 1947, he often felt trapped in his career and sometimes despaired of his chances to achieve his dream of writing full time.

Olson's large and at times almost worshipful following derives in part from personal charisma, but especially from the humanistic philosophy he professed in nine popular books, in magazine articles, and in myriad speeches and interviews. He had a way of writing and speaking about the natural world that touched deep emotions in his audience, and many responded with heartfelt letters. An excerpt from his best-selling first book, *The Singing Wilderness* (1956), shows his unpretentious, yet lyrical, style:

> The movement of a canoe is like a reed in the wind. Silence is part of it, and the sounds of lapping water, bird songs, and wind in the trees. It is part of the medium through which it floats, the sky, the water, the shores.... There is magic in the feel of a paddle and the movement of a canoe, a magic compounded of distance, adventure, solitude, and peace. The way of a canoe is the way of the wilderness, and of a freedom almost forgotten. It is an antidote to insecurity, the open door to waterways of ages past and a way of life with profound and abiding satisfactions. When a man is part of his canoe, he is part of all that canoes have ever known.

In 1974, Olson received the Burroughs Medal, the highest honor in nature writing. His other books include *Listening Point* (1958), *The Lonely Land* (1961), *Runes of the North* (1963), *Open Horizons* (1969), *The Hidden Forest* (1969), *Wilderness Days* (1972), *Reflections From the North Country* (1976), and *Of Time and Place* (1982).

Sigurd Olson believed that the psyche, as well as the physical needs of humanity, were rooted in the Pleistocene environment that dominated the evolutionary history of our species. This, combined with his single-minded focus on spiritual values, distinguished him from other leading philosophers of the wilderness preservation movement. Olson was influenced by the literary naturalists W.H. Hudson and John Burroughs, as well as many other thinkers and social critics of the 19th and 20th centuries, including Henry David Thoreau, Aldous and Julian Huxley, Pierre Teilhard de Chardin, Lewis Mumford, and C.G. Jung. Olson argued that people could best come to know their true selves by returning to their biological roots. As he said at a Sierra Club conference in 1965, "I have discovered in a lifetime of traveling in primitive regions, a lifetime of seeing people living in the wilderness and using it, that there is a hard core of wilderness need in everyone, a core that makes its spiritual values a basic human necessity. There is no hiding it.... Unless we can preserve places where the endless spiritual needs of man can be fulfilled and nourished, we will destroy our culture and ourselves."

Sigurd Olson biography courtesy of the Sigurd Olson Environmental Institute. See www.northland.edu/sustain/soei/ for more information on the institute and its programs.

MASTER
NATURALIST
TOOLBOX

Aldo Leopold

"As a society, we are just now beginning to realize the depth of Leopold's work and thinking."

> — Mike Dombeck, chief emeritus of the USFS; professor of global environmental management, University of Wisconsin–Stevens Point; University of Wisconsin System fellow of global conservation

Considered by many as the father of *wildlife management* and of the U.S. wilderness system, Aldo Leopold was a conservationist, forester, philosopher, educator, writer, and outdoor enthusiast.

Born in 1887 and raised in Burlington, Iowa, Leopold developed an interest in the natural world at an early age, spending hours observing, journaling, and sketching his surroundings. Graduating from the Yale Forest School in 1909, he eagerly pursued a career with the newly established U.S. in Arizona and New Mexico. By age 24, he had been promoted to the post of supervisor for the Carson National Forest in New Mexico. In 1922, he was instrumental in developing the proposal to manage the Gila National Forest as a wilderness area, which became the first such official designation in 1924.

Figure 9. Aldo Leopold was a well-known outdoorsman and conservation scientist.

Following a transfer to Madison, Wisconsin, in 1924, Leopold continued his investigations into ecology and the philosophy of conservation. In 1933 he published the first textbook in the field of wildlife management, and later that year he accepted a new chair in game management — a first for the University of Wisconsin and the nation.

In 1935, he and his family initiated their own ecological restoration experiment on a worn-out farm along the Wisconsin River outside of Baraboo, Wisconsin. Planting thousands of pine trees, restoring prairies, and documenting the ensuing changes in the flora and fauna further informed and inspired Leopold.

A prolific writer, authoring articles for professional journals and popular magazines, Leopold conceived a book geared for general audiences examining humanity's relationship to the natural world. Unfortunately, just one week after receiving word that his manuscript would be published, Leopold experienced a heart attack and died on April 21, 1948, while fighting a neighbor's grass fire that escaped and threatened the Leopold farm and surrounding properties. A little more than a year after his death Leopold's collection of essays, *A Sand County Almanac*, was published. With over 2 million copies sold, it is one of the most respected books about the environment ever published, and Leopold has come to be regarded by many as the most influential conservation thinker of the 20th century.

Leopold's legacy continues to inform and inspire us to see the natural world "as a community to which we belong."

MASTER NATURALIST TOOLBOX

This excerpt about the land ethic from *A Sand County Almanac* captures the essence of Leopold's message:

> The land ethic simply enlarges the boundaries of the community to include soils, waters, plants, and animals, or collectively: the land. This sounds simple: do we not already sing our love for and obligation to the land of the free and the home of the brave? Yes, but just what and whom do we love? Certainly not the soil, which we are sending helter-skelter downriver. Certainly not the waters, which we assume have no function except to turn turbines, float barges, and carry off sewage. Certainly not the plants, of which we exterminate whole communities without batting an eye. Certainly not the animals, of which we have already extirpated many of the largest and most beautiful species. A land ethic of course cannot prevent the alteration, management, and use of these "resources," but it does affirm their right to continued existence, and, at least in spots, their continued existence in a natural state.

Aldo Leopold biography courtesy of the Aldo Leopold Foundation, based in Baraboo, Wisconsin. See www.aldoleopold.org for more information on the foundation and its programs.

MASTER
NATURALIST
TOOLBOX

LESSON 3

Journaling: A Journey Toward a Naturalist's View

Objective

Through nature journaling, participants will cultivate their observation skills and sensitivity to nature.

Audience Type

Teen/Adult

Supplies

☐ The journal you made in Lesson 1

Background

In this chapter, you've learned that a naturalist is an individual who studies nature and natural history. Being a naturalist involves careful observation and reflection on our natural world. Weekly journaling exercises are one important way the Minnesota Master Naturalist Program helps you cultivate those critical skills.

By finding and returning often to a special natural place, you will expand your sensitivity to and familiarity with nature. You will come to know this place on a deeper level, gaining a heightened awareness of its character, patterns, changes, and moods. Journaling will provide you the work space to make sense of your observations and experience. The great naturalists described elsewhere in this curriculum all share a common practice of having spent extended amounts of time exploring, observing, and reflecting on nature. Their experiences moved them to articulate important patterns and meanings they found in the natural world. The rest of us may share or experience these meanings vicariously through their writings and drawings.

Like other journals, a nature journal serves as a workbench where you can freely explore your observations, thoughts, and feelings and then construct meanings from them. In a nature journal, the setting in which those experiences take place is one central character. You, the observer, are another main character.

In a nature journal, you are not limited to words and linear story lines. Threads of writing come and go, start and stop. A satisfying journal entry may start on one subject and end in a completely different, disconnected place. Illustrations, phrases, photos, or botanical samples may punctuate your ideas. Your nature journal is a rule-free space to explore and make visible the interchange that takes place between you and your surroundings.

The journaling exercises found in this book (at the beginning of each "Expand" section) follow a three-step format. Each week when you visit your special place you will begin with a structured, sensory "Experience" that encourages you to observe your spot up close and focused. Next you will "Reflect" on your experience by responding to questions or a guided thought prompt. Last, you will "Record" your observations, impressions, predictions, comparisons, questions, and feelings in your journal. Through this guided process, you will transition from active investigation of the environment toward reflection and creative expression of what you find there. New insights may inspire you to explore further, beginning the cycle anew. These experiences will sharpen your sensitivity to subtle changes or distinctions in the things you see. This sensitivity is a prerequisite to a host of naturalist skills, such as plant identification or weather forecasting.

MASTER
NATURALIST
TOOLBOX

Sigurd Olson wrote in *Listening Point* about his special place:

> From this one place I would explore the entire north and all life, including my own. I could look to the stars and feel that here was a local point of great celestial triangles, a point as important as any one on the planet. For me it would be a listening-post from which I might even hear the music of the spheres.

Activity

1. To get started, choose a natural setting to visit at least weekly for the duration of your Master Naturalist course (and hopefully beyond!). Choose a spot that feels special and interesting to you. Make sure it is convenient to visit: your backyard, the park across the street, or a nearby flower patch. If it takes more than a couple of minutes to get there, it's too far.

2. Spend 10 to 30 minutes experiencing your spot each week and complete the weekly exercise in your nature journal. If it's too cold, wet, or dark when you visit your spot, at least do the "experience" portion of the exercise there and finish "reflect" and "record" in a more comfortable location. Make sure there is somewhere you can sit comfortably at your special spot—a log or flat place on the ground—or bring a folding chair.

3. Follow the prompts presented in the Master Naturalist "Expand" section at the end of each chapter!

MASTER
NATURALIST
TOOLBOX

Conserve

This section highlights organizations that offer opportunities for Minnesota Master Naturalist Volunteers to participate in stewardship and citizen science activities as field naturalists in the North Woods, Great Lakes region. Please visit the websites to learn more.

Minnesota Naturalists' Association

The Minnesota Naturalists' Association (MNA) exists to advance natural and cultural resource interpretation for the purpose of fostering wise stewardship of all resources. MNA strives to achieve this purpose by  1) establishing lines of communication and promoting cooperation among nature centers, environmental education centers, parks, camps, museums, and related facilities; 2) stimulating thought and the exchange of ideas, and, for mutual assistance, maintaining communication with related professionals, administrators, and the public to promote interest in and understanding of natural and cultural interpretation; and 3) encouraging the development of and implementation of programs and training in natural and cultural interpretation. Its members include professional environmental educators, park rangers, naturalists, interpreters, and volunteers throughout Minnesota and beyond. MNA provides a training and information exchange network for its members through naturalist trainings, an annual fall conference, and newsletters. MNA also provides information on jobs, networking with other environmental education organizations, and access to the experience and knowledge of the rest of MNA's membership.

www.mnnaturalists.org

Minnesota Association for Environmental Education

The Minnesota Association for Environmental Education (MAEE) is Minnesota's association for professionals, students, and volunteers working in  the field of environmental education. The MAEE was founded in 1992 to support and advance environmental education throughout the state through an annual conference, events, newsletters, and legislation and by building bridges between educators and other environmental education professionals throughout Minnesota who teach, lead, or provide programs on the environment. The association reflects that goal through a membership and a board that includes representatives from schools, government agencies, environmental learning centers, private and nonprofit groups, business and industry, and others concerned with the quality of life in Minnesota, including classroom teachers and administrators, nonformal educators, outdoor recreation providers, natural resource professionals, and naturalists.

www.minnesotaee.org

Expand

This section suggests some things you can use, do, pursue, read, or join to develop as a naturalist.

Journal

EXPERIENCE Choose a location. Sit there silently for 10 to 20 minutes and just experience the place.

REFLECT What are your first impressions of this place? What did you notice today that you hadn't noticed before? What do you see, hear, smell, and feel here? How did your perceptions change during the course of your first visit? What makes this place special? What could you do to sharpen your observation skills further?

RECORD Describe your special spot in your nature journal. Ask questions and hypothesize about the past, present, and future of this place.

Read

Minnesota's Natural Heritage: An Ecological Perspective

John Tester.
1995. Minneapolis: University of Minnesota Press. 332 pp.

This book is a comprehensive examination of the natural history of Minnesota. It has beautiful pictures and illustrations. Buy it now!

The New Amateur Naturalist

Nick Baker.
2004. Washington, D.C.: National Geographic. 288 pp.

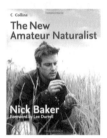

An update of the classic reference, *The Amateur Naturalist* by Gerald and Lee Durrell, this book introduces you to the tricks, techniques, and equipment used by naturalists. Baker, a TV wildlife expert, draws from his worldwide experience to share a variety of skills. Learn about buying binoculars, finding animals in the field, and even estimating the height of trees.

Surf

Bell Museum of Natural History

The James Ford Bell Museum of Natural History is the state's natural history museum. Its mission is to discover, document, and understand nature and promote informed stewardship of our world. Bell Museum scientists work in the treetops of Papua New Guinea's tropical forests, the rivers of southern Minnesota, and the capitals of Europe. Their research provides important baseline data for scientists and conservationists and creates a record of Earth's biological diversity. The museum sponsors events for adults, school children, and families. Visit the museum's website to learn of the ever-changing array of events and find a wealth of information on the natural history of Minnesota.

www.bellmuseum.umn.edu

Minnesota Department of Natural Resources

The Minnesota DNR website has information on all facets of the outdoors in Minnesota. Do you wonder how many lakes exist in the state? Are you looking for details about the deer opener? Do you want to know what naturalist programs are happening at Minnesota state parks? You can find all of that and more on the DNR website.

www.mndnr.gov

Join

Minnesota Master Naturalist

The Minnesota Master Naturalist Program promotes awareness, understanding, and stewardship of Minnesota's natural environment by developing a corps of well-informed citizens dedicated to conservation education and service within their communities. If you are reading this, you are probably already on your way to becoming a Minnesota Master Naturalist Volunteer!

www.minnesotamasternaturalist.org

Additional Reading

Baker, N. (2004). *The amateur naturalist: A new look at a classic subject.* Washington, DC: National Geographic.

Wilson, E. O. (1995). *Naturalist.* New York: Warner Books.

Copyrighted Photographs and Images Used With Permission

Figure 1. Courtesy of The White House Historical Association and Wikimedia Commons

Figure 2. Courtesy of the U.S. Fish & Wildlife Service and Wikimedia Commons

Figure 3. Courtesy of Minnesota Department of Natural Resources

Figure 4. Courtesy of Dawn A. Flinn, Minnesota Department of Natural Resources

Figure 5. Courtesy of USDA Natural Resource Conservation Service

Figure 6. Courtesy of Minnesota Department of Natural Resources

Figure 7. Courtesy of Sarah L. Keefer

Figure 8. Courtesy of Sigurd L. Olson Environmental Institute

Figure 9. Adapted from U.S. Fish & Wildlife Service Region 5

Expand

MASTER
NATURALIST
TOOLBOX

Chapter 1: Rip, Flow, Freeze, and Thaw

Geology and Climate of the North Woods, Great Lakes Region

Sarah L. Keefer

Goal

Understand how geologic and climatic forces have shaped the physical and biological landscape of the North Woods, Great Lakes region.

Objectives

1. Describe how the North Woods, Great Lakes region we see today relates to past geologic events.

2. Identify igneous and metamorphic rock formations in the North Woods, Great Lakes region and describe how they were formed.

3. Describe how the North Woods, Great Lakes landscape is shaped by climate.

Introduction

Minnesota's geologic history begins at the beginning of Earth itself, some 4.6 billion years ago. Early rocks were demolished and reshaped time and again by the tumultuous Earth until roughly 3.8 billion years ago, when rock formations began to appear that still exist today—some of them right here in Minnesota. The geologic history of the North Woods, Great Lakes region includes times in which not only rocks, but also entire mountain ranges, were formed and destroyed.

The Basics

Before you can become a geo-detective and puzzle out what you are really seeing when you look at a mountain, cliff, river, or roadside cut, you need a bit of background on rocks—what they are made of, where they come from, how they change, and how they are pushed around on the landscape.

Recycling Rocks

You may think of a rock as that uniform, unchanging lump that sits at the edge of your garden where you put it after digging. Geologists think of rocks in an entirely different way. They know that over eons, rocks can be melted, eroded, smashed, compressed, heated, squirted out to the surface of the Earth, and eroded again. In fact, they describe rocks as going through a cycle (Figure 1) in which they are constantly being formed, destroyed, and reformed. In other words, rocks are the original recyclable materials, and nature the original recycler!

Because cycles by definition have no end or beginning, we need to pick an arbitrary starting point. Let's begin at the point when magma (molten rock below Earth's surface) cools, forming *igneous rock*. This may occur at or below Earth's surface. The mineral composition of the lava (molten rock above Earth's surface) and how quickly it cools determine the characteristics of igneous rocks. The fine-grained *basalts* found on the North Shore of Lake Superior result from quick cooling and high levels of iron, magnesium, aluminum, oxygen, and silicon. The rough, tough, coarse-grained gabbro of the Duluth Complex, on the other hand, reflects slow cooling

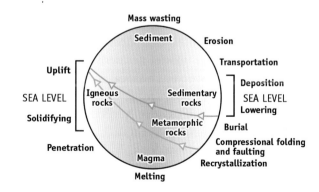

Figure 1. The rock cycle depicts how rocks change from one form to another over time.

below Earth's surface. Geologists call igneous rocks that have squirted to the surface and cooled quickly *extrusive*, while those that stay within the Earth's surface and cool slowly are called *intrusive*.

Igneous rocks at the Earth's surface are subject to the constant but slow process of *erosion*—being worn away by wind, rain, sun, gravity, and ice. The silt, sand, soil, mud, pebbles, and other loose pieces that erode from igneous rocks may wash into rivers, lakes, and oceans and settle into layers of sediment at the bottom. Eventually, compression caused by the weight of more and more layers can cement this hash of ground-up rock into *sedimentary rock* such as sandstone and shale. Some sedimentary rocks form from the squishing of plants (e.g., coal) or shells (e.g., limestone) rather than sediments. Others form from *minerals* left behind when water evaporates (e.g., halite) rather than through a pressure process.

Both sedimentary and igneous rocks can be squeezed and heated until they change and form *metamorphic rock* below the Earth's surface. The calcite crystals in limestone can be reformed into the larger crystals of marble, for example, while the fragile composition of shale can be squeezed into tougher slate. Shale can also turn into schist and granite may turn into *gneiss*. (That's why the old joke goes, "Don't take Minnesota gneiss for granite!") Both sedimentary and metamorphic rocks can, like igneous rock, undergo uplift and erosion. Metamorphic rocks may eventually melt to form new magma.

What Is a Rock?

All of these distinctions might make you wonder about the difference between a mineral and a rock. Well, you're about to find out!

Minerals are naturally occurring substances made up of inorganic matter (matter not derived from living things) with a specific chemical composition. For example, quartz is always made up of one part of silicon to two parts of oxygen. Additionally, components are arranged in a repeating pattern that gives some minerals a crystal look. To identify types of minerals, geologists examine the hardness, luster, streak (color of the powder it makes when crushed), specific gravity, and color. If you run across a mineral with the right combinations of these characteristics,

you will be a wealthy person (think rubies, diamonds, and emeralds).

Rocks are naturally occurring substances made up of one or more minerals. Consequently, a mineral is a rock but a rock isn't necessarily a mineral. For example, quartz is a rock that is also a mineral. Granite is a rock made up of the minerals quartz, feldspar, and mica.

Bedrock is the rock that we see at the surface of the Earth or that lies immediately beneath the soil. Figure 2 illustrates the variety of bedrock found across Minnesota, the result of eons of geologic action.

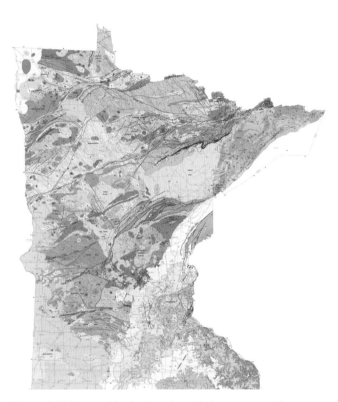

Figure 2. This map of bedrock—the rock that we see at the surface or that lies beneath the soil and plants—layers billions of years of history onto one colorful quilt. Each color represents a different kind of rock, which in turn represents a unique point in the geologic history of Minnesota. Some bedrock formed during times of volcanism and mountain building. Some formed as sediments were deposited in shallow seas. Many are buried by sediment deposited by glaciers. We are lucky in the North Woods, Great Lakes region because much of the rock record is visible at the surface, thanks to glaciers that eroded more material than they deposited. To view a detailed version of this map and a corresponding key, visit: http://conservancy.umn.edu/handle/11299/101466.

A Trip Through Time

The exploration of the geology of Minnesota's North Woods, Great Lakes region will lead us down a time-travel path that stretches all the way from billions of years into the past to right this very minute, as climatic and geologic forces continue to shape the scenes around us (Figure 3). As always, let's start at the beginning.

Earth Birth – The Hadean Eon

Our planet formed some 4.6 billion years ago from material orbiting the young Sun (Figure 4). This "proto-Earth" generated huge amounts of heat due to lingering energy generated from planetary formation, development of a solid core, and an abundance of radioactive elements. As a result, Earth was a ball of lava, with daytime temps in the low 2,000 degrees Fahrenheit.

During the Hadean, Earth collided with another protoplanet, Theia, resulting—scientists currently think—in the formation of our moon. This collision and further pummeling by meteorites set Earth spinning and created its axial tilt with respect to its orbit around the sun, giving us the four seasons.

The Hadean lasted from 4.6 to 4 billion years ago. Rocks formed at this time were all igneous, and none still exists. However, crystals still remain from this time. These include 4.4-billion-year-old zircon crystals found in the Jack Hills of Western Australia and 4.3-billion-year-old crystals found in Northwest Territories, Canada—and potentially in our own Minnesota River valley!

Figure 4. Small rocky debris gravitates to a larger body, a protoplanet. Planets are thought to form by absorbing rocks and other elements from their orbital path around a star. Earth may have formed in this manner over the span of 10 to 20 million years.

Rocky Times – The Archean Eon

The Archean Eon, 4 to 2.5 billion years ago, was a much friendlier time. Earth sweltered under a dense atmosphere laden with carbon dioxide (but not a gasp of oxygen).

It started out with a bang—literally. Numerous asteroids and comets collided with Earth during a period known as the Late Heavy Bombardment, 4.1 to 3.8 billion years ago. These collisions contributed water molecules and additional minerals and elements that would later form the rocks of northeastern Minnesota.

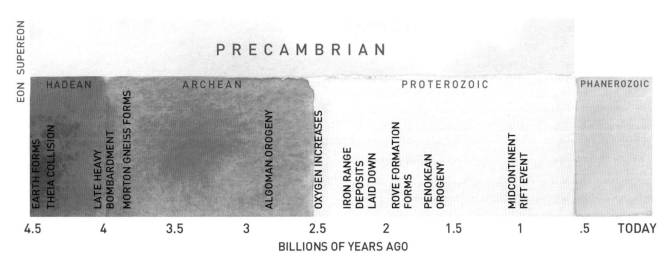

Figure 3. Geologists divide Earth's history into eons, eras, periods, and other units of time. They use *radiometric dating* of rocks, minerals, and meteorites along with observations of our moon and other planets to estimate the age of rock formations and of Earth itself.

SHALLOW OCEAN During the Archean Eon, a single shallow ocean covered our entire planet. Earth had cooled and hardened considerably, but it was still spinning fast. The rotation created superstorms that agitated the waters while our adolescent moon created enormous tides.

Beneath the waves, volcanic activity and earthquakes were rampant. A thin, fragile crust was all that stood between the watery surface and a churning sludge of molten rock that rippled and rolled, hardened, sank, remelted, and occasionally erupted through the crust, forming seething mounds of lava that churned out igneous rock. Over time some of these cones of cooled lava broke the surface of the water, forming volcanic islands.

Plate tectonics most likely started during the Archean, as fragments of crust converged (moved toward one another), diverged (moved apart), or transformed (moved horizontally in relation to one another).

ALGOMAN OROGENY Near the end of the Archean Eon, a plate carrying an arc of oceanic islands moved toward the edge of a part of what is now Canada and northern Minnesota called the Superior Province. This plate convergence was the start of the Algoman *orogeny* (oro is Greek for mountain and genesis is Greek for origin), which began around 2.8 billion years ago. Over 50 to 100 million years mountains lurched skyward (in slow motion) as the arriving plate *subducted*, or slid beneath the crust of ancient northern Minnesota.

The resulting Algoman Mountains formed the earliest known mountain range of Minnesota. They were your average coastal uplift mountains, like the Andes of South America, with estimated heights of an impressive 10,000 to 20,000 feet.

The collision brought with it a familiar cast of characters—earthquakes, volcanoes, and metamorphic power. It also created something we can still see in Minnesota today—the metamorphic rock greenstone. Greenstone began life as molten rock, mostly made up of two minerals: plagioclase feldspar and pyroxene. The liquid cooled relatively quickly (over no more than a few decades), to form basalt, which (due to the rapid cooling) has tiny crystals and an even, darkish-gray color. As the continental plates converged, the pressure on the ocean basins

transformed the minerals in the basalt into chlorite, epidite, actinolite, and other minerals with a greenish hue, forming greenstone. In places such as modern-day Ely, basaltic lava had burbled out of cracks in the ocean floor 3,000 feet below the water's surface. The lava cooled and hardened into gently rounded pillow basalt, which then metamorphosed into pillowed greenstone (Figure 5).

Meanwhile, the interiors of the mountains were smoldering with molten rock made up of the minerals feldspar, quartz, mica, and hornblende. Miles beneath the surface, this magma cooled relatively slowly—on the order of millions of years—into granite. Given this much time, the cooling rock formed crystals we can see with the unaided eye. In the same way oceanic basalt metamorphosed into greenstone, some of this granite metamorphosed into gneiss.

Figure 5. This pillowed greenstone formed near Ely 2.7 billion years ago when molten basalt that had extruded into the depths of an ocean and cooled into rock underwent *metamorphosis*.

Figure 6. *Stromatolites*, such as these in Shark Bay, Australia, form in shallow water when cyanobacteria or other microorganisms trap sedimentary grains and cement them together. They provide records of life on Earth that might date from more than 3.5 billion years ago.

Simple Life – The Proterozoic Eon

The Algoman orogeny marked the end of the Archean Eon and ushered in the Proterozoic Eon, a 2-billion-year period dominated by simple life forms such as single-celled *archaea*—organisms with no cell nucleus—and cyanobacteria. *Cyanobacteria* produce oxygen through *photosynthesis*. Over the tens of millions of years that rocky island archipelagos were inching their way around the planet, cyanobacteria proliferated. Consequently, 2.5 billion years ago there was a tremendous supply of oxygen, first in the ocean and then in the atmosphere.

IRON RANGE ORIGINS In geologic time it seems that no sooner are mountains built than they are turned into grains of sand. Between 2.5 and 1.8 billion years ago the Algoman Mountains eroded, becoming but a footnote in the growing geologic saga of Minnesota.

GONE, BUT NOT FORGOTTEN The dissolved rocks created an ooze among the stromatolite-forming cyanobacteria colonies on the broad continental shelf on the Animikie Basin coast of northeastern Minnesota (Figure 6). Along this shore sediment rich in iron and silica, derived from weathering and volcanic ash, washed in with the tides. In the warm, shallow waters this sediment mingled with surplus oxygen molecules to form hematite and other common iron oxides (Figure 7). The iron oxides settled among the cyanobacteria, which also trapped silt, sand, and mud. Time forged these deposits into banded iron formations, continuous sedimentary rock layers winding their way through the present-day Cuyuna, Mesabi, Vermilion, and Gunflint ranges—like the bathtub ring of a primordial beach.

This sedimentary rock, called *taconite* by the first state geologist, N. H. Winchell, contains at least 15 percent iron layered with bands of sedimentary rocks such as carbonate and chert. Some of the banded materials experienced additional natural processes that swept away more silica or added more oxygen, forming ores with at least 60 percent iron, such as high-grade hematite and goethite.

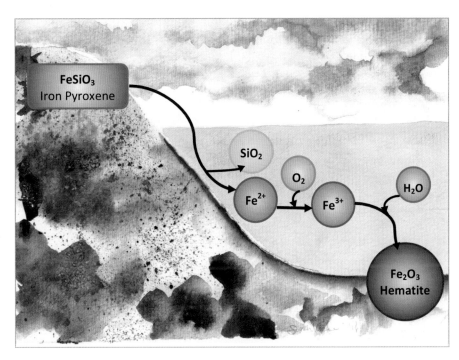

Figure 7. Banded iron is formed in seawater using oxygen released by photosynthetic cyanobacteria. When iron pyroxene ($FeSiO_3$) washes into shallow waters, it dissolves into silica (SiO_2) and ferrous iron (Fe^{2+}). The ferrous iron is oxidized to form ferric iron (Fe^{3+}), which combines with water to *precipitate* as hematite (Fe_2O_3), a common iron oxide.

In addition to the iron formations, there were many layers of sedimentary rock that formed in the Animikie Basin over millions of years. The youngest is known as the Rove Formation, which formed around 1.6 to 1.8 billion years ago. Shale and slate sediments were deposited in the Rove Formation of today's upper northeastern Arrowhead region.

MAKING MOUNTAINS Meanwhile, plate tectonics continued in earnest around the globe, leading to more movement of land around the planet, more mountain building, and more land formation. Around 1.85 billion years ago, yet another mountain-building event began as a plate carrying an island archipelago subducted beneath the southern border of our continental plate (Figure 8). During this event, called the Penokean orogeny, a complex array of rocks formed by uplift, volcanic activity, subduction, metamorphism, folding, faulting, and deposition. Granites took shape in central Minnesota, sediments were deposited along what is now the North Shore

of Lake Superior, and metamorphic "hot spots" led to the reconfiguration of igneous, sedimentary, and metamorphic rocks.

By geologic map standards, it was very colorful! Weathering began instantly, and for the next 600 million years the mountain fragments eroded, exposing the deep igneous and meta-igneous (metamorphosed igneous) core. The continent continued to build beyond the edge of Minnesota, and an identifiable North America emerged.

A TORN CONTINENT So far we've focused on what happens when two plates move together: uplift, volcanoes, and mountains. What would happen to continents if one of the plates they sat on started to split apart? Such continental rifting—which is still happening today—was quite common early on as continents were made and then ripped apart, a new ocean filling the space between them. And it was nearly the fate of the young North American continent during the midcontinent rift event.

For the first few billion years of Earth's geologic history, as more land uplifted and amassed at the edges of the North American *craton* (stable piece of crust), what is now Minnesota became positioned toward the center of the continent, protected from the assault of converging tectonic plates and the corresponding volcanoes and upheaval. Then, about 1.1 billion years ago, the continent began to rip apart. Deep forces like those splitting Iceland now created a 1,000-mile-long rupture that stretched from Oklahoma through Minnesota, curving around into what is now the Great Lakes region (Figure 9). For more than 20 million years, basaltic lava oozed out and formed a 13-mile thick pile (that's a half marathon!) in the widening rift.

On the surface this collection of lava flows formed what we now call the North Shore Volcanic Group, primarily consisting of basalt and rhyolite (the quick-cool version of granite). As these lavas cooled, water vapor and other gases fizzled out of the molten sludge. Some of the bubbles (called *vesicles*) were trapped as the lava hardened to stone. Later, some of these hardened vesicles filled with minerals circulating in the hot fluids to form Minnesota's state gem, the Lake Superior agate. Others formed thomsonite, a relatively

Figure 8. The Penokean orogeny added landmass onto the edge of a young Minnesota 1.85–1.84 billion years ago. Here, an island arc called the Pembine-Wausau terrane is shown colliding with ancient North America. The shoreline of the Animikie Basin can be seen north of this activity, where banded iron formations developed in the shallow, oxygen-rich tidal zone.

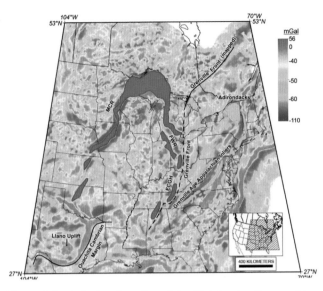

Figure 9. Buried volcanic rock contains high levels of iron and so is denser and more magnetic than surrounding rocks. This map of gravity (mGal) and magnetism (red) shows the bedrock geology generated by the midcontinent rift event 1.1 billion years ago.

rare stone found today along the North Shore of Lake Superior in which pink or white minerals were laid down within the vesicles.

Meanwhile, the giant magma chamber that fed the basalt flows also eventually cooled to form gabbro, the mineralogical equivalent of basalt. Because gabbro cooled slowly, it has large crystals that give it the attractive pepper-and-salt look that, when quarried and polished, is prized for use in monuments, memorials, building facings, and countertops in home kitchens. Gabbro and granite make up the intrusive rock formations of the midcontinent rift event, collectively referred to as the Duluth Complex. The weather-resistant igneous rocks from this time became the Misquah Hills (home of Eagle Mountain, highest natural elevation in Minnesota) and the striking basalt gorge of the Dalles on the St. Croix River at Interstate State Park (Figure 10), where you can actually see separate basaltic lava flows.

But that's not all! Some of the magma extruded during the midcontinent rift event forced its way into cracks in older sedimentary rock formations and lava flows, slowly cooling to form diabase and anorthosite *sills* (igneous rock formations that form in cracks running parallel to the rock layers) and *dikes* (igneous rock formations that form in cracks that run through rock layers). Split Rock Lighthouse is on a cliff composed of diabase and anorthosite. The cliff began as a sill or dike contained within the host rock that became exposed when the coarser-grained rock around it weathered away. In the Rove Formation, east-west fractures in the older sedimentary rocks were also intruded by diabase. In times to come, the soft sedimentary rocks will erode, leaving diabase-edged valleys that will fill with water.

When the continental tearing finally stopped, probably helped by some far-away continental collision along the eastern seaboard, the hot igneous rock that had pooled in the rift cooled and sank. The rift was also squeezed shut a bit by the collision, and these events resulted in a tipping of the formerly flat-lying lava flows and rift-filling sediment layers. Some are even now standing on end such as the upended igneous rocks that form the Sawtooth Mountains. The sediments formed impressive rocks you can see today along the North Shore of Lake Superior (Figure 11).

Figure 10. Cliffs made of basalt that formed during the midcontinent rift event form the edges of the St. Croix River gorge. At least 10 distinct layers of basalt are distinguishable, representing intervals of volcanic upheaval and inactivity. Hundreds of millions of years later, advancing and retreating seas and later glacial ice sculpted the formation we see today.

Visible Life – The Phanerozoic Eon

Beginning around 542 million years ago, something very exciting happened. Life forms larger than the archaea and cyanobacteria we met earlier in the Proterozoic Eon began to evolve, as evidenced by the presence of their fossils in sedimentary rocks formed during this time, such as sandstone, shale, and limestone. During this Phanerozoic (from the Greek for "visible life") Eon, tectonic plates continued to move apart and toddle back together again, crust continued to accumulate, the major landmasses Gondwana and Laurasia appeared, and living things continued to evolve.

TROPICAL SEAS, ANCIENT LIFE At the beginning of the Phanerozoic Eon, life evolved quickly. Over a period of just 20–25 million years—a chunk of time now known as the Cambrian explosion—nearly all major animal phyla appeared, as witnessed by fossils trapped in sedimentary rocks laid down by rivers and tides.

Figure 11. Rust-colored sedimentary rock with an overlaying basaltic lava flow near Good Bay Harbor on the North Shore of Lake Superior tells a story of a quiet period between eruptions of the midcontinent rift event 1.1 billion years ago, when rivers resumed their course and seas lapped onto the cooling rocks. Sediment was deposited on potentially still hot rocks, and hot fluids moving through the sediment oxidized the iron, giving the sedimentary rock its reddish hue. The next lava flow covered the sediment, and the cycle began again.

From the Cambrian period to the Permian period (the Paleozoic Era, a subdivision of the Phanerozoic Eon, a time spanning about 288 million years), Minnesota was a tropical destination. The state danced around the equator as seas waxed and waned unencumbered over the sands and gentle hills of the midcontinent.

Gondwana and Laurasia (of which North America was a member) united to form Pangaea during the Paleozoic Era, around 300 million years ago.

MIDDLE LIFE Life continued to diversify during the Mesozoic ("middle life", another subdivision of the Phanerozoic) Era. Plants began to dominate the land, providing great green habitats for the first dinosaurs, mammals, lizards, and birds. Plants and animal life spread out across Pangaea like moss across a shaded rock. Then, just when things seemed to be settling down 100 million years ago, our old and ever-present friend plate tectonics separated Gondwana and Laurasia once more.

Like an inside look at life in the Mesozoic? Check out the fossil shark teeth, fish and turtle bones, clams, and other sea creature fossils at Hill Annex Mine State Park near Calumet on Minnesota's Mesabi Iron Range. These 86-million-year-old fossils are testament to the ocean that once covered our state.

COVERED BY ICE Scientists use the term "ice age" or "glacial age" to indicate any geological period in which ice sheets and glaciers exist. A few Snowball Earth episodes (periods of massive global glaciation) occurred in the Archean and in the Proterozoic and Phanerozoic eons. And we are in an ice age right now! Specifically, we are in Marine Isotope Stage 1, an *interglacial* (warmer) time within the Quaternary Period glaciation, which began around 2.58 million years ago.

During the Quaternary, several major glaciations have advanced across the entire state, reshaping the landscape with each pass. Minnesota was most recently glaciated in Marine Isotope Stage 2, also known as the Wisconsin Glaciation, beginning around 50,000 years ago and peaking 20,000 years ago.

A continental ice sheet, or glacier, is born of countless snowflakes falling, gathering, and not melting year to year, decade to decade, millennium to millennium.

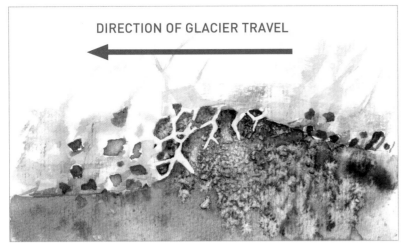

DIRECTION OF GLACIER TRAVEL

Figure 12. Pressure from the weight of a glacier causes ice to melt at rock outcrops. The water may then refreeze on the side of the rocks away from the direction the ice sheet is traveling. The refreezing traps the rocks, which then become abrasive forces that scour and scratch other bedrocks "downstream."

ICE ON THE ROCKS Lobes of ice from the Laurentide ice sheet—the last great ice sheet to cover North America—invaded what is now Minnesota many times from different directions, importing sediment from various parts of what is now Canada. The crust was scraped of *regolith* (loose material covering solid rock) and the sediment was incorporated into the ice or dragged along beneath it. Wherever the ice began to stagnate and retreat the till piled up, eventually accumulating in rumpled hills along the edge. The final ice lobe melted out of the Lake Superior basin, which was scoured out by the Superior lobe, approximately 10,000 years ago.

As the snowpile grows, the flakes are packed and crushed together until they metamorphose—just like a rock!—into glacial ice. This action squeezes most of the air out of the ice or condenses it into tiny bubbles.

As the glacier thickens, the crystals making up the ice slide past one another, causing the whole glacier to spread outward in all directions like pancake batter over a griddle. This kind of movement is fastest where the ice is thickest—near the center of the ice sheet.

The glacier also slides, especially where there is a thin film of water. Pressure alone can melt ice, even if the temperature is well below freezing; ice sheets melt first where pressure is concentrated on rock protuberances. Water that forms under these conditions may refreeze when it flows to a lower pressure area—say, behind the protuberance. This is one way in which bits of the rock may get frozen into the bottom of the glacier, giving it a "scouring pad" texture (Figure 12).

Clinging to the underbelly of the glacier like course sandpaper, the quarried rocks abrade the bedrock, are ground into smaller sizes, or simply ride the ice to a new location. Glacial ice transports massive amounts of every size and kind of rock (collectively called *till*).

Lasting Impressions

The glaciers that once covered Minnesota left behind numerous signs of their passing. The jagged rocks and grit embedded in the underside of the glaciers (Figure 13) smoothed and polished the rough edges of bedrock outcrops and left lasting scratch marks, called striations, on exposed surfaces. In northern Minnesota, where erosion was greater than deposition, the soil and regolith that developed during warmer times were stripped away and carried southward, leaving many areas with rugged exposed bedrock.

Figure 13. The Taku Glacier, an outlet of the Juneau Ice Field in southeastern Alaska, pushes a small moraine into willows and its meltwater stream. The sediment in the moraine is an unsorted mixture of sand, silt, clay, and rocks. Meltwater sorts the sediment according to size. The bottom of the glacier is loaded with sediment that eventually will be released by melting.

Many Minnesota lakes owe their origins to the glaciers. Some formed in the irregular, rumpled hilly terrain along former ice margins. So-called "kettle lakes," such as those found today in the Brainerd area or even Lake Minnetonka, filled in the depressions created as blocks of ice buried beneath sediment melted away. Proglacial lakes, such as lakes Agassiz, Upham, and Aitkin, formed at the terminus of glacial lobes. Here, great deposition of fine particles created the setting for shallow, poorly drained lakes. Many of these low-lying areas would go on to form bogs and *peatlands*, special relatives of the lake that we'll explore more in Chapter 6.

Still other lakes developed in basins created by the differential chemical weathering of different rock types during the previous tropical conditions and during subsequent removal of the regolith by the ice. Many of the lakes along the Canadian border and in the Boundary Waters Canoe Area Wilderness (BWCAW), including Gunflint Lake, formed in this way.

Perhaps one of the most impressive reminders of the ice age is one of the least visible: glacial isostatic adjustment, sometimes called continental rebound.

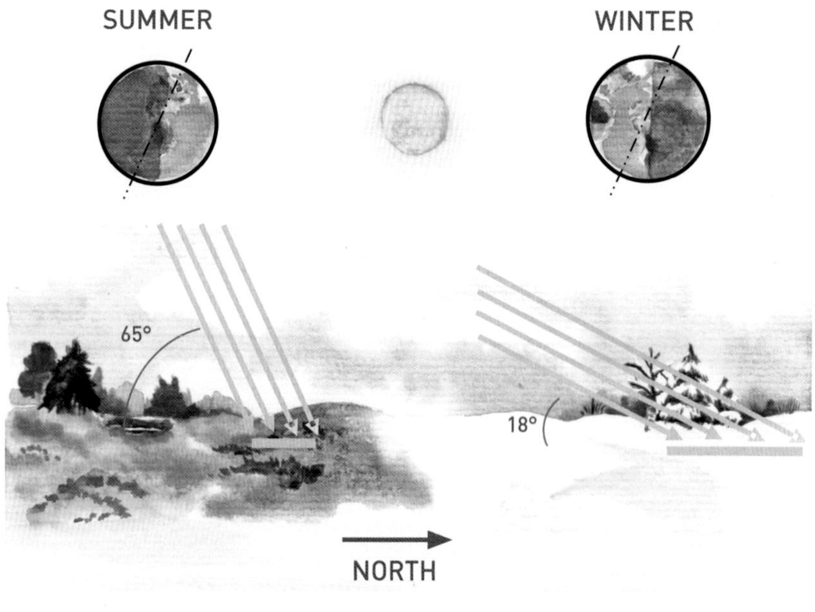

The continental glacier that entombed Minnesota and northern North America was so gargantuan that it depressed the crust of the North American plate in the same way you might depress a sofa cushion if you sat upon it a long time. This weight pressed the crust into the fluid *mantle* below. When the ice sheet melted, the crust began to rise again—much as that sofa cushion returns to its original shape when you stand up. Because of this phenomenon, the land in northern Minnesota around Lake Superior currently continues to rise nearly a tenth of an inch per year!

Climate

The rocks of the North Woods, Great Lakes region and the thin, nutrient-poor, slow-forming soil that developed from them help shape the flora and fauna buzzing, burrowing, and budding all around. Glacial activity helped form the basins that hold many of the aquatic habitats found here. The landscape is further shaped by seasonal changes in temperature and moisture—in other words, climate.

If weather is the somewhat unpredictable atmospheric conditions we experience day to day, then climate is what the daily weather should be like based on past averages. So, for example, on any given day in northern Minnesota during July, the average high temperature "should" be in the 60–70 °F range—but occasionally it will dip to near freezing. This was the case in the summer of 2013, which prompted unconfirmed rumors of July snowflakes in the BWCAW! In effect, climate is what you expect, and weather is what you get.

Minnesota's climate is a product of Earth's tilt with respect to its orbit around the sun, the state's position in North America, and the origin of prevailing winds—all of which affect temperature and precipitation.

Figure 14. In the summer, Earth's Northern Hemisphere tips toward the sun and the rays strike the surface at a 65-degree angle, concentrating the energy over a small area. In the winter, the Northern Hemisphere is tipped away from the sun, and the rays arrive at a much shallower angle, spreading the energy over a greater area. The angles shown in the image are for 47 degrees north latitude in June and December.

Tilt and the Four Seasons

Summers in Minnesota can get so hot and humid that it's tempting to think that Earth is closer to the sun than in the winter. On the contrary, Earth is farther from the sun by about 3.1 million miles. Remember Earth's collision with protoplanet Theia 4.5 billion years ago? The impact tilted the axis of the planet (the imaginary line it spins around over the course of a day) to the point where it is now at an angle of about 23.5 degrees from the plane defined by Earth's orbit around the sun. Simply, it's hotter here in summer than in winter because the Northern Hemisphere is tilted toward the sun, so the angle at which the sun's rays strike Earth is steeper, concentrating the energy over a smaller area (Figure 14). Additionally, in summer the sun shines on Minnesota for more time each day—nearly 16 hours in mid-June compared with 8.5 hours in mid-December.

Prevailing Winds

Wind patterns have a huge influence on Minnesota's climate. In the winter a jet stream—a band of moving air miles above Earth's surface—pushes cold, dry air south, burying the North Woods, Great Lakes region beneath Arctic chill. The effect is strongest in northern Minnesota, where places near Tower and Embarrass gain national notoriety for record-setting temperature extremes—down to –60 °F in 1996. In summer, warm, moist air from the Gulf of Mexico wafts northward into Minnesota (Figure 15). Mingling of these air masses creates thunderstorms capable of producing other weather extremes—strong winds, lightning, hail, and tornadoes.

Temperature

The average annual temperature in Minnesota follows a predictable gradient of hotter in the south to cooler in the north (Figure 16). This is due to Minnesota's distance from the equator, the decreasing intensity of sunlight as one moves farther north, and the lack of ocean currents that redistribute heat along continental coasts. Northern Minnesota averages fewer than 100 frost-free days each year—a big deal for gardeners anxious to plants their tomatoes and petunias as well as for native plant species, which have adapted to a cold, short growing season.

But latitude isn't everything. In Minnesota, Lake Superior (which we'll learn lots more about in

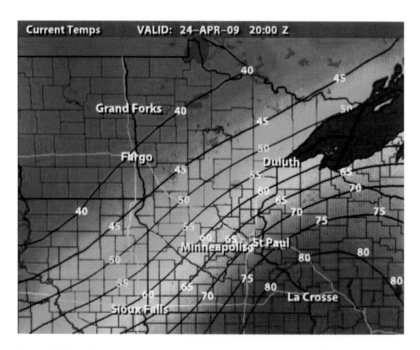

Figure 15. Meeting air masses produce local weather extremes, which may include strong winds, sudden downpours, lightning, hail, or tornadoes. Temperature variation was substantial in Minnesota on April 24, 2009. Warm air had arrived from the Gulf of Mexico, but the cold northern air seemed reluctant to leave.

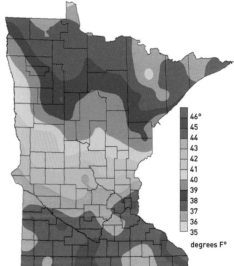

Figure 16. Surprise—it's cooler in the north and warmer in the south! Normal annual averages are around 34 °F in the north and 40 °F in the southern range of the North Woods, Great Lakes region.

Chapter 7) has a powerful moderating effect on the temperature along its shoreline. Due to its massive size, the lake is slow to change temperature with the seasons, so human and nonhuman residents along its shore enjoy relatively cooler temperatures in summer and warmer temperatures in winter than they would at similar latitudes and elevations elsewhere. The temperature discrepancy even influences the timing of natural events: Flowers bloom and leaves change color later along the North Shore than elsewhere in the North Woods, Great Lakes region.

Precipitation

Both seasons and Lake Superior influence the amount of precipitation that falls in the North Woods, Great Lakes region. The greatest rainfalls and snowfalls in the region occur along the North Shore, thanks to the availability of additional moisture from Lake Superior (Figure 17). In winter, this "lake effect" can mean accumulations of several feet of snow near shore but merely inches a few miles inland. Both snow and rain replenish the region's groundwater, lakes, and bogs.

Evapotranspiration

Temperature affects the amount of water available in an environment. When the water lost from the system through runoff, evaporation, and plant transpiration is subtracted from the water added to the system, we get a colorful map that coincides with the dominant vegetation cover across the state (Figure 18).

The part of Minnesota with the most available moisture is the coniferous forest of the North Woods, Great Lakes biome. As we shall see in upcoming chapters, this influences the ecology of both terrestrial and aquatic organisms of the region.

All Together Now

Bottom line, the North Woods, Great Lakes region we see today is the product of dramatic changes over eons of time, starting around 4.5 billion years ago when a young Earth collided with a rival planet to create the moon and the axial tilt that today gives us seasons. Billions of years of crust shaping, mountain building, volcanic eruptions, and erosion produced the bedrock that forms the region's foundation. More recently, glaciers scoured the surface, leaving a blank canvas that living things moved onto as the ice melted. Today, temperature and precipitation interact with this geologic landscape to shape the Coniferous Forest biome—23 million acres of rock, lakes, bogs, and forests.

Normal Precipitation Annual (1981-2010)

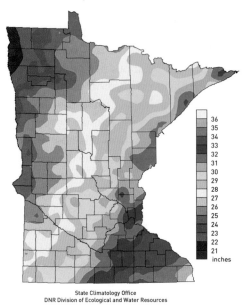

State Climatology Office
DNR Division of Ecological and Water Resources

Figure 17. Northeastern Minnesota receives an average of 24–32 inches of precipitation each year, with the greatest average along the eastern edge.

Annual Precipitation Minus Potential Evapotranspiration

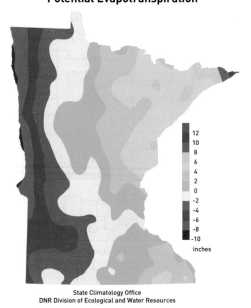

State Climatology Office
DNR Division of Ecological and Water Resources

Figure 18. The dominant vegetation of a habitat is directly related to water availability (a measure of precipitation minus evapotranspiration).

Explore

This section highlights great examples of places you can learn more about geologic and climatic features of the North Woods, Great Lakes region. Please check them out online, then head out to discover them in real life!

Lake Vermilion–Soudan Underground Mine State Park – Soudan, Minnesota

WHAT The Soudan Underground Mine sits atop one of the richest iron ore deposits in the world. It produced more than 15 million tons of ore during its operation from 1882 to 1962, and in its peak production year of 1892, employed 1,800 workers. Today, you can ride the cage down the original mine shaft nearly a half-mile underground. From there you can take the underground train to one of the last mined ore bodies. Back above ground, explore the banded iron formation, Minnesota's deepest open mine pits, and hiking trails that take you through a northern hardwood conifer forest and along 10 miles of rugged shoreline ridges that date back more than 2.7 billion years.

WHEN The park is open Memorial Day weekend through Labor Day, 10 a.m.– 4 p.m. Call or visit the website for information on fall and spring tour schedules.

WHERE Follow U.S. 169 to Soudan and follow the signs.

WHO Lake Vermilion–Soudan Underground Mine State Park, P.O. Box 335, Soudan, MN 55782, (218) 300-7000

FOR MORE INFORMATION www.mndnr.gov/soudan

Tettegouche State Park – Silver Bay, Minnesota

WHAT The North Shore of Lake Superior is a combination of rock cliffs, pebble beaches, and bold headlands. The landscape owes its character to the upheaval of the midcontinent rift event, which leaked lava that cooled to form the bedrock of the North Shore. More than a billion years of settling caused the flows to tilt— creating formations such as Palisade Head and Shovel Point, which are made of rhyolite rather than the basalt more common along the rest of the shore. Glacial action shaped the scenic views at Tettegouche State Park by excavating the Lake Superior basin and scraping away regolith, revealing numerous rock outcroppings. Tettegouche also offers a sampler of the North Shore drainage system, made up of short, steep rivers with many waterfalls and deeply eroded gorges.

WHEN Visit year-round for camping, cabin lodging, trail use, and visitor center exhibit viewing.

WHERE The park is located in Lake County, 4.5 miles northeast of Silver Bay on State Highway 61.

WHO Tettegouche State Park, 5702 Highway 61 East, Silver Bay, MN 55614, (218) 226-6365

FOR MORE INFORMATION www.mndnr.gov/tettegouche

Interstate State Park – Taylors Falls, Minnesota

WHAT Interstate State Park is another product of the midcontinent rift event. The steep basalt walls reveal layers of vesicles (gas bubbles) that identify at least 10 separate lava flows during that time. When glacial meltwater rushed through this rock fracture, it formed the magnificent Dalles of the St. Croix—widened, but still standing, bald-faced cliffs of basalt. Even more spectacular here are the rare potholes that were drilled into the basalt as glacial meltwater raged across the solid basalt when the crack took a 90-degree turn. To add to your geological frenzy, hike the Sandstone Bluffs Trail to walk among evidence of the seas that covered the area 530 million to 70 million years ago. Interstate State Park gets its name from being an interstate (connecting different states) state park. If you still have time for more, check out the sister Wisconsin Interstate State Park just across the river!

WHEN The visitor center is open and camping is available spring through late fall. Due to the rough landscape, the trails are not maintained in winter.

WHERE The pothole area is located just across U.S. Highway 8 from downtown Taylors Falls. The park office, campground, and boat landing can be accessed one mile south on U.S. Highway 8.

WHO Interstate State Park, 307 Milltown Road, Taylors Falls, MN 55084, (651) 465-5711

FOR MORE INFORMATION www.mndnr.gov/interstate

Moose Lake State Park Agate and Geological Interpretive Center – Moose Lake, Minnesota

WHAT The Moose Lake Agate and Geological Interpretive Center contains a magnificent collection of Lake Superior agates and tells the story of our geological heritage through interpretive displays. "Rock around the clock" to brush up on your geological time line. After discovering the variety of Minnesota's geological landscapes, ponder how minerals provide the basis for everything in our daily lives.

WHEN The center is open daily from Memorial Day through Labor Day. Check online or call ahead for hours.

WHERE The park is located in Carlton County one-half mile east of Interstate Highway 35 at the Moose Lake exit. The park entrance is off County Road 137.

WHO Moose Lake State Park, 4252 County Road 137, Moose Lake, MN 55767, (218) 485-5420

FOR MORE INFORMATION www.mndnr.gov/mooselake

MASTER
NATURALIST
TOOLBOX

Teach

MASTER NATURALIST TOOLBOX

This section features lesson plans for activities on Minnesota geology. You may experience some of these activities as a student in your Master Naturalist class. The lessons are adaptable to a wide range of audiences, ages, and settings. Feel free to use them to teach others what you have learned!

LESSON 1

Amateur Geologist — Identifying Rocks

Objective

Participants will use observation skills to describe, define, and identify major rock types of the North Woods, Great Lakes region.

Audience Type

Teen/Adult

Supplies

- ☐ Good samples of granite, rhyolite, basalt, and gabbro
- ☐ North Woods, Great Lakes Linnaeus List
- ☐ Hand lenses or magnifying glasses
- ☐ Map of northern Minnesota

Background

Billions of years ago, mountain-building activity created granite and greenstone belts across what is now northern Minnesota. Basaltic lava bubbled out of deep sea vents to form pillowed basalt, which later metamorphosed into greenstone. Continental rifting 1.1 billion years ago created the gabbro, rhyolite, and basalt of the Duluth Complex and North Shore Volcanic Group. Through eons of erosion, uplift, and glaciation, these rocks emerged in northern Minnesota, prominently visible in rock outcrops and road cuts and along the North Shore of Lake Superior.

Geologists identify rocks in the field by observing the location and provenance of the rock formation and determining the basic rock group (igneous, metamorphic, or sedimentary), grain size, pattern, color, hardness, and mineral composition. Despite the ease with which geologists may be able to identify the rocks, novices may be understandably bewildered because, until a sudden interest gripped them, a rock was just a rock—that thing in nature upon which lichen grew or a red fox stood sentry, or that was quarried or mined. Our goal here is for participants to be able to identify four major rock types found in the North Woods, Great Lakes region: basalt, gabbro, rhyolite, and granite. These four types represent a large percentage of visible rocks in northern Minnesota and have relatively straightforward identifiable characteristics.

Basalt

Basalt (Figure 19) is a gray to bluish black rock made up of small crystals (undetectable to eye) with iron-rich minerals in exposed surfaces oxidizing to brown or rust colored. It may have vesicles (empty holes/bubbles) or *amygdules* (filled vesicles). An igneous extrusive rock, it formed during the midcontinent rift event 1.1 billion years ago, cooling above ground or underwater over months and years (decades at most). Probably the most common volcanic rock on our planet, basalt is found along the Lake Superior shoreline and the Dalles of the St. Croix.

Figure 19. Basalt

Gabbro

Gabbro (Figure 20) has a dark gray or black background color with flecks of large, light-colored, coarse-grained crystals. An igneous rock with large, coarse-grained crystals, it cooled deep underground over millions of years. The intrusive equivalent of basalt, gabbro is sometimes called "black granite." Although this rock makes up most of the Duluth Complex of the Arrowhead region, the best places to see it are the Lake Superior beaches and exposed hilltop outcrops of Duluth. It formed during the mid-continent rift event 1.1 billion years ago.

Figure 20. Gabbro

Rhyolite

Rhyolite (Figure 21) is light red to salmon-colored with small crystals (undetectable to eye). An igneous extrusive rock, it cooled above ground over months and years (or faster). Rhyolite may have vesicles or amygdules and commonly forms at the surface of cooling lava. You can find rhyolite pebbles on any of the beaches of Lake Superior, and see particularly nice rhyolite formations at Palisade Head and Tettegouche State Park. Rhyolite formed during the midcontinent rift event 1.1 billion years ago.

Figure 21. Rhyolite

Granite

Granite (Figure 22) is gray or pink with flecks of large, coarse-grained light and dark crystals. An igneous rock, it cooled deep underground over millions of years. It is probably the most common rock making up Earth's crust and is the intrusive equivalent of rhyolite. Bedrock granite in northern Minnesota formed during the Algoman orogeny 2.6 billion years ago. Granite pebbles along the North Shore were carried in from Canada by glaciers during the most recent ice age, and probably date to the Algoman orogeny.

Figure 22. Granite

MASTER
NATURALIST
TOOLBOX

The purpose of this activity is to get participants (in groups) to make their own observations about their rock samples, form descriptions of them in their own words, and then teach the class how to identify their given rocks. The purpose is not to learn technical geological terms or to learn the complex natural history and mineral composition of the rocks. After this activity, participants should be able to point at a rock and say, "that's basalt (or gabbro or rhyolite or granite)!"

Activity

1. Divide the class into four groups. Give each group a basalt, gabbro, rhyolite, or granite rock (don't tell them which one they are getting); a hand lens or magnifying glass; and a North Woods, Great Lakes Linnaeus List.

2. Have students:
   - identify the rock using their Linnaeus List
   - determine if it is igneous, metamorphic, or sedimentary (and if igneous, extrusive or intrusive), also using the Linnaeus List
   - describe the rock in their own words
   - develop a method for identifying and remembering the name of their rock.

3. Have groups take turns being the "expert" on their rock and present observations and identification tricks to the rest of the class. For example, one group related an anecdote where they would mistakenly pick up round red rhyolite rocks while they were harvesting small red potatoes from their garden, since they looked so similar. Everyone remembered the red rhyolite potatoes!

4. After the presentations, discuss what was learned about basic identification skills. What were some challenges? Were some rocks easier to identify than others? Why? What do all these rocks have in common? How do rocks that do not originate in Minnesota get here? Have fun!

Resources

Ojakangas, R. W. (2009). *Roadside geology of Minnesota*. Missoula, MT: Mountain Press Publishing Company.

Stensaas, M. S., & Kollath, R. (2000). *Rock picker's guide to Lake Superior's North Shore*. Duluth, MN: Kollath-Stensaas Publishing.

Strauss, A. L.; Blair, R. B.; Meyer, N. J.; Rager, A. R. B. (2010). *North Woods, Great Lakes Linnaeus List*. St. Paul, MN: Regents of the University of Minnesota.

MASTER
NATURALIST
TOOLBOX

LESSON 2

How Glaciers Move

Objective

Participants will understand how glaciers move and respond to gravity. They will observe how friction can slow movement and how underlying water affects speed.

Audience Type

Teen/Adult

Supplies

For making glacier goo

- ☐ One teaspoon borax powder
- ☐ 1.25 cup warm water
- ☐ One cup white glue
- ☐ Food coloring
- ☐ Two mixing bowls
- ☐ Popsicle sticks for stirring
- ☐ Rubber gloves

CAUTION

Glue and borax are toxic and should not be ingested. We therefore advise against allowing young children to play with the compound unsupervised. Glacier goo should not stick to clothes, hair, or skin.

Other supplies

- ☐ Chute made from PVC pipe (three feet long, three inches wide, sliced in half lengthwise)
- ☐ Books to prop up chute
- ☐ Airtight container to store goo
- ☐ Dry erase marker
- ☐ Ruler
- ☐ Timer
- ☐ Plastic drinking straw
- ☐ One teaspoon water

Background

Despite their massive sizes and seeming permanence, glaciers are always on the move. Gravity pulls glacial ice downhill and causes it to deform under its own weight. As glaciers move across the landscape, erosion and deposition of soil, rock, and debris change the underlying surface. Most glaciers creep along at a pace that's too slow to detect with the naked eye (about a foot a day). But sometimes conditions are just right to cause glaciers to surge forward at speeds of 100 feet or more per day!

Figure 23. Glacier goo runs its course.

MASTER NATURALIST TOOLBOX

Ice is a special substance. Under steady pressure, such as that exerted by the weight of a glacier, ice will bend and flow. Under a lot of stress, ice will break. This is how crevasses form in glaciers.

Glue, water, and borax combine to make a goo that bends and flows very much like ice and therefore makes an excellent medium for simulating the movement of glaciers (Figure 23). In this activity you will make a model glacier out of this "glacier goo." Additionally, you will observe how subglacial water affects glacial flow. Glaciers and ice sheets can have a water layer beneath them. This helps them flow by providing a lubricating film of water that allows the glacier to slide.

Activity

1. In the first bowl, combine 3/4 cup warm water and one cup glue. Stir until well mixed. In the second mixing bowl, combine 1/2 cup warm water and one teaspoon of borax powder and stir until the powder is fully dissolved. Combine the contents of the two mixing bowls and stir until a glob forms. Put half of the glob back into the first mixing bowl. Add a few drops of food coloring. Use your hands to knead the mixture in each bowl until it is well mixed (about two to three minutes). Wear rubber gloves to prevent staining your hands with the food coloring. (Note: This step can be done ahead of class to save time. Glacier goo can last for months if stored in an airtight container.)

2. Break off fist-sized chunks of white goo and colored goo. Lay them out in strips of alternating color into one end of the valley (PVC chute). Pat the strips together to reform a single striped glob of goo.

3. Prop up one end of the PVC chute with books so the glacier will be able to flow downhill. Use the dry erase marker to mark the position of the front end of the glacier on the side of the chute. Set your timer for five minutes. Mark the new location of the glacier terminus. Measure the distance the goo traveled from start to finish at the center, the left side, and the right side of the glacier. Determine the rate of flow for all three by dividing distance by time. Record your results.

4. Level the chute, reset the goo, and mark the terminus of the glacier. Set your timer for five minutes. Poke the plastic drinking straw through the goo as close to the top as possible. Make sure the goo doesn't plug the straw. Tilt the chute again and add one teaspoon of water through the straw to simulate meltwater seeping down through the glacier. Predict how you think the glacier will flow compared with the first time you ran the experiment. Measure the distance the goo traveled from start to finish at the center, the left side, and the right side. Determine the rate of flow with water. Record your results.

5. Let the glacier continue to flow as you discuss the following ideas: What causes glaciers to flow? When the glacier initially flowed, what shape did the front of the glacier take? What part of the glacier flows the fastest? Why? Describe the difference between the flow rates before and after you introduced water. Why do you think this change occurs? Why is it important for scientists to find out how fast glaciers are moving? How does this exercise demonstrate glacial dynamics experienced by Minnesota?

Resources

Link to original glacier activity: http://serc.carleton.edu/eslabs/cryosphere/3c.html

MASTER NATURALIST TOOLBOX

Conserve

This "Conserve" section highlights organizations that offer opportunities for Minnesota Master Naturalist Volunteers to participate in stewardship and citizen science activities related to geology and climate in the North Woods, Great Lakes region. Please visit the websites to learn more.

National Map Corps

The National Map Corps consists of citizens who devote some of their time to provide mapping information to the U.S. Geological Survey's National Map. Members may be invited to participate in projects within mutually determined work areas. The only requirements are owning a GPS receiver and having internet access. The National Map is a consistent framework for geographic knowledge needed by the nation. It provides public access to high-quality geospatial data and information from multiple partners to help support decision making by resource managers and the public.

http://nationalmap.gov/TheNationalMapCorps

Natural Resources Conservation Service Earth Team Volunteers

Since 1935, the Natural Resources Conservation Service (originally called the Soil Conservation Service) has helped America's private landowners and managers conserve their soil, water, and other natural resources. NRCS employees provide technical assistance based on sound science and suited to a customer's specific needs. The NRCS created the Earth Team Volunteers program so people can help right in their own communities, whatever their talents may be. Minnesota Earth Team Volunteers have led the nation by contributing 87,315 hours of time helping to protect and conserve natural resources. Volunteers plan and implement conservation practices on the land, conduct natural resource inventories, improve wildlife habitat, organize conservation tours and exhibits for school groups, organize data, prepare newsletters, take photos, write articles, produce artwork, and much more.

www.mn.nrcs.usda.gov/about/volunteer

Minnesota Volunteer Precipitation Observing Program (MNgage)

The DNR Minnesota State Climatology Office's Minnesota Volunteer Precipitation Observing Program (MNgage) harnesses the observation and reporting skills of hundreds of volunteers statewide. Participants report daily precipitation measurements online; observations are invaluable for laying the groundwork for forecasting in a shifting climate.

MNgage

http://climate.umn.edu/HIDENsityEdit/HIDENweb.htm

Expand

This section suggests some things you can use, do, pursue, read, or join to develop as a naturalist.

Journal

EXPERIENCE Find a rock, any rock. You don't even need to go outside. Look around you—what do you see? The homes and buildings that shelter us are made from rocks and trees. Can you find glass (melted sand), a stone countertop, a ceramic mug, or a brick wall?

REFLECT Where did these rock materials come from? How did the original rock form, and how did they get where they are now? What does the future hold for these materials 100 or 10,000 or 1 million years from now?

RECORD Answer this question in your journal: Are humans a geologic force? Think of two reasons why we might be considered so, and two why not.

Read

Roadside Geology of Minnesota

Richard Ojakangas.
2009. Missoula, Montana: Mountain Press Publishing Company. 368 pp.

This guide begins with a tidy review of the mechanisms of geology and an overview of the geologic history of Minnesota. The book is then divided into regions of exploration, highlighting exposed rock outcrops and road cuts for convenient observation around the state. Don't leave home without it!

Rock Picker's Guide to Lake Superior's North Shore

Mark Sparky Stensaas and Rick Kollath.
2000. Duluth, Minnesota: Kollath-Stensaas Publishing. 48 pp.

This is a succinct and handy guide to all of the rocks you will find on the beaches of the North Shore (and almost anywhere in the North Woods, Great Lakes region). With beautiful illustrations and well-written text, it provides an introduction to Minnesota geology, profiles for different beaches along the North Shore, and detailed information on your favorite finds.

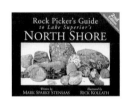

Surf

The Paleontology Portal

Click on "Exploring Time & Space" and let the journey begin! You can select from different countries or U.S. states and then select a time period to see information and view a map of the bedrock geology. For example, select "Minnesota" during the "Precambrian" to see where the oldest rocks in Minnesota can be found.

www.paleoportal.org

Minnesota Geological Survey

Burning to know more about the nitty-gritty details of Minnesota geology? Click on "Rocks and Minerals" for an in-depth look at native rocks, or click on "Glacial Geology" to learn more about the ice age. Or simply get lost poring over the many maps illustrating bedrock geology!

www.mngs.umn.edu/mngeology.htm

Join

Your Local Rock, Gem, and Mineral Club

Minnesota boasts at least ten local gem and mineral clubs, three of which are in the North Woods, Great Lakes Region: Cuyuna Rock, Gem & Mineral Society (http://webdom.org), Carlton County Gem and Mineral Club, and Itasca Rock and Mineral Club. Visit the website for meeting locations and times.

www.rockhounds.com/rockshop/clubs/minnesota.shtml

Geological Society of Minnesota

The Geological Society of Minnesota is a public-spirited, nonprofit educational organization that sponsors an annual program of stimulating lectures in the winter and field trips in the summer. It also conducts outreach activities in Twin Cities area elementary schools.

www.gsmn.org

Additional Reading

Green, J. (2005). *Geology on display: Geology and scenery of Minnesota's North Shore state parks.* St. Paul: Minnesota Department of Natural Resources.

Okajangas, R., and Matsch, C. (1982). *Minnesota's geology*. Minneapolis: University of Minnesota Press.

MASTER
NATURALIST
TOOLBOX

Copyrighted Photographs and Images Used With Permission

Figure 1. Courtesy of Minnesota Department of Natural Resources

Figure 2. Courtesy of Jirsa, M. A., Boerboom, T. J., Chandler, V. W., Mossler, J. H., Runkel, A. C., and Setterholm, D. R. (2011). Bedrock geologic map of Minnesota. Minnesota Geological Survey State Map Series S-1

Figure 3. Courtesy of Sarah L. Keefer

Figure 4. Courtesy of Macmillan Publishers Ltd. (Nature 473[7348], 460–461, 2011)

Figure 5. Courtesy of Pam and Michael Pagelkopf

Figure 6. Courtesy of Paul Harrison, Wikimedia Commons

Figure 7. Courtesy of Sarah L. Keefer

Figure 8. Courtesy of Sarah L. Keefer

Figure 9. Courtesy of Carol A. Stein, Seth Stein, Miguel Merino, G. Randy Keller, Lucy M. Flesch, Donna M. Jurdy. Was the Midcontinent Rift part of a successful seafloor-spreading episode? http://onlinelibrary.wiley.com/doi/10.1002/2013GL059176/full, John Wiley and Sons

Figure 10. Courtesy of Wikimedia Commons

Figure 11. Courtesy of Sarah L. Keefer

Figure 12. Courtesy of Sarah L. Keefer

Figure 13. Courtesy of Carrie Jennings

Figure 14. Courtesy of Sarah L. Keefer

Figure 15. Courtesy of Paul Purington

Figure 16. Courtesy of State Climatology Office – Minnesota DNR Division of Ecological and Water Resources

Figure 17. Courtesy of State Climatology Office – Minnesota DNR Division of Ecological and Water Resources

Figure 18. Courtesy of State Climatology Office – Minnesota DNR Division of Ecological and Water Resources

Figure 19. Courtesy of John Geissler, Boulder Lake Environmental Learning Center

Figure 20. Courtesy of John Geissler, Boulder Lake Environmental Learning Center

Figure 21. Courtesy of John Geissler, Boulder Lake Environmental Learning Center

Figure 22. Courtesy of John Geissler, Boulder Lake Environmental Learning Center

Figure 23. Courtesy of Leigh Stearns, Climate Change Institute

MASTER
NATURALIST
TOOLBOX

Chapter 2: The Forest and the Trees

Plant Communities of the North Woods

Laura Duffey, Joe Walewski, and Danielle M. Hefferan

Goal

Understand how geography, disturbance, and management shape the distribution of plant communities in the North Woods.

Objectives

1. Describe how the plants in the North Woods are adapted to geography, soil conditions, and disturbance.

2. Define major plant communities in the North Woods.

3. Describe how forests have layers.

4. Describe why and how forests change over time.

5. Use a dichotomous key to identify trees common to the North Woods.

Introduction

Take a walk through a Minnesota forest and you may get the sense that it's a relatively settled place—as though it always has been what it is now. True, those towering pines didn't arrive yesterday, and their staid presence gives the forest a feeling of permanence that farmland and city subdivisions just don't share. Yet even the least disturbed, most "natural" areas of our state have seen many changes. These magnificent *ecosystems* are the result of millennia of transformations. And they are still changing. In this chapter, we'll take a look at the big picture of Minnesota's forests, then focus in on specific plants and plant communities that comprise the forests of the North Woods, Great Lakes region.

The Big Picture

If you've spent any time in the woods, you know that different forests have different "feels." Bushwhacking in the Chippewa National Forest near Cass Lake gives you a different sense than tromping around in the Big Woods at Nerstrand State Park near Rochester, which gives you a different sense than ambling through Forestville State Park in southeastern Minnesota. Though the differences in these forests may seem obvious to you, they may be hard to define exactly—and it may be tough to point to the place where one type of forest ends and another begins. Is the forest near Hibbing different from one near Hinckley? Is the forest near Hinckley different from the one near Mille Lacs? Where do the forests switch from being typical of the North Woods to being typical of the Big Woods?

Don't feel alone if this leaves you befuddled. Plant ecologists have spent their entire careers attempting to describe these differences and determine why they exist.

Big, Broad Biomes

A big part of the "why" is climate—specifically, average annual temperature and precipitation. As we learned in Chapter 1, average annual temperature is higher in southern Minnesota than it is in the north; average annual precipitation is higher in the east than in the west.

What does that mean from a forest's perspective? Well, forests are often defined by their trees, and trees come in (mainly) two kinds: deciduous and coniferous. The typical deciduous tree is a lot like Goldilocks: It wants its growing conditions "just right" (not too hot, not too cold, not too wet, not too dry). As a result, Minnesota has a band of deciduous forest running diagonally from the northwest to the southeast (Figure 1). Coniferous forests, on the other hand, thrive in colder, damp conditions and find northeastern Minnesota—the North Woods, Great Lakes region—

just to their liking, while plants that like it warm and dry inhabit the Prairie Grassland biome to the southwest, and those that favor cold and dry make up the Tallgrass Aspen Parklands biome in the north.

Communities and Assemblages

While understanding the major biomes in the state sheds light on the varying nature (literally) of Minnesota's forests, it's important to realize that

Figure 1. The Coniferous Forest biome to the northeast and the Prairie Grassland biome to the southwest are separated by the Deciduous Forest biome in the south and the Tallgrass Aspen Parklands biome in the north.

biomes aren't homogeneous habitats. The forest around Ely isn't identical to the forest around Cloquet, even though they are both part of the Coniferous Forest biome. Different species of trees and other plants dominate under different conditions in different localities.

For example, oaks occur throughout Minnesota, but northern red oaks reach all the way to the Boundary Waters while white oaks tend to be found in the southeastern part of the state (Figure 2). This means that an oak woodland near Bemidji will have a different feel to it than one near Rochester.

Similarly, naturally occurring white cedar is limited to the northeastern part of the state. In contrast, its needle-leaved cousin, the tamarack, reaches far enough west and south to cover almost two-thirds of the state (Figure 3).

These variations have led to a longstanding disagreement among plant ecologists. Some believe that different types of forests are long-evolved associations that function almost as a single entity. They believe that a northern wet ash swamp, for example, can be considered a superorganism with its

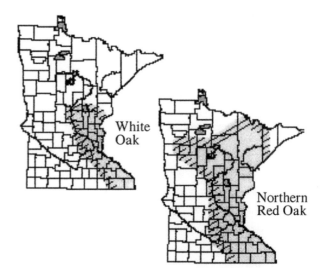

Figure 2. Many species of trees reach the northern limits of their distribution in Minnesota, but those limits are not the same for all species.

own traits and characteristics. Others, however, view forests as *assemblages*, which are collections of species that happen to be occupying the same piece of land at the same time. They think that most of the trees in a forest are there merely because they find the physical conditions of the forest to be a good fit for them. Their ability to do so is the result of sometimes narrow climatic requirements, and the ever-changing nature of ecosystems means that their residence in any given area is somewhat temporary. Despite this difference, both sets of plant ecologists refer to the different types of forest by the names listing the main tree species

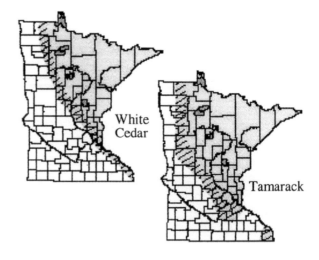

Figure 3. Many species of trees reach their southern limits of distribution in Minnesota. Not surprisingly, the limits vary from species to species.

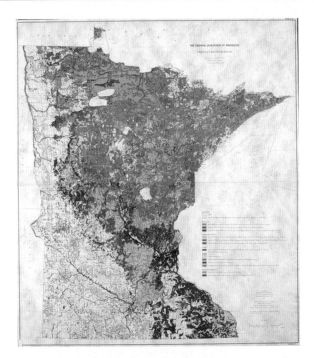

Figure 4. The natural vegetation of Minnesota at the time of the public lands survey in 1847–1907 was a mix of prairies, wetlands, broadleaf trees, and conifers.

The Marschner Map

In 1930, Francis J. Marschner, a research assistant for the U.S. Department of Agriculture, created a map of Minnesota's presettlement landscape by meticulously combing more than 200 volumes of the 1847–1907 public land surveys and determining what plant communities grew in every township in the state. The resulting map, known as the Marschner map, today provides valuable insights into the vegetation of Minnesota before it was disturbed by European settlement.

that are found there, such as spruce-fir, aspen-birch, or tamarack.

What determines which type of forest grows where? A look at a map of vegetation in Minnesota before European settlement (Figure 4) makes it easy to see that average annual temperature and precipitation are not the only things that affect what grows where in Minnesota. Other factors that determine whether the

forest outside your door is aspen-birch or jack pine barrens include soils, topography, ecological history, available moisture, and a dash of unpredictability. And, of course, on top of these natural influences, humans also dramatically shape the look and location of forests in Minnesota. We'll talk more about that in Chapter 8.

North Woods Mosaic

Now that we've learned the broad story of how trees and other plants are distributed across Minnesota, let's take a closer look at those found in the North Woods, Great Lakes region.

The northeastern third of the state is part of the Coniferous Forest biome, which stretches north into Canada. This biome is defined by a relatively moist, cool climate with a short growing season. In many parts thin soils cover bedrock, and fierce north winds bring temperatures plunging far below zero during long, dark winters. These conditions favor the growth of conifers, which are able to photosynthesize in winter and hang onto *nutrients* needed to survive in the thin soils. They also favor trees such as paper birch, quaking aspen, and balsam poplar that have special adaptations for surviving temperatures of −40 °F and colder (Figure 1).

Before 1850, the Coniferous Forest biome was an intricate mosaic of mostly northern hardwoods, peatlands, and various pine forests. Forest categories in the Marschner map for this part of the state include aspen-birch, big woods (oaks, elm, ash, basswood, and maple), conifer and bog swamps, jack pine barrens, mixed hardwood and pine, mixed white pine and Norway pine, pine flats, and white pine. Although the Coniferous Forest biome we see today is quite different than before European settlement, portions of these various forest types still remain.

Meet the Plants

The cast of plant characters found in the various forests that make up the Coniferous Forest biome fall into five main categories: mosses and liverworts, ferns and fern allies, algae, conifers, and flowering plants. Let's meet a few of them!

Mosses and Liverworts

Mosses and liverworts belong to a group of plants known as *bryophytes*. Bryophytes lack many of the basic parts we're used to finding in plants. Instead of flowers and seeds, they reproduce via spores. They don't have vascular tissues — the specialized structures other plants have for carrying water and nutrients — or the support material *lignin*, so they can't grow taller than a couple of inches.

Mosses are commonly found in cool, damp places (Figure 5). You've probably heard they tend to grow on the north sides of trees. In fact, especially in the North Woods, they grow on all sides of trees.

Sphagnum moss (commonly known as peat moss) grows on the ground in acidic wetlands known as *bogs* and *fens*. It provides habitat for a long list of peatland plants, including sedges, blueberry, leatherleaf, bog laurel, bog rosemary, cranberry, snowberry, Labrador tea, orchids, and carnivorous plants such as pitcher plants and sundew.

Feathermosses are a major component of black spruce swamps, and when you see them you'll immediately know how they earned their name. Pincushion moss can be found on the floors of drier pine forests.

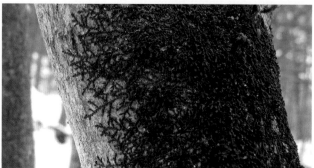

Figure 5. Many mosses and liverworts can maintain a brilliant green even into winter.

Polytrichum mosses (hair cap mosses) are common on rocky outcrops.

Liverworts (Figure 5) are commonly found in moist areas. There are two main groups: thallose liverworts have a flattened, ribbon-like structure, and leafy liverworts have thin, leaflike flaps on either side of a main stem. Look for species of the leafy liverwort, including *Frullania* spp., on maple bark. When dry they are dark brown to purple, and when wet they take on a green tone.

Ferns and Fern Allies

Like mosses and liverworts, ferns lack flowers and seeds. But they do have vascular structures to carry water through their tissues. Around 350 to 300 million years ago they were the dominant feature of the landscape. When dinosaurs roamed the earth, some ferns stood more than 100 feet tall.

Ferns and fern allies of the North Woods, Great Lakes region include ferns, horsetails, clubmosses, quillworts, and spikemosses. There are approximately 100 species in the region — some common and others extremely rare. You can find them in a wide range of habitats, including swamps, rocky outcrops, disturbed areas, and forests of all types.

Ferns are generally featherlike in appearance. Most have spore-bearing structures on the backs of their leaves. Some, such as interrupted ferns and moonworts, produce distinctive spore-bearing structures.

Horsetails (Figure 6) and scouring rushes have an upright stem, often with wispy branches that give them a look of a horse's tail. The spore-bearing "cones" are often perched at the top of the main stem.

Have you ever seen what look like miniature pine trees on the *forest floor*? These plants, commonly called princess pine or ground pine, are actually clubmosses (Figure 7) — even though they are neither mosses nor pines. Along with quillworts and spikemosses, clubmosses belong to a group known as *lycophytes*. Clubmosses produce underground or surface runners from which new plants arise. If you see one clubmoss, you will most likely see many others.

Figure 6. The only remaining member of an ancient family of plants that have vascular tissues but reproduce via spores instead of seeds, *Equisetum*, or horsetail, is quite common in all sorts of plant communities, including the floor of North Woods forests.

Spikemosses are easily overlooked. Small and very similar in appearance to mosses, they can be a challenge to locate.

You'll need to wade — or even snorkel — to observe quillworts. These plants are found in shallow water along shorelines or even in clear, cold lakes as deep as 10 feet. They have leaves similar in shape to porcupine quills.

Spotlight Species – Sphagnum Moss

Vast stretches of northern Minnesota are covered by peat bogs, wet areas with unique vegetation. They owe their existence to a type of tiny bryophyte known as *sphagnum* (Figure 8). Lightweight and feathery, sphagnum moss plants are made up of two kinds of cells. Chlorocytes, which are living cells, are in charge

Figure 7. Clubmosses and princess pines such as this *Dendrolycopodium dendroideum* are neither mosses nor pines, but vascular plants that reproduce with spores.

of capturing sunlight and transforming it into more sphagnum. Hyalocytes are hollow dead cells that readily fill with water — so much so that a clump of sphagnum can weigh 20 times wet what it weighs dry. (Aren't you glad you're not made of sphagnum?) As sphagnum absorbs nutrients from its surroundings, it gives off hydrogen ions, acidifying its environment. The natural acidity of the sphagnum, even when dry, gives it antiseptic qualities. It was used in World War I in bandages for major wounds.

Figure 8. Look for sphagnum mosses such as *Sphagnum angustifolium* in bogs and fens in the North Woods, Great Lakes region.

Sphagnum makes more of itself in three ways: by branching, by sprouting new plants from bits of old ones, and by producing spores. As it does, it creates vast, waterlogged mats of highly absorbent plant tissue that thicken as one layer piles on top of the previous one. This layering process sometimes creates floating platforms that can support the weight of large mammals such as humans and even massive moose!

When the lower layers of sphagnum moss die, they partly decompose to form peat, a rich, organic, soil-like substance that stores vast amounts of the greenhouse gas carbon dioxide. Peat accumulates slowly — at a rate of inches per millennium. In different parts of the world, including Minnesota, it's mined for *horticultural* use and sometimes for fuel. Recent commercial uses are for treating and cleaning pool and spa water.

Algae

Algae are extremely varied in structure and size. They also grow under a wide variety of conditions. Though algae play a particularly big part in aquatic systems, you can find them just about everywhere.

Ecologically, algae serve many roles. Diatoms, dinoflagellates, and other microscopic algae, known as *phytoplankton*, are part of the food base of many aquatic ecosystems. We'll learn more about that in Chapter 6.

Chara are algae that resemble land plants with stemlike and leaflike structures. They grow submerged, attached to muddy lake bottoms, in water with relatively little oxygen. Anglers sometimes call these "weeds" when their lures get tangled in them. They aren't weeds at all, but important components of a healthy ecosystem.

Algae of the genus Trentepohlia (Figure 9) grow on tree trunks and wet rocks. They sometimes are part of the symbiotic system of lichens (see sidebar). They can be orange or red.

Figure 9. We most expect to find algae in ponds, but you can easily see terrestrial algae if the substrate is white — such as this reddish *Trentepohlia* species on birch bark.

Conifers

Coniferous ("cone-bearing") trees are icons of the North Woods, Great Lakes region. They reproduce by cones, with small male cones producing pollen that fertilizes seeds in larger female cones. Most conifers produce male and female cones on the same tree. Junipers and yew, however, produce pollen and seed on separate male and female plants.

The pines of the North Woods, Great Lakes region — red, white, and jack — have long needles in bunches and large cones that take two years to mature. Needles grow every year and last two to five years, depending on the species. Fallen needles can produce a layer several inches thick on the ground. Combined with

the shade pines produce, this duff can make it hard for other plants to grow under pines.

Spruces (black and white) and firs (balsam) are common members of northern forest communities. Like pines, they are adapted to cold, dry winters and heavy snows.

The northern white cedar is most commonly found today in wetlands. However, early data collected by surveyors suggest that cedar once thrived in drier habitat. White-tailed deer (a relatively new addition to the North Woods) eat cedar, and it appears that where there are deer there is little or no cedar regeneration.

Tamaracks (Figure 10) are easy to spot in the autumn when their needles turn a deep gold. They are unusual among conifers in that they also are deciduous, meaning they shed their leaves. Like cedars, tamaracks were once widely distributed over the landscape, including wetlands and uplands. A warming climate, which helps the tamarack-pestering eastern larch beetle thrive, makes it unlikely that you will see tamaracks anywhere other than a wetland.

Figure 10. Not all conifers are evergreens, and not all evergreens are conifers. The tamarack *(Larix laricina)*, a conifer, drops its needles each fall.

Flowering Plants

Flowering plants can be found in every plant community in both aquatic and terrestrial systems. Not all have conspicuous flowers; those that do tend to be pollinated by insects and other animals, while those with inconspicuous flowers tend to use the wind to spread their pollen.

Figure 11. Most flowering trees lack "showy" flowers, but look closely to see diminutive magenta female flowers of the beaked hazel *(Corylus cornuta)* in early spring. The male catkin flower is below in this image.

All trees except conifers are flowering plants (Figure 11). Birch, alder, and poplar produce vast amounts of pollen that is carried by the wind. Cherry, juneberry, basswood, and willow depend upon animal pollinators and produce far less pollen.

In addition to flowering trees, the Coniferous Forest biome is home to a wide variety of *herbaceous* flowering plants. They come in many shapes and sizes and have many different adaptive strategies. Some even lack chlorophyll (Figure 12)! Different plants flower at different times, creating a rainbow of color spread through the growing season.

Early spring flowers are commonly white or only lightly pigmented. Instead of investing their energy in making pigments that visually attract pollinators, these plants produce odors that draw moths, beetles, and flies. Many early spring flowers, including Solomon's seal, Canada mayflower, and bellwort, belong to the lily family. Other early bloomers include spring beauty, wood anemone, trillium, wild leek, marsh marigold, and bloodroot. All take advantage of the sunlight before trees grow leaves and the resulting canopy shades the forest floor.

As the canopy forms and less sunlight reaches the forest floor, midsummer flowers emerge: columbine, sarsaparilla, twisted stalk, baneberry, strawberry, and thimbleberry. Elaborate orchids and colorful flowers of the rose family also take the stage.

Finally come the late-summer flowers. This group is dominated by asters, goldenrods, thistles, and plants of disturbed areas including ox-eye daisy, hawkweed, tansy, fireweed, and a variety of clovers.

Sedges, rushes, and grasses are wind pollinated and lack showy flowers (Figure 13). You can find these flowering plants in every plant community. It is worth your time to learn more about these plants. A good place to start is with this mnemonic for telling them apart: "Sedges have edges, rushes are round, and grasses have nodes and grow from the ground."

Fens and bogs contain plants in the Ericaceae family, which includes blueberry, leatherleaf, bog laurel, bog rosemary, cranberry, snowberry, and Labrador tea. Carnivorous plants, such as pitcher plant, sundew, and bladderwort, have adapted to the difficulty of

Figure 12. Some flowering plants lack chlorophyll. This Indian pipe *(Monotropa uniflora)* gets its energy not from the sun but from a symbiotic relationship with a mycorrhizal fungus.

Figure 13. Not all flowers attract pollinators. Those of grasses, rushes, and sedges, all wind pollinated, are far less showy and fragrant than those pollinated by insects, birds, and other pollinators.

obtaining nitrogen from the nutrient-poor soils commonly found in such habitats by absorbing what they need from insects they trap and kill.

Lakes, *marshes*, ponds, and other communities inundated by water may be home to marsh cinquefoil, wild iris, calla, pickerelweed, and loosestrife along the shorelines. Water lilies, pondweeds, coontail, and eelgrass are flowering plants routinely found in shallow and even deep rich waters of lakes and ponds.

Spotlight Species – Paper Birch

Figure 14. The flaky bark of paper birch trees can be spotted throughout the North Woods.

Stark white against the blue sky, golden-leaved in fall, paper birch (Figure 14) are among the most iconic trees of the North Woods, Great Lakes region. They sprout in sunny spots, such as clearings left behind by fire or harvest, preferring well-drained soil with plenty of moisture. When they reach maturity, each tree produces both male and female flowers in the form of catkins that sprout from the branches in spring. Seed crops are cyclical, with large numbers produced every three to four years. Many animals use paper birch as a food source. Deer, moose, rabbits, and porcupines

nibble the branches. Birds such as ruffed grouse and chickadees eat its seeds, buds, and catkins. Insects such leafminers and birch borers thrive on the leaves or bark.

If you've spent much time in Minnesota's North Woods, you've probably observed that birch often grow in clumps. What's that all about? Individual birch trees are not known for living long lives, but when wind, disease, or age gets them down (literally), new stems often sprout up around the main one — a form of vegetative growth called *stump sprouting.*

Another striking feature of paper birch trees is their "eyes" — the dark spots that speckle the bark. Known as *lenticels*, these breaks in the bark allow air to get under the birch's otherwise relatively impermeable skin.

Humans derive bountiful benefits from birch. American Indians have long used the tree's pliable bark to make baskets, canoes, and other useful objects. Campers find bits of oily bark picked up along the trail handy for starting campfires — although the wood from downed birch is notoriously bad for burning. North Woods loggers harvest birch for paper, plywood, and other forest products. Birch is a source of home remedies, and scientists in recent years have discovered the bark contains chemicals with anticancer, antimicrobial, and other useful properties. You will often find that when a birch tree rots, it leaves behind a tube of bark.

Birch trees represent an early stage of *succession* in a forest. As the trees mature, large scrolls of loose bark can hang from the trunks. These provide fuel for fires moving through the forest, and the scrolls can be lifted into the air to light spot fires ahead of the fire front. Interestingly, this creates the kind of clearing that allows the birch forest to regenerate itself through stump sprouting and its windborne seed.

Birch trees are not very tolerant of tough conditions, particularly heat or drought. They have been dying in droves along the North Shore of Lake Superior in recent years, victims of drought and browsing by increasingly prolific white-tailed deer.

A relative of the paper birch is bog birch (*Betula glandulosa*), which is a dwarf tree with small, coin-shaped leaves, found in bogs.

Neither Animal nor Plant

When we think of living things, we often think of plants and animals. But when it comes to life, these are just the tip of the iceberg! Most living things are members of other groups, neither animals nor plants. Two of these less-considered kinds of living things that play important roles in North Woods, Great Lakes ecosystems are bacteria and fungi. A third, lichens, are a mash-up of a fungus with a bacterium or alga.

Bacteria

With approximately 150,000 known species worldwide, bacteria are extremely diverse. They are also abundant: There can be billions of bacterial cells in a single ounce of soil! In fact, the total weight of all bacteria on Earth exceeds that of all plants and animals combined.

Bacteria are big stuff when it comes to keeping ecosystems functioning. They make most of the oxygen we breathe. They break down plant and animal material, releasing nutrients so other living things can use them. They pull nitrogen — one of the main building blocks of life — from the air to make it available to living things. They help animals digest their food. *Frankia* species form root nodules with sweet fern and alder that help supply the plant with nitrogen. *Rhizobium* species form a similar relationship with *legumes* such as clover.

Even though individually they are invisible to the naked eye, bacteria leave signs in the environment that remind us of their presence (Figure 15). Black stains, scums, and odors are all clues that bacteria are in the neighborhood.

Cyanobacteria (aka blue-green algae) can grow in large quantities in nutrient-filled waterways. Development of lakeshore property (with the potential for leaky septic systems and yard fertilizer runoff) increases the risk of such "algae blooms." Some cyanobacteria, such as *Trebouxia* species, can partner with fungi to make lichens (see below). Rock tripes and dog pelts are two kinds of lichens

Figure 15. Bacteria are most obvious in dense black colonies on tree bark and as root nodules of clover and speckled alder. The maple on the left is coated with bacteria.

formed in this way. *Agrobacterium* is one of the organisms responsible for the formation of galls and burls in plants.

Bacteria produce methane in swamps and bogs and in the form of "wet wood," as seen as the dark black stains on poplars, birch, and maple.

Fungi

Fungi play a vital role in all ecosystems. Some serve as decomposers. Others form mycorrhizal associations — symbiotic relationships with other organisms to help provide micronutrients. With more than a million species worldwide, this group is wildly diverse and complex. Fungi include zygomycetes, ascomycetes, basidiomycetes, and lichenized fungi.

Zygomycetes are found on decaying organisms and as mycorrhizal fungi. They form the white "threads" we find in soil and rotting wood. Zygomycetes help keep nutrients "on the move" rather than stuck in one place in an ecosystem.

Figure 16. Ascomycetes come in all shapes and sizes. Some — like *Apiosporina morbosa*, shown here — even look like raccoon scat on a branch.

Ascomycetes (Figure 16) are fungi with saclike structures where spores form ("asco" comes from a Greek word meaning "sac"). We see examples all around us, including morels, cup fungi, dead man's fingers, and lobster fungi.

Basidiomycetes (Figure 17) include that typical mushroom form we think of when we hear the word "fungus" – the toadstool shape with a stipe (stalk) and cap. Examples include bracket fungi, jelly fungi, coral fungi, and stinkhorns. Basidiomycetes reproduce through spores held in clublike structures called basidia.

Figure 17. When we think of fungi, we often think of basidiomycetes such as *Amanita muscaria*, which has a typical "toadstool" stalk and cap.

Lichenized Fungi

Lichens (Figure 18) are fascinating life forms made up of two or three unique organisms forming a mutually beneficial relationship called a *symbiosis*. One partner is always a fungus; the other(s) may be bacteria and/or algae. The fungus creates the body of the lichen, and the alga or cyanobacterium, embedded within, contributes the ability to capture energy from the sun. Lichens get their scientific names from the fungi involved in the partnership.

You can find lichens on the ground, on rocks, and on trees virtually everywhere in the North Woods. The wide variety of surfaces, moisture and temperature conditions, air quality, and human disturbance levels means there's a wide variety of lichen species to like!

All told, Minnesota is home to about 750 species of lichen. In fact, if you look hard enough you can find more than 700 species in the North Woods, Great Lakes region! Many have colorful names, such as old man's beard, elegant sunburst lichen, and common greenshield. Perhaps the most familiar are the ones that form scaly, crustlike surfaces on rocks and tree bark. Other common ones are British soldiers lichen (*Cladonia cristatella*) and reindeer moss (*Cladonia rangiferina*), which are often found on flat, rocky outcrops in the Sawtooth Mountains along the North Shore of Lake Superior. Lichens provide food for deer, small mammals, birds, and insects.

Figure 18. Lichens such as these (a mix of at least three species) are among the most obviously overlooked organisms. Lichens grow on rock, soil, and tree bark and are very common in the North Woods.

Spotlight Species – Bunchberry

If you're the kind of person who appreciates plant and animal names that provide a clue as to what their namesake looks like—goldfinches, bluegills, spotted skunks—you'll like the bunchberry (dwarf dogwood).

Figure 19. Bunchberry (Cornus canadensis) is a distinct flower of our northern forests. It looks much like what most of us think of when we think of a flower.

A common inhabitant of the forest floor throughout much of the North Woods, Great Lakes region, in spring this low-growing plant with strongly veined, pointed oval leaves sports clusters of tiny flowers surrounded by four white bracts—specialized leaves often mistaken for flower petals (Figure 19). The flowers attract bees and flies. When an insect touches the bunchberry flower, a pollen-filled structure explodes, showering the visitor with pollen grains. The insect then carries these to other bunchberry blooms, fertilizing them. By midsummer the flowers ripen into (surprise!) bunches of bright red berries, each containing two seeds.

The berries quickly become food for robins, spruce grouse, deer, bears, and other animals, which then spread the seeds in their droppings. But seeds are not the only—or even the most important—way bunchberry reproduces. This plant also spreads underground.

Although it occurs in a wide range of settings, you'll often find bunchberry near rotting logs in coniferous forests. Where spreading is by *rhizomes* it can form large mats.

Slime Molds

Slime molds, or amoebozoa (Figure 20), are found in similar habitat as fungi and can look like fungi, but they are not fungi. While they are more closely related to both animals and fungi than to plants, they are still included in the botanist's realm.

Figure 20. Slime molds such as this Trichia species are actually social amoeba—an intermediate organism that falls taxonomically between fungi and animals.

Biologists recognize almost 1,000 species of slime mold. They currently classify them (these things tend to change over time) into three groups: protosteloids, dictyostelids, and myxomycetes.

Protosteloid amoebae live on dead plant matter and eat bacteria, yeasts, and fungal spores. They are considered *predators* in the decomposer community.

Dictyostelia are cellular slime molds. When food is readily available, these social amoebae feed and divide normally. When food is in short supply, they gather together to form a grex or "slug" that can migrate to find food.

Myxomycetes are the acellular amoebozoa that live in open forests most commonly on dead wood. Slime molds include blackberry slime, chocolate tube slime, red berry slime, and tapioca slime. Yummy names, but you can't eat them.

Forest Change

It's easy to look at a forest with its towering trees and imagine it has always looked just like this. In reality, forests change, sometimes dramatically, over time. Factors that alter forests include succession, fire, wind, and human activities.

Nothing Succeeds Like Succession

The patchwork we saw on the Marschner map reflects the amount of water, nutrients, and sunlight available in different areas. As the availability of such resources changes, conditions may favor a different set of plants, and these new plants will become more abundant. This causes a shift in the makeup of the forest known as *succession*. In effect, the new plants succeed the old, creating a slightly different community. So even before European settlers dramatically altered the landscape, change was a constant feature of the North Woods, Great Lakes region.

Succession also occurs after land is disturbed by fire, tree harvest, or other human activities. If you've had the opportunity to observe a clear-cut forest over a number of years, you've seen succession in action. After a boreal forest is clear-cut, grasses and other nonwoody plants typically move in. Seeds from shrubs such as raspberry and other plants that have been biding their time in the tree-shaded soil burst into life. Birds bring in additional seeds, and some fall from trees and other plants along the periphery of the open space. Eventually, light-loving trees such as aspen, paper birch, and jack pine may sprout in the clearing. After several more years, these trees can become so large and the canopy so thick that their seeds, which need sunlight, may be unable to sprout. Other, more shade-tolerant tree species such as white pine, balsam fir, and white spruce find themselves at a competitive advantage, and the species composition of the forest slowly shifts. The older sunlight-loving trees die out and their more shade-tolerant successors take over — until the next disturbance. Figure 21 shows how a typical plot of bare land may change across several decades in Minnesota.

Traditionally, plant ecologists called a forest of large, shade-tolerant trees a *climax community* because they thought that this forest was the end of forest succession. They assumed that succession was an orderly march toward status as a mature forest — just as children progress toward adulthood, eventually actually arriving. In reality, succession in forests is a bit more unpredictable than the idealized version because the orderly march occasionally gets upset and the process starts all over again. Ecologists use the word *disturbance* to describe the processes that set the game back.

Gone With the Wind

Strong winds can disrupt vast stretches of forest in one fell swoop (so to speak). On July 4, 1999, a powerful straight-line windstorm flattened tens of millions of trees in Cass, Itasca, Aitkin, St. Louis, Lake, and Cook counties, including large areas within the BWCAW, Superior National Forest, and several state forests. Two additional major wind events occurred near Sandstone in the St. Croix State Forest on July 1 and July 19, 2011, leveling 185,500 acres of trees.

Most instances of wind damage, however, don't involve millions of trees and thousands of acres. Usually wind events are limited to a single tree or two that has been weakened by insect damage, disease, or age. When a single tree falls in a forest it creates a light gap where sun can reach the forest floor directly. This oasis of light allows sun-loving pioneer species such as aspen, birch, and red pine to thrive, and also allows the saplings of shade-tolerant species to gather enough energy to shoot up to the canopy. Consequently, light gaps are often an important source of tree species diversity in a forest.

Burning Issues

Forest fires can start when lightning strikes, an ember escapes from a bonfire, or a spark escapes from a train. Soil layers near Itasca State Park contain thin lines of ash from past fires, indicating that the area burned about every 30 years in presettlement times. These low-intensity fires rarely reached the crowns (tops) of trees, but burned plant matter on the forest floor, clearing out shrubs and brush, recycling nutrients, and giving species that depend on fire a chance to thrive. The records suggest that hotter, crown-burning fires occurred much less frequently — every 110 years or so. It's the high-intensity fires that are more capable of transforming the species of plants growing on a site.

The charred land that remains in the wake of a fire becomes friendly terrain for the first pioneers. Some trees have special adaptations that help them move readily into a burned area. Aspen, for instance, is not very fussy about the soil conditions it grows under (wet or dry, acid or alkaline, nutrient rich or poor), and because new trees can sprout from roots left behind after a fire, aspen can recolonize a burned forest in a few years. Jack pine cones are *serotinous*,

Figure 22. In growing recognition of the importance of fire to the ecological health of forests, Smokey Bear's slogan changed in 2001 to "Only You Can Prevent Wildfires."

meaning that the seeds stay trapped within the cones until released by heat (120 °F or higher). When a fire burns through an area littered with these cones, they open, scattering seeds on the land.

Even though forest fires seem devastating, they are an important part of the cycle of life in a forest. If we prevent forest fires in places that commonly had fires before European settlement, combustible material can build up. Then, when a fire does occur, it can wreak havoc on both natural and human communities. When fires are allowed to burn periodically, however, woody debris doesn't build up and the fires that do occur are relatively tame. That's why forest owners and managers may let fires burn as long as they don't threaten buildings or human lives (Figure 22).

Human Hands

Perhaps the biggest source of change to North Woods forests over the years has been human activity, including logging, fragmentation, urbanization, active management, introduction of invasive species, and climate change. Following we'll look in detail at these factors, and also in Chapter 8.

YOUNG   OLDER   DISTURBANCE   YOUNG

Figure 21. Succession occurs after a forest is disturbed. Typically the plant communities change from grasses to mixed ages of trees, but actual patterns may vary.

Forest Layers

When you think of a forest, you probably think of what you see at eye level on a walk through the woods. But if you look up or look down, you quickly see that's not all there is to it. Forests are made up of layers, each with its own unique community of plants and animals.

Imagine, for a moment, standing in a sun-filtered stand of mature aspen interspersed with a few white and red pines, remnants of the great northern forest that once stretched across the brow of Minnesota. Some 60 feet above you is the top layer, or *canopy*. The contains millions of leaves busily making oxygen and sugar — key ingredients for living things — from sunlight, carbon dioxide, and water. Canopy trees include white and red pines, northern red oak, balsam fir, white cedar, mountain maple, aspen, and birch. Animals that inhabit the canopy include eagles, bats, insects, and mammals such as squirrels and porcupines.

In the *mid-story*, where chokecherry, alder, and young trees absorb whatever sunlight reaches them, a variety of birds such as warblers eat their suppers and make their nests. Many understory trees are biding their time waiting for a canopy tree to fall so they can stretch their branches into the newly available sunlight and join the other canopy trees.

Beneath that, the head-high *shrub layer* is made up of saplings and smaller woody plants such as alder, red-osier dogwood, and chokecherry. Here, berries and berry-eaters abound. The shrub layer is also home to black flies, mosquitoes, and browsers such as white-tailed deer and rabbits.

Even lower, in the *herb layer*, seedlings, grasses, and *forbs* — nonwoody flowering plants other than sedges, grasses, and rushes — live and die, providing food and habitat for mice, chipmunks, insects, frogs, and more.

The forest floor, though not their exclusive home, is the kingdom of the decomposers such as pillbugs, bacteria, and a rainbow of fungi, mosses, and lichens. Millions of deciduous leaves and conifer needles fall to the floor every fall, and create a layer of *duff* — important for the germination and early survival of many plants and seedlings. Decomposers break down leaves, plants, and animal matter into nutrients, which combine with eroded rock to create soil. The soil in turn provides the nutrients and moisture trees and other plants need to thrive — and the cycle begins again.

Modern Forest Management

Much of the Coniferous Forest biome today is dominated not by pine but by quick-growing aspen, birch, and red and jack pine that grew up after the great pine forests were logged and burned. Although shade-tolerant spruce and fir have returned to some of these forests, more than one-third of Minnesota's forested acres are primarily aspen, which thrive in the sunny, open, disturbed clearings left by logging. Aspen grow quickly from seeds and even faster from roots remaining after they are cut.

Over time, we've learned a lot about what we can do to help forests stay healthy. Today, foresters manage forests. While specific techniques may differ, the goal of forest management is similar around the world: to maintain forests that are renewable; support a diversity of plants and animals; enhance water quality; and provide timber, paper, fiber, carbon storage, clean air, healthy animal *populations*, healthy environments for humans, and the many other forest amenities humans depend on.

Sound complicated? It is! Foresters rely on centuries of experience and decades of research to determine how to manage each forest to provide the right mix of benefits while keeping it healthy. A big part of this is identifying the harvest method that best meets current and future goals for the land.

Clear-cutting is a harvest method used to regenerate tree species that need full sunlight — typically species that regenerate naturally after catastrophic fire. Here, all trees in a stand are harvested at once, so that a new even-aged stand becomes established. The new stand generally develops either from stump or root sprouts of cut trees or from newly planted seedlings. Clear-cutting works well for trees that require full sunlight, such as aspen, jack pine, and red pine.

In a *shelterwood cut*, the forester marks specific trees for removal over a period of years. Early cuttings improve the vigor and seed production of remaining trees and prepare the site for new seedlings. Partial shade reduces growth of shade-intolerant species, allowing mid-tolerant species to become well-established. Later cuttings remove most or all of the "shelter" trees, allowing the new even-aged stand to grow freely in full sunlight.

Selection harvests involve removal of single trees or small groups. The selection system generally favors more shade-tolerant species such as spruce, fir, maple, and basswood. Regeneration in selection systems can be from planting under the trees, but generally occurs through stump sprouting and natural seed fall from surrounding trees.

To create an uneven-aged stand, foresters may use single-tree selection. With this management approach, individual trees are harvested as they mature. Seedlings or sprouts grow in the spaces, creating a stand that contains trees of many ages and sizes. This system favors species that thrive in low light, such as maples and ash.

A twist on this technique is *group selection* — harvesting small groups of trees rather than individual trees. The new trees that grow in the small openings are part of a larger stand containing trees of many ages.

Reseeding or replanting is an important part of managing forests. The Minnesota State Forest Nursery supplies seedlings to replant state lands. It strategically breeds, harvests, and tests native seeds that are expected to be able to thrive in the face of *invasive* species, climate change, and land-use change. Several commercial nurseries carry native seeds as well.

Forest Fragmentation and Urbanization

Whether from logging or fire, the continuous forest ecosystem that once graced the North Woods, Great Lakes region became fragmented in the 1800s, leaving groups of trees edged with forest openings. Roads and development further broke up habitat. Soon abandoned roads, dams, and old railway tracks also left openings. Patches of second-growth forest altered the trees and understory such that they, too, fragmented habitat.

Fragmentation changes forest life in many ways. Animals that need large tracts of deep forest may move on to new territory, while others thrive along the new edges. Edges bring exposure to predators, invasive species, wind and temperature differences, loss of browse, and other factors influencing a plant's or animal's success. Smaller forest interiors lead to crowding and greater competition.

Corridors designed to connect fragments may help some animals, but leave others at risk of predation.

Caribou, moose, and large cat populations have declined in the North Woods, Great Lakes region as a result. Migrating birds have chosen different breeding grounds. Pine marten, northern goshawk, and other species have become threatened or endangered.

As cities and towns are developed, domestic animals that can disrupt wildlife move in. The mix of wildlife that thrive in an area changes, with adaptable animals that find human backyards habitable — raccoons, deer, coyotes — thriving while other, more reclusive or particular species decline.

Fragmentation and urbanization change forest soils and their inhabitants as well. Formed by layers of needles, leaves, and other organic matter, boreal soils had lain undisturbed, accumulating from several inches to a foot or more over the years. Specialized fungi and bacteria in such soil that support shrubs and wildflowers unique to the habitat can be lost as humans alter the balance of nature. Symbioses are often lost upon disruption.

Plant Community Types

The plants we've met in this chapter are individual inhabitants of the North Woods. Just as human inhabitants create human communities, each with its own characteristics, these plants in various combinations shape ecological communities with distinct traits we can use to distinguish them from each other. Although organisms from all of the plant groups can be found in every North Woods community, they don't all serve as indicators of those unique plant communities.

Botany and forestry experts would likely cringe at this crude lumping of plant community types, but for our purposes we'll use these to take a closer look at six kinds of plant groupings you're likely to encounter in the North Woods.

Wet Meadow and Marsh

Wet meadows/shrub carr communities such as those found in Cass County experience moderate annual flooding that causes soils to fluctuate between aerobic (oxygen-rich) and anaerobic (lacking oxygen) conditions. Soils range from mineral soils to muck and peat. Unlike open rich peatlands, however, wet meadows aren't thousands of years old. Rather, they were formed by relatively recent changes such as beaver activity. Surface water comes from runoff, streams, or groundwater. Plants are adapted to waterlogged conditions and can generally tolerate long wet periods. Vegetation is abundant but not extremely diverse and varies with moisture levels.

Marshes, such as those found in Crow Wing County, are dominated by wetlands with standing or slow-flowing water. Seasonal flooding is not a big deal for these wetlands, but drought cycles are. The dominant plants here tolerate persistently deep water; their stems, leaves, and roots have air spaces within the cells that store oxygen and transport it from above-water parts to below-water parts. When the soil surface is occasionally exposed during periods of low precipitation, beggarticks and smartweeds germinate. Other vegetation can be rooted on floating mats, such as duckweeds, cattails, bulrushes, arrowheads, and white water-lily.

Mesic Hardwood

Upland sites with moist soils, *mesic* hardwood forests are usually protected from fires. The soils in these communities drain well, yet retain enough moisture to buffer the system from seasonal drought. Wind-throw, disease, and other small disturbances drive change in this system. The lower layers can be starved of light — trees and shrubs capture as much as 98 percent of direct sunlight before it can reach the forest floor.

Peatland

Remember those low-lying areas left behind by the glaciers we met in Chapter 1? Over the millennia, poor drainage and cool temperatures led to the accumulation of dead but undecomposed sphagnum moss and other vegetation, creating remarkable ecosystems known as peatlands. Although all northern Minnesota peatlands share some common traits — lack of oxygen in the soil, low temperatures, and acidic conditions that inhibit plant decomposition— they also come in several different "flavors" characterized by different vegetation and physical conditions.

FORESTED RICH PEATLAND Formed on the poorly drained basins of former glacial lakes, forested rich peatlands have a dense mossy ground layer. You can see these communities today in the Leech Lake area and Lake of the Woods County.

Plants able to succeed in the low-nutrient conditions of forested rich peatlands have a variety of adaptations to survive. Evergreens, for example, retain their leaves from year to year and are able to prevent nutrient loss.

ACID PEATLAND Found in the Red Lake area, acid peatlands have a low pH (less than 5.5) and few nutrients. They get most or all water from precipitation. Few plant species thrive in these areas; in fact, some bogs may have as few as 25. Those that thrive tend to be stunted conifers, shrubs, orchids, and grasses or sedges with thick, leafy membranes to reduce moisture loss. Some plants found in these nutrient-poor peatlands capture and digest insects as a source of nitrogen. Plant survival in this system is strongly linked to associations with mycorrhizal fungi — fungi that live in and around plants' roots, helping them to access the nitrogen, phosphorus, and water they need to thrive, while the plants provide them with carbohydrates they need in turn.

Figure 23. A variety of plants and lichens cling to the bedrock along Lake Superior.

OPEN RICH PEATLAND Characterized by a cool climate, poor drainage, and lots of rain and snow, open rich peatlands are dominated by mosses, grasses, sedges, and low shrubs. Nutrients are provided (or not) by groundwater. The peat is always saturated, and plants that thrive here are adapted to high sunlight, saturated soils, low nutrients, and high minerals. Trees and shrubs are rare, but where floating mats allow some oxygen in the soil, you might find willows, bog birch, and speckled alder. Look for open rich peatlands in Lake of the Woods County.

Pine/Spruce/Fir (Fire Dependent)

Pine/spruce/fir forests such as those found in parts of the Superior National Forest depend on fire for their existence. Soils are typically sandy and gravelly over bedrock and can routinely become very dry since repeated fires have removed the organic matter. Many of the plants are evergreen — capable of retaining their leaves most years, thus retaining nutrients.

Rocks (Cliffs, Talus Slopes, Outcrops)

Along the North Shore of Lake Superior, sheer bedrock towers over slopes of fractured rock and exposed hillsides, creating challenging habitat for plants. But life finds a way! Vascular plants are often limited to crevices, ledges, or the undersides of protective overhangs. Wet seeps can create a vastly different plant community than those found in dry, south-facing situations (Figure 22).

In places like Voyageurs National Park in St. Louis County, rock outcrops are characterized by bedrock or thin soils over bedrock. Consequently, they are open or shrub-dominated. Plants are adapted to greater environmental extremes, such as evaporation, exposure to direct sunlight, strong winds, rapid temperature changes, and lower nutrient levels. Lichens cover exposed rock surfaces, and there are more shrubs and far fewer trees.

Wet Forest/Swamp

Wet forests occur in narrow bands along lakes, rivers, and peatlands. They also crop up in areas where the groundwater is very near the surface. The soils are saturated, and roots rarely penetrate into the deeper, oxygen-deprived soil layers. As a result, trees are easily blown over by wind, creating new habitat for other plants and animals. Flooding due to beaver activity or simply a wet year can kill the big trees, converting the community to a marsh.

Conclusion

If you used to think the Coniferous Forest biome was a forest of conifers, you know better now! Rather, the Coniferous Forest biome is a magnificent *mélange* of many different forest types, each with its own mix of plants. You also know that many factors contribute to the appearance of forests today, and many factors, such as wind, fire, and human influence, will continue to change these forests over time.

Community Snapshots

Following are trees, shrubs and other vegetation commonly found in different communities.

Wet Meadow and Marsh Community Snapshot

TREES	SHRUBS	OTHER VEGETATION
Tamarack (*Larix laricina*)	Willows (*Salix* spp.)	Cattails (*Typha* spp.)
Northern white-cedar (*Thuja occidentalis*)	Dogwoods (*Cornus* spp.)	Lake sedge (*Carex lacustris*)
Quaking aspen (*Populus tremuloides*)		Bluejoint (*Calamagrostis canadensis*)
Balsam poplar (*Populus balsamifera*)		Sphagnum mosses (*Sphagnum* spp.)
		Marsh bellflower (*Campanula aparinoides*)
		Tufted loosestrife (*Lysimachia thyrsiflora*)

Mesic Hardwood Community Snapshot

TREES	SHRUBS	OTHER VEGETATION
Sugar maple (*Acer saccharum*)	Northern bush honeysuckle (*Diervilla lonicera*)	Rice grass (*Achnatherum hymenoides*)
Basswood (*Tilia* spp.)	Canada yew (*Taxus canadensis*)	Pennsylvania sedge (*Carex pensylvanica*)
Paper birch (*Betula papyrifera*)	Mountain maple (*Acer spicatum*)	Large-flowered bellwort (*Uvularia grandiflora*)
Quacking aspen (*Populus tremuloides*)	Mountain ash (*Sorbus americana*)	Wild sarsaparilla (*Aralia nudicaulis*)
Northern red oak (*Quercus rubra*)	Green alder (*Alnus viridis*)	Woodland horsetail (*Equisetum sylvaticum*)
Heart-leaved birch (*Betula cordifolia*)	Bearberry (*Arctostaphylos uva-ursi*)	Beech fern (*Phegopteris hexagonoptera*)
Occasionally these areas will host:	Shrubby cinquefoil (*Dasiphora fruticosa*)	Maidenhair fern (*Adiantum pendatum*)
Red pine (*Pinus resinosa*)	Juneberry (*Amelanchier arborea*)	
Northern white cedar (*Thuja occidentalis*)	Creeping juniper (*Juniperus horizontalis*)	
	Nine bark (*Physocarpus opulifolius*)	

Peatland Community Snapshot

TREES	SHRUBS	OTHER VEGETATION
Black spruce (*Picea mariana*)	Red-osier dogwood (*Cornus sericea*)	Sphagnum moss (*Sphagnum* spp.)
Northern white cedar (*Thuja occidentalis*)	Speckled alder (*Alnus incana rugosa*)	Feather moss (*Hylocomium splendens*)
Tamarack (*Larix laricina*)	Willow (*Salix* spp.)	Labrador tea (*Ledum groenlandicum*)
Speckled alder (*Alnus incana rugosa*)		Creeping snowberry(*Gaultheria hispidula*)
Paper birch (*Betula papyrifera*)		Bunchberry (*Cornus canidensis*)
Balsam fir (*Abies balsamea*)		Starflower (*Trientalis borealis*)
Bog birch (*Betula pumila*)		Three-leaf goldthread (*Coptis triflora*)
		Small cranberry (*Vaccinium oxycoccus*)
		Three-leaf false Solomon's seal (*Maianthemum trifolium*)
		Leatherleaf (*Chamaedaphne calyculata*)
		Bog laurel (*Kalmia polifolia*)
		Labrador tea (*Rhododendron groenlandicum*)
		Bog rosemary (*Andromeda polifolia*)
		Pitcher plant (*Sarracenia purpurea*)
		Round-leaved sundew (*Drosera rotundifolia*)
		Three-fruited bog sedge (*Carex trisperma*)
		Buckbean (*Menyanthes trifoliata*)

Pine/Spruce/Fir (Fire Dependent) Community Snapshot

TREES	SHRUBS	OTHER VEGETATION
Pines (*Pinus* spp.)	Blueberry (*Vaccinium boreale*)	Scattered lichens with bare patches of soil form the ground layer, along with:
Spruce (*Picea* spp.)	Juneberry (*Amelanchier arborea*)	Bunchberry (*Cornus canadensis*)
Fir (*Abies* spp.)	Red maple (*Acer rubrum*)\	Twinflower (*Linnaea borealis*)
	Beaked hazel (*Corylus cornuta*).	Sweetfern (*Comptonia peregrina*)
		Thimbleberry (*Rubus parviflorus*)
		Polypody ferns (*Polypodium virginianum*)

Rocks (Cliffs, Talus Slopes, Outcrops) Community Snapshot

TREES	SHRUBS	OTHER VEGETATION
Sugar maple (*Acer saccharum*)	Chokecherry (*Prunus virginiana*),	Rockshield (*Xanthoparmelia cumberlandia*)
Basswood (*Tilia* spp.)	Fly honeysuckle (*Lonicera canadensis*)	Rock posy (*Rhizoplaca melanophthalma*)
Paper birch (*Betula papyrifera*)	Beaked hazel (*Corylus cornuta*)	Rock foam (*Stereocaulon saxatile*)
Quaking aspen (*Populus tremuloides*)		Sunburst lichen (*Xanthoria candelaria*)
Northern red oak (*Quercus rubra*)		Reindeer lichen (*Cladonia rangiferina*).
		Herbaceous plants might include:
		Rusty woodsia (*Woodsia ilvensis*)
		Fragrant fern (*Dryopteris fragrans*)
		Fragile fern (*Cystopteris fragilis*)
		Polypody (*Polypody virginianum*)
		Harebell (*Campanula rotundifolia*)
		Pussytoes (*Antennaria*)
		Sedges (*Cyperaceae*)
		Three-toothed cinquefoil (*Sibbaldiopsis tridentat^a*)
		Spikemoss (*Selaginella*)

Wet Forest/Swamp Community Snapshot

TREES	SHRUBS	OTHER VEGETATION
Black ash (*Fraxinus nigra*	Speckled alder (*Alnus incana rugosa*)	Sedges (*Carex* spp.)
Northern white cedar (*Thuja occidentalis*)	Mountain maple (*Acer spicatum*)	Mosses (*Sphagnum* spp.)
Balsam fir (*Abies balsamea*)		Marsh marigold (*Caltha palustris*)
		Bunchberry (*Cornus canadensis*)
		Dwarf raspberry (*Rubus arcticus*)
		Lady fern (*Athyrium filix-femina*)

Explore

MASTER
NATURALIST
TOOLBOX

This section highlights great locations for exploring forests of the North Woods, Great Lakes region. Please check them out online, then head out and discover them in real life!

Itasca State Park – Park Rapids, Minnesota

WHAT At Itasca State Park, the mighty Mississippi River begins its 2,552-mile journey to the Gulf of Mexico. Established in 1891 to preserve remnant stands of virgin pine and to protect the basin around the Mississippi's source, this park has become a famous natural and cultural landmark. Within the park you'll find the Itasca Wilderness Sanctuary Scientific & Natural Area (SNA). In 1938 this became the first site in Minnesota set aside for research and interpretation of its natural attributes. It contains a large virgin stand of white and red pine, mostly 100 to 300 years old, and provides habitat for two of the state's rarer plant species, bog adder's mouth and matricary grape-fern. The Bohall Wilderness Trail leads to a lovely overlook on Bohall Lake.

WHEN The best time to visit is when woodland wildflowers are blooming, although a walk through the majestic pines is rewarding any time of the year. Note: Most SNAs do not allow pets.

WHERE Itasca State Park is 20 miles north of Park Rapids on U.S. Highway 71. The SNA is on Wilderness Drive within the park.

WHO Itasca State Park, 36750 Main Park Drive, Park Rapids, MN 56470, (218) 699-7251

FOR MORE INFORMATION www.mndnr.gov/state_parks/itasca (park information), www.mndnr.gov/snas (plant list for the SNA)

Lost 40 Scientific & Natural Area – Alvwood, Minnesota

WHAT The Lost 40, named for a surveying slip-up in 1882 that left this chunk of land unmapped and so relatively undisturbed, is in the Big Fork State Forest. Here, a narrow peninsula extending from a large upland esker is flanked by a black spruce and tamarack bog on one side and a willow and alder marsh on the other. The area contains 28 acres of red pine forest and 18 acres of spruce-fir forest. White pine over 300 years old can be found on the site. A walking trail provides easy access.

WHEN Early to mid-summer is a good time to see wildflowers in bloom, including fringed polygala, bluebead lily, twinflower, and Canada mayflower.

WHERE From Alvwood, Minnesota, travel 11 miles east on County Highway 29, then two miles north on County Highway 26 to Forest Road 2240. Go west less than one mile to parking lot.

WHO Minnesota Department of Natural Resources, 500 Lafayette Road, St. Paul, MN 55155, (651) 296-6157 or (888) 646-6367

FOR MORE INFORMATION www.mndnr.gov/snas

Caribou Rock Trail – Gunflint Trail, Minnesota

WHAT A 3/4-mile well-traveled walk takes you to a beautiful overlook of West Bearskin Lake; another 3/8-mile hike and you are overlooking Moss Lake. Continue walking over rugged and scenic terrain to Stairway Portage and Rose Lake. When you get there, your prize is a panoramic view of the 1999 Fourth of July blowdown.

WHEN Head out after the black flies and before the ground freezes.

WHERE Take the Gunflint Trail (County Road 12) 28 miles north from Grand Marais, turn right (north) onto County Road 65 and travel two miles to the trailhead sign.

WHO Superior National Forest, Gunflint Ranger District, 2020 W. Highway 61, Grand Marais, MN 55604, (218) 387-1750

FOR MORE INFORMATION www.fs.fed.us/r9/forests/superior/recreation/hiking/hiking_trails.php (click on "North Shore Area")

Boulder Lake Environmental Learning Center - Duluth, Minnesota

WHAT Boulder Lake's 18,000-acre classroom is a regional leader in fostering connections to natural resource stewardship through education, research, and recreation. Educational programs showcase resource management, including hydroelectric power generation and a working forest environment, and illustrate the many social, biological, and economic benefits of that forest. Open to the public; hiking, cross-country skiing, boating, and camping are just a few of the outdoor activities to enjoy. The Environmental Learning Center was established in 1994 and features a strong and unique partnership of University of Minnesota Duluth's College of Education and Human Service Professions, Minnesota Power, and Saint Louis County Land and Minerals Department. Boulder Lake's natural resources are managed by Minnesota Power, St. Louis County Land and Minerals Department, and the Minnesota Department of Natural Resources.

WHEN Land is open all year long, education center only open during business hours.

WHERE Take Rice Lake Road (County Hwy 4) north from Duluth about 18 miles. Just past Island Lake Inn turn left onto Boulder Dam Road.

WHO Boulder Lake Environmental Learning Center, 7328 Boulder Dam Road, Duluth, MN 55803, (218) 721-3731

FOR MORE INFORMATION www.boulderlake.org/index.html

MASTER NATURALIST TOOLBOX

Teach

MASTER
NATURALIST
TOOLBOX

This section features lesson plans for activities on North Woods forests. You may experience some of these activities as a student in your Master Naturalist class. The activities are most appropriate for adults and children ages 12 and up. Feel free to use them to teach others what you have learned!

LESSON 1

Using a Dichotomous Key

Objective

Participants will learn how to use a dichotomous key to identify common trees.

Audience Type

Teen/Adult

Supplies

☐ One copy of *A Beginner's Guide to Minnesota Trees* for each participant (www.extension.umn.edu/environment/trees-woodlands/beginners-guide-to-mn-trees/)
☐ Sample leaf types
☐ Sample twigs with buds
☐ Snack foods (gumballs, triangular tortilla chips, potato chips, cheese puffs, cookies)
☐ Overhead, slide, poster, or chalkboard drawing of the snack food key (see below)

Background

Have you ever found a leaf and wondered about the name of the tree to which it belongs? You could ask someone, randomly flip through a tree field guide (frustrating and time-consuming), or try your hand at using a dichotomous key to identify the specimen yourself.

A dichotomous key is a tool that allows the user to determine the identity of items, such as trees, wildflowers, reptiles, rocks, and fish. Dichotomous means "divided into two parts," and a dichotomous key consists of a series of paired statements describing mutually exclusive characteristics. The user decides which of the two statements applies most to the specimen. The key then directs the user to another couplet with additional distinctions, and so on until the series of choices leads the user to the correct identification of the specimen. Dichotomous keys usually begin with general characteristics and lead progressively to specific characteristics. Some employ numbering or coding systems.

Using a dichotomous key may require familiarity with vocabulary used by scientists to describe a species. When you use a tree key, understanding a few botanical terms (e.g., simple and compound leaves) will greatly aid in making correct choices. Use the illustrations in *A Beginner's Guide to Minnesota Trees* to help you recognize a few key visual characteristics of trees and leaves.

Tips for using a key:

- Always consider both choices. Although the first may seem to fit your sample, the second may be even better.

- Be sure you understand the meaning of the terms involved. Do not guess. You may need to use additional reference material.

- When measurements are given, use a scale or ruler. Do not "eyeball" it.

- Work with multiple samples of your specimen whenever possible. Living things are always somewhat variable, and keys reflect typical presentations of a species' characteristics.

- If the choice is not clear, try pursuing more than one sequence of couplets. After working through a few more descriptors, it may become apparent that one line of choices does not fit your sample. If you end up with multiple possible answers, read the descriptions of the choices to help you decide.

- Arriving at an answer in a key is not the end! Be sure to check the description of the organism and a picture or an illustration to see if these agree with what you have.

Preparation

Display botanical samples and the snack foods where everyone can see them. If you can't be outdoors, bring in a variety of tree specimens (leaves, branches, etc.) for participants to identify.

Activity

1. Begin by asking participants how many trees they can correctly identify. How can you distinguish one type of tree from another? If there's a tree you don't recognize, how can you learn what it is? Introduce the concept of dichotomous keys and explain their uses in multiple settings.

2. Walk the participants through the Snack Food Key. After identifying all the snack foods, discuss the following:

   What terminology is necessary to use this key properly?

   Which snack food characteristics were difficult to classify?

   How can you use this sample to prepare to use more complex keys (more types of snacks, snacks very similar to each other)?

   > SNACK FOOD KEY
   > 1a Snack items are flat: go to 2
   > 1b Snack items are not flat: go to 4
   > 2a Snack items are round: go to 3
   > 2b Snack items are triangular: tortilla chips
   > 3a Snack item is thinner than ¼ inch: potato chip
   > 3b Snack item is ¼ inch or thicker: cookie
   > 4a Snack item is tubular: cheese puff
   > 4b Snack item is spherical: gumball

   Once all participants understand how the key works, eat the snack foods!

MASTER
NATURALIST
TOOLBOX

3. Instruct participants to study the illustration of various leaf types on pages 2 and 5 of *A Beginner's Guide to Minnesota Trees*. Discuss the terminology used in the booklet: deciduous, coniferous, simple, compound, doubly compound, bundled, clustered, opposite, alternate, smooth, toothed, doubly toothed, lobed, leaflet, leafstalk, leaf base, vein, and bud. Show students real-life examples of as many leaf, branch, and bud types as possible to illustrate these terms.

4. Go outside and locate a sample tree to identify (or use the samples you brought indoors). Walk the students through the tree key found in *A Beginner's Guide to Minnesota Trees*. Review the tips listed above for successfully using tree keys.

5. Have participants practice identifying trees using the dichotomous key alone or in small groups.

6. After participants have used the dichotomous key, wrap up the lesson with the following discussion points:

   What strategies helped you to be successful using the dichotomous key?

   What skills, knowledge, and qualities are helpful when using a dichotomous key?

   In what ways is using a dichotomous key easier and harder than other methods of tree identification (asking someone, flipping through a field guide, etc.)?

   Which tree species are easiest to recognize? Which are hardest to tell apart?

ADVANCED OPTION To help participants really understand how dichotomous keys work, encourage them to construct their own keys. They might make a key of breakfast cereals, shoes, beans, cartoon characters, or even their classmates.

OPTION FOR YOUNGER GROUPS Younger participants can learn how to identify some non-leaf features to help identify deciduous trees with a simple twig identification activity. Collect pairs of deciduous twig samples. Give participants each one twig and ask them to carefully observe it using their senses of sight, touch, and smell, noting features such as patterns, aromas, textures, and branching patterns (opposite vs. alternate). Have them find the person who has a twig from the same type of tree. Then have them explain which features helped them find their match. If you know, you can tell them the names of the trees their twigs came from — but not until the activity is over! You can also do this activity with pairs of deciduous leaves or bundles of coniferous needles. Note: Even though younger groups can do this activity, it's a good, fun introduction for all ages that reminds us how to observe using all our senses.

Resources

A beginner's guide to Minnesota trees by David Rathke (1995) is a great basic guide and dichotomous key to 35 of the most common Minnesota trees. It's available online at www.extension.umn.edu/environment/trees-woodlands/beginners-guide-to-mn-trees.

Minnesota trees, also written by David Rathke and published by University of Minnesota Extension in 1995, is a more complete guide (100 trees instead of the most common 35).

Leafsnap electronic field guide is available for low-cost purchase for iPhone or Android. www.leafsnap.com

MASTER
NATURALIST
TOOLBOX

Forest Management

Objective

The learner will describe how forest management goals lead to the selection of management techniques and suggest management techniques that would fulfill a client's goals.

Audience Type

Teen/Adult

Supplies

- ☐ 11" x 17" sheet of paper
- ☐ Pens or pencils
- ☐ Four Client Cards
- ☐ Real forest management plans if possible
- ☐ Sample Forest Management Map

Background

Many of the products and resources we use daily are the result of managing and harvesting forests. In addition, Minnesotans enjoy a wide variety of recreational activities in forests. Because forests are so important to our lives, caring for and maintaining our forests is an important job.

It's easy to assume that if humans just leave a forest alone it will be fine. Because humans have needs and wants associated with both public and private forests, forest management processes can help make sure the needs and wants of people today are fulfilled, while at the same time preserving forests' capacity to continue filling society's needs into the future. Choosing to take no management action on a parcel of land is still a management decision that has consequences.

The forest manager's role is to help landowners (who may be private citizens, corporations, or units of government) manage land to achieve specified goals while protecting soil, water, and living things. When developing *management plans*, forest managers consider relevant local, state, and federal laws and regulations, such as endangered species regulations or conservation easements, as well as their own knowledge of ecological processes and best management practices. Students may not be familiar with the many technical guidelines that managers draw on and comply with to develop their management plans. This activity provides an introduction to the types of questions and issues that forest managers may encounter in developing forest management plans.

Preparation

Fold the 11" x 17" sheet of paper into four equal quadrants. Unfold the paper. Refer to the sample map. Draw on the paper a river that transects each of the quadrants. Add lakes, wetlands, tributaries, etc., so that each quadrant has something interesting. Then add a highway and roads, as well as natural features such as rock outcroppings, beaver dams, etc. Draw lines to delineate forest types and other land uses, such as maple/ basswood, lowland hardwood, oak, aspen/birch, former cropland, and former pasture. Number each quadrant, then cut the paper along the fold lines. Make a copy of the Client Cards page and cut along the outer dotted line, then cut between the cards.

Activity

1. Introduce students to the concept of forest management by discussing management plans for sites nearby or familiar to the students. Have real plans and maps on hand, if possible, to discuss the relationship between management plans and what you see in the forest today. Be sure to discuss the importance of goals and priorities in making decisions about forest management.

2. Tell participants that they are going to become forest management consultants during this activity. Divide participants into four groups and distribute one quadrant of the hypothetical map to each group. Mention that one inch square equals 10 acres on the map.

3. Provide one Client Card to each group, and let participants know that their task is to fulfill the needs of the client listed on their card. They should consider the client's goals as well as the other limitations mentioned on the card.

4. Instruct small groups to develop a few recommendations for managing the property. They may draw on their maps to indicate areas where management activities will take place. Remind them to keep in mind both short-term and long-term plans for their land.

5. Have groups report to the class their proposed courses of action. Then put the four maps together to make one big map.

6. Discuss:

   How would the plan for each quadrant affect the other quadrants?

   What additional information did you need in order to develop your plan?

   How much will it cost to implement your plan? What resources besides money will you need? Can your clients afford it?

   How would your plan have been different if your client's goals had been different?

Useful Trees

Trees provide more than just wood! This list is just a small sampling of products that come from Minnesota trees.

- Adhesives
- Bioenergy
- Carpeting
- Cellophane
- Cellulose fiber for use in fabrics, plastics, and other products
- Chemical extracts used in sunblocks and medicines
- Chewing gum
- Cosmetics
- Crayons
- Erosion control
- Fences
- Furniture
- Imitation leather
- Lumber
- Medicines
- Mulch
- Nuts and fruits
- Paint thinner
- Paper products of all sorts
- Perfumes
- Plywood
- Printing ink
- Renewable fuel
- Syrup
- Waxes
- Windbreaks

MASTER NATURALIST TOOLBOX

Sample Forest Management Map

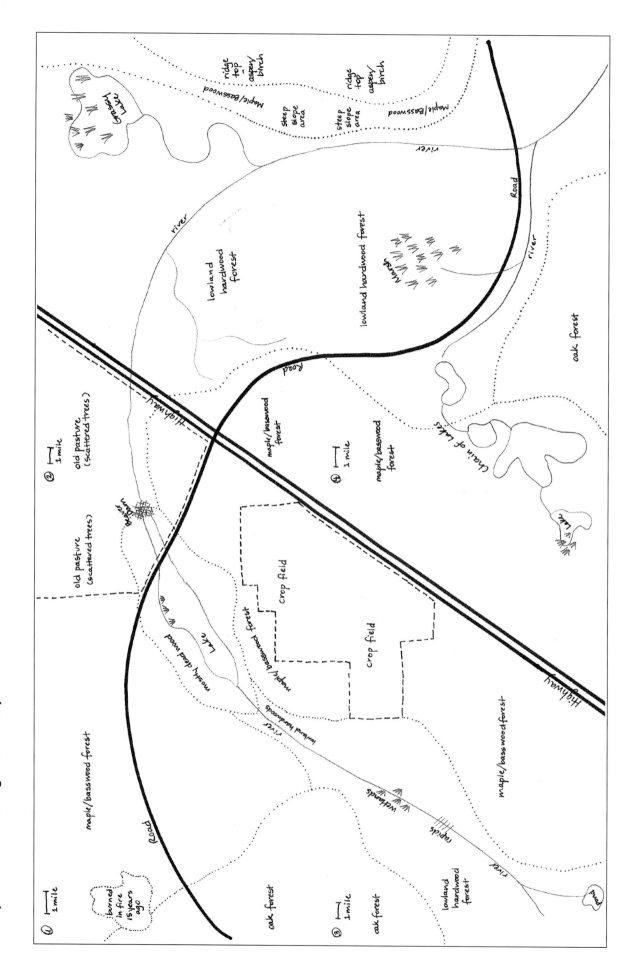

Client Cards

RETIRED HOMEOWNER

We bought this parcel of land so we can build a lovely retirement home that our children and grandchildren will visit and eventually inherit. We need to identify a suitable home-building site with aesthetic views in all directions and easy access to the main road. We hope to go for quiet walks and view wildlife on our property. As we age, we won't be able to do any land management activities ourselves or afford much help, but we are very worried about the possibility of forest fires destroying our home.

What are your recommendations for developing and managing our property?

HUNTER

I bought this land so I can have my own private hunting grounds. I like to hunt or trap small game, deer, and rabbits. Since these species like forest edges, I'll want to increase the edges and early successional areas on my land. I spent most of my savings buying the land, so I don't have much money for improvements, but I consider this land a long-term investment and want to increase its value somehow. I live in another state and will be able to visit once or twice a year. I'm very worried about trespassers.

What are your recommendations for developing and managing my property?

TIMBER COMPANY

Our company bought this land because we want to harvest the trees for a continuous cycle of timber sales. The land is somewhat hilly, and we want to take measures to prevent erosion and other environmental damage. We only have rough estimates for an inventory of the tree species present on the land. We want to maximize the efficiency of the harvest, so we will need some access roads.

What are your recommendations for developing and managing this property?

RECREATION OUTFITTER

I want to start a business offering guided wilderness trips on my land. I'll need to build trails, campsites, a headquarters building, and access roads. Because I hope to draw high-end customers, I will want to offer discrete trip supports, such as hidden supply caches, trail shelters, etc. I will host multiple groups at once, and to preserve their sense of adventure they must not encounter each other. My clients will expect to see lots of wildlife on these trips, so I must ensure animals are abundant on my land. My primary promotional hook will be the pristine solitude of my wilderness setting. Maintaining these is my highest priority.

What are your recommendations for developing and managing my property?

Resources

Woodland stewardship: A practical guide for midwestern landowners (2nd edition, 2014) is designed to help family forest landowners identify goals for their woodlands and work with professional foresters to choose management practices that will help meet those goals. It's available at www.woodlandstewardship.org.

Standing tall, a 2014 publication of the Minnesota Department of Natural Resources, showcases Minnesota's forests and how DNR's Division of Forestry takes care of them. You can download this publication at www.mndnr.gov/forestry/index.html.

MASTER
NATURALIST
TOOLBOX

Conserve

This section highlights organizations that offer opportunities for Minnesota Master Naturalist Volunteers to participate in stewardship and citizen science activities related to forestry in the North Woods, Great Lakes region. Please visit the websites to learn more.

Minnesota State Forests and Minnesota State Parks

State forests and state parks need campground hosts. Hosts live in campgrounds for at least four weeks between May and October. Hosts help campers by answering questions and explaining rules, do light maintenance work, post naturalist events in kiosks, and set good examples by being model campers. For application, background check information and questions, contact campground.host@state.mn.us or call (888) 646-6367 or (651) 259-5607.

www.mndnr.gov/volunteering/stateparks/campgroundhost.html

Scientific & Natural Areas

SNAs are premier state lands displaying examples of native prairies, old growth forests, geological features, and habitat for rare and endangered species. The state SNA program needs volunteers to work on projects throughout the state. Projects are typically carried out on Saturdays from 10 a.m. to 2 p.m. unless otherwise noted. Activities include collecting seeds, planting seedlings, removing exotic species, pulling buckthorn, and cutting and burning brush.

www.mndnr.gov/volunteering/sna/index.html

Superior National Forest

The USFS needs your help! While each visitor is responsible for following rules and regulations, picking up litter, and following minimum-impact camping practices, successful preservation of the Superior National Forest, including the BWCAW, depends on the help of Superior National Forest volunteers—visitors who are willing to spend a little more time and effort in their role as caretakers of their national forest. Volunteer commitments can range from spending a few extra minutes picking up trash to spending an entire summer as a wilderness rehabilitator, restoring worn BWCAW campsites to a more natural condition. Volunteer opportunities are available both in and outside the wilderness. Projects also are available for groups to work on for a weekend or a week. Positions include wilderness ranger, wilderness rehabilitator, back-country ranger, recreation aid, campground host, wildlife aid, timber aid, and naturalist

http://www.fs.usda.gov/main/superior/workingtogether/volunteering

Expand

This section suggests some things you can use, do, pursue, read, or join to develop as a naturalist.

Journal

EXPERIENCE Explore a coniferous forest and find at least two different types of conifer needles. Notice where each was found and what was around you. Examine each needle closely with a magnifying glass and smell your needles.

REFLECT Did you like one needle over the other? Why or why not? What are the advantages of their different shapes? What did you notice about the trees the needles came from?

RECORD Write a description of what each needle looks, smells, and feels like. Sketch the needles and fine details you notice. Describe which is your favorite and why.

Read

Trees and Shrubs of Minnesota

Welby Smith.
2008. Minneapolis: University of Minnesota Press. 640 pp.

Who better to learn from about trees than Minnesota's state botanist? This volume is chock-full of information about more than 200 species found in the state.

All About Minnesota's Forests and Trees: A Primer

Division of Forestry, 2008. St. Paul: Minnesota Department of Natural Resources. 58 pp.

This book provides a user-friendly introduction to Minnesota's trees and forests, from basic tree biology to past, present, and future human uses of trees.

Field Guide to the Native Plant Communities of Minnesota: The Laurentian Mixed Forest Province

2003. St. Paul: Minnesota Department of Natural Resources. 352 pp.

Brimming with maps, fact sheets, keys, descriptions, and tables, this field guide is a valuable resource for becoming familiar with native plant communities of the North Woods, Great Lakes biome.

Canoe Country Flora: Plants and Trees of the North Woods and Boundary Waters

Mark Stensaas.
1996. Minneapolis: University of Minnesota Press. 224 pp.

This book is a concise guide to the 96 most common trees, shrubs, wildflowers, fungi, ferns, lichens, and other plants you're likely to encounter in the north woods. "Sparky" Stensaas has served as a buyer and marketing director for Duluth Pack. Formerly he was a ranger for the National Park Service, biologist for the Minnesota DNR, stuntman for Walt Disney, and pizza deliverer. Consequently, this is not your typical field identification manual but a rich trove of information.

Surf

Plants of Minnesota

This section of the Minnesota DNR's website serves as a portal to all of the DNR's information on plants—including trees and shrubs. You can explore the state's distribution of mosses in the moss atlas, learn how to plant a butterfly garden, find the biggest individual of every tree species in the state, and learn how to identify our most common trees.

www.mndnr.gov/plants/index.html

MyMinnesotaWoods.org

This site provides one-stop shopping for the private landowner who wants to know more about the stewardship of his or her forested land. It includes information on everything from sustainable management to how to organize a timber sale, and even information about conservation easements. The site is a project of University of Minnesota Extension and was financed by the Blandin Foundation.

http://myminnesotawoods.org

Join

Wild Ones: Native Plants, Natural Landscapes

Wild Ones promotes environmentally sound landscaping to maintain biodiversity through the preservation, restoration, and establishment of native plant communities. Wild Ones is a not-for-profit environmental education and advocacy organization with chapters in Minnesota.

www.for-wild.org

Minnesota Chapter of The Nature Conservancy

The mission of The Nature Conservancy is to preserve the plants, animals, and natural communities that represent the diversity of life on Earth by protecting the lands and waters they need to survive. The Minnesota chapter protects dozens of sites across the state, sponsors events and field trips, and offers statewide volunteer opportunities

http://www.nature.org/ourinitiatives/regions/northamerica/unitedstates/minnesota/volunteer/index.htm.

Minnesota Tree Care Advocate

Minnesota TCA, a program of University of Minnesota Extension, educates citizens about urban forests and provides an opportunity for them to volunteer to care for trees in their neighborhoods and communities. Volunteer positions include tree care advisor and citizen pruner.

www.mntca.org

MASTER NATURALIST TOOLBOX

Additional Reading

Minnesota Department of Natural Resources. (2003). *Field guide to the native plant communities of Minnesota: the laurentian mixed forest province.* St. Paul: Minnesota Department of Natural Resources Ecological Land Classification Program, Minnesota County Biological Survey, and Natural Heritage and Nongame Research Program.

Walewski, J. (2007). *Lichens of the north woods.* Duluth: Kollath-Stensaas Publishing.

Copyrighted Photographs and Images Used With Permission

Figure 1. Courtesy of the Minnesota Department of Natural Resources

Figure 2. Courtesy of Minnesota Forest Resources Council

Figure 3. Courtesy of Minnesota Forest Resources Council

Figure 4. Courtesy of the Minnesota Department of Natural Resources

Figure 5 Courtesy of Joe Walewski, Wolf Ridge Environmental Learning Center

Figure 6. Courtesy of Joe Walewski, Wolf Ridge Environmental Learning Center

Figure 7. Courtesy of Joe Walewski, Wolf Ridge Environmental Learning Center

Figure 8. Courtesy of Joe Walewski, Wolf Ridge Environmental Learning Center

Figure 9. Courtesy of Joe Walewski, Wolf Ridge Environmental Learning Center

Figure 10. Courtesy of Joe Walewski, Wolf Ridge Environmental Learning Center

Figure 11. Courtesy of Joe Walewski, Wolf Ridge Environmental Learning Center

Figure 12. Courtesy of Joe Walewski, Wolf Ridge Environmental Learning Center

Figure 13. Courtesy of Joe Walewski, Wolf Ridge Environmental Learning Center

Figure 14. Courtesy of Dawn A. Flinn

Figure 15. Courtesy of Joe Walewski, Wolf Ridge Environmental Learning Center

Figure 16. Courtesy of Joe Walewski, Wolf Ridge Environmental Learning Center

Figure 17. Courtesy of Joe Walewski, Wolf Ridge Environmental Learning Center

Figure 18. Courtesy of Joe Walewski, Wolf Ridge Environmental Learning Center

Figure 19. Courtesy of Joe Walewski, Wolf Ridge Environmental Learning Center

Figure 20. Courtesy of Joe Walewski, Wolf Ridge Environmental Learning Center

Figure 21. Courtesy of Sarah L. Keefer

Figure 22. Courtesy of the U.S. Forest Service

Figure 23. Courtesy of Dawn A. Flinn

Expand

MASTER
NATURALIST
TOOLBOX

Chapter 3: Wolves and Moose and Grouse, Oh My!

Creatures of the North Woods

Andrea Lorek Strauss

Goal

Understand that animals have physical and behavioral adaptations that help them survive in the north woods and that humans manage wildlife for a variety of reasons and with a variety of methods.

Objectives

1. Define adaptation; provide examples of physical and behavioral adaptations.

2. Understand the relationship between forest communities and wildlife species.

3. Describe why and how humans manage wildlife.

Introduction

Animals have specific ways to eat, grow, reproduce, avoid being eaten, and generally do things that help them stay alive in the place they call home: their habitat. The details, of course, vary a great deal from one species to another. A turkey vulture is better at soaring on thermals and sniffing the air for *carrion* than a hummingbird, while a hummingbird is better at hovering and spotting nectar-bearing red flowers than a vulture. These strategies illustrate the different way each bird obtains the energy it needs to survive — to make a living in its habitat. In this chapter we'll explore how these peculiarities allow different animals to live in the various communities that make up Minnesota's north woods.

Adaptation: Survival in the North

How does the black-capped chickadee get the energy to keep warm all winter and flit around finding seeds? How does a 70-pound wolf capture and eat a 1,200-pound moose? How does a blue-spotted salamander catch enough insects while maintaining a high enough level of moisture to survive and not becoming dinner for a great blue heron? Each of these organisms has a way to obtain energy so it can grow and reproduce in its environment. Each also has a way to avoid being eaten and becoming someone else's source of energy!

These strategies are known as *adaptations*. From an evolutionary viewpoint, an adaptation is a characteristic of an organism that improves its chances of surviving and reproducing. An adaptation may be behavioral, such as when a beaver builds a dam to raise the water level of the surrounding area or when wolves hunt *prey* as a pack, or it may be anatomical or physiological, such as the fangs on a spider (Figure 1). These traits are part of the genetic makeup of the organism. In fact, biologists get snippy if you say a wild fox has adapted to life in your living room, even if it learns not to tear up the couch.

Figure 1. Adaptations may be anatomical or physiological, such as this porcupine's predator-deterring quills, or they may be behavioral, such as the chattering sound it makes to warn potential enemies before they try to take a bite.

Life in the Cold: The Ultimate Test

As if it isn't challenging enough to find a sufficient supply of food to survive under relatively easy (summer) conditions, plants and animals living in the north woods experience a special challenge — a landscape covered in ice and snow for almost half of the year. This is one reason the diversity of critters here is relatively low compared to that of other biomes.

In a typical north woods winter, with temperatures well below freezing and snow falls of 70 to 80 inches, quite a lot of the food supply is either dead or hidden under the snow. As a result, every species inhabiting the north uses at least one of three strategies for securing and conserving energy in winter: move, adapt, or die (MAD).

Move

In anticipation of dramatic seasonal changes in food availability, some creatures migrate, or move to areas where food is available (Figure 2).

You can probably list a whole slew of migratory birds off the top of your head — songbirds, waterfowl, raptors, and more. Migration presents its own challenges, including the dangers and energy required to travel long distances. But the prize is continued food availability in the warmer location. It makes you wonder why birds would bother to return north when a year-round food supply is available in the balmy south! But producing offspring requires lots of energy, and competition for food and nesting sites is high in

Figure 2. Trumpeter swans are among many North Woods, Great Lakes birds that migrate in the spring and fall. They may winter as close as central Minnesota or as far away as Texas.

the overwintering areas. The energy expense of migrating north to Minnesota each spring is worth it because food and nest sites are more plentiful and days are longer here than in their winter homes, so there are plenty of resources to raise young and store energy for the long flight back south.

White-tailed deer also move in the winter, although not so far. They often gather in "deer yards" or herds in winter (Figure 3). These hooved creatures are hindered when snow is a foot deep or more. Coming together in dense conifer stands provides some shelter from snow and allows for collective trampling of trails to ease movement. The downside of living in close quarters is the heavy pressure on the limited food supply at a time when deer must take in more calories to stay warm. Decreased overall activity and repeated use of packed trails help compensate for the additional energy required.

Figure 3. White-tailed deer often gather in sheltered "deer yards" in winter, where the trampled snow makes it easier to move around.

Adapt

Many North Woods, Great Lakes region species have evolved adaptations for coping with the snowy cold. The river otter has thick, oily fur that protects it in frigid water. Beavers have a layer of fat that keeps them warm — and even store fat in their tails as a winter food supply. Cued by shortening daylight hours, snowshoe hare and ermine (short-tailed weasel) switch out their brown fur for white, improving camouflage in snow. Lynx and snowshoe

Figure 4. A snowshoe hare's big feet help it travel through snow without getting bogged down.

hare have large feet that act like snowshoes to help them maneuver in deep snow (Figure 4). Chickadees reduce their body temperatures at night to conserve energy.

Deep hibernation, another adaptation, is a physiological state in which body temperature is dramatically reduced without the harmful effects of hypothermia. This decreased body temperature is accompanied by slowed heart rate, slowed breathing, and decreased metabolism. Ground squirrels and other hibernators can drop their body temperatures as low as 30 °F (and you thought YOU got cold in winter!). Hibernation usually involves periodic arousal in which body temperature and metabolism return to near normal for short periods. This allows for the restorative effects of sleep, which apparently doesn't occur at such low body temperatures. Hibernators draw on stored fat to sustain them through months of hibernation. While a number of species radically decrease their activity in winter, very few are considered true hibernators — and all the true hibernators are mammals. In Minnesota, bats (little brown, big brown, and eastern pipistrelle), woodchucks, chipmunks, and ground squirrels are the only known true hibernators.

Black bears also hibernate, but their winter state is different from deep hibernators and is often termed winter lethargy (Figure 5). They reduce their activity and draw on stored fat reserves, but decrease their body temperatures less than 10 °F and are mildly alert. And talk about a weight loss plan: a female bear can start winter weighing more than 250 pounds, give birth to several cubs while in a state of lethargy, nurse those cubs most of the winter, and then wake up and leave the den in the spring weighing less than half of her pre-winter weight.

Most small mammals, such as rodents, undergo a briefer state of lowered heart, respiratory, and metabolic rates and body temperature in winter. Termed *torpor*, this state lasts from a few hours to several days.

Reptiles, amphibians, and some insects use sleeplike periods of dormancy to make it through the winter. Many reptiles and amphibians spend winter in a burrow below the frost line or nestled in the sediment of a lake or pond. Wood frogs temporarily freeze solid over winter (frogsicles!) and thaw in spring. They survive by filling their cells with glucose to protect them from the damage normally caused by freezing.

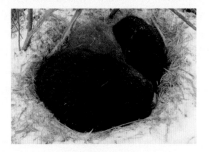

Figure 5. Black bears go into hibernation September to November, emerging in late March to early April. Here a mother and two yearlings, one black and one brown, are sleeping in an open den. A fair number of bears, especially males and in northwestern Minnesota, den in open nests.

Die

Ever wonder how insects magically appear in the spring, after having been absent all winter long? Some, such as spittle bugs, lay their eggs in the fall, then die. The eggs, which are cold hardy, survive and hatch in the spring. Other insects lay eggs that *desiccate* (dry up) for several years, then rehydrate and hatch when conditions become favorable. Adult dragonflies, mosquitoes, and other insects with aquatic life stages die before winter. Their nymphs or larva survive in the frigid water under the ice at the bottom of lakes, ponds, and streams in the colder months (Figure 6). In the spring they continue their process of metamorphosis, with adult stages emerging in the warmer months.

Figure 6. Dragonflies survive winter underwater in an immature stage known as a nymph.

They would prefer that you say the fox has become *acclimated* to its new surroundings. Populations adapt to their environments through changes in the frequency of different genes within the population, or evolution. This can only occur over many generations. Individuals may be able to acclimate within their lifetimes, such as the fox in the living room or when you learn to favor a bum knee. But true adaptation takes generations, such as the process of wild canids evolving into man's (and woman's) best friend over many thousands of years.

Everywhere you look at living things you'll see adaptations at work. They create the wide diversity of organisms that exist on Earth. Different plant species grow in wet, dry, or mesic soil. Different birds nest on the forest floor, in a wetland, or in a tree. Each has its own strategy to survive.

Exploring in depth the adaptation of every species in Minnesota's north woods would be entertaining but also overwhelming. To keep things simple, this chapter will focus on one especially important set of adaptations: the ways animals get the energy they need.

Herbivores: Eating Green

Herbivores are the vegetarians of the north woods. They gain energy by eating plant parts. Herbivores are the most numerous contingent of animals in the woods, and insects are by far the most numerous group of herbivores.

It might seem like being a plant eater would be an easy job with all the plants available in the north woods. But in truth, herbivores don't eat every plant in the forest. Many have "favorite" foods, just as you and I do (chocolate, anyone?). For instance, white-tailed deer prefer eating the growing tips of white pine and northern white cedar trees to such an extent that large deer populations can make it hard for white pine and white cedar seedlings to survive. Herbivores can also compete with each other for food. For example, forest tent caterpillars can strip aspen trees of their leaves, leaving slim pickings for deer.

The digestive systems of herbivores are adapted to gaining energy from these favored foods. Deer and moose are efficient at digesting *cellulose* from leaves

and twigs. Similarly, birds are good at digesting their preferred seeds or fruits. Because many herbivores specialize on a few specific foods, they depend on the north woods communities where those plants grow.

Carnivores: Eating Red

Carnivores eat other animals to gain energy (Figure 7). There are far fewer carnivores in the woods than herbivores, because it takes quite a few herbivores to support each carnivore (more on that in Chapter 4). We may think of carnivores, such as snakes, as controlling populations of prey, such as mice. However, research suggests that food is the major limiting factor for carnivores, which means that a prey population probably has a bigger impact on the predator population than the other way around.

Carnivores have to overcome their prey's defenses to gain the upper hand. What's more, the effort expended on capturing prey has to provide a sufficient return on the energy invested to make the effort worth it. For example, a gray wolf could spend all day chasing and eating mice, but it wouldn't get much energy back. It's much more efficient to spend the same amount of energy chasing a deer or moose where the reward is (literally) much bigger. The dangers of hunting deer and moose are great — those hooves and antlers aren't just for show — so it's a gamble, and one that occasionally pays off.

Figure 7. There's no such thing as a free lunch, even for a wild carnivore. These wolves expended substantial energy and risked injury from flailing hooves to capture and kill a white-tailed deer.

Omnivores: Eating It All

An *omnivore* can derive energy and nutrients from both plants and animals. Some omnivores hunt and eat prey, but many will scavenge dead animals. Their teeth are adapted to both biting into things and grinding things. Because they can make use of diverse food sources, they are well-suited to living in human-altered environments.

Figure 9. A beaver lodge usually has an underwater entrance and an interior den above the water line.

Spotlight Species – Beavers

Quick: Name the animal that has the biggest impact on the north woods environment! If you answered "humans" you're right. But the beaver (*Castor canadensis*) runs a close second (Figure 8).

The beaver, North America's largest rodent, is considered the civil engineer of the natural world. In response to the sound of running water, beavers use sticks, mud, grass, and stones to create leaky dams that slow a river or stream enough to form a pond. This deeper water creates habitat for the beaver and a suite of other warm-water-loving creatures, such as panfish, pond insects, great blue herons, frogs, and toads.

Using the same architectural styling as the dam, beavers also build mud-and-stick lodges with an interior den above the water line (Figure 9). An underwater entrance makes the lodge a very secure fortress, protecting residents from predators such as wolves, bears, coyotes, cougars, and bobcats. If you see a beaver dam but can't locate an obvious lodge,

scan the banks of the lake or river for smaller piles of sticks and mud along a steeper edge. When a muddy riverbank or lakeshore is available, a beaver is just as likely to burrow into the mud to create its lodge, sometimes adding the equivalent of a foyer to the existing hillside.

Beavers get their energy from tree bark and leaves as well as soft green plants such as cattails, pond lilies, grasses, and ferns. Their favorite trees include aspen, alder, birch, cottonwood, and willow, all trees that grow near rivers and lakes (Figure 10). Although mammals usually do not have the *enzymes* necessary for getting energy from cellulose, a special digestive system allows beavers to use up to 30 percent of the woody material they consume—much like rabbits, porcupines, and horses.

Beavers' bodies are well-adapted to traveling efficiently in water, but they need to waddle up onto dry land to acquire food. This is when they are most vulnerable to predators, so they minimize the time they spend out of the water by caching sticks and branches in the water near the entrance to their lodge. This cache is critical in winter when the beaver pond is covered in ice.

Figure 8. Beavers use their large teeth and powerful jaws to fell aspen, alder, and other trees they use for food and to build dams and lodges.

Figure 10. A stick or log gnawed to pencil-point shape is a good clue that a beaver lives in the neighborhood.

Figure 11. Pine martens may be cute, but they are also deadly to small animals. Martens hunt both in trees and on the ground for squirrels, birds, and other prey.

Spotlight Species – Pine Marten

The pine marten (*Martes americana*) wins the prize for most adorable carnivore (Figure 11). Its small, rounded ears, pug nose, dark eyes, and slender furry body just make you want to pick one up and cuddle it. But don't be fooled! Pine martens are competent predators, hunting in trees for red squirrels, birds (they love to visit bird feeders), and eggs. They also sometimes hunt on the ground for snowshoe hare and mice. At 24–30 inches long, including tail, this four-pound, light brown member of the weasel family generally keeps to a home range of two to four square miles.

Pine martens were once thought to prefer coniferous forest habitats, hence their name. Today we know that pine martens live in any type of northern Minnesota forest: deciduous or coniferous, old or young.

Martens were nearly decimated by the removal of Minnesota forests in the early 1900s logging era. As the forests regenerated, the marten population rebounded as well. Today the population is estimated to be more than 10,000.

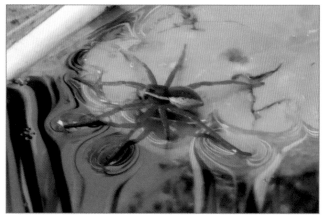

Figure 12. The six-spotted fishing spider relies on good eyesight, speedy movements, and powerful fangs to capture its prey.

Spotlight Species – Six-Spotted Fishing Spider

Forget what you thought you knew about spiders (they all weave webs, have poor eyesight, and talk to adorable pigs). The six-spotted fishing spider (*Dolomedes triton*) is an impressive reminder of the wide diversity of spider natural history.

The largest of the north woods spiders (females can be as much as 2¾ inches long!), the six-spotted fishing spider hangs out on docks, along shorelines, and under rocks or leaf litter near shore. It has a dark body with light lines down both sides of its body. It also has two rows of light-colored spots on its topside. It gets its name from six dark-colored spots on its underside.

This carnivore obtains its food the same way many other predators do — by lying in ambush and then using keen eyesight and quick movements to catch prey (Figure 12). It perches on floating vegetation with a couple of legs resting on the surface of the water to detect ripples made by prey. In pursuit of aquatic insects and sometimes tadpoles and small fish, it can even dive under water for up to 30 minutes. It uses its fangs and venom to overpower prey. Then it uses its fangs and strong stomach muscles to suck out the innards.

Since they catch aquatic critters to eat, six-spotted fishing spiders don't build typical webs, although the female will spin a small "nursery web" to shelter the egg sac and young spiderlings until they are mature enough to emerge. Young six-spotted fishing spiders, like other spiders, go through several "molts" before reaching adult size.

Figure 13. With their intelligence, versatile diet, and ability to store food for winter, gray jays are among the most successful of north woods birds.

Spotlight Species – Gray Jay

The gray jay, or timberjay (Figure 13), is a member of the corvid family, which also includes blue jays, crows, and ravens. *Corvids* are known for their intelligence, their problem-solving ability, and their propensity to eat many kinds of food, including human garbage, roadkill, and crops. What sets the gray jay apart from other corvids is that it's only common in boreal forests and mountains.

These grayish birds eat insects, berries, nestling birds, carrion, and mushrooms. The diversity of their diet allows them to take advantage of the most available food source at any given time, such as berries in the fall. If a common food source is rare one year — perhaps a lower deer population leads to less carrion left over from wolf kills — these adaptable birds can switch to another food source, or even experiment with new foods, such as campers' lunches. A gray jay has even been seen landing on a moose's back to pick off engorged ticks (yummy!).

The adaptation that has made gray jays one of the most successful boreal bird species is their ability to store food in tree hollows and cracks or under tree bark during the summer, then retrieve it in the winter. This means they don't have to spend much time foraging for food in the winter, which saves them energy. It also means they have ample food on hand for when the female lays and incubates her eggs in the relatively cold and snowy months of March and April.

Moose Mystery

Moose numbers are dropping in Minnesota and other northern states, and no one is sure why (Figure 14). In the 1990s, Minnesota supported two healthy moose populations, one in northwestern Minnesota and one in northeastern Minnesota. Between 2006 and 2014, the northwestern population almost disappeared from a high of 4,000 to fewer than 100. The northeastern population dropped from 8,800 to 2,800.

There are several possible causes for the steep population declines, but most can be traced to climate change. Potential culprits include parasites such as brainworms, liver flukes, and winter ticks that don't die off in as high a number in milder winters. Heat stress that comes with higher temperatures and humidity is another big factor, as are changes in habitat and food availability. Even more worrisome, almost half of moose tracked by researchers die of undetermined causes.

Wildlife biologists use radio collars to track moose so they can determine causes of death. They receive a text message when the moose hasn't moved and is presumed dead so they can find it very quickly to study the remains. Stay tuned as they work to unravel this mystery.

Figure 14. Magnificent moose were once far more abundant in Minnesota. Scientists are working to figure out why populations have plummeted in recent years.

Spotlight Species – Squirrels and Chipmunks

If the natural world hosted a TV show about hoarders, members of the chipmunk family (Figure 15) would be regular guest stars. To be fair, they need to gather and store a reliable supply of food to help them through the cold months. Sometimes it's hard to distinguish which critter just zipped through your yard or campsite. Here's a quick primer on the squirrels and chipmunks of the Boreal Forest biome, in order from smallest to largest:

LEAST AND EASTERN CHIPMUNKS These two ground-loving species are hard to tell apart, both sporting dark and light stripes behind their eyes and along their backs.

The least chipmunk, the smaller of the two, is just seven to eight inches from nose to tip of the tail, while eastern

Figure 15. Least Chipmunk

chipmunks typically reach nine to ten inches in length. Both feast on seeds, nuts, leaves, buds, berries, and even slugs and insects (Figure 15). Both have internal cheek pouches they use to carry food (60 to 70 sunflower seeds at a time!) to an underground "granary," where they stash it for winter. They hibernate atop their food pile so they can have a quick snack during those periodic arousals.

NORTHERN FLYING SQUIRREL If one of these things is not like the others, it's the northern flying squirrel (Figure 16). This squirrel is nocturnal and stays active all winter. About nine to 12 inches long, it has disproportionately large eyes. A flap of skin between the wrist and ankle stretches when the squirrel leaps from tree to

Figure 16. Northern Flying Squirrel.

tree, giving it the extra lift of a hang glider as it covers 20 to 30 feet with each jump. It prefers forests with large trees.

RED SQUIRREL You'll hear a red squirrel before you see one. These are the critters making the loud chittering sound warning you away from their feeding grounds. With reddish brown fur, they are the largest of our contingent at 11 to 14 inches long (Figure 17).

Figure 17. Red Squirrel
Most chipmunks and squirrels store food for winter consumption.

Red squirrels are the smallest of the tree squirrels and prefer coniferous forests, where they feed on seeds, nuts, cones, bird eggs, mushrooms, sap, buds, grasses, beetles, and grubs (Figure 18). They stash food in hollow logs and tree branches and find them by memory and smell. Antagonistic, especially over food, they sometimes strike each other with their front feet.

Other members of the squirrel family (*Sciuridae*) not found in the north woods include prairie dogs, various ground squirrels, and a couple of other types of tree squirrels. They serve an important role as food for carnivores, particularly foxes, owls, snakes, and bobcats.

Figure 18. A telltale sign that a red squirrel has been at work is a midden pile. Red squirrels will sit in a safe place and pull apart a pinecone, devouring the nutritious pine seeds and discarding the fibrous parts.

Biting Buggers

If you've ever been to the north woods, you've been bitten by at least a few parasites, such as mosquitoes (Figure 19), blackflies, horseflies, deerflies (Figure 20), or ticks (Figure 21). The bites can be itchy or painful! The saliva of these biting buggers contains a protein that prevents clotting and allows them to feed and escape undisturbed — a brilliant adaptation that aids their survival. Not so brilliant for humans, though. The saliva triggers an immune response in our bodies in the form of redness, welts, and itchiness to combat this foreign substance.

For all these insects and arachnids (ticks are part of the spider family), only the females bite — they use blood as extra protein to make and lay their eggs. Males feed on nectar instead. A female mosquito finds victims by using her antennae to sense the carbon dioxide they give off. She then follows the carbon dioxide trail to her meal.

Figure 19. Minnesota is home to more than 50 species of mosquito; although some are generalists, many specialize on the blood of birds, mammals, frogs, or turtles.

Mosquitoes and blackflies lay their eggs in water with the larval and pupal stages of development taking place entirely under water (Figure 22). During this phase mosquitoes can tolerate a wide range of aquatic conditions, including extreme variations in temperature, pH, and salinity, though they do not survive well in moving water. Blackflies, on the other hand, require relatively clean, moving water. The adults emerge

Figure 20. Deerflies are common biting insects in Minnesota.

from the water, dry off, and then fly around in search of blood for egg development (Figure 23).

Many insect repellents contain a chemical called DEET (diethyl-meta-toluamide). Researchers think DEET either interferes with a mosquito's ability to sense carbon dioxide, or it gives the wearer a scent mosquitoes don't like. Either way, it seems to work. While the U.S. Environmental Protection Agency allows the sale of repellents with 100 percent DEET, concentrations above 50 percent don't seem to provide an added benefit.

Some health experts recommend using repellents with no more than 10 percent DEET for children and 30 percent DEET for teens and adults to minimize potential health impacts. Keep in mind that if DEET solutions greater than 30 percent have a potentially harmful effect on something so large as a human body, consider what effect it may have on something fragile or tiny, such as a butterfly or dragonfly that may inadvertently land on your skin or treated clothing.

Figure 21. Blacklegged ticks (aka deer ticks) can transmit diseases such as Lyme disease and babesiosis to humans.

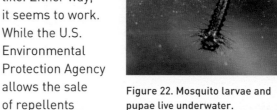
Figure 22. Mosquito larvae and pupae live underwater.

Figure 23. Like mosquitoes, blackflies need blood to reproduce.

Community Snapshots

The following community snapshots list animal species that are particular to each type of forest community found in the north woods. These do not include species such as gray wolves or barred owls that can be found in a variety of forest types; rather, these are the species that, when you see them together, indicate you have made it — you are standing in a specific forest community.

Wet Meadow and Marsh Community Snapshot

INDICATOR PLANTS	MAMMALS	BIRDS	REPTILES & AMPHIBIANS
Cattail (*Typha* spp.)	Mink (*Mustela vison*)	American bittern (*Botaurus lentiginosus*)	Smooth green snake (*Opheodrys vernalis*)
Lake sedge (*Carex lacustris*)	Muskrat (*Ondatra zibethicus*)	Common yellowthroat (*Geothlypis trichas*)	Boreal chorus frog (*Pseudacris maculata*)
Willows (*Salix* spp.)		Marsh wren (*Cistothorus palustris*)	Northern leopard frog (*Lithobates pipiens*)
Dogwoods (*Cornus* spp.)		Sedge wren (*Cistothorus platensis*)	
Sphagnum moss (*Sphagnum* spp.)		Sora (*Porzana carolina*)	
		Swamp sparrow (*Melospiza georgiana*)	
		Brown thrasher (*Toxostoma rufum*)	
		Eastern meadowlark (*Sturnella magna*))	

Mesic Hardwood Community Snapshot

INDICATOR PLANTS	MAMMALS	BIRDS	REPTILES & AMPHIBIANS
Sugar maple (*Acer saccharum*)	Eastern chipmunk (*Tamias striatus*)	Eastern wood-peewee (*Contopus virens*)	Blue-spotted salamander (*Ambystoma laterale*)
Basswood (*Tilia* spp.)	White-footed mouse (*Peromyscus leucopus*)	Great crested flycatcher (*Myiarchus crinitus*)	Eastern garter snake (*Thamnophis sirtalis*)
Paper birch (*Betula papyrifera*)	Gray fox (*Urocyon cinereoargenteus*)	Hairy woodpecker (*Picoides villosus*)	Ringneck snake (*Diadophis punctatus*)
Quaking aspen (*Populus tremuloides*)	Coyote (*Canis latrans*))	Ovenbird (*Seiurus aurocapilla*)	Wood frog (*Lithobates sylvaticus*)
Northern red oak (*Quercus rubra*)		Pileated woodpecker (*Dryocopus pileatus*)	
		Red-bellied woodpecker (*Melanerpes carolinus*)	
		Red-eyed vireo (*Vireo olivaceus*)	
		Scarlet tanager (*Piranga olivacea*)	
		Veery *(Catharus fuscescens)*	
		Wood thrush (*Hylocichla mustelina*)	
		Ruffed grouse (*Bo umbellus*)	

Peatland Community Snapshot

INDICATOR PLANTS	MAMMALS	BIRDS	REPTILES & AMPHIBIANS
Sphagnum moss (*Sphagnum* spp.)	Masked shrew (*Sorex cinereus*)	Chipping sparrow (*Spizella passerine*)	Mink frog (*Lithobates septentrionalis*)
Black spruce (*Picea mariana*)	Red squirrel (*Tamiasciurus hudsonicus*)	Nashville warbler (*Oreothlypis ruficapilla*)	Green frog (*Lithobates clamitans*)
Northern white cedar (*Thuja occidentalis*)	Short-tailed shrew (*Blarina brevicauda*)	Olive-sided flycatcher (*Contopus cooperi*)	Red-bellied snake (*Storeria occipitomaculata*)
Tamarack (*Larix laricina*)	Northern bog lemming (*Synaptomys borealis*)	Pine siskin (*Spinus pinus*)	
Speckled alder (*Alnus incana rugosa*)		Purple finch (*Haemorhous purpureus*)	
Red-osier dogwood (*Cornus sericea*)		Red-breasted nuthatch (*Sitta canadensis*)	
Willow (*Salix* spp.)		Veery (*Catharus fuscescens*)	
		White-throated sparrow (*Zonotrichia albicollis*)	
		Yellow-rumped warbler (*Setophaga coronate*)	
		Swamp sparrow (*Melospiza georgiana*)	
		Winter wren (*Troglodytes hiemalis*)	

Pine/Spruce/Fir (Fire Dependent) Community Snapshot

INDICATOR PLANTS	MAMMALS	BIRDS	REPTILES & AMPHIBIANS
Pine (*Pinus* spp.)	Least chipmunk (*Tamias minimus*)	Blackburnian warbler (*Setophaga fusca*)	Blue-spotted salamander (*Ambystoma laterale*)
Spruce (*Picea* spp.)	Red fox (*Vulpes vulpes*)	Chipping sparrow (*Spizella passerine*)	
Fir (*Abies* spp.)	Red squirrel (*Tamiasciurus hudsonicus*)	Red crossbill (*Loxia curvirostra*)	
	White-footed mouse (*Peromyscus leucopus*)	White-winged crossbill (*Loxia leucoptera*)	
	Woodchuck (*Marmota monax*)	Dark-eyed junco (*Junco hyemalis*)	
	Porcupine (*Erethizon dorsatum*)	Eastern wood-peewee (*Contopus virens*)	
		Evening grosbeak (*Coccothraustes vespertinus*)	
		Hermit thrush (*Catharus guttatus*)	
		Ovenbird (*Seiurus aurocapilla*)	
		Red-breasted nuthatch (*Sitta canadensis*)	
		Yellow-rumped warbler (*Setophaga coronate*)	

Rock (Cliffs, Talus Slopes, Outcrops) Community Snapshot

INDICATOR PLANTS	MAMMALS	BIRDS	REPTILES & AMPHIBIANS
Lichens (including Rockshield, Rock posy, Rock foam, Sunburst lichen, and Reindeer lichen) Mosses (*Bryophyta*)	Little brown bat (*Myotis lucifugus*)	Bank swallow (*Riparia riparia*) Barn swallow (*Hirundo rustica*) Chimney swift (*Chaetura pelagica*) Eastern phoebe (*Sayornis phoebe*) Cliff swallow (*Petrochelidon pyrrhonota*) Northern rough-winged swallow (*Stelgidopteryx serripennis*)	This habitat is inhospitable to reptiles and amphibians!

Wet Forest/Swamp Community Snapshot

INDICATOR PLANTS	MAMMALS	BIRDS	REPTILES & AMPHIBIANS
Black ash (*Fraxinus nigra*) Northern white cedar (*Thuja occidentalis*) Speckled alder (*Alnus incana rugosa*)	Eastern chipmunk (*Tamias striatus*) Least chipmunk (*Tamias minimus*) Masked shrew (*Sorex cinereus*) Red fox (*Vulpes vulpes*) Red squirrel (*Tamiasciurus hudsonicus*) Short-tailed shrew (*Blarina brevicauda*) White-footed mouse (*Peromyscus leucopus*) Star-nosed mole (*Condylura cristata*) Arctic shrew (*Sorex arcticus*) Snowshoe hare (*Lepus americanus*)	Blue-headed vireo (*Vireo solitarius*) Boreal chickadee (*Poecile hudsonicus*) Chipping sparrow (*Spizella passerine*) Hermit thrush (*Catharus guttatus*) Magnolia warbler (*Setophaga magnolia*) Nashville warbler (*Oreothlypis ruficapilla*) Northern waterthrush (*Parkesia noveboracensis*) Olive-sided flycatcher (*Contopus cooperi*) Ovenbird (*Seiurus aurocapilla*) Pileated woodpecker (*Dryocopus pileatus*) Pine siskin (*Spinus pinus*) Purple finch (*Haemorhous purpureus*) Red-breasted nuthatch (*Sitta canadensis*) Spruce grouse (*Falcipennis Canadensis*) Veery (*Catharus fuscescens*) White-throated sparrow (*Zonotrichia albicollis*) Yellow-rumped warbler (*Setophaga coronate*)	Eastern gray treefrog (*Hyla versicolor*) Eastern red-backed salamander (*Plethodon cinereus*) Red-bellied snake (*Storeria occipitomaculata*) Spotted salamander (*Ambystoma maculatum*) Spring peeper (*Pseudacris crucifer*) Wood frog (*Lithobates sylvaticus*)

Managing Wildlife

If we just leave wildlife alone, won't it be fine without us? On one hand, yes: If wildlife had free run of healthy, undisturbed ecosystems, they would find food and reproduce in balance with nature. However, since humans occupy—or at least affect—most every corner of the globe, we have a huge influence over animals' fate. That's why we manage wildlife rather than just let them work out their balance with nature on their own.

When Europeans first settled the United States, they had a very utilitarian approach to natural resources. Plants and animals were so abundant that the settlers made use of them in whatever ways they could. People exploited species such as beaver and egrets that provided fur, feathers, medicine, and other goods (Figure 24). Other species, such as wolves, bears, and hawks, were killed because they were perceived as dangerous to humans or as competition for food. Little thought was given to long-term sustainability. But as time passed, people began to observe changes in wildlife populations and to regulate how wildlife should be treated.

Today, wildlife management—the application of scientific knowledge and technical skills to influence animals' habitat, behavior, and abundance—is a common practice. The choices and priorities set by wildlife managers, public agencies, or individual landowners reflect a set of values. For example, humans often manipulate the living conditions of various fish in order to create a bountiful harvest for anglers.

Wildlife Management Practices

In the United States, each state typically has jurisdiction over the plants and animals within its borders. States usually have an agency charged with managing wildlife. Employees of these agencies make and carry out decisions to ensure the long-term viability of the plants and animals in their state. The federal government has jurisdiction over nearly all birds (they migrate across state boundaries), endangered species, and marine mammals.

Some species are considered desirable, so their populations are nurtured to benefit humans. Other species are considered a nuisance, or *vermin*, and their populations are minimized to limit their impact on humans. To influence an animal's habitat, behavior, or abundance, wildlife managers may use any of the following tools:

PROTECTION – state or federal laws that make any injury to a species a crime

REGULATED HARVEST – controlled number of permits or licenses to hunt or fish a certain species

SEASONS – certain times of year people may harvest a species to meet population goals (maximize reproduction for game species; minimize reproduction of vermin)

BAG LIMIT – maximum number of animals an individual may catch within a specified time period

SIZE LIMIT – maximum or minimum weight or length of a species, usually fish, that may be caught and kept in order to protect smaller or larger individuals

SLOT LIMIT – range of sizes of fish that are protected (i.e., fish that are within the length range must be immediately returned to the water) or unprotected and thus may be harvested

POPULATION MONITORING – estimate of the overall size of a species' population by counting individual

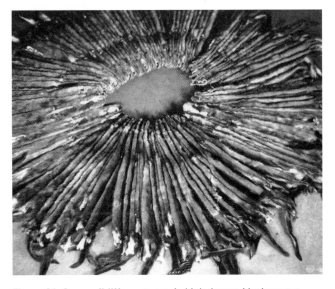

Figure 24. Some wildlife parts are in high demand by humans, such as these illegally harvested mink skins, seized in 1951. Furbearer harvest is carefully managed by state and federal wildlife managers to achieve population goals and prevent the collapse of a population.

animals or locating scats, tracks, nests, and so on, to provide data for management decisions

HABITAT ANALYSIS – data collection about key habitat elements

HABITAT PROTECTION – laws that preserve key food, water, shelter, or space for the target species

HABITAT IMPROVEMENT – adding or improving key food, water, shelter, or space components

HABITAT REMOVAL – removing, destroying, or erecting barriers to food, water, shelter, or space for undesirable species, such as mosquitoes

CONTROL – removing individual animals of a certain species

CONTRACEPTION – limiting reproduction of a species

EDUCATION – providing information to the public about wildlife habits and needs

These tools are commonly used on public lands over which the wildlife management agency has jurisdiction. However, public lands are only part of the picture. As a result, many wildlife management agencies bring private landowners and public land managers together to collaboratively preserve and improve habitat.

Figure 25. Wildlife managers use bear collars to gather data on movements and habitat.

Figure 26. A wildlife manager installs a flying squirrel nest box.

A Management Plan

Most wildlife species are under the jurisdiction of state wildlife agencies, which employ biologists to formulate and carry out species management plans. The biologists outline the needs and outcomes desired for a given species, identify its habitat needs (food, water, shelter, space), determine the optimal population level, and identify any limiting factors that are keeping the species from maintaining the desired population level. They then use the tools above to create a plan designed to maintain the target species at the desired population level or in the desired range. As they do so, they keep in mind that actions that benefit one species may harm another, and that a species' needs may change over time.

A management plan usually includes details about when, where, and how long any management strategies will be used. For example, under the Minnesota DNR's management plan for black bears,

bears are hunted by licensed hunters regulated by a quota system in northeastern Minnesota during a fall hunting season. In parts of western and southern Minnesota, where the habitat is not as good and the potential for bear-human conflicts is greater, harvest quotas are not imposed on bear hunting during the hunting season. The DNR also provides quality bear habitat through a variety of forestry practices, supports research to improve understanding of bear behavior and needs (Figure 25), and provides information to the public about how to live with bears.

Biologists usually seek input when preparing management plans. Citizens may comment at public hearings or participate in special interest groups that offer opinions about the planning process. Wildlife management plans often must undergo a rigorous approval process with the agency or lawmakers, depending on prevailing laws.

A wide variety of wildlife management activities take place across the state (Figure 26). Wetlands are protected to provide habitat for waterfowl. Population surveys determine whether lynx and boreal owls are permanent residents of, or temporary visitors to, an area. Black spruce stands are managed to favor boreal owl nesting. Reflectors are installed to frighten white-tailed deer from highways, and population survey information is used to regulate the deer harvest each year. Lake stocking, dams that control water levels, and erosion management benefit walleyes by preserving clean water. Prescribed burns and winter brush shearing maintain sharp-tailed grouse dancing grounds. Forested travel corridors benefit solitary species such as fishers and martens as they move though the landscape.

Many species have very healthy population levels and don't need special management. The Minnesota DNR doesn't actively manage animals such as porcupines, mice, skunks, toads, or garter snakes, although these species may benefit indirectly from the management of other species.

Conclusion

To sum it all up, each animal has adaptations that allow it to live in a certain way in a certain environment. Consequently, each has a specific niche, with specific strategies for eating, growing, reproducing, and avoiding being eaten in the place they call home. North woods creatures are adapted to a climate with short summers and long, cold winters and comprise a smaller cohort of herbivores, carnivores, and omnivores than creatures that live in warmer climates. Wolves expend energy to catch deer and moose, which provide a much greater energy return than smaller prey. Gray jays can make use of a very wide range of foods so they don't suffer when certain foods are scarce. Squirrels and chipmunks become much less active in the coldest winter months to conserve energy. Beavers go so far as to change their environmental conditions by building dams to protect themselves from being eaten. All of these organisms are adapted to their environments; their environments can tell you a bit about how they live, and their physical and behavioral adaptations can tell you a bit about their environment. Humans manage wildlife to our benefit and to help them deal with special challenges our activities impose on them.

Explore

This section highlights places in the North Woods, Great Lakes region where you can do some great wildlife watching. Please check them out online, then head out and discover them in real life!

Zippel Bay State Park – Williams, Minnesota

WHAT Minnesota's northernmost state park, located along the shore of Lake of the Woods, is home to a suite of wildlife characteristic of the north woods. Look for signs of black bear, coyote, deer, moose, mink, fisher, otter, pine marten, and gray wolf onshore or inland. On the lake you'll find a variety of shorebirds and waterfowl, such as American white pelicans, Franklin's and Bonaparte's gulls, double-crested cormorants, and several species of terns. Ospreys, bald eagles, and the rare piping plover nest in the area. The park has nine miles of hiking trails, but the crown jewel of the park is the gorgeous white sand beach. If you're an angler, you'll appreciate the fishing pier and protected marina.

WHEN Visit in summer when you can relax on the beach, view the abundant waterfowl, or throw in a fishing line.

WHERE From the west end of Baudette, take State Highway 172 ten miles north to County Road 8. Go west on County Road 8 for six miles to the park entrance.

WHO Zippel Bay State Park, 3684 54th Avenue NW, Williams, MN 56686, (218) 783-6252

FOR MORE INFORMATION www.mndnr.gov/state_parks/zippel_bay

International Wolf Center – Ely, Minnesota

WHAT The International Wolf Center is a private, nonprofit organization supported by memberships, program fees, and donations that seeks to advance the survival of wolf populations by teaching about wolves, their relationship to wild lands, and humans' role in their future. To accomplish this, the center offers a wide range of educational programs and exhibits centered on a captive wolf pack viewable through the windows of the visitor center. The legendary "Wolves and Humans" exhibit traces the folklore, history, and biology of the wolf/human relationship through history. If you bring along the family, be sure to stop in the "Little Wolf" exhibit that follows the seasonal adventures of a wolf pup's first year. Call ahead to reserve your seat at a "What's For Dinner?" program, where you can watch the ambassador pack receive its weekly meal.

WHEN The center is open seven days a week in the summer, but only on weekends from October to early May. Check the website for exact hours and admission fees. Summer can be crowded, especially if the pack is welcoming pups. Winter is less busy, and the ambassador pack's appearance and social behavior is especially dramatic, especially during February. Learning Adventure programs, seminars, and workshops are offered year round.

WHERE The International Wolf Center is located at the eastern edge of the town of Ely along U.S. Highway 169. Follow the brown signs.

WHO International Wolf Center, 1396 Highway 169, Ely, MN 55731-8129, (218) 365-4695

FOR MORE INFORMATION www.wolf.org

Sax-Zim Bog – Cotton, Minnesota

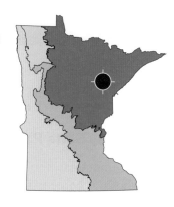

WHAT Designated as an Important Bird Area, this old-growth black spruce and tamarack habitat is pockmarked with mossy bogs throughout. Frequently observed are the great gray owl, black-backed woodpecker, boreal chickadee, yellow-bellied flycatcher, white-winged crossbill, pine grosbeak, common redpoll, hoary redpoll, Connecticut warbler, and relatively rare northern hawk owl. Bobcat, lynx, pine marten, and fisher also use this habitat. A recent BioBlitz documented 300 species in the area! The bog is a mix of state, county, and private land. You can drive throughout the area and bird from your car, set up a spotting scope, or park yourself near the feeders at the Welcome Center.

WHEN The Welcome Center is only open mid-December through mid-March when the birding is especially good. You'll see warblers in late May and waterbirds, wildflowers, butterflies, and other wildlife in the warmer months.

WHERE From Cotton, go west on County Road 52/Arkola Road about 11.5 miles. Turn south on County Road 203/Owl Avenue and go about 1.5 miles to the Sax-Zim Bog Welcome Center.

WHO Friends of Sax-Zim Bog, P.O. Box 3585, Duluth, MN 55803, info@saxzim.org

FOR MORE INFORMATION www.saxzim.org

Rice Lake National Wildlife Refuge – McGregor, Minnesota

WHAT If you're looking for waterfowl in the north woods, Rice Lake National Wildlife Refuge is a worthy destination. Established in 1935 to protect Rice Lake's shallow wild rice beds and waterfowl habitat, the refuge provides a valuable resting place for more than 70,000 waterfowl during the fall *migration*. A variety of forest types surround the lake, including upland hardwoods and lowland forest along the Rice River. The refuge has been designated a globally important bird area by the American Bird Conservancy due to the importance of the lake and its wild rice as a food source to migrating waterfowl, especially ring-necked ducks. The refuge has also been designated as a state important bird area (as part of the larger McGregor Important Bird Area) by the National Audubon Society. Check out the 12-mile self-guided auto tour (you can download an auto tour interpretive guide before you go!) and observation deck overlooking 3,600-acre Rice Lake.

WHEN Visit in the fall to view migrating waterfowl.

WHERE In Aitkin County, about five miles south of McGregor. From State Highway 65, go west on 363rd Lane about 2.5 miles to the refuge headquarters.

WHO Rice Lake National Wildlife Refuge, 36289 State Highway 65, McGregor, MN 55760, (218) 768-2402

FOR MORE INFORMATION www.fws.gov/refuge/Rice_Lake

MASTER NATURALIST TOOLBOX

102   NORTH WOODS, GREAT LAKES | CHAPTER 3: WOLVES AND MOOSE AND GROUSE, OH MY!

Teach

This section features lesson plans for activities that will reinforce the concepts presented in this chapter. The lessons are adaptable to a wide range of audiences, ages, and settings. Feel free to use them to teach others what you have learned!

LESSON 1

Mammal Tracking

Objective

Participants will learn to identify several common track patterns.

Audience Type

All ages

Supplies

☐ Track identification field guides
☐ Camera or sketching supplies

Background

Finding animal tracks in mud, snow, or wet sand is exciting! When you encounter tracks, you can try to ascertain what animal left the tracks, what the animal was doing, and where the animal went. Here are some things to consider when interpreting animal tracks:

SHAPE Learn to recognize the basic shapes of mammal footprints. Some are very distinctive, such as deer tracks. Others are hard to differentiate by shape alone.

SIZE OF THE ANIMAL As a general rule, larger animals leave larger tracks. A larger mammal will have a longer stride (the distance between each step). It may also have a wider straddle (the distance between left and right feet) and make a deeper footprint than a smaller mammal.

SUBSTRATE CONDITIONS Is the substrate in which the track was made wet or dry? Dry ground doesn't displace easily, so even a heavy animal won't make a very deep track. Tracks in the snow may become distorted over time in bright winter sun, or may get filled in with new snow.

TRAIL PATTERN North woods mammals can be divided into three categories based on the typical trail pattern they leave behind:

- **Ambler** These animals typically walk or trot one foot at a time: left, right, left right. Examples of amblers are deer, bear, fox, and beaver.

AMBLER	HOPPER	TRAILING-FOOT HOPPER

- **Hopper** These animals typically hop, putting two feet down at a time. They have larger hind feet that often fall ahead of the smaller front feet in trail patterns. Notable hoppers are snowshoe hare and chipmunks.

- **Trailing-Foot Hopper** This gait looks like hopping if you watch it happen, but the overall pattern incudes two feet down at a time, often with one slightly behind the other. Typically all four feet are the same size, such as with weasels and skunks, though a few species have hind feet larger than front feet, as with raccoons and opossums. Hind feet often land exactly (or nearly so) on top of the spot where the front feet left a track, a pattern called direct register.

Keep in mind that these patterns will vary depending whether the critter is in a hurry. A weasel may walk when it is exploring and a deer may gallop to escape a predator. A few species, such as mice and voles, have highly variable gaits with no pattern deemed typical. Always use multiple clues, including size and shape, to identify tracks and trails.

A few more tips for interpreting the stories behind animal tracks and trails:

- You can determine the animal's direction of travel by looking for toe prints. The toes point in the direction the animal was traveling.

- Look for overall trail patterns. The critter is unlikely to have dropped out of the sky. It had to come from somewhere and go somewhere, even if it stopped leaving prints. Do the tracks end at the base of a tree? Perhaps the critter climbed the tree.

- Beware of the "single track" phenomenon. One single imprint is unlikely to be an animal track. More likely, something dropped in that spot, such as snow from an overhead tree branch.

- Look for additional markings as part of the overall trail pattern. For example, muskrats and mice often drag their tails behind them, leaving a line along with the footprints.

- Be on the lookout for other signs, such as chew marks, scat, and burrows.

- Avoid stepping on the tracks or otherwise obliterating them. Point out the tracks to other members of your party and tell them to step around tracks so others may see them. A simple way to do this is to straddle the tracks while others file by.

Activity

After reviewing common animal tracks and trail patterns, go outdoors and search for tracks and trails. Snow is often great for animal tracking. In warmer months, your best chance of seeing tracks will be in places with open mud or sandy soil after a rain.

Try to determine where an animal trail begins and ends. Look for factors that influence where and how animals travel, such as food, water, and shelter.

Try to construct a story based on evidence and information in your field guide(s). If you are unsure which critter made a track, photograph and/or sketch the track for later research.

MASTER
NATURALIST
TOOLBOX

Optional: Make a Track Pad

You may think of a laptop computer when you hear the words "track pad." But in the world of animal tracking, a track pad is a whole different thing — a substrate used to collect animal tracks. Here's how to make one:

1. Remove rocks and plants from an area of soil about four feet by four feet. Dig down about two inches to loosen the soil. Mix in some sand and water if desired. Rake the soil to make it smooth and soft.

2. Provide food such as seeds or nuts.

3. Leave the area for 24 to 48 hours, then return to see if any critters left behind any tracks.

4. Rain will wipe the slate clean. Rake the area frequently to keep the soil clean and smooth. Add water as necessary to keep it moist. Check back frequently to see who has visited!

Resources

Forrest, L. (1988). *A field guide to tracking animals in snow.* Harrisburg, PA: Stackpole Books.

Rezendez, P. (1999). *Tracking and the art of seeing: how to read animal tracks and sign,* 2nd ed. New York: HarperCollins.

MASTER
NATURALIST
TOOLBOX

LESSON 2

Landscaping for Wildlife

Objective

Participants will learn to describe several methods for enhancing wildlife habitat.

Audience Type

All ages

Supplies

- ☐ "Planning Habitat Improvements" worksheet
- ☐ Pens or pencils
- ☐ Reference material
- ☐ Brush
- ☐ Wildlife habitat and requirements reference materials
- ☐ PVC pipes (optional)
- ☐ Suet
- ☐ Birdseed
- ☐ Oats
- ☐ Peanut butter
- ☐ Saucepan
- ☐ Small containers
- ☐ Plastic wrap

Background

Humans have altered Minnesota's landscapes to such a degree that it's a wonder wildlife can survive here at all any more. OK, that may be extreme, but there certainly are a lot of places we've changed to meet our own needs, forgetting that wildlife also need a place to live. We can help wildlife thrive alongside humans in these altered habitats with a few simple steps.

All animals need four things to survive: food, water, shelter, and space. Helping wildlife fill their survival needs makes conditions for reproduction more optimal, allowing the populations of target species to grow. But, in many cases, humans benefit from these activities, too. For example, growing berry-producing trees and shrubs not only provides food for wildlife, it may also provide shade and thus energy conservation for nearby buildings and prevent erosion to boot. Areas with increased wildlife activity provide better bird watching and photography opportunities, perhaps even windbreaks or play areas for kids. And of course, wildlife-rich environments are likely to be aesthetically attractive, too.

Keep in mind that when choosing plants as food or shelter for wildlife, it's always better to rely on native species. These are more readily recognized by wildlife, are already adapted to grow in local conditions, and require less maintenance than non-native species.

FOOD The nutritional needs of many wildlife species change with age and season. Plants with nuts, acorns, berries, or other seeds make great food sources, especially those that keep the food available through winter. Flowering plants provide nectar; multiple species blooming at different times can provide food throughout the growing season. Feeders (e.g., corn or black-oil sunflower) can provide a food source for birds and other animals.

WATER Many species are attracted to liquid water year round. Birdbaths, especially in shaded areas, attract multiple species. Fountains provide dripping and splashing, which many species prefer. Nearby ponds, creeks, and wetlands provide food and water for wide-ranging species. Rain gardens have water available periodically and are suitable for some species.

SHELTER Animals need protection from adverse weather and predators and places to raise young. Conifers provide useful shade and cover year round. Nest boxes, when cleaned annually

MASTER
NATURALIST
TOOLBOX

and suitably located, help nesting birds. Brush and rock piles provide hiding spots and nest sites for a variety of mammals. Grasses and shrubbery in multiple locations provide escape routes and nest sites.

SPACE Many species maintain a home range or have territorial requirements. Snags, logs, and perches are useful in several locations. Dust beds and grit help some species "bathe." If the patches are small they may not attract cats.

Activity – Part A

1. Ask participants to brainstorm actions humans take that help wildlife.

2. Review basic survival needs of wildlife (food, water, shelter, space). Refer to wildlife habitat reference materials to help with ideas. Ask participants to provide specific examples of how various species fill these needs.

3. Identify three species whose habitat you want to improve.

4. Use the worksheet to build lists of how participants can provide food, water, shelter, and space for various species.

5. Plan how to reasonably implement the habitat improvement strategies listed.

6. Discuss: Which of these methods have you seen used? How successful were they in attracting wildlife? What downsides are there to implementing these habitat strategies?

MASTER
NATURALIST
TOOLBOX

Planning Habitat Improvements

Instructions: Use this worksheet to brainstorm actions you can take to improve habitat at your selected site.

Site: _____

Target Species:			
FOOD	**WATER**	**SHELTER**	**SPACE**

Target Species:			
FOOD	**WATER**	**SHELTER**	**SPACE**

Target Species:			
FOOD	**WATER**	**SHELTER**	**SPACE**

Activity – Part B

1. Build a Rabbitat

A Rabbitat is a glorified brush pile that provides shelter for small critters such as rabbits, chipmunks, weasels, and even birds. Choose a site in a forested area, away from houses, gardens, and roads. Begin by placing a few large rocks, piles of smaller rocks, or medium-size logs a few feet apart. A few PVC pipes can help preserve space for tunnels. Pile on brush loosely, interlocking branches to preserve airspace. Place a few larger branches on top to keep the pile from coming dislodged. The pile can be any size up to eight feet high and eight feet wide; larger piles will provide habitat for more animals!

For more detailed instructions, visit http://dnr.wi.gov/files/PDF/pubs/wm/WM0221.pdf

2. Make suet feeders

Suet is beef or mutton fat, or tallow, and is usually raw. It melts at high heat but remains in a mostly solid state at room temperature. You can acquire it from a butcher or meat market, but make sure it is ground with no meat or other material in it. If suet is not available, lard is an acceptable alternative.

Suet gives birds much-needed fat in fall and winter. It provides high-calorie food for migrating and nesting birds, and is a good substitute for insect-eating birds in low insect years. Mixed with other bird-appropriate foods such as seeds and fruits, suet cakes provide a variety of dietary benefits.

Make suet cakes using the recipe below, hang them outdoors, and watch to see who comes to feed on them.

Easy Suet Cakes
2 pounds beef suet, ground
1/2 cup birdseed
1/2 cup oats
3 tablespoons crunchy peanut butter

Melt suet in a skillet or saucepan. Mix in other ingredients. Pour the mixture into small plastic containers to a depth of one to two inches (or use mini-Bundt pans for special holiday gifts). Refrigerate or freeze before removing from the pan. Cakes store well if wrapped airtight in plastic. Feel free to experiment with contents, including dried fruit, nuts, seeds, cornmeal, etc.

Resources

Henderson, C. (1987). *Landscaping for wildlife.* St. Paul: Minnesota Department of Natural Resources.

Henderson, C. L., C. Dindorf, F. Rozumalski. (1998). *Lakescaping for wildlife and water quality.* St. Paul: Minnesota Department of Natural Resources. 176 pp.

Henderson, C. L. (2009). *Woodworking for wildlife* (3rd edition). St. Paul: Minnesota Department of Natural Resources. 112 pp.

MASTER NATURALIST TOOLBOX

Conserve

MASTER NATURALIST TOOLBOX

This section includes opportunities for Minnesota Master Naturalist Volunteers to participate in stewardship and citizen science activities related to the creatures in the North Woods, Great Lakes region. Please visit the websites to learn more.

Moosewatch Expeditions

So much of what we know about the ecological relationships among wolves, moose, and north woods forests comes from research conducted on Isle Royale. Started in 1958, it is now one of the longest-running ecological studies anywhere — and volunteers are essential to helping find out how all the ecological pieces fit together. A Moosewatch Expedition is a rugged, seven-day, off-trail, backpacking trip with a goal of collecting bones from moose carcasses. These bones help reconstruct a story about the size, age, and health of the individual animal as well as contributing to the understanding of the moose population at large. Excellent physical fitness is a must!

www.isleroyalewolf.org

Minnesota Loon Monitoring Program (MLMP) and LoonWatcher

These two Minnesota DNR programs help professional biologists monitor population levels of the common loon and the health of loons' lake habitats. MLMP volunteers report sightings of adult and juvenile loons during specified periods in summer and also provide details about factors such as weather and shoreline conditions. LoonWatcher volunteers report on their lake at the end of the season, providing information on nesting success, number of loons observed, interesting occurrences, and problems that may harm the loons.

www.mndnr.gov/eco/nongame/projects/loon_survey.html
www.mndnr.gov/eco/nongame/projects/mlmp_state.html

HerpMapper

If you dig reptiles and amphibians, why not get involved in their conservation? Volunteers with the HerpMapper project document observations of reptiles and amphibians around the world by submitting to the website a photo or audio recording of species they observe. Participants can keep a "life list" of their observations on the site and see what other volunteers are reporting. Agencies and organizations working on herp conservation use the data for research and conservation projects, though exact locations are hidden from the public to protect rare species.

www.herpmapper.org

Expand

This section suggests some things you can use, do, pursue, read, or join to develop as a naturalist.

Journal

EXPERIENCE Examine your special spot for the diversity of things present. Look for, tally, and differentiate the types of plants, animals, soil particles, clouds, etc. Use a field guide to learn the names of things you don't recognize.

REFLECT How many different things were you able to find? How can you categorize what you found? What other categories can you use? How is your experience with an object or species different when you have a formal name for it? How does your awareness of an object or species change when you sketch it?

RECORD Make a list of the plant and animal species you find. Use a field identification guide to help you make the list as long as possible. Sketch at least three things you find.

Read

Canoe Country Wildlife: A Field Guide to the North Woods and Boundary Waters

Mark Stensaas.
2004. St. Paul: University of Minnesota Press. 240 pp.

This book is a friendly reference guide describing the life and habits of the forest inhabitants you are most likely to see outdoors in the north woods. In this cross between a field guide and coffee table book, author "Sparky" Stensaas recounts tales of wildlife antics he's observed while delivering a wealth of scientific information on the biology of each species.

Northwoods Wildlife: A Watcher's Guide to Habitats

Janine M. Benyus
1989: Minocqua, WI: NorthWord Press. 453 pp.

Many wildlife reference books are organized by the taxonomy of the species described, but not this book. Here you'll find that each chapter describes a different north woods habitat type — from shrub swamp to upland needleleaf forest — and the corresponding wildlife to be observed in each, along with a description of the unique qualities of each habitat type. Also look for wildlife-watching hot spots and observation tips.

Surf

Birding and Wildlife in Voyageur Country of Northeast Minnesota

This website offers a variety of information, maps, and checklists of birds and wildlife in Voyageurs National Park and surrounding areas. A nature blog reports current bird sightings. Look for several maps of area hiking trails.

www.BirdVNP.com

USFS Fire Effects Information

Ever wonder how wildfire affects salamanders, ruffed grouse, or moose? This website is your chance to find out. Here you can browse monographs detailing fire effects on specific species or download the comprehensive document "Wildland Fire in Ecosystems: Effects of Fire on Fauna." Don't let the technical look of this website scare you off. It is surprisingly straightforward and readable.

www.fs.fed.us/rm/pubs/rmrs_gtr042_1.pdf (Wildland Fire article)
www.feis-crs.org/feis/ (database search)

Join

Minnesota Chapter of the Wildlife Society

The Wildlife Society is the professional organization for wildlife managers. The Minnesota chapter is extremely active and is a great source of information for people interested in wildlife and habitat information in the state.

http://wildlife.org/minnesota

Minnesota Herpetological Society

Reptiles and amphibians tend not to get much notice, so take a look at this organization dedicated to the study and conservation of these creatures. The organization provides grants for herp conservation and research as well as educational outreach about herps' ecological value.

www.mnherpsoc.org

Additional Reading

Burt, W. (1972). *Mammals of the Great Lakes region.* Ann Arbor, MI: The University of Michigan Press.

Weber, L. (2003). *Spiders of the northwoods: A handy reference to our most common northern spiders.* Duluth, MN: Kollath-Stensaas Publishing.

MASTER
NATURALIST
TOOLBOX

Copyrighted Photographs and Images Used With Permission

Figure 1. Courtesy of Jerri Waddell

Figure 2. Courtesy of National Park Service, Wikimedia Commons

Figure 3. Courtesy of Ken Thomas, Wikimedia Commons

Figure 4. Courtesy of Tim Rains, National Park Service

Figure 5. Courtesy of Dave Garshelis, Minnesota Department of Natural Resources

Figure 6. Courtesy of Ami Thompson

Figure 7. Courtesy of Kelly Godfrey

Figure 8. Courtesy of Jim Kearns via Flickr. No changes were made.

Figure 9. Courtesy of Wikimedia Commons

Figure 10. Courtesy of Andrea Lorek Strauss

Figure 11. Courtesy of U. S. Fish and Wildlife Service, Wikimedia Commons

Figure 12. Courtesy of Chris Serani

Figure 13. Courtesy of Gavin Schaefer via Flickr. No changes were made.

Figure 14. Courtesy of Dave Pauly

Figure 15. Courtesy of Wikimedia Commons

Figure 16. Courtesy of Larry Master, U.S. Fish and Wildlife Service, Wikimedia Commons

Figure 17. Courtesy of Wikimedia Commons

Figure 18. Courtesy of Andrea Lorek Strauss

Figure 19. Courtesy of Jeff Hahn

Figure 20. Courtesy of Jeff Hahn

Figure 21. Courtesy of Jeff Hahn

Figure 22. Courtesy of David Israel

Figure 23. Courtesy of Jeff Hahn

Figure 24. Courtesy of U.S. Fish and Wildlife Service, Wikimedia Commons

Figure 25. Courtesy of Minnesota Department of Natural Resources

Figure 26. Courtesy of U.S. Fish and Wildlife Service

Wildlife management information in this chapter was adapted with permission from:

Strauss, A.L. (Ed.). (2006). *Gray wolves, gray matter: Exploring the social and biological issues of wolf survival* (2nd ed.). Minneapolis: International Wolf Center.

MASTER
NATURALIST
TOOLBOX

Chapter 4: Putting the Pieces Together

An Introduction to Ecology

Rob B. Blair, Karen S. Oberhauser, and Tommy Rodengen

Goal

Understand the basic principles of ecology.

Objectives

1. Define the term *ecology*.

2. Describe how energy flows through an ecosystem.

3. Explain how water, carbon, and nitrogen flow through ecosystems.

4. Describe how species interact at the population, community, and landscape scale.

5. Explain why biodiversity is important.

6. Describe what the endangered species list does for plants and animals.

7. Describe what restoration can provide for an ecosystem.

Introduction

We've learned some great basics about the rocks, soils, climate, plants, and animals of the North Woods, Great Lakes region. But that's like entertaining yourself with a jigsaw puzzle by looking at the pieces. It's interesting, of course — but what's *really* interesting is to put the pieces together to see the big picture of how all the pieces fit together. That's what ecology is all about.

Ecologists study the distribution and abundance of organisms and their connectedness with their environment (including other organisms) to understand what lives where, and why. Their work is every bit as fascinating and delightful as putting together a puzzle and watching the big picture emerge. As a naturalist, a good grasp of basic ecology will help you understand the processes going on in your local ecosystem. That in turn will help you be able to "put things in order" when you're wandering in a forest or visiting your favorite lake. Once you become familiar with a natural area, you have expectations of what you will (and will not) see, and so have important context you can use to conserve — and help others conserve — that ecosystem.

In this chapter, we'll explore the basics of ecology so you will be able to build and share the story of why Minnesota (and the North Woods, Great Lakes region in particular) is such a marvelous place.

While ecologists are united in wanting to explain the distribution and abundance of organisms, different ecologists have different ways of approaching the puzzle. Some focus on how energy flows through an ecosystem. Others use the physical factors that limit which organisms live where as their organizing principle. Still others base their studies on how species interact with one another. As a result, ecologists use a variety of approaches, looking at different facets of ecosystems and working at different scales, to "put things in order."

Focus on Energy

One approach ecologists use to explore and explain the living world is using the framework of energy: where it comes from, where it goes, and how it moves among organisms. And no wonder: Without energy, every organism would be dead and your favorite forest or pond would be a mighty boring place. (Not that it would matter — you wouldn't have the energy to get out and see it anyway!) Let's peek over the shoulders of ecologists who use this organizing principle to see how the flow of energy helps us understand the way the world works.

Photosynthesis and Respiration

Almost all energy on Earth comes from the sun. Plants, algae, and cyanobacteria transform the sun's energy into a form that is useful for themselves and other living things through the amazing process of photosynthesis. (A very small portion of energy comes from heat and hydrogen sulfide in deep sea vents that bacteria convert into usable energy, but because that process doesn't take place in Minnesota, we won't address it here.)

In photosynthesis, energy from the sun drives a biochemical process that rearranges the atoms constituting carbon dioxide and water (very simple molecules) to form carbohydrates (sugars, which are more complex molecules), oxygen, and water. In chemistry shorthand, this reaction is represented by:

PHOTOSYNTHESIS

Carbon Dioxide + Water + Energy $\longrightarrow$
Sugar + Oxygen + Water

— OR —

$6 \, CO_2 + 12 \, H_2O + Light \longrightarrow$
$C_6H_{12}O_6 + 6 \, O_2 + 6 \, H_2O$

Water is on both sides of the equation because the water molecules that go into the reaction are not the same water molecules that come out of it. In other words, photosynthesis actually makes water molecules (although fewer than it uses).

Wish you could try this yourself? Sorry: It takes more than a wish to zap carbon dioxide and water with energy to get sugars. You also need a special molecule that can trap the sun's energy so it can be used to carry out the chemical reaction. Plants and algae use a molecule called *chlorophyll* to do this, usually in structures within cells called *chloroplasts*.

The first photosynthesizers in the world were probably cyanobacteria. These amazing bacteria played a big role in driving the evolution of biodiversity (and thus us!) by adding oxygen to the earth's atmosphere. Their descendants are incredibly genetically diverse, and live in many ecosystems all over the earth. Most cyanobacteria use light harvesting protein complexes called phycobilisomes to carry out photosynthesis, but a few use chlorophyll. Interestingly, many evolutionary biologists think that the chloroplasts in plants actually evolved from cyanobacteria that used chlorophyll! That's right, today's plants are probably carrying around the descendants of a group of cyanobacteria. They may have gotten together when algae ingested the cyanobacteria, or as a result of a symbiotic relationship in which the cyanobacteria lived inside the algae. Wow!

Chlorophyll comes in several varieties, conveniently called a, b, c, and d. Land plants mainly use chlorophyll a and b. Algae sometimes use a, sometimes b, and sometimes c. Some cyanobacteria use chlorophyll b, and others used different molecules found only in cyanobacteria.

So, thanks to photosynthesis, the sun's energy is trapped in sugar molecules. Now what? Respiration, my dear Watson!

You probably think of respiration as the process of breathing in and out. In ecology, it has a different (though related) meaning. When we're talking about the flow of energy between living things and their environment, respiration refers to the process within cells that breaks down sugars to release energy in the form of a molecule known as *ATP* (adenosine triphosphate). Chemically speaking, it's the opposite of photosynthesis. Animals (including you!) use respiration to release the energy they need to do everything from scratching and blinking to swallowing and breathing. Plants use respiration to release the energy they need to do everything from growing new cells to making seeds and roots to releasing chemicals that help them communicate with other plants and animals.

The chemical shorthand for respiration is:

RESPIRATION

Glucose + Oxygen $\longrightarrow$
Carbon Dioxide + Water + Energy

— OR —

$C_6H_{12}O_6 + 6 \, O_2 \longrightarrow$
$6 \, CO_2 + 6 \, H_2O + Energy \, (in \, the \, form \, of \, ATP)$

Notice anything interesting? The ingredients and end products of respiration are almost the exact opposite of photosynthesis.

Why should we care about photosynthesis and respiration? The short answer is that we need both to stay alive. The more nuanced answer is that the ability of virtually all creatures to live and pass life along to future generations depends on the ability to do these things well. The vast diversity of life forms among us has been shaped over millennia by the pursuit of different and better ways to photosynthesize, get ahold of the energy captured by photosynthesis, and use it as it is released in the process of respiration. In other words, photosynthesis and respiration make the living world go 'round!

Food Chains and Food Webs

Ecologists who focus on energy and ecosystems are interested in more than how energy is captured for use by plants and animals. They also want to know how energy is transferred from one living thing to another.

A simple way of thinking about how energy flows through an ecosystem is to visualize it traveling along pathways called food chains. In short, food chains are simplified descriptions of what eats what, starting with the plants that capture the sun's energy. In food chain language, plants are known as *producers* because they capture the sun's energy and produce the sugar that keeps an ecosystem functioning. This is somewhat of a misnomer because the sun is the actual producer of energy in almost all ecosystems (except those chemosynthetic bacteria at the bottom of the ocean); plants merely have the unique ability to capture that energy and transform it into a form the other living things can use.

Animals, in contrast, are known as *consumers* because they eat the producers. Consumers come in a variety of flavors (pun intended). Primary consumers, such as forest tent caterpillars, eat producers. Secondary consumers, such as phoebes, eat primary consumers. Tertiary consumers, such as goshawks, eat secondary consumers. At the top, or bottom (depending on your perspective) of the food chain are the, creatures that gain their energy by eating dead things. Some ecologists refer to primary consumers as herbivores, secondary and tertiary consumers as carnivores, and living things that eat anything as omnivores. The various links in the chain eat-and-be-eaten are called *trophic levels*. The higher the trophic level, the further away the organism is from the original source of the energy — the sun. Higher trophic levels contain less energy than lower ones, since organisms at each level use energy for the business of living.

In reality, ecosystems are more complicated than simple food chains. A better way to depict who eats

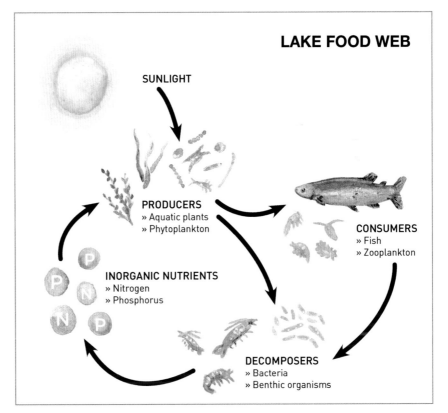

Figure 1. In this example of a food web in a lake in the North Woods, Great Lakes region, sunlight supports aquatic plants and phytoplankton. These producers are consumed by consumers or die and are consumed by decomposers. Once the consumers or decomposers die, they are converted back into nutrients, which are in turn used by the producers.

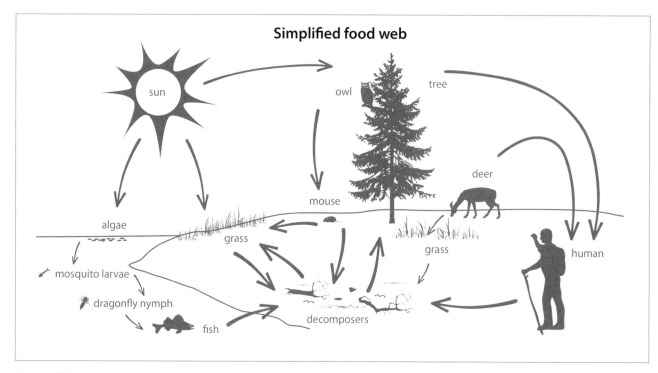

Simplified food web

Figure 2. This simple food web illustrates the players in the eat-and-be-eaten world of North Woods, Great Lakes.

whom — and how energy flows — is with a food web (Figure 1). A *food web* shows the major pathways of energy flow in a specific ecosystem.

Though it may sound straightforward, it's actually quite difficult to create a food web for a specific habitat, determining every organism, what it eats, and what eats it. One ecologist, R. D. Bird, carried out this painstaking task for a willow forest in Canada. Though the resulting depiction is simple (for a food web), it included trees, birds, spiders, insects, frogs, snails, and garter snakes. Figure 2 is a simplified version of the web he described. The arrows show the direction energy flows in the system. As you can see, even in its simple form, the food web is a complicated world.

Energy Pyramids

Ecology energy mavens not only care about who eats whom in an ecosystem, they also want to know how much everyone is eating of everyone else. Consequently, food web ecologists try to quantify how much energy is passed along a food chain. One way to do this is to count every organism in an ecosystem and classify it as producer, primary consumer (or carnivore), secondary consumer (or top carnivore), and so on.

Some ecologists did this for a field of bluegrass in Kentucky (Figure 3). They found that 5,842,424 plants fed 708,624 herbivores, which fed 354,904 carnivores, which fed three top carnivores. Notice a trend in those data? Each level of consumption supports far fewer individuals. Ecologists refer to this

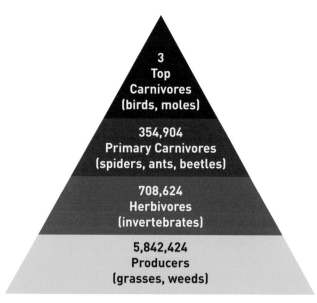

Figure 3. This food pyramid shows how the number of organisms (and the amount of energy they embody) decreases as trophic level increases in a bluegrass field in Kentucky. In general, about 90 percent of energy is lost from the base to the apex of the pyramid.

depiction of the flow of energy through living things as a food pyramid (not the same as the ones on the side of cereal boxes that encourage you to eat three servings of chocolate, six servings of trans fat, and one serving of potato chips a day — or something like that).

Why is the food pyramid a pyramid? The answer is that only about 10 percent of the energy in one level is passed on to the next. For example, a mouse (an herbivore) might eat 100 calories of nutritious grass (a producer), but will only pass on 10 of those calories in the form of tasty mouse parts to the snake that eats it. It uses the other 90 calories of grass to conduct its daily activities: digesting grass, running around, making babies, taking a nap, and leaving scat behind. Similarly, animals at every level of the pyramid expend energy surviving, thus reducing the energy available to the next higher level.

In a more controlled assessment of energy flow in an ecosystem, Lamont Cole, a scientist at Cornell University, quantified the energy pyramid of Cayuga Lake in New York (Figure 4). He found that for every 1,000 calories (a measure of energy) algae produced, only 150 calories were transferred to the miniscule herbivores, called *zooplankton*, that ate the algae. Of the 150 calories stored in the zooplankton, only 30 made it into the smelt that ate them. Of the 30

calories that made it into the smelt, only 6 made it to the trout that ate the smelt. Of the 6 calories that made it into the trout, only 1.2 made it to the humans who ate the trout. In other words, of the 1,000 calories originally found in the algae, only 1.2 calories reached human consumers, four links up the food chain, as useful energy. This loss of energy from one trophic level to another explains why agriculture can feed more people with plants than it can with plants and animals.

Studies such as these have led ecologists to devise what is known as the "10 percent rule" — typically, only 10 percent of the energy of one trophic level is found at the next level. As you may have noticed, however, 30 is not 10 percent of 150. Because ecological relationships are so hard to measure, many ecologists get excited when they come within an order of magnitude. For them, 150 is about an order of magnitude different than 30 and, consequently, they translate that to 10 percent. The "10 percent rule" is a helpful concept, not a precise measure.

Focus on Physical Factors

In contrast to the reductionist ecologists who focus on energy flow in ecosystems, the accountants in the world of ecology explain the way the world works in terms of *limiting nutrients*: what is in abundance (surplus), what is deficient (deficit), and how organisms find the nutrients they need to maintain the biological processes that keep them alive.

These ecologists study biogeochemical cycles, the flow of elements and molecules among living (bio-) and nonliving (geo-) parts of an ecosystem. Typically, they study materials that are critical to life, such as water, carbon, nitrogen, and phosphorus.

Water Cycle

The water, or hydrologic, cycle (Figure 5) is probably the most well-known of all biogeochemical cycles because water is critical for all organisms. Plants, algae, and cyanobacteria need water to photosynthesize. Both plants and animals release water through respiration. Without water, the world would be a lifeless place.

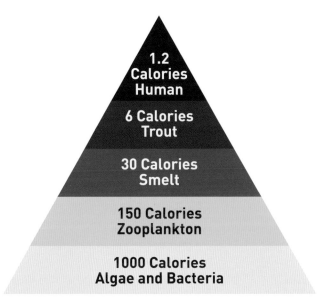

Figure 4. This energy pyramid from Cayuga Lake in upstate New York shows how few of the energy calories captured from the sun end up in trout and the humans who eat them.

You probably learned about the water cycle in school with a narrative something like this: Water falls from the sky as rain, sleet, snow, or hail. It soaks into the ground, is taken up by living things, or flows into a stream and eventually into the ocean. The sun causes it to evaporate somewhere along the way and the process starts all over again.

While this is a simple and instructive image, water molecules in the real world usually follow a more circuitous path.

Individual water molecules can follow myriad routes. One might cycle back and forth from the ground to a cloud to the ground and then eventually soak into the ground and become part of groundwater for millennia. Another may be incorporated into the wood of a tree and become trapped for a hundred years. Another may end up in the ocean, evaporate, and fall back in an afternoon shower. In other words, the "water cycle" might be better titled the "serendipitous wandering of a water molecule around Earth."

To illustrate this, let's follow the flow of water from a Grand Rapids backyard. Precipitation in the form of rain or snow falls in that backyard fairly often throughout the year. In the summer, some of the rain that falls flows across the surface of the ground into a rivulet and then into a pond—an example of surface water—near that backyard. However, much of the rain that reaches that backyard soaks into the soil and becomes groundwater, which makes up 96 percent of the freshwater in North America.

Figure 5. The hydrologic cycle describes the flow of water among living and nonliving components of ecosystems.

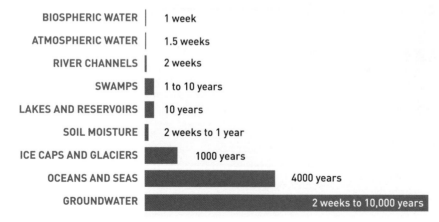

BIOSPHERIC WATER	1 week
ATMOSPHERIC WATER	1.5 weeks
RIVER CHANNELS	2 weeks
SWAMPS	1 to 10 years
LAKES AND RESERVOIRS	10 years
SOIL MOISTURE	2 weeks to 1 year
ICE CAPS AND GLACIERS	1000 years
OCEANS AND SEAS	4000 years
GROUNDWATER	2 weeks to 10,000 years

Figure 6. Residence time varies among the various components of the hydrologic cycle.

If the rainwater finds its way to the pond it can take different paths. Some might evaporate, changing into water vapor that will become the clouds that will rain on another part of Minnesota. Some of it will soak into the ground to become groundwater. Some might satiate a Labrador retriever and be released on a fire hydrant. And some of it will flow or seep from the pond into the Mississippi River. Once it reaches the Gulf of Mexico, the water can circulate for a while,

The Hierarchical Perspective

We can view the web of life at different levels (Figure 7).

At the **individual** level, each species is unique and can be described by its physical, biochemical, and behavioral attributes. These characteristics come from genetic variation among the individuals that compose the species.

Populations are groups of interbreeding individuals of the same species. The abundance of a given population changes over time in response to things happening in the environment that affect four variables: birth rate, immigration rate, death rate, and emigration rate. Eventually, all populations approach a carrying capacity — a population level that can be supported by available resources. Populations that exceed their carrying capacity are not sustainable and eventually crash to smaller abundance and sometimes to extinction. Populations can also crash for other reasons, such as the sudden occurrence of a deadly disease or habitat loss.

To answer questions about how species interact, we delve into the realm of ecological **communities**. A community is a bunch of different populations that occur in the same time and place and that interact. Each species within a community uses resources in the environment and interacts with other species. Its role, or job, in the community is called its *niche* (pronounced "neesh"). Some niches are very specific and some are

very broad. For example, the stemless lady's-slipper needs a very specialized niche of just the right conditions of shade and well-buffered acidic and nutrient-poor soils. The American bald eagle has a very broad niche, a factor that has contributed to its removal from the endangered species list.

Of course, living things don't exist in a vacuum — they are surrounded by soil, air, water, sunlight, and other nonliving things. Together, the life forms that make up a community and the other components of their physical environment are known as an **ecosystem**.

On yet larger scales, **biomes** are groupings of ecosystems that have things such as climate, vegetation, and animals in common. The **biosphere** is the collection of all of Earth's biomes — in other words, all of the living things on our planet along with the nonliving things that are influenced by and influence them shape and are shaped by them.

| Individual | Population | Community | Ecosystem | Biome | Biosphere |

Figure 7. From the individual to the planet, the web of life has many levels of organization.

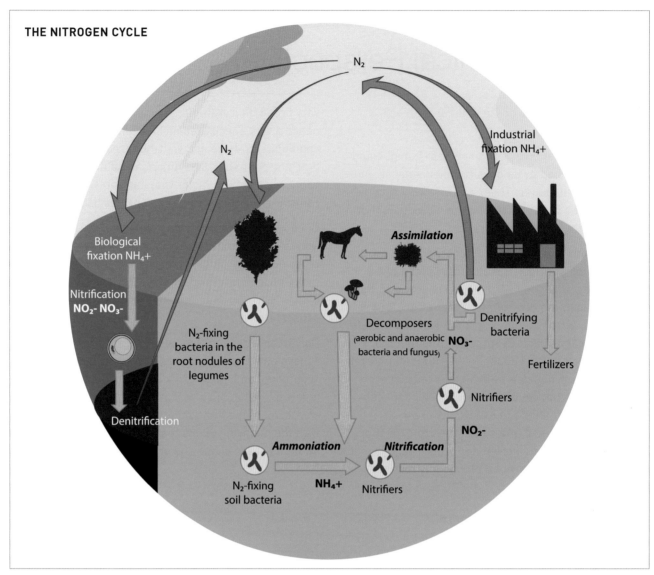

THE NITROGEN CYCLE

Figure 8. The nitrogen cycle depicts the movement of nitrogen among components of the living and nonliving world.

but eventually it will evaporate and supply rain clouds for some other part of the world. Even if the rainwater from that backyard enters the groundwater, its job isn't over. It may stay underground for many years. But eventually it will seep into a lake, pond, or ocean or be drawn up through a well, and eventually evaporate and join the water in clouds.

These multiple paths mean that the water cycle is an intricate dance of many different routes that take different times to complete. Hydrologists call the time a molecule of water stays in a specific state its *residence time* (Figure 6). Residence time can range from hours to centuries.

Key to understanding the water cycle (and every other cycle) is being able to identify the portion that is "bio" (part of a living system), the portion that is "geo" (*abiotic*), the major reservoirs (places where water is stored for long periods of time), and the processes that cause it to travel between different portions of the cycle.

In the case of the *hydrologic cycle*, water enters the biotic portion of the cycle when living things absorb or drink it. Plants give water back to the atmosphere through a process called *evapotranspiration*. The main reservoirs are groundwater, lakes, rivers, and oceans. You might be thinking of other reservoirs; certainly glaciers store a lot of water, but until quite recently, the water in glaciers was there for so long that it could almost be considered to have left the cycle. However, with a warming climate, some of that water is returning to the cycle, and is likely to increase ocean levels, with lots of problems for people and other living things that inhabit ocean coasts. Some plants store water for fairly long periods of time, but the process of evapotranspiration usually limits the time any given water molecule stays in a plant. And water generally moves quite quickly into and out of the atmosphere. The sun powers the cycle via evaporation and precipitation.

Nitrogen Cycle

Another vital substance that cycles through ecosystems is nitrogen (Figure 8). This element is a key ingredient of protein, DNA, RNA, and even chlorophyll. Without it, life as we know it would not exist.

The good news is, there's plenty of nitrogen on our planet — in fact, nitrogen in the form N_2 makes up 78 percent of the atmosphere by volume. Interestingly, it also is the limiting factor for growth in most

GLOBAL OVERLOADING OF NITROGEN

Global sources of biologically available (fixed) nitrogen	Annual release of fixed nitrogen (teragrams)
Anthropogenic Sources	
Fertilizer	100
Legumes and other plants	20
Fossil fuels	20
Biomass burning	40
Wetland draining	10
Land clearing	20
Total from human sources	**210**
Natural Sources	
Soil bacteria, algae, lightning, etc.	100
Total from natural sources	**100**

Figure 9. Natural sources of fixed nitrogen in our environment are overwhelmed by human-generated releases.

ecosystems. That's because most organisms can't use N_2. Instead, they obtain the nitrogen they need from ammonia (NH_3) or nitrate (NO_3). Most of this "biologically active" nitrogen is harbored in organic matter in soil and is quickly absorbed by plants when that matter decays. Occasionally, some is lost to the atmosphere when bacteria process it back to N_2.

This low-level loss of nitrogen from the "bio" portion of the biogeochemical cycle is balanced by combustion in the atmosphere (usually by lightning or volcanoes) and by nitrogen-fixing and nitrifying bacteria, which convert N_2 to NH_3 and nitrogen oxide (NO_x). If you're interested in the chemistry of this process, it basically frees the nitrogen atoms in the N_2, which are held tightly together by a triple bond. Some microorganisms are able to carry out this process using enzymes called *nitrogenases*.

Since 1940, humans have doubled the annual amount of nitrogen available to living things (Figure 9). Some of this increase is due to wetland draining and land clearing, which releases nitrogen held in organic matter. Most, however, is due to manufacturing NH_3 from N_2 for fertilizer, burning biomass, and using fossil fuels.

This excess of available nitrogen has led to a number of ecosystem changes. It has contaminated groundwater in agricultural areas, altered the chemistry and biology of lakes and rivers, and created a "dead zone" in the Gulf of Mexico and other coastal areas. Excess nitrogen has also altered soil chemistry and led to the loss of other nutrients such as calcium, magnesium, and potassium that plants need to grow.

Carbon Cycle

Carbon is the basis of all organic matter, making up the central chain in molecules of proteins, fats, DNA, RNA, chlorophyll, hemoglobin, and almost every large molecule in your body. It is also the key molecule in energy transfer — as we saw earlier, CO_2 is taken up in photosynthesis and released in respiration.

The vast majority of carbon on Earth exists as rock, mostly as calcium carbonate. Because of this, carbon scientists actually think of two pools of carbon that cycle: the geologic cycle, which occurs over millions of

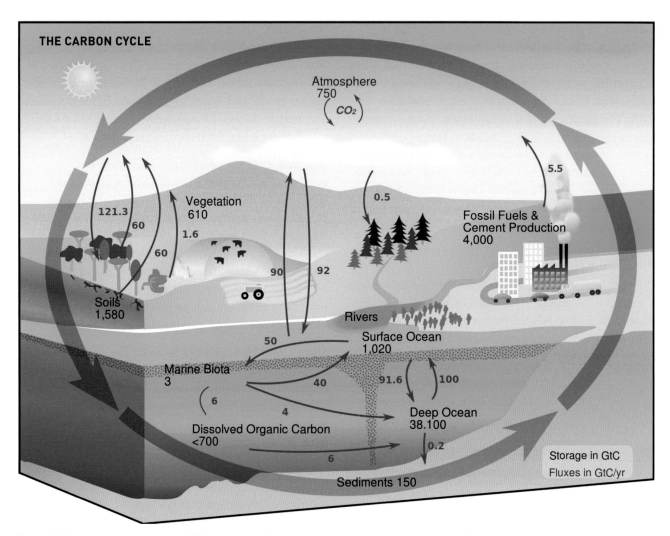

THE CARBON CYCLE

Atmosphere
750
CO₂

Vegetation
610

121.3   60   1.6

60

Soils
1,580

90   92

0.5

Fossil Fuels &
Cement Production
4,000

5.5

Rivers

Surface Ocean
1,020

50

Marine Biota
3

40   91.6   100

6   4

Deep Ocean
38.100

Dissolved Organic Carbon
<700

0.2

6

Sediments 150

Storage in GtC
Fluxes in GtC/yr

Figure 10. In any given year, tens of billions of tons of carbon move between the atmosphere, hydrosphere, and geosphere. Human activities add about 40 billion tons per year of CO₂ to the atmosphere.

years, and the biological/physical cycle, which is the one we will tackle here.

Figure 10 illustrates the biological/physical carbon cycle. The arrows represent flux, or pathways where carbon changes form. The words represent the major reservoirs of carbon, with most being sequestered in the oceans. The major pathways of change between forms of carbon are photosynthesis, respiration, and, increasingly, combustion.

Humans have been altering the carbon cycle significantly since the Industrial Revolution by clearing land and burning fossil fuels. Currently we add about 40 billion tons of carbon to the atmosphere every year. This is a major concern because the amount of CO₂ in Earth's atmosphere is directly correlated with the temperature of the atmosphere.

The atmosphere today holds more CO₂ than it has in more than 160,000 years, and this is having important impacts on Earth's climate.

Methane, CH₄, is second to CO₂ in human induced climate change impact, contributing to 20% of post-industrial global warming. As a result of human activities, the atmospheric CO₂ concentration continues to increase. Figure 11 shows the rise of CO₂ in the atmosphere since 1850. In the absence of strong control measures, CO₂ emissions projected for this century could result in concentration increasing to a level that is roughly two to three times the highest level occurring over the glacial-interglacial era that spans the last 800,000 years or more.

Hubbard Brook: An Example

Biogeochemical cycling implies that ecosystems tend to reuse resources, but catching a community in the act of cycling is easier said than done. One group of ecologists in New Hampshire tried to do this in a now-famous (okay, famous among ecologists) experiment.

The ecologists wanted to find out how nutrients in a forest were recycled. They wanted to see what was being cycled, how much, and how fast, and decided to focus on the forest near one New Hampshire stream called Hubbard Brook. To measure everything entering their piece of the forest, such as the water and nutrients brought in by raindrops, they set up rain gauges to catch precipitation throughout the forest. To measure all of the biogeochemicals leaving the forest, they first defined the edges of the study area as the watershed of Hubbard Brook.

To discover what was happening with the cycling of nutrients in the Hubbard Brook watershed, the ecologists built a small dam — or weir — at the base of a mountain stream that drained the watershed. The watershed was sealed off by an impermeable layer of bedrock that forced all nutrients leaving the forest to flow through this brook and past this weir. By measuring precipitation and outflow and taking water samples at the weir, the ecologists were able to measure all of the nutrients and water entering and leaving the watershed.

What did the ecologists learn? There were some surprises. First, a lot more water fell on the forest as rain than left the watershed through the weir. The ecologists concluded that the trees used a lot of the rain to grow and photosynthesize, some rain evaporated, and some soaked into the ground.

Second, the ecologists knew the forest needed more than rain to survive and grow; the trees needed other nutrients, such as CO_2, nitrogen, potassium, and calcium but the ecologists didn't know the source of all of these nutrients. They knew that CO_2 is abundant

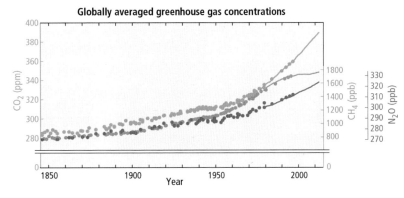

Globally averaged greenhouse gas concentrations

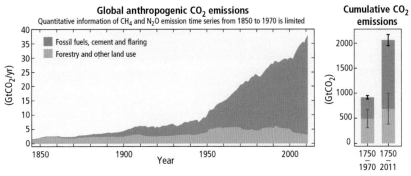

Global anthropogenic CO₂ emissions
Quantitative information of CH₄ and N₂O emission time series from 1850 to 1970 is limited

Cumulative CO₂ emissions

Figure 11. The graphs above show the increase of greenhouse gas concentrations and the correlations with CO_2 emissions.

in air, but suspected that other nutrients came from within the watershed. They reasoned that if these nutrients were being cycled in the watershed by the trees, they could measure this process by cutting down the forest and comparing the amount of nutrients coming out of the cut watershed to those that had come out of the watershed when it was intact.

So the ecologists cut down the trees. What did they learn? First, the amount of water flowing over the weir increased by 40 percent! This meant that the forest had been retaining and presumably using a lot of water. Not only that, but, the flow of nutrients past the dam also went up dramatically. As shown in Figure 12, the flow of nutrients increased as well compared with the flow of a nearby, uncut watershed that was used as an experimental control. The scientists concluded that before the area was clear-cut, the trees growing there absorbed the nutrients from trees that died and decomposed. After the clear-cut, there was nothing to trap and reuse the nutrients.

Focus on Interactions

The third way ecologists approach their work is by focusing on how organisms relate to one another

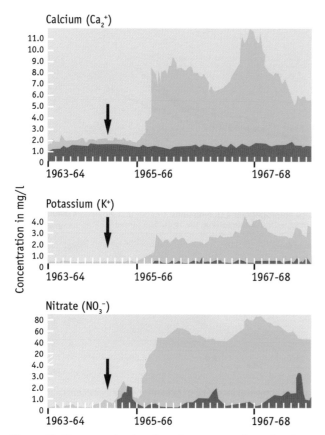

Figure 12. These graphs show how the concentrations of various nutrients flowing past the weir at Hubbard Brook changed over time. The dark arrow indicates when the watershed was clear-cut.

and their world. Questions ecologists using this approach ask include: What does an organism need to thrive and reproduce? How does it interact with other organisms? What can it do to change those interactions?

Resources and Niches

Resources are anything a plant or animal needs to thrive and reproduce. Typically, ecologists categorize these as food, water, shelter, and space. They include everything from the fish that hosts *neascus* (the parasite that makes some fish fillets look like they've been sprinkled with pepper) to the vast forest that a moose calls home.

Resources of a Loon

To illustrate the concept, let's consider the resources of the common loon (Figure 13) — our state bird and the mascot of the Minnesota Master Naturalist Program. These big black-and-white birds spend their summers on lakes in the northern United States

(including Minnesota!) and Canada. They have webbed feet for swimming and are master divers. Their long, pointed bills help them catch fish. Their dense feathers keep them warm and dry even though they spend most of their time in or on water. Their chicks can swim within hours of hatching. They leave the water only when they are flying, mating, or incubating eggs in spring. In winter, loons fly to the coasts of North America to feed, rest, and wait for their summer lakes to thaw.

What resources do loons need during the summer? First, like all animals, they need water to drink and food to eat. Adults are exclusively *piscivores* (fish-eaters), but they may occasionally feed their chicks an invertebrate or two. One researcher calculated that an adult loon eats about 50 times its weight each summer. If you weighed 110 pounds, you would have to eat 5,500 pounds of fish in one summer to keep up with a loon. That's about 60 pounds of fish per day!

Their food needs determine the type of water loons need. Because they chase fish underwater, they need clear water. If a lake is too cloudy, loons can't see well enough to fish successfully. However, the lake also must have a lot of producers (plants and phytoplankton) to feed the herbivores that feed the fish that the loons eat. This creates a conundrum; lakes with lots of producers tend to be cloudy because of all of the producers, mostly algae, in the water. There is actually a fairly narrow window of conditions that meet loons' demanding water quality standards.

Like other organisms, loons also need shelter and space. They require a large expanse of water for use as a "runway" to take off. Unlike most ducks,

Figure 13. Common loons summer on lakes across Minnesota.

which can take flight from a standstill, loons need to build up speed before they become airborne. If they land on a pond that is too small, they may become trapped because they don't have the required distance to lift off. The lakes they live on also need to be big enough to support the fish they need to eat. Large lakes are also more likely to have small islands for nesting. Islands are less likely than the mainland to have predators, such as raccoons, which might attack nesting loons or their eggs. Because of these space requirements, loons usually spend summers on lakes that have more than 100 acres in surface area, and an island or two makes the lake even more attractive to loons on the lookout for prime real estate.

Resources of a Showy Lady's-Slipper

Plants have resource needs as well. If you have a "brown thumb" when it comes to houseplants, you know how hard it is to provide the resources a plant requires to thrive and reproduce.

Let's take a quick look at the resources of the showy lady's-slipper (Figure 14). This delicate flower needs to keep its roots wet, so it grows in swamps, fens, and other wet drainages. It requires alkaline (non-acidic) soils and, consequently, typically grows in regions with calcium-rich soils and bedrock. It also needs plenty of light, so it is only found in open areas of these wet, calcium-rich places. Finally, the showy lady's-slipper takes up to 16 years to reproduce. Therefore, it needs a habitat that is not subject to frequent disturbances.

Ecologists use the term *niche* to describe the specific range of resources each type of organism needs to thrive and reproduce. Loons need just the right kinds of water (clear), space (plenty), and food (fish), so

Figure 14. The rare and protected showy lady's-slipper is Minnesota's state flower.

lakes with this magical combination provide loons the perfect niche for them. Showy lady's-slippers find some areas too wet (think Lake Superior) or too dry (my backyard in August) or too alkaline (waste piles at cement plants) or too acidic (your friendly nearby bog) to thrive and reproduce. Consequently, these places are outside the niche of a showy lady's-slipper.

Species Interactions

No organism exists in a vacuum. Plants are crowded out by other plants, eaten by animals, used for shelter, stepped on, and uprooted. Animals eat plants and other animals, are eaten by other animals, and often use plants for shelter. In other words, every organism interacts with other organisms.

Ecologists spend considerable time studying the interactions among organisms. One way to do so is to take the point of view of each organism in the interaction to see if the interaction is good or bad for that organism, then assign plus, minus, or zero signs to the outcome for each player in the interaction. For example, if they see a spider catch a fly in its web, they say that the interaction is good for the spider because the spider gets dinner but not so good for the fly, because it is dinner. In this case, one organism wins while the other loses—a plus-minus (+/−) interaction. Sometimes both organisms win (+/+). Sometimes both organisms lose (−/−). Sometimes one isn't even affected by the interaction (+/0 or −/0). Figuring out various interactions in this way is an interesting, and not always obvious, challenge.

COMPETITION Ecologists define competition as what happens when one species uses a resource in such a way that another cannot use it. In competition, both organisms are affected negatively (−/−). For example, if two species of birds eat the same kind of seed, they may compete with each other for those seeds. Another example is if one species of tree competes for water with another by growing roots that spread out over a larger area or go down farther into the soil. Competition occurs only when a resource is in short supply; trees may compete for water but they rarely compete for CO_2.

Organisms often compete without directly interacting with one another. For example, researchers working in the Ausable River in Michigan found that both brook trout and brown trout (Figure 15) like to rest at the

Figure 15. The native brook trout (top) and the introduced brown trout (bottom) compete for the same resting spots in streams.

bottom of a streambed, but they are never seen resting in the same location. The brook trout prefer to rest in shady areas of the stream where the water doesn't flow very fast. The brown trout like these areas, too, and when they are present, the brown trout take up those spots and the brook trout use less preferred habitat. The two types of trout compete for space in the river without ever directly interacting. The same thing occurs in northern Minnesota streams.

Sometimes competition occurs when two organisms actually fight to gain control of the resources within a certain area called a territory. For example, hummingbirds (Figure 16) fight over flower nectar. They may guard several flowers in a territory and chase away other hummingbirds that try to feed from "their" flowers. When they chase other members of their species, they are engaging in *intraspecific* competition. However, they also engage in *interspecific* competition — for instance, chasing away moths that try to sip nectar.

Another example of interspecific competition happens between cormorants and anglers. Cormorants eat fish, and some anglers feel the cormorants are eating the fish they could catch. A few anglers have illegally tried to thwart this competition, whether real or perceived, by shooting cormorants and destroying their nesting colonies, a common

practice prior to the Migratory Bird Treaty Act. The Minnesota DNR addressed this controversy by sponsoring a research project on Leech Lake from 2004 to 2007. The analysis indicated that predation pressure by the expanding cormorant population could have been sufficient to affect young walleye survival. Management activities at Leech Lake have reduced the cormorant population to a level where fish consumption by cormorants now has had little effect on the fishery.

PREDATION, HERBIVORY, AND PARASITISM Another sort of species interaction occurs when one organism eats another one. Depending on who's involved and the outcome, these interactions are called *predation*, *herbivory*, or *parasitism* (Figure 17). In all of these interactions, one species wins and the other loses. Let's consider each of these +/− interactions separately.

Predation. Predation occurs when one animal eats another animal — the whole thing! When a gray wolf eats a deer, that's predation. When a great-horned owl eats a mouse, or when a raven eats the eggs of another bird, or when a dragonfly eats a mosquito or black fly, that is also predation. Many ecologists are interested in how predator and prey populations affect each other. One of the most famous examples is that of lynx and snowshoe hares in northern Canada. For over a hundred years, hunters trapped lynx and hares and sold their pelts to the Hudson's Bay Company. Throughout this time, the company kept careful records of the number of pelts they bought each year.

Ecologists realized that the Hudson's Bay Company records were a great source of information on lynx and hare populations. They graphed the numbers of each type of pelt bought each year, assuming that

Figure 16. Male ruby-throated hummingbirds guard flowers in their territories.

Figure 17. A white pine weevil, an insect in the North Woods, Great Lakes region, commits an act of herbivory.

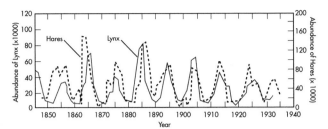

Figure 18. Changes in abundance of lynx and hares in northern Canada from 1845 to 1935 show a cyclical pattern.

the number of pelts reflected how well lynx and hare populations were doing.

Figure 18 shows what they discovered. The dotted line represents the number of hare pelts each year and the solid line represents the number of lynx pelts. Both numbers move up and down in cycles. For example, in 1869, almost no hares were caught. In 1875, more than 100,000 were caught.

The interesting thing in these records is that the number of lynx closely follows the number of hares. When there are a lot of hares, there are also a lot of lynx. This makes sense; when there are a lot of hares around, the lynx can easily feed themselves and their kittens, so the number of lynx increases. In years when there are few hares to be caught, not many lynx kittens survive and the number of lynx goes down. Of course, who is regulating whom is a complicated question, and ecologists still don't agree on whether the lynx follow the hares, which cycle for some other reason, or if lynx cause the hares to cycle.

What can a prey species do to avoid being eaten? One answer is *camouflage*. With camouflage, an animal (or plant) can blend in with its surroundings so well that predators have a tough time finding it. Insects are

probably the biggest masters of camouflage. Moths often look like the bark of the trees upon which they rest. Katydids (Figure 19) look like leaves when they fold up their wings. Walking sticks look like, well, sticks, and you would never know they were insects unless you saw them move.

Larger animals use camouflage, too, but usually in an effort to hide themselves from their prey instead of their predators. One amazing example is the American bittern (Figure 20), a big brown-and-white wading bird that hunts along the edges of freshwater lakes. Bitterns have long brown streaks that run up their white necks. They stand with their beaks in the air so that the brown streaks line up with the plants around them. To add to their camouflage deceit, they sway with the breeze, in rhythm with the plants surrounding them.

Prey animals also avoid predation by running, kicking, climbing, diving, tunneling, gathering in herds or flocks, playing dead, tasting or smelling offensive, mimicking another offensive animal, or standing down a predator, depending on the species and the situation. This delicate balance between predator and prey is a constant source of interest (and, in some cases, mystery) to ecologists.

Herbivory. Animals that eat plants are called *herbivores* (omnivores eat both plants and animals, so they can be considered both predators and herbivores). Herbivory occurs when an animal eats a plant. In some cases, such as when a deer browses on a white pine seedling, a whole plant can be killed. In these cases, herbivory is similar to predation. However, sometimes the animal doesn't eat the whole plant; for example, a monarch caterpillar rarely gobbles an entire milkweed plant, and forest tent caterpillars never actually consume an aspen tree. In this case, herbivory is more like our next kind of +/− interaction, parasitism. (Patience—we'll get to that soon!)

Herbivores actually have a pretty tough job—literally. Animals can't digest cellulose, which is found in all plant cell walls. Some have developed a partnership with bacteria that live in their

Figure 19. Katydids are among animals that are protected from predation by camouflage.

Figure 20. American bitterns hide from their prey by swaying in the breeze like a plant.

guts to help get around this limitation. The bacteria get food and shelter, and in exchange, they break down the cellulose for their animal hosts. Deer and moose are examples of organisms that have this kind of relationship with gut bacteria. The rest of us are less efficient plant eaters, and eliminate a lot of plant material we eat as waste.

While many animals escape their predators by running away, plants don't have this luxury. They do, however, have ways to defend themselves against their animal enemies. Their defenses fall into three broad categories.

Mechanical defenses include things like spines, sticky sap, and thorns. Wild roses are one example of plants found in the north woods that use this method to deter herbivores.

Some plants have tissues, such as wood, that are particularly *hard to digest*. This makes them more difficult to completely demolish.

Still others produce *chemical defenses* such as toxins or poisons that are sometimes called *plant secondary compounds*. The nutrients that go into producing plant secondary compounds aren't available for growth or reproduction. In some cases plants minimize that "cost" of defense by waiting until something tries to eat them to produce large amounts of secondary compounds.

The resins found in pine, fir, and spruce trees provides a good example of both mechanical and chemical defenses. Chemicals called terpenes that are part of these fragrant, sticky substances give off the characteristic "north woods" evergreen fragrance that reminds us of holidays and time in the woods. But they have a much bigger job than just evoking pleasant thoughts in humans. The same chemicals that make them smell pleasant to us make eating evergreens unpleasant for insects. When an insect does chomp into a tree, the sticky resin can trap and eventually kill it. The resin also seals the wound, preventing infections from getting inside the tree. Of course, true to the never-ending battle between eater and eaten, some insects have evolved tools for getting around this defense.

An interesting side note: We humans owe a lot to these plant defenses. Pine terpenes are an important source for turpentine. Terpenoid substances are what give mint, basil, cinnamon, oranges, and many other herbs, spices, and other foods their appealing fragrance and flavor.

Parasitism. Parasites obtain food from a host organism, often by living inside it. They include things you've probably heard a lot about, such as tapeworms and fleas. They also are things you may not consider parasites at all, such as bacteria that cause infections. The difference between *parasitism* and predation is that parasites usually don't kill their host in one fell swoop.

One fascinating parasite is the lamprey, a kind of jawless fish that attaches itself to the sides of other fish (Figure 21), then scrapes out a shallow wound and feeds on the body fluids that leak out. Minnesota has two species of native lampreys that are rare and apparently don't play havoc with our fish. We also are home to nonnative sea lampreys, which moved into the Great Lakes from the Atlantic Ocean along the St. Lawrence Seaway. These nonnative, invasive lampreys contributed to the decline of the Great Lakes fishery (more about that in Chapter 7). Controlling sea lamprey has been a huge focus of research and action for several decades, and the Lake Superior population is finally almost under control. There are still sea lampreys around, but many fewer than there were in the 1980s and early 1990s, thanks to the use of poisons in lamprey spawning grounds (tributary streams), barriers that prevent movement of adults into these streams, and a few other methods of control.

Figure 21. Parasites, such as the lampreys attached to this fish, usually don't kill their host immediately.

Figure 22. This cow moose is exhibiting signs of brainworm.

Another parasite, the brainworm *Parelaphostrongylus tenuis,* has caused trouble in recent years for one of the north woods' most magnificent mammals — the moose (Figure 22). This parasite is fairly common in white-tailed deer, and causes damage to the central nervous system of its host. While symptoms in moose were reported as early as 1912 (but the cause of these symptoms wasn't discovered until 1963), it didn't become common until recently, when the old dividing lines between deer and moose habitat became blurry. The northward movement of deer into moose ranges has been facilitated by climate change (deer are not well-adapted to extremely cold winters), logging, and increasing human development. While deer aren't immune to brainworms, they've been co-existing for so long that the evolutionary arms race between them has resulted in a degree of immunity in the deer. But brainworms haven't been common in moose populations, and infection often results in death due to a nervous system condition called *cerebrospinal nematodiasis.*

Plants can be parasites, too. The Indian pipes we met in Chapter 2 don't produce chlorophyll and consequently don't get energy from the sun. Instead, they obtain their energy from mycorrhizal fungi growing on or in the roots of trees. These mycorrhizal fungi in turn get their energy from the tree to which they are attached in exchange for helping the tree absorb water and nutrients. Which brings us to …

MUTUALISM Every interaction between two species isn't necessarily a win-lose (+/–) or lose-lose (–/–) situation. Sometimes two species help each other out. Ecologists call this type of +/+ interaction *mutualism.* Remember the bacteria in the guts of deer and moose?

Thinking About Extinction

We hear a lot these days about plants and animals becoming threatened, endangered, and even extinct. But don't all species go extinct eventually?

In fact, all species do become extinct eventually. The problem today is that species are going extinct at a much faster rate than at any other time in the fossil record — and it's due to humans' drastic alteration of many of the Earth's ecosystems. Passenger pigeons (Figure 23) are extinct and American chestnut trees are endangered, which means they may soon become extinct. In both cases, humans probably are at least partially responsible; we overhunted passenger pigeons and imported a disease

from Europe that killed most of the chestnut trees. While no one knows exactly what the current extinction rate is, recent calculations by leading scientists estimated that it is 1,000 to 10,000 times greater than it would be naturally.

Figure 23. The passenger pigeon, which became extinct in 1914, was abundant in the North Woods, Great Lakes region until the late 1800s. It's likely the bird that gave the Pigeon River and Pigeon Bay their names.

All Together Now

Let's use Itasca State Park to illustrate the different levels of biological diversity. First, the park has a high level of ecosystem diversity. Its many and varied ecosystems include swamps, bogs, old-growth pine forest, deciduous forest, streams, and the headwaters of the Mississippi River.

Near the headwaters of the Mississippi, you can find myriad species. Collectively, these represent the species diversity in the headwaters. Some of the species you might find are dragonflies, wild rice, mallards, brook trout, and humans. A group of well-trained naturalists could probably identify hundreds of other species (most of them insects) within spitting distance of the rocks that mark the beginning of this great river.

If you looked more closely, you could also find genetic diversity within any of the species. A very visible example of genetic diversity might be an albino red squirrel. Every once in a while a squirrel is born lacking the gene that produces melanin, the pigment that lends a brownish color to hair, skin, and eyes. These squirrels instead have white fur and pink eyes.

However, most genetic diversity within a species is not quite so visually striking. For example, this squirrel and its friends and neighbors likely differ to some extent in their ability to resist different diseases or tolerate extremely cold temperatures, or in the length of their tails or how big they grow. All of this variation could contribute to the squirrels' ability to survive and thrive in a variety of habitats and conditions.

Their relationship with their hosts is an example of mutualism: The bacteria help their hosts access plant energy by breaking down plant cell walls, while the hosts provide shelter and food.

Remember the lichens we learned about in Chapter 2? They're another common north woods example of mutualism. Although a lichen may look a bit like a plant, it's actually a collaboration between a fungus and an alga or cyanobacterium.

Figure 24. This bumblebee is pollinating a blueberry plant. Pollination is an example of mutualism.

Probably the most biologically important form of mutualism is that existing between flowering plants and pollinators (Figure 24). Many plants depend on another organism, usually an animal, to carry pollen from one flower to another so they can make seeds. Most pollinators are insects, but birds, bats, and even a few mammals help plants out this way. In return, the animals often gain a calorie-rich treat in the form of nectar.

At the other end of the reproductive process, many seed-bearing plants also depend on animals to help spread their seeds, and produce some type of treat — for example, fruit or nuts — that provide animals with an incentive to do so.

Biological Diversity

Imagine if there were just one species of butterfly — or, worse yet, just one species of insect. What a boring world it would be! Not only that, but it would be a world teetering on the edge. If something went wrong for that species (for example, if its food source was wiped out by disease) it would be curtains for everyone. In the world we really have, however, other species can step in to keep the ecosystem functioning while the species under siege recovers.

Biologists call the variety of life on Earth *biological diversity*. They tend to focus on three levels of

biological diversity: ecosystem diversity, species diversity, and genetic diversity. In general, the more biodiversity, the more *resilience* — ability to recover after disturbance — a community has.

Ecosystem Diversity

Ecosystem diversity has to do with the variety of life in an entire ecosystem. An ecosystem is the big, happy family created by all living things in an area, the nonliving physical and chemical factors, and the processes that connect them, such as biogeochemical cycling and energy flow. To a certain extent, the boundaries of an ecosystem, like the boundaries of other big, happy families, are in the eye of the beholder: An ecosystem can be as small as a pond (just as you might define your family as you and immediate relatives) or as big as the entire planet (just as you might consider your family to be everyone on Earth). When we speak of ecosystem diversity, we usually mean the variety of habitat types found in an ecosystem.

The more variety of plants, animals, insects, and other species, the more biologically diverse the ecosystem and the greater variety of species interactions. Increased ecosystem diversity also creates more biomass, and the community tends to be more stable.

Species Diversity

Species diversity is a bit easier to define. Most people, and many biologists, define a species as a group of organisms that are so much alike they can successfully reproduce with each other. Yellow-rumped warblers, sarsaparilla, and black bears are all different species. At first thought, you might think species diversity would be the number of species in an area. However, ecologists also consider the relative numbers of individuals within each species. Say, for example, that two ecosystems are each home to five bird species — but one of these has 20 individuals of each species, and the other has 96 of one species and one each of the other four. Which do you think is more diverse? If you thought the first one, you're right! One way to think about this is to consider the chances of drawing two of the same species if you randomly draw two individuals from the population. In the first example, there's a good chance that your two individuals will be different, so the population is more diverse. But in the second example, you're likely to draw two of the very common species.

Genetic Diversity

Genetic diversity has to do with how many different genes are present in an ecosystem, population, or species. Genes are segments of DNA that give living things inherited traits such as hair color or leaf shape. Some species contain a lot of genetic diversity; think of the differences among the humans or dogs you know (Figure 25). Others are less diverse; for example, scientists have recently learned that all of the cheetahs in the world are virtually genetically identical. (In other words, if you thought that one cheetah looked a lot like any other cheetah, you were right.)

Environmental events such as fires, floods, and disease can reduce the gene pool of a population. Sometimes a lack of genetic diversity is due to human impacts — isolating breeding populations from each other or reducing the number of individual animals left in a species. Lack of genetic diversity may make extinction more likely for cheetahs and other species.

Figure 25. An albino (lacking pigment) eastern gray squirrel is due to a gene variation. Gray squirrels can also be brown, black, and different shades of gray.

So What?

As much as 30 percent of mammal, bird, and amphibian species are threatened with extinction because of human activity. Destruction of habitat is the biggest contributor to loss of species biodiversity. By using 25 percent more of the natural resources than the planet can sustain, humans have directly threatened biodiversity.

Why does biological diversity matter? Who cares if ecosystems host fewer habitat types or habitats have fewer species, or species have less diverse genetic material? For one thing, we know that species interact with other species all the time. All of these species interactions affect one another and create healthy, functioning communities. If we remove one species, the community is altered. If we remove several species, the changes can be so drastic that the community no longer functions. Consider what would happen, for example, if all decomposers suddenly became extinct. We would soon be up to our necks in dead animals and plants that could not decay. Biogeochemical cycling would stop. Eventually, no new organisms would be able to grow because they couldn't get the nutrients locked up in all of the dead bodies. Or consider what would happen if all pollinators suddenly disappeared. The many plants that depend on pollinators to carry their pollen from one flower to another would no longer be able to reproduce, sending the entire ecosystem into a cascade of potentially life-threatening unintended consequences.

A second reason to preserve biological diversity is its current and future economic value. All of our domestic crops and animals originally came from wild species. Researchers often study the wild forms of these organisms to see if they can use them to improve crop plants — perhaps breed more drought-tolerant wheat or a more pest-resistant potato. Similarly, about one-third of all modern medicines come from different types of plants and molds, and drug companies continually test many wild plants to see if they have medicinal value. In fact, two drugs that have revolutionized the treatment of leukemia came from a little-known plant called the Madagascar periwinkle. The plant grows wild in the few remaining areas of rainforest on the island of Madagascar, off the southeastern coast of Africa. We don't know which wild species may be useful for humans in the future, so it makes sense that we should do our best to avoid losing them today.

A third reason to preserve biological diversity is aesthetics. Many people enjoy walking in the woods, strolling along the beach, or climbing a mountain — at least partly because they enjoy nature's diversity. More than 20 percent of Americans are birders,

"To keep every cog and wheel is the first precaution of intelligent tinkering."

— Aldo Leopold

according to the U.S. Fish and Wildlife Service. More than one out of every three families feeds birds for fun, spending over half a billion dollars a year doing it! Humans are instinctively bonded with living systems. Naturalist E. O. Wilson termed this bond *biophilia*, which he defined "the urge to affiliate with other forms of life." Numerous recent studies have shown specific and measurable ways in which spending time in nature or even simply viewing nature contributes to our health and well-being.

Yet another reason for preserving biodiversity is ethics. Is it our right to destroy the entire habitat of the golden-winged warbler? Is it our right to hunt all of the blue whales, the Earth's largest animal? Many ethicists have argued that all species have a right to exist, whether or not they serve a human need.

Conclusion

We have been focusing on how ecologists think about the Earth and how it functions. Ecologist and activist Barry Commoner offered a different and practical take on ecology by encapsulating it into four "laws" of ecology. These laws may not fully reflect the way scientists view the functioning of ecosystems, but they provide useful windows into the ways humans fit into the world.

1. Everything is connected to everything else.
2. Everything must go somewhere.
3. Nature knows best.
4. There is no such thing as a free lunch.

Think back to the ecological principles presented in this chapter. You learned about how the sun's energy flows within an ecosystem; food chains and webs; species interactions; and water, nitrogen, and carbon cycles. Commoner's laws can serve as a practical summary to remind us of the complex, delicate balance of life on Earth.

Explore

This section highlights great examples of places where you can learn more about the ecological side of Minnesota—places that emphasize how things work and interrelate rather than simply what they are. Please check them out online, then head out to discover them in real life!

Headwaters Science Center – Bemidji, Minnesota

WHAT The Headwaters Science Center is dedicated to science education and environmental awareness. It features hands-on exhibits, a live animal collection, and special events.

WHEN Monday through Saturday, 9:30 a.m. – 5:30 p.m.; Sunday, 1 – 5 p.m.; open late on Thursdays.

WHERE The Headwaters Science Center is located near the headwaters of the Mississippi River in downtown Bemidji.

WHO Headwaters Science Center, 413 Beltrami Avenue, Bemidji, MN 56601, (218) 444-4472

FOR MORE INFORMATION www.hscbemidji.org

Wolf Ridge Environmental Learning Center – Finland, Minnesota

WHAT Since 1971, Wolf Ridge has provided lifelong learning experiences to more than half a million children, families, and adults from all walks of life. Each year 15,000 schoolchildren, teachers, and chaperones spend three to five days at the Wolf Ridge campus. An additional 3,000 families, elders, and youth attend during the summer.

WHEN Wolf Ridge offers programming throughout the year.

WHERE Follow U.S. Highway 61 approximately 66 miles north from Duluth to County Road 6 in Little Marais. Turn left on County Road 6. Travel three miles to the Wolf Ridge driveway (Cranberry Road). Follow the driveway three miles to the ridgetop.

WHO Wolf Ridge Environmental Learning Center, 6282 Cranberry Road, Finland, MN 55603, (218) 353-7414

FOR MORE INFORMATION www.wolf-ridge.org

Northland Arboretum – Baxter, Minnesota

WHAT The member-supported nonprofit Northland Arboretum encompasses over 500 acres in the heart of Brainerd/Baxter, including a former 40-acre landfill site that is now home to a grassland, a Norway pine plantation, land leased from Crow Wing County, and close to 200 acres of jack pine savanna owned by the Nature Conservancy. Visitor attractions include a Monet bridge and pond, a DNR Landscaping for Wildlife project, a Girl Scout secret garden, numerous flower beds, an orienteering course suitable for amateurs and experts alike, and 12 miles of hiking and cross-country ski trails.

WHEN The arboretum is open dawn to dusk seven days a week.

WHERE Take State Highway 371 through Baxter to Excelsior Road. Turn east and go 0.8 miles to Conservation Drive. Turn left (north) and drive to the end of the road.

WHO The Northland Arboretum, 14250 Conservation Drive, Baxter, MN 56425, (218) 829-8770

FOR MORE INFORMATION http://northlandarb.org

MASTER
NATURALIST
TOOLBOX

Teach

MASTER
NATURALIST
TOOLBOX

This section features lesson plans for activities that will reinforce the ecological concepts presented in this chapter. The lessons are adaptable to a wide range of audiences, ages, and settings. Feel free to use them to teach others what you have learned!

LESSON 1

Species Area Curve and Plant Diversity

Adapted from Horn, H.S. (1993). "Biodiversity in the backyard." *Scientific American*, January 1993.

Objective

Participants will learn the relationship between biodiversity (species richness) in a given area and the size of that area.

Audience Type

Teen, adult

Supplies

- ☐ Flagging tape or rope (about 160 yards; can use less, or none, if necessary)
- ☐ Stakes for marking study area
- ☐ A big piece of butcher paper to tape plant specimens onto
- ☐ Transparent tape
- ☐ Measuring tape (at least 50 feet long if possible)
- ☐ Data sheets (see sample), enough for one per group
- ☐ A large lawn, field, or forested area with some plant diversity (if you can walk across it and count about 10–12 obviously different species quickly, it should work)

Background

Measuring the species richness of a given area can help us plan how best to conserve biodiversity in a given patch of land. Such surveys not only help us determine what land should be preserved to maximize the conservation of biodiversity, they also help us design conservation reserves. In this lesson, participants will experimentally discover how the number of species found in a plot varies with the size of the plot and learn how conservationists, ecological planners, and policy makers use such information to estimate how much land is needed to preserve natural flora and fauna.

The relationships between the area of a piece of land and the number of species found on that land are referred to as species-area curves. Ecologists Robert MacArthur and E. O. Wilson (for you ant and ecology lovers: Yes — that E. O. Wilson) formally studied species-area curves in the 1960s. They developed "island biogeography theory" to explain the relationship between the area of ocean islands and the number of species living on these islands. While you won't be studying actual islands, much of the natural habitat left in the world is similar to islands, in that it is divided into fragments surrounded by very different habitat.

This activity helps participants learn about species-area curves by counting plant species on a lawn. At the same time they learn about classification, explore a habitat, and gain experience graphing and analyzing data. The project can be done at many levels of complexity.

Activity

1. Ask participants: How does the area of a habitat affect the number of plant species present? They might have the following hypotheses:

    - Area has no effect on the number of plant species present (the area could affect the number of individuals within each species, but not actually the number of species).

    - The number of species increases proportionally as the size of the habitat increases.

    - The number of species increases and then levels off as the size of the habitat increases.

2. Lay out a nested grid of plots of increasing size (see Figure 26). You can either do this ahead of time, or have the participants help with the task. Mark the plots with stakes and flagging tape if you have them. You may want to increase or decrease the area depending on the number of species that appear during a quick investigation. The area is the right size and has enough diversity for the activity to work if you can walk across it and count at least seven to ten obviously different species.

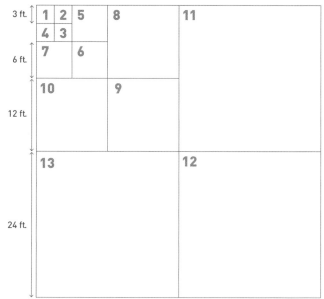

Figure 26. Sampling plots for Lesson 1.

3. Assign one or two (depending on the size of your group) people to be the curator (whose task is describe in #4). Divide the rest of the participants into teams of two, and assign each team to one or more squares in the grid. (You may want to assign the smaller squares to one participant, or a team of two participants to several smaller squares) and the larger ones to larger teams. Ideally, you should have at least 16 people, with one curator; two or three each in squares 11, 12, and 13; one or two in squares 8, 9, and 10; one or two assigned to 5, 6, and 7; and one or two assigned to 1–4 combined.)

4. Have the participants explore their plots for new plant species and bring a sample of each to the herbarium. If it is the first of its type to appear in the herbarium, the curator should write the name of the species on the butcher paper and tape the specimen to the paper above the name. The "discoverer" of a species can name it if he or she doesn't already know its name. Just as professional taxonomists do, they may use names of friends or defining characteristics of the specimen (like "Hairy Harry" or "Itty-Bitty"). They can be creative.

MASTER
NATURALIST
TOOLBOX

5. Tally the species present in each plot and in the entire area sampled by filling in the Species and Plots Data Table (see next page). Keep track of both the number of species in each square and a running count of the numbers, starting with those from the smallest square and then adding new ones from subsequent blocks until you have included the entire plot.

6. Look at patterns in the plots in which various species appear. Notice that some species are common to nearly every square, while others are rare. Some appear as lone or scattered individuals, while others are in scattered clumps.

7. Graph the relationship between the area sampled and the number of species found. To explore for patterns graphically, plot the number of species against the area surveyed in several ways. First, graph the numbers of species for each surveyed square, starting with the most subdivided corner with one-yard squares. You should see that larger blocks tend to have more species. Then graph the cumulative number of species (the number in plot 1; the number in plots 1 and 2; the number in plots 1, 2, and 3; and so on. Connect the dots showing cumulative species. You should see that larger blocks tend to have more species. Discuss with participants:

   - Do you notice any different characteristics of common and widespread, clumped, and rare and scattered species?

   - If you were a land manager making recommendations about how much of this area to protect, what would you recommend?

   - Is it worth it to protect large additional areas just to protect a few additional rare species?

   - Comment on this statement: "Rare species are common, and common species are rare."

Resources

Groom, M., Meffe, G. K., and Carroll, C. R. (2006). *Principles of conservation biology, 3rd Edition.* Sunderland, Mass.: Sinauer Associates.

Horn, H. S. (1993). "Biodiversity in the backyard." *Scientific American*, January.

MASTER
NATURALIST
TOOLBOX

Species and Plots Data Table

SPECIES	PLOT NUMBER												
	1	2	3	4	5	6	7	8	9	10	11	12	13
TOTAL IN THIS PLOT													
CUMULATIVE PLOT													
AREA OF PLOT													
CUMULATIVE AREA													

Food Chain Tag

Adapted with permission from MinnAqua, an aquatic education program of the Minnesota DNR.

Objective

Participants will be able to illustrate how energy is transferred through an aquatic food chain, understand carrying capacity, and explain how organisms in a food chain depend on one another for survival.

Audience Type

Youth grades 5 and up, teen, adult

Supplies

☐ Aquatic Food Chain Sheet (see page 147)
☐ Aquatic Food Chain Cards (see pages 148–151)
☐ Scissors
☐ Glue
☐ Construction paper or card stock
☐ Clear contact paper or laminating material
☐ Food Chain Identification Tags (see pages 152–154)
☐ Clothespins or other clips, string, or yarn to thread through identification tags so they can be worn necklace-style
☐ Paper plates, one per participant (optional)
☐ Markers (optional)
☐ 500 poker chips (or other tokens) to simulate plankton
☐ Plastic cups or plastic sandwich bags, one per participant, to simulate stomachs
☐ Hula-hoops, two or more to simulate cover
☐ Several laminated illustrations of lily pads
☐ Masking tape, for creating boundaries that simulate cover
☐ Rope, 50–100 feet long, or several field cones, to define lake boundary
☐ Whistle or other noisemaker

Background

Food chains illustrate how energy flows through a sequence of organisms and how nutrients are transferred as one organism consumes another. Ecosystems consist of many, often interlinked food chains. A food web is a diagram of a complex, interacting set of food chains within an ecosystem.

Parts of a Food Chain

The sun provides light, the ultimate energy source for all freshwater aquatic food chains. The food chains themselves consist of producers, consumers, and decomposers.

MASTER
NATURALIST
TOOLBOX

PRODUCERS Plants are called producers because they produce simple nutrients and sugars using the sun's light energy to drive photosynthesis. The food energy produced by phytoplankton—free-floating microscopic plants and bacteria suspended in the water—supports much of the other life in the water.

CONSUMERS Consumers are organisms that obtain energy from eating other plants or animals. Herbivores, or primary consumers, eat only producers. Carnivores, or secondary consumers, eat other animals. An animal that hunts, captures, and consumes other animals is a predator. Northern pike and eagles are predators, for example. An animal consumed by a predator is described as prey.

DECOMPOSERS Decomposers, such as bacteria and fungi, complete the food chain by breaking down dead plants and animals and freeing nutrients and carbon dioxide to become inputs further up the food chain. They also keep the landscape tidy—imagine what it would be like if decomposers didn't break down dead plants and animals!

A relatively large quantity of plant material is required to support primary consumers. Primary consumers, in turn, support a smaller number of secondary consumers. That's because most of the food energy consumed by organisms fuels growth and other functions and is lost from the system rather than converted into *biomass*—organic plant or animal material. Because energy is lost at each level, most food pyramids contain at most four trophic levels.

Nutrients

Nutrients are the materials required for life, and they build and renew organisms as they cycle through food chains. Plants use the sun's energy to convert carbon, hydrogen, and oxygen (in the form of carbon dioxide and water) into carbohydrates. Then these atoms cycle through consumers. When consumers die, bacteria and fungi decompose them, releasing these molecules and others (phosphorus, nitrogen, and sulfur) needed for life into the soil, water, and air. These nutrients are available to plants again, which use them to convert the sun's energy into carbohydrates. Decomposers are often referred to as nutrient recyclers because they break down dead material to provide the nutrients producers need to continue the cycle. Each living thing is composed of nutrients that have been—and will be—used by other organisms in a continuous cycle. This sharing and recycling of nutrients is known as the nutrient cycle.

Food Chains and Webs Are Systems

Producers, primary consumers, secondary consumers, and decomposers are all connected, like links in a chain. Harm to one link eventually affects all organisms in the food chain or food web.

As they evolved together over time, producers, consumers, and decomposers have developed ecological relationships. These relationships, of one species to another and between each species and its environment, maintain population levels and balance within ecosystems.

Carrying Capacity

The maximum number of individuals or inhabitants that an environment can support without detrimental effects on the habitat or to the organisms over time is referred to as *carrying capacity*. Habitats contain limited amounts of food, water, cover, space, and other resources. The quantity and quality of these resources influence the carrying capacity of a habitat. Because resources are limited, population growth slows as a species approaches the habitat's carrying capacity. At times, a population may exceed carrying capacity, but it will decrease eventually.

MASTER
NATURALIST
TOOLBOX

Population numbers tend to fluctuate over time, depending on seasons and changes in weather, climate, and other environmental shifts. Other influences include excessive predation, the introduction of exotic species, disease, pollution, overharvesting, poaching, development, agriculture, and recreation.

If a fish population grows dramatically, becoming larger than the carrying capacity of the lake ecosystem, the fish consume resources much faster than they can be naturally replenished. Eventually, this can result in serious habitat degradation and a reduced carrying capacity. And because all organisms are interconnected, other species are affected, too. Excessive numbers of one type of fish competing for food and other resources will eventually lead to the death of many individuals if balance isn't restored. Fish sometimes emigrate (leave an area) and the size of the population in the habitat decreases. This, in turn, affects the predators that normally depend on that type of fish for food and eventually affects the entire food chain.

Balance

Food chains are part of a larger system of cycles, checks, and balances that maintain stable ecosystems—those that function continuously and remain viable over time. An ecosystem that can sustain itself over time is said to be in balance. An ecosystem in balance is sustainable.

Activity

1. Before starting, make aquatic food chain cards and food chain identification tags. Copy and cut out cards, then glue each to construction paper or cardstock and laminate. Make 36 minnow cards, 12 yellow perch cards, three northern pike cards, two angler cards, and two bacteria cards. Attach clothespins or other clips, string, or yarn so the tags can be worn necklace-style. Mark the boundaries of your lake ecosystem (an area approximately half the size of a basketball court) using a rope or field cones. Scatter plankton (poker chips) randomly around the lake, reserving approximately 100 for later use.

2. Ask participants where they get their energy. Ask them to diagram the flow of food energy from the previous night's dinner back to the sun. Then ask them to think about how fish get the energy they need.

3. Choose six volunteers. Give each one an aquatic food chain card. Ask the volunteers to try to line up in the order of a food chain (without talking). How did they do? Explain food chains, food webs, and predator-prey relationships.

    Ask participants: Which organisms in our food chain are predators? Which are prey? Can an animal be both? (The perch is one example of a species that is both predator and prey. Perch eat minnows and are also eaten by larger fish such as northern pike.)

4. Have volunteers remove food chain cards.

5. ROUND 1 Distribute a minnow identification tag and a "stomach" (plastic cup or sandwich bag) to each participant. Put all the "minnows" in the lake.

MASTER
NATURALIST
TOOLBOX

Teach

6. Tell participants that when you blow the whistle they should fill their "stomachs," one poker chip at a time, with as much "plankton" as they can. Share the rules of the lake: 1) Walk, don't run. 2) Stay within the lake boundary. 3) Stop when you hear the whistle again.

7. Blow the whistle. Let the feeding continue until the minnows have eaten all the plankton.

8. Ask who filled their stomach with 15 or more poker chips. Those minnows survived!

9. Introduce the term carrying capacity. What will happen in our lake now that all the food is gone? Thinking about the food chain, how could we balance the lake?

10. Have participants return plankton to the lake.

11. ROUND 2 Put two hula-hoops into the lake. Tell the participants the hula-hoops represent cover and are safe places for prey. Only one participant at a time may hide in a hula-hoop, and only for five seconds at a time. Tell participants that they can't stand next to the cover and go in and out. They must move to other areas of the lake before they can return to cover.

12. Exchange several participants' minnow tags for perch tags. The number of perch will depend on the size of the group. If your group size is about 15, you may wish to start with four perch. If your group size is closer to 35, try starting with eight or nine perch.

13. Tell participants both perch and minnows can eat plankton—but perch are predators and can also eat minnows. Predators catch their prey by tagging them. When tagged, the minnow, or prey, must empty the contents of its stomach into the stomach of the predator, which is the perch. The tagged fish is now "dead" and must sit down at the edge of the lake.

14. Begin the feeding and continue until most of the plankton have been eaten before blowing the whistle to stop feeding.

15. How many minnows and perch have plankton in their stomachs? Those fish survived! What would happen to the food if we kept playing? Is anything missing from our lake?

16. Have participants return plankton to the lake.

17. ROUND 3 Select one or two of the minnows to be bacteria. Tell participants the bacteria break down the dead plants and animals into nutrients, and they're called decomposers. In this round, when the minnows are tagged, they must sit down and wait to be decomposed by the bacteria. The bacteria will take them to the edge of the lake. Give the 100 reserved poker chips to the bacteria. The bacteria toss a few poker chips back into the lake when they take a tagged minnow to the edge of the lake. This represents the nutrients the bacteria release, which provide new phytoplankton growth in the lake. The phytoplankton, in turn, provide food for zooplankton and other consumers.

18. Start the game again. You may wish to periodically add a few minnows (the ones that get tagged) back into the game as this round progresses, to show reproduction of minnows.

19. Let the feeding occur until most of the plankton are consumed or after several minutes of your aquatic ecosystem functioning in balance.

20. How many minnows survived? How did the bacteria affect the lake ecosystem? Is our ecosystem balanced? What does our ecosystem need? (You may need to adjust the ratio of minnows, perch, and bacteria to better balance the system.)

21. Ask participants if anything else could be missing from the lake. Can they think of another predator to add to the lake? Have participants return the plankton to the lake.

22. ROUND 4 Exchange up to three minnow tags from the remaining minnows for northern pike tags, depending on the size of your class. You may also wish to have some minnows and perch trade roles, giving more participants opportunities to be predators. The northern pike are predators that feed on the perch. When a perch gets tagged, the participant must empty half the contents of its stomach into the stomach of the northern pike and sit down to wait for the bacteria to take them to the edge of the lake. Then they give their remaining poker chips to the bacteria to scatter back into the lake as phytoplankton. (The northern pike can eat perch or minnows. But remind the participants that northern pike usually go after the perch because they're larger and give them more food energy for less work. Perch still eat both minnows and plankton. Minnows eat only plankton.)

23. Both minnows and perch may hide in the cover (hula-hoops), but the same rules apply: only one fish in a hula-hoop at a time, and for only five seconds. They must then move around the lake.

24. Restart the game. When much of the plankton is gone, or when the system has been operating in balance for several minutes, stop the game. Determine how many survivors remain in the lake. Are there minnows left? How many perch are left? Did the northern pike survive? A northern pike has survived if it has food in its stomach. A healthy, balanced lake will have more prey individuals than predators. How could you adjust the numbers so this occurs? (An approximate ratio of six minnows to three perch to one northern pike balances this simulated lake. Participants should begin to understand that energy flows through ecosystems and is constantly being replenished by the sun as nutrients cycle or circulate through the ecosystem. Tell participants that an ecosystem is defined as all living and nonliving things interacting within a defined place. One way that living and nonliving things interact is by means of a food chain. Have participants return the plankton to the lake.

25. ROUND 5 Discuss how people are part of the ecosystem, and how they might affect it. Select one or two of the minnows to be anglers. Give each an angler tag to wear. Explain that anglers must first find bait by tagging one minnow before they can fish. While linking arms, the minnow and angler must then try to catch a perch or northern pike by having the minnow tag that fish. (Only one fish can be caught at a time.) The angler will then take the fish's food and escort the fish to the edge of the lake. Ask participants what happens to the food from the fish the angler catches. Remind participants that the fish can still use the cover to hide from predators and anglers.

MASTER
NATURALIST
TOOLBOX

26. When most of the plankton are gone, stop the game. Determine which species survived. If the lake ecosystem is in balance, there should be more minnows than perch and more perch than northern pike.

27. Have participants discuss the results of this round. Is the lake balanced, or is it headed for trouble? How did anglers affect the lake ecosystem? If the impact was dramatic, what could be done to limit the anglers' impact on the lake? (Examples include creating regulations such as designating fishing seasons for certain species or establishing catch limits.) What would happen if the number of northern pike exceeded the carrying capacity? (Eventually, they could be the sole remaining fish and have no more food to eat.) Could the northern pike survive this situation?

28. If time permits, try to balance the lake by varying the ratios of different fish species in the lake, then play more rounds and discuss what happens. Have the participants determine what adjustments need to be made after each round to balance the ecosystem.

29. Try adding more anglers and introduce fishing regulations to maintain a balanced ecosystem.

30. Hand out copies of the aquatic food chain sheet and review definitions of food chain, ecosystem, and carrying capacity.

31. Discuss: What was it like to be a prey species? A predator? Why? What would happen if anglers caught too many predators? Would the ecosystem be balanced?

This lesson was simplified from *Fishing: Get in the Habitat!* — The leader's guide for the Minnesota DNR MinnAqua program. Find more activities and information at www.mndnr.gov/minnaqua.

MASTER
NATURALIST
TOOLBOX

Aquatic Food Chain Sheet

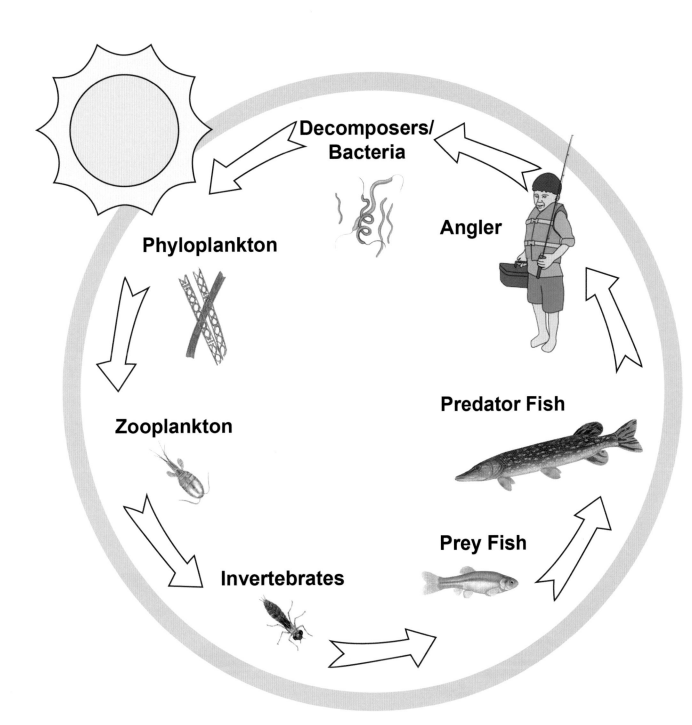

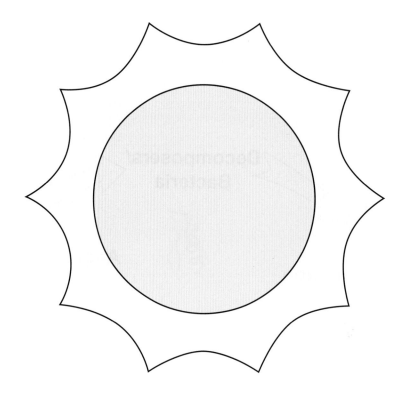

Sun

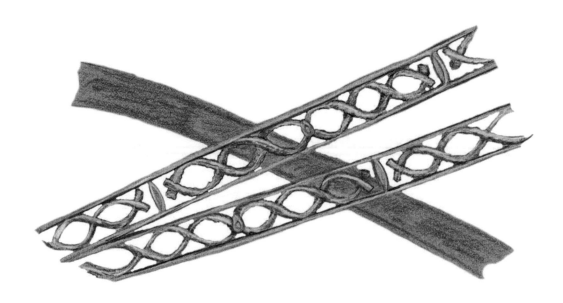

Phytoplankton: Spirogyra

Aquatic Food Chain Cards

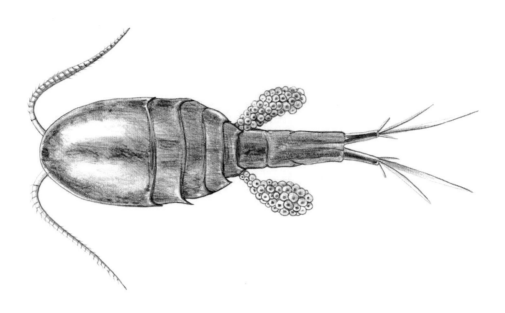

Zooplankton: Cyclops (Copepod)

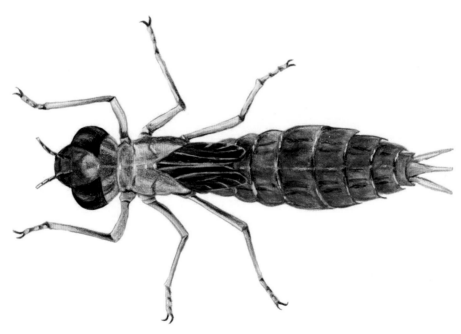

Dragonfly Larva

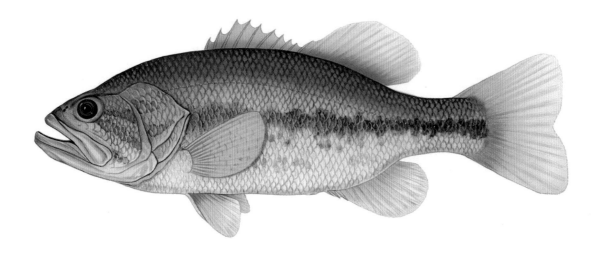

Largemouth Bass

Green Sunfish

Aquatic Food Chain Cards

Angler

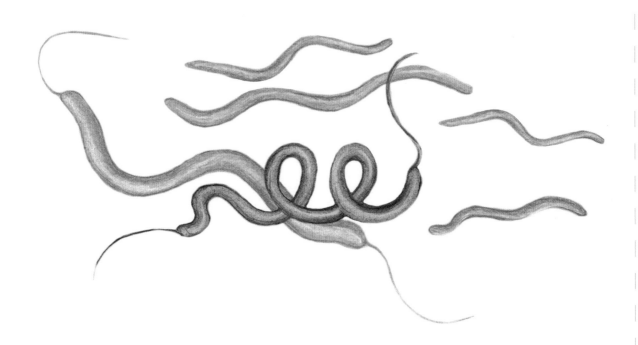

Decomposer: Bacteria

Food Chain Identification Tags

Make six copies of this page.

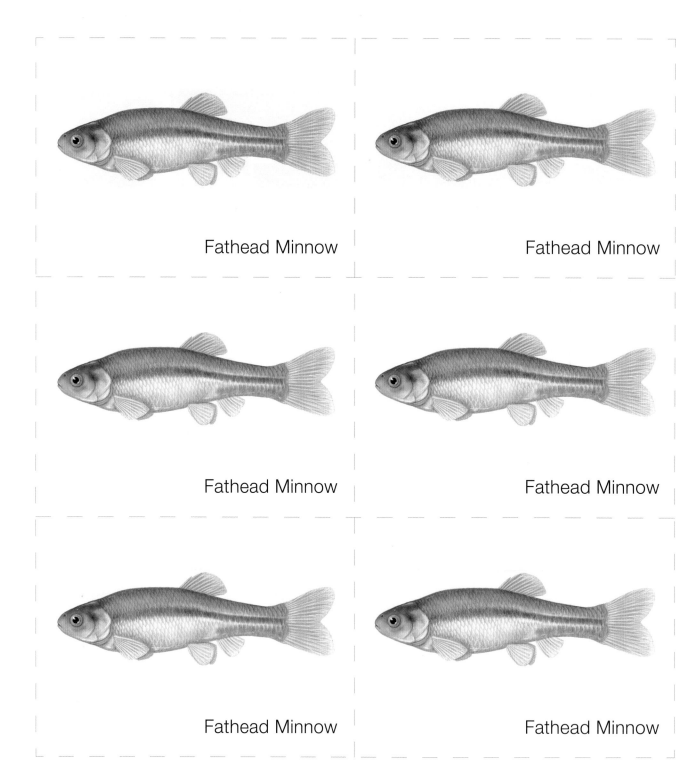

Fathead Minnow

Fathead Minnow

Fathead Minnow

Fathead Minnow

Fathead Minnow

Fathead Minnow

Food Chain Identification Tags

Make three copies of this page.

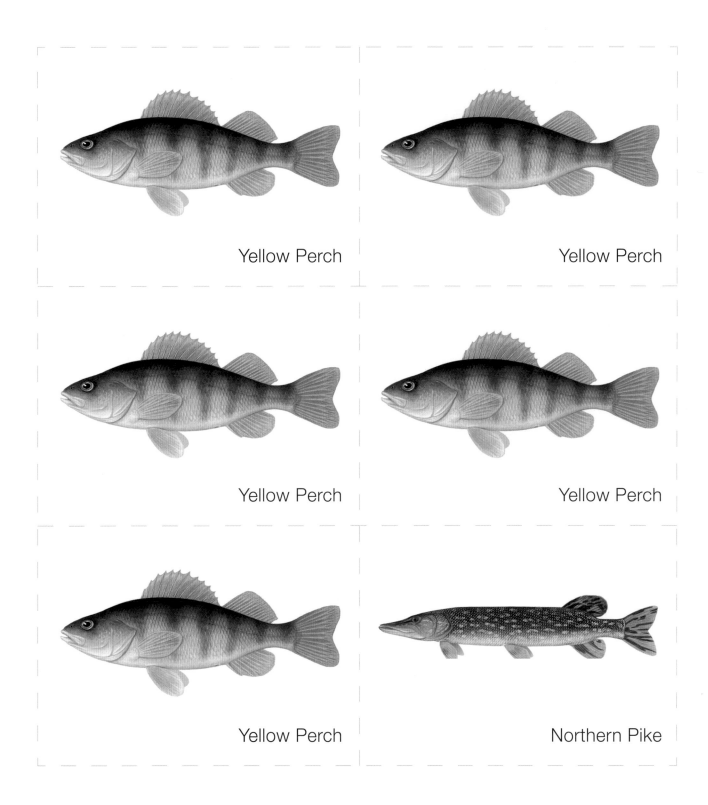

Yellow Perch

Yellow Perch

Yellow Perch

Yellow Perch

Yellow Perch

Northern Pike

Food Chain Identification Tags

Make one copy of this page.

Angler

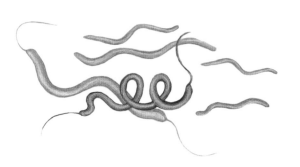

Bacterial Decomposer

Angler

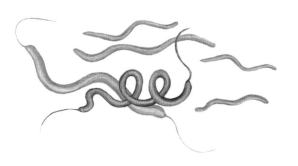

Bacterial Decomposer

Conserve

This section highlights organizations that offer opportunities for Minnesota Master Naturalist volunteers to participate in stewardship and citizen science activities related to ecology in the North Woods, Great Lakes region. Please visit the websites to learn more.

Citizen Science Central

CitizenScience.org aims to harness the knowledge gained by practitioners and researchers across the field of citizen science to build collaboration, community and credibility.

http://citizenscience.org/

CITIZEN SCIENCE ASSOCIATION

USA National Phenology Network

Phenology is the study of seasonal natural phenomena, such as the timing of various climate, plant, and animal events for a given locale. The USA National Phenology network has developed Nature's Notebook, a tool that collects observations from citizen scientists and standardizes them. The standardized data can then be made available to influence decisions related to allergies, wildfires, water, and conservation. You can help by collecting phenology data for Nature's Notebook in your yard or local area.

http://usanpn.org

USA npn
National Phenology Network

Expand

This section suggests some things you can use, do, pursue, read, or join to develop as a naturalist.

Journal

EXPERIENCE While sitting in your special spot, consider the following quote: "When we try to pick out anything by itself, we find it hitched to everything else in the Universe." – John Muir

REFLECT What songs, poems, or other artistic works come to mind when you're in your special spot? Reflect on the ways that art in all its forms expresses the inexpressible. What is inexpressible about your spot?

RECORD Write a poem based on some aspect of your special spot. You could compose a simple rhyme, a haiku, or a whole sonnet. Free-form poetry and song lyrics are welcome, too!

Read

The Boundary Waters Wilderness Ecosystem

Miron Heinselman.
1996. University of Minnesota Press: Minneapolis. 384 pp.

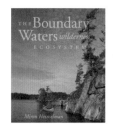

This book is a great introduction to the ecology of the Boundary Waters region and all of northern Minnesota. Among the topics discussed are the origins of the lakes and landforms, forest communities, early human history, logging, the role of mammals and birds in the ecosystem, the effect of visitors, and the future of the area. Heinselman mapped all the forest stands and uncut portions of the Boundary Waters region, and the book includes a fascinating discussion of the integral role fire plays in this ecosystem.

North Shore: A Natural History of Minnesota's Superior Coast

Chel Anderson and Andelheid Fischer.
2015. University of Minnesota Press: Minneapolis. 601 pp.

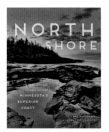

This is a great example of a coffee table textbook. North Shore has clear and well-presented information on a wide variety of subjects relating to the Lake Superior coast and nearby inland area accompanied by beautiful photographs and illustrations. The book is topical, with subjects such as coaster brook trout management, mining, and climate change. *North Shore* complements key scientific references and often recounts the current sentiment of researchers and citizens. At 601 pages, this book will stay on your coffee table for a good while, but every time you pick it up again you will be met with new, or strange, information together with professional photography of the Lake Superior coast.

Minnesota Conservation Volunteer

Minnesota Department of Natural Resources.
Since 1940

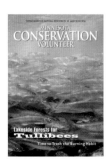

Minnesota Conservation Volunteer is a bimonthly magazine that has reports on a wide variety of ecological issues specific to Minnesota. Readership is as varied as the issues covered. Readers include anglers, birders, hunters, hikers, paddlers, armchair ecologists, and adventurers. Past contributors include Sigurd Olson, Jim Brandenburg, and Les Blacklock.

Surf

The Wolves and Moose of Isle Royale

This site includes video essays, research reports, technical publications, photos, and information on research taking place on Isle Royale.

www.isleroyalewolf.org

Encyclopedia of the Earth

A fantastic resource to provide background information on any of the terms covered in this chapter. The information is expert-reviewed and easy to read. The "Feature Articles" section gives well-referenced textbook examples of a host of ecological topics.

http://editors.eol.org/eoearth/wiki/Main_Page

Join

Your Local Environmental Learning Center

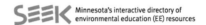

Minnesota has a great network of environmental learning centers where Minnesotans of all ages can learn about the ecology of their neighborhoods and regions. SEEK — Minnesota's web-based interactive directory of environmental education resources — keeps track of all of them for you in one place. From the main SEEK page, select "Destinations" and click the region of the state you are interested in. That will bring you to a list of (and links to) facilities. Go explore your local nature center today!

www.seek.state.mn.us/index.cfm

Audubon Minnesota

You may think of Audubon as being a group that is involved solely in bird conservation, but it does much more than that in Minnesota and across the nation. Audubon Minnesota, the state office of the National Audubon Society, shares Audubon's 100-year heritage of working to protect our environment as well as the Audubon mission to conserve and restore natural ecosystems, focusing on birds, other wildlife, and their habitats. Audubon Minnesota has its own statewide programs and pursues its own funding for Minnesota efforts. Audubon has 12 local chapters in Minnesota. Visit the website to locate and find contact information concerning the chapter nearest you.

http://mn.audubon.org

Additional Reading

Carson, R. (1962) *Silent spring.* Houghton Mifflin: Boston, Massachusetts. 378 pp.

Leopold, A. (1949) *A Sand County almanac and sketches here and there.* Oxford University Press: Cary, North Carolina. 240 pp.

MASTER NATURALIST TOOLBOX

Copyrighted Photographs and Images Used With Permission

Figure 1. Courtesy of Caileigh Speck

Figure 2. Courtesy of Minnesota Department of Natural Resources Forestry Division, adapted from All About Minnesota's Forests and Trees

Figure 3. Courtesy of University of Minnesota

Figure 4. Courtesy of University of Minnesota

Figure 5. Courtesy of U.S. Climate Change Science Program, 2002

Figure 6. Courtesy of United Nations Environment Programme, 2002, modified

Figure 7. Courtesy of Sarah L. Keefer

Figure 8. Courtesy of Wikimedia Commons

Figure 9. Courtesy of Vitousek, P.M. et al. 1997. Human alterations of the global nitrogen cycle: Causes and Consequences. Issues in Ecology 1:4-6, modified

Figure 10. Courtesy of Wikimedia Commons

Figure 11. Courtesy of United States Global Change Research Program

Figure 12. Courtesy of Rob Blair (modified from Blair 1996)

Figure 13. Courtesy of Carrol Henderson, Minnesota Department of Natural Resources Nongame Wildlife Program

Figure 14. Courtesy of Brett Whaley

Figure 15. Courtesy of Donald Biemborn

Figure 16. Courtesy of Wikimedia Commons

Figure 17. Courtesy of Sandra Jensen, Cornell University, Wikimedia Commons

Figure 18. Courtesy of Rob Blair (modified from Blair 1999, original MacLulich 1937)

Figure 19. Courtesy of Mary Holland, www.naturallycuriouswithMaryHolland.com

Figure 20. Courtesy of Andrea Westmoreland, Wikimedia Commons

Figure 21. Courtesy of and copyright by M. Gaden, Great Lakes Fisheries Commission

Figure 22. Courtesy of University of Minnesota

Figure 23. Courtesy of Dawn A. Flinn, Minnesota Department of Natural Resources

Figure 24. Courtesy of Janet Allen

Figure 25. Courtesy of Peter Trimming, Wikimedia Commons

Partial text throughout chapter 4. Courtesy of CK-12 Foundation
CK-12 Curriculum Material is made available to users in accordance with the Creative CommonsAttribution-Noncommercial 3.0 Unported (CC BY-NC) License (http://creativecommons. org/licenses/by-nc/3.0/) , as amended and updated by Creative Commons from time to time (the "CC BY-NC License"), which is incorporated herein by this reference.

MASTER
NATURALIST
TOOLBOX

Chapter 5: Why Is This Meaningful?

Communicating Your Message Through Environmental Interpretation

Dawn A. Flinn

Goal

Understand environmental interpretation and interpretive techniques.

Objectives

1. Define what environmental interpretation means to you.

2. Give an example of a theme.

3. Explain the steps in the ADDIE model.

4. Identify three methods of interpretation.

5. Know how to use signs, brochures, and other interpretive products.

> "Nature is personal. It is about moments experienced by individuals, and interpretation is about making those moments more valuable, or even possible in the first place."
>
> — Paul Caputo
> National Association for Interpretation

Introduction

As a Minnesota Master Naturalist Volunteer, you'll likely have many opportunities to help others understand and appreciate nature. In general, the process of clarifying meaning or explaining something is known as interpretation. You've heard of sign language interpretation and foreign language interpretation, and in these cases, the interpretation process translates meaning from one language into another. In this chapter we focus on "environmental interpretation," which is another form of translation — in the words of the National Association for Interpretation, "a communication process that forges emotional and intellectual connections between the interest of the audience and the inherent meaning in the resource." In other words, environmental interpretation is an engaging translation of the natural world for human understanding.

Two people were instrumental in building a foundation for environmental interpretation: Enos Mills (Figure 1), born in 1870, a guide who led trips in the Rocky Mountains; and Freeman Tilden (Figure 2), born in 1883, a newspaper reporter, author, and commentator interested in effective techniques for reaching the public.

Enos Mills once said, "A nature guide (interpreter) is a naturalist who can guide others to the secrets of nature. It is not necessary for a guide to be a walking encyclopedia. He arouses interest by dealing in big principles—not with detached and colorless information."

In 1957, Freeman Tilden wrote *Interpreting Our Heritage,* the first book dedicated to the profession of interpretation. He wrote, "Thousands of naturalists, historians, archaeologists, and other specialists are

Figure 1. Enos Mills was a founder of Rocky Mountain National Park and one of the first people to practice natural history interpretation.

Figure 2. Freeman Tilden gave form and substance to the field of natural history interpretation when he published his seminal book, *Interpreting Our Heritage*, in 1957.

engaged in the work of revealing, to such visitors as desire the service, something of the beauty and wonder, the inspiration and spiritual meaning that lie behind what the visitor can, with his senses, perceive."

In *Interpretation: Making a Difference on Purpose* (2013), Sam Ham (Figure 3) defined environmental interpretation as "a mission-based approach to communication aimed at provoking in audiences the discovery of personal meaning and the forging of personal connections with things, places, people, and concepts."

In *The Interpreter's Guidebook* (2015), a team of authors, including Ron Zimmerman and Michael Gross (Figure 3), explores a meaning-centered philosophy of interpretation and introduces the concept of heritage interpretation vs. environmental interpretation. They define heritage interpretation as "a communication process that guides visitors to discover meaning in objects, places, and landscapes." The use of the word *heritage* expands the interpretive focus beyond the environment.

What do these descriptions have in common? Each states how interpretation is a method of stimulating interest in, and appreciation of, a variety of things, including nature. Interpretation aims to do more than simply convey facts; it also inspires and conveys interest and meaning in the subject area. An environmental interpreter needs to be an entertainer, a translator, and a revealer of secrets!

The Interpreter's Guidebook discusses Three Pillars of Interpretation—the essential aspects of the interpretive experience. These combine to determine the best messages and techniques to use. The pillars are:

Figure 3. Sam Ham (left), Ron Zimmerman (center) and Michael Gross (right) have helped define the field of environmental interpretation as well as train thousands of college students and others in interpretive techniques. Their books are excellent "how-to" manuals for almost any form of interpretation.

ORGANIZATION MISSION AND GOALS Knowing these and integrating them into your programs and resources will help guide the direction of your interpretive messages. A volunteer program for the DNR may have a much different goal than a volunteer program of the Minnesota Historical Society.

NEEDS AND INTERESTS OF AUDIENCE If audience members aren't interested, they aren't going to have a positive experience. They must hear what you have to say and you must meet their needs and interests to be effective. This can be challenging because sometimes you don't know who your audience will be until they arrive. Do your research ahead of time to find out who will most likely be visiting.

SIGNIFICANT SITE RESOURCES Focus on the things that make your site unique (Figure 4). It is probably the reason the visitors are there in the first place. Being knowledgeable about these key resources is an important part of helping people connect to the site.

By integrating these three pillars you will create a worthwhile experience for both the visitor and the site organization.

Principles of Interpretation

While there are as many variations on interpretation as there are interpreter and audience combinations, there are some simple things to keep in mind for any interpretive situation. Following are six principles Tilden developed for interpretation. Although they may not suit all occasions (for example, sometimes you'll want to convey the incredible minutiae that make the world so wonderful, and sometimes you will have a range of ages in the same audience) they are still useful guides. If you find yourself straying from Tilden's principles, as we hope you will have occasion to do, be sure you know why you're straying. Your most important goal is to ensure an effective interpretive experience for your audience.

Figure 4. Good interpretation involves both the visitor and the site. Paddling as a group to Split Rock Lighthouse and interpreting the site from lake level provides a different perspective from programs held at the lighthouse itself.

Freeman Tilden's Principles of Interpretation, from *Interpreting Our Heritage*, 1957

1. *"Any interpretation that does not somehow relate what is being displayed or described to something within the personality or experience of the visitor will be sterile."*

   In other words, interpretation connects the concepts or ideas you're trying to convey with your audience's own real-life experiences. This means you need to understand your audience (more on that later).

2. *"Information, as such, is not interpretation. Interpretation is revelation based upon information. But they are entirely different things. However, all interpretation includes information."*

   Telling a string of facts is not interpretation. We're not only conveying information when we interpret, we're revealing nature's secrets in a dramatic way. Revelation is the feeling in those "aha" moments that occur when you "get it" or "see it." Effective interpretation gives just enough information for your audience to realize or deduce meaning relevant to their lives. For example, a naturalist might show visitors the serrated edge of an owl wing feather, then swing a frayed rope and an unfrayed rope through the air to demonstrate how one makes noise and the other is silent. Rather than telling visitors the adaptive value of the owl feather's unusual feature, the interpreter provides them with a clue from which they can deduce the answer.

3. *"Interpretation is an art, which combines many arts, whether the materials presented are scientific, historical, or architectural. Any art is in some degree teachable."*

   Being creative and using a variety of imaginative techniques brings interpretation to life. You are an

Figure 5. Interpretation for children should follow a fundamentally different approach than interpretation for adults.

actor, a scientist, a storyteller, an artist, maybe a singer and more. All of these characteristics come together to create good interpretation.

4. *"The chief aim of interpretation is not instruction, but provocation."*

As Mills said, we don't need to be walking encyclopedias. Our goal is to provoke and inspire. We want our audience to leave with an appreciation of nature and a desire to learn more.

5. *"Interpretation should aim to present a whole rather than a part and must address itself to the whole man rather than any phase."*

We usually want to convey the big picture and put our setting into a broader context. We also need to appeal to all aspects of our audience — their aesthetic, emotional, and intellectual levels — and to provide both sides of the story.

6. *"Interpretation addressed to children should not be a dilution of the presentation to adults, but should follow a fundamentally different approach. To be at its best, it will require a separate program."*

Children are not miniature adults. Interpreting for them requires a different mind-set than interpreting for adults (Figure 5). If you know you will be working with children, be sure to prepare activities appropriate to their level of development. Since parents love sharing interpretive experiences with their children, interpretation for a combined audience of adults and children together can be tricky if you aren't well-prepared.

The ADDIE Model

Though good interpretation may seem casual and effortless, it requires a huge amount of planning, implementation, and practice before it becomes so. The ADDIE model, developed by Florida State University, is an instructional systems design that works for almost any type of educational effort but particularly well for interpretation. It consists of five steps:

THE ADDIE MODEL	
ANALYZE	theme, audience, setting
DESIGN	instructional strategies, media
DEVELOP	materials
IMPLEMENT	presentation, product
EVALUATE	how to improve

Step One: Analyze

First, consider your theme, audience, and setting.

THEME A successful interpretive presentation must have a theme (a.k.a. instructional problem, or framework for the story you're planning to tell, Figure 6). Once you determine the theme, it will be easy to pinpoint the message you want to convey, and identify clear goals and objectives.

Figure 6. A theme should be narrowed down to a message you would like people to understand.

Identifying your theme is as easy as 1–2–3:

1. Select your topic. This should fit your setting and the goals and objectives you would like to achieve. For example, you might choose the importance of pond life as a topic if you're at a nature center with a pond and you'll be interpreting on a warm summer day.

2. Narrow your topic. You won't be able to cover everything about the pond in one day, so you might choose to focus on aquatic invertebrates.

3. Write your theme statement — the take-home message for your presentation. Word it so it answers the "so what?" question. For example, "Aquatic invertebrates are a vital link in the food web of a pond."

In selecting and developing your theme, be sure to ask yourself:

Is the theme important to this site, and will it enrich the visitor's experience? Scooping for aquatic invertebrates or walking through a marsh will enrich most people's experience. They will see things they may not have noticed before, understand the value of the pond in a new way, and have fun in the process.

Will audience members be able to relate to this theme, and will they recognize the take-home message? If visitors enjoy fishing or duck hunting, they will understand the importance of aquatic invertebrates to their sport.

If they like watching great blue herons feed along a lakeshore, they will understand the interdependence of aquatic invertebrates and predatory birds in the pond's food web.

Is this a theme I care about? You need to be enthusiastic if you want to convey enthusiasm to your audience. Choose a theme that excites you!

Do I have the information I need to develop the presentation? Plan to include only information that supports your theme. You don't need to shower your audience with facts. If you don't have the information you need, what resources do you need to gather, and where can you find them?

AUDIENCE Will your audience include families, children, people with disabilities, school groups, senior citizens, people who speak English as a second language? Or will it be a mixture of all of the above? Knowing your audience is critical to successful interpretation.

One way to engage a variety of audience types is to consider the eight multiple intelligences, or ways people learn (see box). Most people draw on a variety of intelligences to make sense of a new situation or concept. If you design your programs to appeal to multiple intelligences — for example, use props, sounds, touch, movement, pictures, and written words — you will satisfy more visitors.

If you work with children, remember that they learn differently than adults. There are great resources available to clarify some of these differences. For ideas about designing developmentally appropriate and engaging environmental activities, see *Natural Wonders: A Guide to Early Childhood for Environmental Educators,* an online publication available through SEEK, Minnesota's environmental education website (www. seek.state.mn.us).

If you aren't sure how to work with a particular audience, get advice from someone who is familiar with this audience. Also, keep in mind that participants may turn out to be different than you

> "Education is not filling a bucket, but lighting a fire."
>
> — William B. Yeats

Best Practices for Differing Learning Styles

In their book *Best Practices for Field Days,* University of Minnesota Extension Environmental Science Education team members developed the following suggestions for reaching audience members with different learning styles.

Imagine that you are planning and leading a program. Go through each of these lists and check off at least one teaching method that you would most enjoy using to reach your audience members.

Linguistic

- Learning through reading, writing, and speaking
- In activities, learners should:
  - ☐ read and write stories, poems, or essays that illustrate main ideas
  - ☐ give answers and discuss ideas out loud
  - ☐ discuss the meanings of important words/language
  - ☐ develop mnemonic devices to remember key terms (e.g., ROY G BIV for the colors of the rainbow).

Logical

- Learning through reasoning, argument, calculating, problem solving
- In activities, learners should:
  - ☐ list and detail connections between main ideas and/or activity steps
  - ☐ describe things in terms of numbers (square feet, trees per acre, etc.)
  - ☐ identify and debate multiple sides of issues
  - ☐ develop solutions for real-world issues.

Visual-Spatial

- Learning through creating mental and physical images, maps, etc. (see Figure 7)
- In activities, learners should:
  - ☐ draw pictures, take photos, create models, etc.
  - ☐ use photographs to illustrate main ideas and/or activities
  - ☐ map and diagram main ideas (concept maps, Venn diagrams, flowcharts, etc.)
  - ☐ use directions, landforms, and coordinates to explore landscapes.

Musical

- Learning through music, tone, and rhythm
- In activities, learners should:
  - ☐ play background music softly during activities
  - ☐ sing and play instruments during activities
  - ☐ compose songs and/or rhythms to remember main ideas.

Kinesthetic

- Learning through movement, balance, and manipulation of objects
- In activities, learners should:
  - ☐ perform tasks and/or build things that describe main ideas (plant trees, build models, band birds, etc.)
  - ☐ be physically active during activities (use binoculars, take a hike, leap like a frog, etc.)

Figure 7. Visual-spatial and kinesthetic learners will learn more from using a working model to demonstrate how glacial features are formed than from reading about it in a book.

☐ detail activities in terms of actions and discuss finer points of these actions

☐ describe the way things feel to touch.

Interpersonal

- Learning through working with and seeking to understand others
- In activities, learners should:
  ☐ complete and/or discuss activities in groups
  ☐ interview other students and describe how they understand main ideas
  ☐ describe how their actions affect others
  ☐ explore and develop solutions for real-world conflicts, considering how others feel.

Intrapersonal

- Learning through self-reflection, understanding, control, and action
- In activities, learners should:
  ☐ relate main ideas and activities to past experiences and understanding
  ☐ work individually or with a mentor to complete activities and hone skills
  ☐ set personal goals for improvement and ways to achieve their goals
  ☐ explore the question, "Why does this matter to me?"

Naturalist

- Learning through connecting with and understanding the natural world.
- In activities, learners should:
  ☐ get outdoors
  ☐ explore and detail natural flora and fauna
  ☐ describe how their attitudes and/or actions affect their environment
  ☐ explore and develop solutions for real-world environmental issues, considering social, economic, and environmental implications.

Now that you have checked off one item in each category, you have identified the ways you prefer to teach, taking into consideration the fact that people in your audience have varying learning styles. Great job! This list may seem familiar to you, since your instructor may have given you a short questionnaire at the beginning of this course to assess your own preferred learning style categories. Now you can see this list from the perspective of a teacher/interpreter!

anticipated. If that happens, don't despair! Be flexible and enjoy yourself. Remember, your audience wants you to succeed.

SETTING Consider the physical setting. Does the location contain any unusual features or hidden mysteries you should mention? What larger concepts, stories, or issues should you connect to your interpretation? Are there any dangers or major changes to which your audience should be alerted? Are there rare plants or animals you should avoid to encourage their survival?

The analysis phase of interpretive planning is key to ensuring that your interpretive program or product will succeed. Beginning your interpretive planning with an analysis of theme, audience, and setting is like eating breakfast — it starts you off right.

Step Two: Design

After you have analyzed your theme, audience, and setting, you are ready to pull together your presentation. Remember that visitors like sensory involvement, humor, new information, and an enthusiastic interpreter. Most people do not enjoy dry monologues or long technical programs. People like to interact, ask questions, and share their own experiences. Do your best to relate to your audience by linking your theme with their lives.

An interpretive program should contain four main components:

1. POW! Capture the group's attention with a powerful introduction. For example: "In the next 100 years, climate change could cause the northern forests to retreat north by as much as 300 miles."

2. BRIDGE The bridge explains what the Pow! statement means and why the audience should care. For example, "Experimentation with planting a variety of tree species in the northern forests could help us figure out what will grow there in the future."

3. BODY The body contains the main message of the program. When you plan the body, look over your goals and objectives and make sure you cover them all. For example, you could conduct an interpretive walk or an illustrated talk showing the different tree plantings and how successful they have been.

4. CONCLUSION Summarize what you have said and perhaps give a call to action. For example, you might explain why continued research, experimentation, and restoration of northern forests is important and how individuals can help. Or describe how different cultures might be affected if the forest moves northeast.

Note that it works best if you write the body and the conclusion first and then the introduction.

Step Three: Develop

Developing your program depends so much on the first two steps that it's difficult to write one-size-fits-all directions here. If you've done a good job analyzing and designing, this step will be very clear. You might collect images or posters, build a PowerPoint presentation, or walk a trail to check it out. Be sure to think through the entire interpretive activity carefully: Will your visuals be visible? Will people be able to hear you? How will you transition from one activity to the next? What props will make your presentation more interesting and clear? The better you prepare, the more smoothly your presentation will proceed. Remember to practice, practice, practice!

Step Four: Implement

Finally, you're ready for an audience! In some cases, you may go out and give a single presentation. However, we hope you'll be able to do it again and again and maybe even train others to present your interpretive product.

Step Five: Evaluate

The agency or organization for which you're interpreting may have specific evaluation requirements. Even if it doesn't, program evaluations can be an important way to find out how people perceived your presentation, get kudos to inspire you to keep doing this kind of thing, and gain feedback that will help you do an even better job the next time.

There are many ways to evaluate your interpretive activities. You may simply ask your audience to share what they learned or enjoyed. Or you may give them a few written questions, such as: What did you most enjoy about this presentation? What was the most important (or interesting) thing you learned? What do you wish had been covered that wasn't? Do you have any suggestions for improving future presentations? Another easy way to evaluate a presentation is to ask a friend or colleague to join your audience and provide feedback later on what went well and what didn't.

Interpretive Forms

Interpretation can take on many forms, including programs, signs, brochures, electronic products, and exhibits. Entire books have been written on each of these topics. We will only touch the surface of a few that you may use as a Minnesota Master Naturalist Volunteer.

Programs

Two important goals of interpretive programs are to interpret the site and involve the visitor. When you interpret your site, focus on what makes it special. Is it the plants, animals, history, or geology? Stick to interpreting things found at your site. For example, there are few occasions when it would be appropriate to talk about African lions in Minnesota, unless there is a relevant connection to your location. To involve your audience members, don't just talk at them. Engage them through questions, hands-on activities, and action. This makes their experience more interesting and fun, and they'll learn more. Remember the old proverb, "I hear and I forget. I see and I remember. I do and I understand."

There are many ways to provide an interpretive experience, ranging from a casual conversation to costumed characterization. There is no single best method, nor are there secrets about interpretation. Your best bet is to observe how a variety of professionals interpret nature, then experiment with different approaches to see what works for you. Give yourself time and be patient as you build on your successes and learn from your mistakes. Most importantly, have fun, be enthusiastic, and involve the audience. Your enjoyment will rub off on your audience members, and they'll learn more if they're engaged and having a good time.

Below is a list of things to consider when implementing almost any interpretive program.

1. Check equipment and props ahead of time to make sure everything is working properly (Figure 8). This includes items such as a projector, computer, props with moving parts, or any other device you may be using.

2. Arrive early. Allow time to set everything up before your audience arrives and to greet participants, answer questions, and socialize.

3. Start promptly. Be respectful of those who show up on time, and try not to interrupt the flow of your presentation if people arrive late.

4. Dress appropriately. Dress neatly but comfortably for the weather and location. Remember that you represent your message and organization. Also, anticipate what audience members might wear; you don't want to be dressed much more casually or formally than they are.

Figure 8. Good interpretation takes lots of work before you even meet your audience. By providing props and bug netting, you can help participants feel more comfortable and engaged.

5. Use notes appropriately. It's fine to refer to notes during your presentation, but avoid reading from them. Use them as a backup to help keep you on track or to remind you of facts and figures.

6. Speak clearly. Enunciate well and use inflection. Make sure you face your audience and use a microphone if you need to. Avoid distracting words such as ah, um, cool, OK, like, and you know.

7. Use pictures when possible to make a point. When using projected images always make sure they are high quality and large enough to see. Face the audience while you speak and don't say "This is a..." as you move through each image. Project images for no longer than 10 to 15 seconds.

8. Use props to engage the audience. These could include natural items, field equipment, books, and even demonstrations. Allow your participants to touch the props if they're not too fragile. Wait until the end to pass objects around to your audience, or be aware that attention will be drawn away from you.

There are a few additional things to keep in mind on interpretive walks or guided tours:

1. Safety first! If possible, inform participants before going on a walk about appropriate attire such as hats, sunglasses, sturdy shoes, raincoats, snow boots, or mittens. During tick season or around poison ivy or stinging nettle, recommend long pants tucked into socks, and shoes or boots (not sandals).

2. Be seen and heard. When talking to a group, try to move to the middle or to a high point so everyone can see and hear you. If someone needs to face the sun, it should be you and not your audience (Figure 9). Don't wear sunglasses so people can see your eyes.

3. Provide an overview. Before you start, tell your audience what to expect, how long the tour will be, where and if bathrooms are available, if there are any special guidelines to follow, and if you will run into hazards along the way. Map out the time but be flexible to allow for "teachable moments."

Figure 9. Always consider the safety and comfort of the visitors when leading a walk. This naturalist is making sure the sun is at the children's backs for easier viewing. Appropriate clothing for a cold winter day is also important.

4. Be a leader. Walk in front. If the group is large, ask a participant to volunteer to be at the end throughout the tour. This makes is easier to tell if everyone is together at a stop.

5. Plan specific stops. Stops should be brief, have a clear purpose, and connect with the theme. A good rule of thumb is five stops per hour. The remainder of your time should be spent on self-discovery, observation, answering questions, and spontaneous interpretation.

6. Keep your interpretation flexible so you can respond to "teachable moments" as they arise. If you are teaching about pond invertebrates and an eagle flies overhead, address the eagle, tie it to your theme if you can, and return to your program.

7. Have a plan for encouraging—and limiting—sharing. Engaged participants will want to share their own experiences, and for the most part

"Do not try to satisfy your vanity by teaching a great many things. Awaken people's curiosity. It is enough to open minds; do not overload them. Put there a spark. If there is some good inflammable stuff, it will catch fire."

— Anatole France

their stories will enrich your own. Occasionally, however, you'll find a participant straying from the topic at hand or dominating the conversation. If possible, gently direct attention to other participants or back to your own presentation. If necessary, you can thank the person for sharing but note that it's time to hear from others. You can also invite him or her to continue the conversation with you later.

A few other common ways to interpret a site are by doing roving interpretation, having information stations, or providing first-person interpretation (Figure 10). Roving interpreters move throughout a site or facility answering questions and interpreting a variety of features as visitor interest warrants. Information stations can be tables with artifacts set up in a busy location or positioning yourself at an interesting place, such as a tree that was used as a scratching post by a black bear. These stations help draw visitors' attention to something you want to highlight. First-person interpretation involves dressing in costume as a character from the past, along with interpreting as if the past is the present, helping to bring days gone by to life.

At an information station, your main goals are to make the visitor feel welcome and comfortable and to encourage questions. It's a good idea to have touchable artifacts that relate to your site. You need to be familiar with notable features, plants, and wildlife of the site so you can direct people to these items or answer questions about them.

As a final note, it's impossible to anticipate every question or situation that will arise during any interpretive program. Don't be afraid to say, "That's a great question. I don't know." Ask for help and information from other participants. Offer to help find answers at the end of your program, or give ideas on where the questioner could go for more information. Learn from experience, and be prepared for questions that can be anticipated.

Signs

Signs should be visually appealing, sturdy, and appropriate to the setting. As with verbal interpretation, the best message is short and concise

Figure 10. Roving interpretation and interpretive stations involve interpreting your site during impromptu encounters with visitors.

Figure 11. Signs should have a short and concise message. This sign explains that you should wipe your feet before starting on the trail to prevent dispersal of the seeds of the invasive tansy.

(Figure 11). A good graphic and short title may be all that is needed. Interpret what is important to the site and what the visitor can see while standing in front of the sign. If there are multiple signs, connect them with a common content theme and design.

If you provide more information than just a label, use pictures to illustrate your point and include a theme-based title or large heading. Odd numbers of things are pleasing to the eye, so think about having three columns rather than two, or five pictures rather than four. Also note that many of the tips for brochures below also apply to designing signs.

Brochures

Just as with other interpretive forms, a brochure should have a target audience and an objective or theme. A tri-fold brochure (Figure 12), constructed by folding an 8 1/2" x 11" sheet of paper twice to create three panels on each side, is a handy format that can fit in a standard business envelope. Use each panel to provide a different part of your message:

FRONT PANEL The front cover should catch the reader's attention, be visually appealing and provide enough content to invite the reader to pick up the piece, open it, and read more.

BACK PANEL In most cases, the back panel should be limited to credits, contact information, and perhaps a testimonial. This is the panel people are least likely to read, so avoid putting important messages here.

INSIDE FRONT PANEL This is an important panel because it will be seen immediately when the brochure is opened. Use it to provide a summary of your message. Brochure designers recommend you design this panel last. Writing the rest of the inside spread first will give you a better idea of what you want to say here.

INSIDE THREE-PANEL SPREAD Use these three panels to develop your theme and accomplish your educational objective.

Make sure the brochure is visually appealing and inviting to read. Use the rule of thirds when laying out your brochure. Divide the page into thirds both vertically and horizontally. Imagine where lines cross, these are great places for important visual elements such as a headline or image. Avoid clutter. Use space to create an open look and develop your message so it is clear and concise. Use only high-quality photographs or images (at least 300 dots per inch), and include permissions and credits for borrowed material and logos. For example, Minnesota Master Naturalist Volunteers developing final projects should use the official Minnesota Master Naturalist Program logo provided at the program website and give proper credit to any source of information or images.

Regardless of how attractive your brochure or sign is, it will only be as good as the information it provides. Ensure that information is factual, at the appropriate reading level for the audience, and understandable. Avoid technical jargon and other forms of communication that alienate readers or obscure your message. Finally, avoid being longwinded. Short, sweet, and to the point is a good rule to follow.

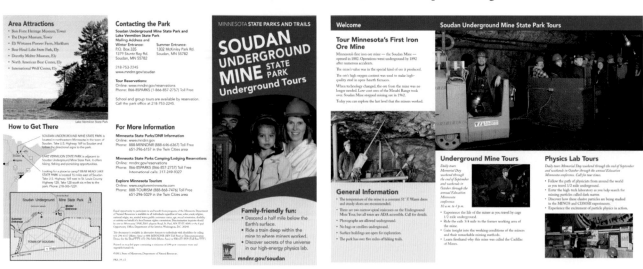

Figure 12. A tri-fold brochure includes a front panel, inside front panel, back (center panel) and an inside three-panel spread.

What's In Your Backpack?

On the Trail with Interpretive Props

Every field interpreter should put together an "interpretive backpack" (Figure 13) composed of safety equipment and teaching props to have on hand. These will become your essentials, whether they help you respond to an emergency or help the visitor understand and appreciate the central message of your presentation. Use the following list as an idea generator for your own interpretive backpack. What goes in your pack will depend on you, your audience, and your location. You'll also want to consider the season, the size of your group, and your own area of expertise.

Figure 13. Naturalists can capitalize on the moment by having a well-prepared interpretive backpack full of props and safety equipment.

☐ **First aid kit** — Having items to help with scrapes, stings, and other injuries is extremely valuable. If you carry nothing else, carry a first aid kit and know how to use what's in it.

☐ **Water bottle** — Water comes in handy to quench someone's thirst or wash away soil to show interesting striations on a rock.

☐ **Snack** — A quick pick-me-up on a long hike is usually a welcome surprise. Because of allergies, it's good to avoid peanuts.

☐ **Watch** — A watch is handy to keep track of time and clock velocity of streams.

☐ **Sunscreen and bug repellent** — Bring along items that will help protect you and others.

☐ **Cell phone or two-way radio** — These items can help you communicate with others in case of emergency.

☐ **Magnifying glass** — Magnifying glasses of any power can enhance the visual senses.

☐ **Pocketknife** — A pocketknife is a "must-have" item for many naturalists for opening seeds, looking for fly larvae in goldenrod galls, or cutting rope. Just be sure to not have it in your carry-on if you're flying to your interpretive event!

☐ **Field guides and local keys** — Depending on where you are and the theme of your presentation, field guides to birds, mammals, insects, reptiles, amphibians, animal tracks and signs, wildflowers, rocks and minerals, weather, and more are all useful tools. The Golden Guide series books are small, lightweight, inexpensive, and interpretive.

☐ **Smartphone applications** — Many smartphone applications are available to enhance your interpretation. Some identify trees by their leaves, show constellations and planets in the night sky, play bird songs, or even act as a flashlight.

☐ **Binoculars** — Great for viewing not only birds but also a distant geological feature, a dragonfly on a water lily, or a star.

Electronic Products

Technology is changing all the time! Electronic communication products can often help get your message across. They include phone and tablet applications, magnification tools, measuring devices, trail or nest cameras, interactive screens in nature centers, and more. Who knows what else the future will bring? All require a variety of skills to use appropriately and effectively. If you choose to use one or more to communicate your message, make sure you have done your homework and get help as needed from those who are familiar with these tools.

Electronics can be a great hook to pull people into exploring nature, but be careful not to let it get distracting. "Oooh, is THAT the new (fill in the blank) phone?" might be the comments you hear from participants instead of the "Wow" that could have come from nature discovery. Keep in mind that the Kaiser Family Foundation reported that today's kids ages 8–18 spend an average of between 8 and 12 hours per day in front of some kind of electronic media. In contrast, The National Wildlife Federation reports that kids spend less than five minutes per day outdoors engaging in unstructured play. When communicating with kids, recognize that most of the younger generation sees the world through a technology lens and doesn't spend much time outdoors. The good news is that many of the things you show them outdoors will be novel and exciting for them!

Learning by Doing

Combining interpretation with service projects that benefit the environment such as collecting native seeds, planting a rain garden, or picking up litter can help participants learn, build skills, have positive hands-on experiences, and gain the satisfaction of making a difference, thereby fostering stewardship. Service projects can be done with all ages as long as the task is developmentally appropriate. Be sure to choose projects that meet real environmental needs and use the ADDIE model to develop the interpretation portion. When the project is complete, reflect on the experience with the group. Record observations, how the project could be improved next time, what worked well, and next steps. Then put on your party hats and celebrate the difference you made for the environment.

Go Forth and Interpret!

You now have a basic understanding of a variety of ways to do successful interpretation. Like anything, it takes practice. Remember to have fun with, learn from, and enjoy the people you come in contact with through your Minnesota Master Naturalist Volunteer experiences.

Explore

This section highlights locations of great examples of interpretation and environmental education. Please check them out online, then head out to discover them in real life!

Your Local State Park's Interpretive Displays

WHAT All Minnesota state parks interpret their site for visitors to some degree. You may know of the Mary Gibbs Mississippi Headwaters Center in Itasca State Park, but did you know that Moose Lake State Park, just minutes off of Interstate Highway 35, has the Agate and Geological Interpretive Center? There are 67 interpretive jewels out there just waiting to be discovered!

WHEN Minnesota state parks are open year round.

WHERE State parks are located throughout Minnesota.

WHO Division of Parks and Trails, Minnesota Department of Natural Resources, 500 Lafayette Road, St. Paul, MN 55155, (651) 296-6157 or (888) MINNDNR

FOR MORE INFORMATION www.mndnr.gov/state_parks

Bell Museum – Minneapolis and St. Paul, Minnesota

WHAT The James Ford Bell Museum of Natural History was established in 1872 to collect, preserve, prepare, display, and interpret our state's animal and plant life for scholarly research, teaching, and public appreciation, enrichment, and enjoyment. The Bell is home to many dioramas that depict Minnesota's biomes, a touch-and-see room, and traveling exhibits that change regularly.

WHEN Check the Bell Museum website for current hours of operation.

WHERE At the time of this writing the Bell Museum is at the corner of University Avenue and Church Street S.E. in Minneapolis. A new building with a planetarium is expected to open in 2018 at the corner of Larpenteur and Cleveland Avenues in Falcon Heights.

WHO The Bell Museum of Natural History, University of Minnesota, 10 Church Street S.E., Minneapolis, MN 55455, (612) 624-7083.

FOR MORE INFORMATION www.bellmuseum.umn.edu.

Hawk Ridge Nature Reserve – Duluth, Minnesota

WHAT A unique area atop a bluff overlooking Lake Superior, Hawk Ridge is a great place to watch migrating hawks in the fall. Open to the public and owned by the city of Duluth, the 365-acre reserve is managed by a nonprofit organization.

WHEN Fall migration begins mid-August through November, with best viewing between 10 a.m. and 2 p.m. when winds are from the west or northwest. Naturalists are available September 1 through October.

WHERE Hawk Ridge is at approximately 3980 E. Skyline Parkway in Duluth on a gravel road. Parking is along the edge of the gravel road.

WHO Hawk Ridge Bird Observatory, P.O. Box 3006, Duluth, MN 55803-3006, (218) 428-6209.

FOR MORE INFORMATION www.hawkridge.org.

MASTER
NATURALIST
TOOLBOX

Teach

This section features lesson plans and pointers for improving your skills in interpretation (or other means of communication). You may experience some of these activities as a student in your Master Naturalist class. The lessons are adaptable to a wide range of audiences, ages, and settings. Feel free to use them to teach others what you have learned!

LESSON 1

What's It All About?

Objective

Participants will develop a well-crafted theme for an interpretive project.

Audience type

Teen/Adult

Supplies

☐ Paper
☐ Pencil/pen/markers

Background

This activity deals with the concept of theme — the one particular idea you want to plant in the minds of the audience for your interpretive presentation. Themes are basically the story you want to tell. They have a beginning, a middle, and an end. The theme for this activity is that themes are the first step in making any interpretation memorable and effective.

What is a Theme?

Most people are a little vague on the definition of a theme and use it in different ways in everyday conversation. Here, we will be very specific in its use, and we hope to convince you to be specific in its use as well.

The most common source of misunderstanding is the difference between a topic and a theme. A topic is the general subject of your interpretive event — for example, birds, water, logging, or the water cycle. You'll notice that all of these can be the subject material of a message but are not the intent of the communication. So what about birds? So what about water? So what about logging?

Themes, on the other hand, are the message in your communication. They answer the "So what?" of the message. You might select the topic of "pine forest" for your event, but then you would need to focus on what you want your visitors to know about the pine forest — that is, your theme. Some examples of potential themes for a pine forest–oriented interpretive presentation might be:

- Minnesota's pine forests helped build large cities like Chicago.
- The pine forests of Minnesota are disappearing.
- There is a lot of activity in the pine forest at night.
- A variety of resources and products come from the pine forest.
- Many animals need the pine forest for survival.
- Pine forests have been used by native cultures for many centuries.

Why Bother?

Themes make life simpler by organizing your interpretive product and creating more effective communication. They focus your effort when you're developing your presentation. Once you have a designated theme, you can judge whether specific activities, visits, signs, or sections fit into the presentation or if they are out in left field and should not be included.

Themes increase the chance participants will remember your message by providing a framework on which they can hang the information you present. Themes also make the interpretation interesting. Finally, participants will remember themes even if they forget the specific details you offer them.

Activity

Use the following steps to identify a theme for a future interpretive product.

1. Brainstorm a bazillion topics.
    Write down any topic idea that comes into your head. Ask others for suggestions.
    Some ideas will be silly (flannel), some will be too serious or complex (forest carbon sequestration), but some will have a core of an idea that will develop into your theme.

2. Pick one topic and add the details.
    Next, take a likely topic from your brainstorm and flesh out the details. Birds may be interesting and you may have a lot of birds at your interpretive site, but what do you want people to know about birds? Do you want people to know about their evolution, that they migrate, that red-tailed hawks eat still-squirming squirrels? Fleshing out the main points of your message will help you determine the theme.

3. Complete the sentence:
    "At the end of the day, I want the participants to know_____."
    This will help you focus your content and end up with a theme.

4. Make sure your theme passes "quality control." It should:
    - be a short, complete sentence
    - contain only one idea
    - reveal the overall point of the interpretive activity or product
    - be specific
    - be catchy.

MASTER
NATURALIST
TOOLBOX

Ask yourself, "Does my theme tell an important story that will enrich the participants' experience?" For example, if you are showcasing a particular natural area you may want to emphasize why the site has been preserved and its ecological or historical interest. Also ask yourself if the theme will be interesting to the audience. Finally, ask if you have the interest and resources to develop the theme.

Extension

Incorporate the theme throughout your interpretive event or product.

1. Include the theme in the name of and promotion for your interpretive event or product. "Water Days" may express the topic of a conservation field day, but also mention what you want your participants to know about water at the end of the day.

2. Introduce the theme at the opening of a presentation or product such as a brochure or leaflet. Let participants know the theme at the outset, have all of your activities reinforce the theme, and end the day on the theme.

3. Be sure all aspects of your interpretive product (events, exhibits, activities, stops on a walk, major points of a talk, etc.) support the theme.

    Every station, activity, statement, and event should add depth and texture to your theme. They should flesh out the ideas initiated in the theme so participants can add more to their knowledge. For example, if your theme is "Raptors are predators of the sky," you might have parts on feeding adaptations, hunting styles, flying, and raptor identification. Throwing in a demonstration on candle-dipping would be distracting and not further your message.

4. Each major activity has its own theme that builds on and supports the overall theme. You can even develop a subtheme for a specific activity that supports the overall theme.

5. Have five or fewer supports for your theme. While each event, major support, or activity should have its own message and reinforce the overall theme, don't overwhelm the audience. People can only remember a few major points. (How many times have you successfully exited the grocery store with all six things that were on your mental shopping list?)

6. Return to the theme in your closing, end, conclusion, or finale. Remind participants how the activities or supports endorsed the theme, and tie the whole presentation into a neat package they can easily take home with them. As the saying goes, "Tell them what you are going to tell them. Tell them. Tell them what you told them." People need reinforcement. Don't be shy about giving it to them.

Resources

Meyer, N. J., Blair, R. B., Carlson, S. P., Bilotta, J. P., Montgomery, K. L., Ostlie, K. M., Prax, V. J., & Rager, A. R. B. (2005). *Best practices for field days: A program planning guidebook for organizers, presenters, teachers and volunteers.* St. Paul: University of Minnesota Extension Service.

MASTER
NATURALIST
TOOLBOX

LESSON 2

iNaturalist – A Digital Resource

Objective

Participants will learn how to use iNaturalist.

Audience Type

Teen/Adult

Supplies

- ☐ Smartphone or tablet
- ☐ Digital camera
- ☐ Computer
- ☐ iNaturalist application

Background

Technology is becoming an increasingly useful tool in the field of interpretation. iNaturalist is an online social network of professional and nonprofessional nature enthusiasts together identifying, mapping, and sharing plant and animal observations from across the world.

Originally created by students at the University of California, Berkeley, iNaturalist utilizes the Catalog of Life, a global index of 1.5 million species, as well as other resources to help participants identify and record species. The goal of iNaturalist is to help build awareness of local biodiversity and encourage exploration of local environments. A perfect fit for a Minnesota Master Naturalist Volunteer!

Besides recording observations, both written and photographic, participants can create their own identification "guides" for their areas and record species for a specific event like a BioBlitz or for an individual park or natural area. Don't know a plant or animal? iNaturalist contributors can help identify it for you. Bring iNaturalist on an interpretive hike and have visitors help enter species or pull up species to share with them, or use it during a presentation to visually show what plants and animals can be found in your area.

Activity

1. Sign-up for an iNaturalist account by visiting www.inaturalist.org. Learn how by watching the "Creating and Account & Changing Account Settings" video at www.inaturalist.org/pages/video+tutorials.

2. Once you have created an account, download the iNaturalist application to your smartphone or tablet.

3. Visit the Getting Started page at www.inaturalist.org/pages/getting+started to learn what an observation is. You will also learn about adding photographs and creating your own species lists.

4. View the "Adding and Observation" video at www.inaturalist.org/pages/video+tutorials to learn how to use your computer to add an observation to the iNaturalist site.

5. Browse other pages on the iNaturalist website for more information on how to use this great resource. You are now ready to start exploring.

6. Bring your camera to a local park, natural area, or even your own backyard and take photos to upload later. Or practice using the iNaturalist app with your smartphone camera. The more you use iNaturalist, the easier it gets. Soon you will have an entire collection of species that you discovered at your fingertips.

MASTER NATURALIST TOOLBOX

Conserve

This section highlights organizations that offer opportunities for Minnesota Master Naturalist Volunteers to participate in activities related to interpreting the natural history of Minnesota's North Woods, Great Lakes region.

Project Learning Tree

Project Learning Tree (PLT) is an international award-winning environmental education program. It uses the forest as a "window on the world" to increase students' understanding and stewardship of our complex environment. PLT teaches not only about trees, but also about land, air, and water. PLT of Minnesota offers workshops to anyone interested in environmental education.

www.mndnr.gov/plt

Project WET

Project WET (Water Education for Teachers) is an international, interdisciplinary water science and education program for formal and nonformal educators of K–12 students.

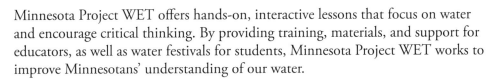

Minnesota Project WET offers hands-on, interactive lessons that focus on water and encourage critical thinking. By providing training, materials, and support for educators, as well as water festivals for students, Minnesota Project WET works to improve Minnesotans' understanding of our water.

www.mndnr.gov/projectwet

Project WILD

Project WILD is one of the most widely used wildlife-focused conservation education programs for formal and nonformal educators of K–12 students. The Project WILD and Aquatic WILD guides contains fun, hands-on lessons that build an understanding of our natural world. You can get the guides by participating in workshops throughout Minnesota.

www.mndnr.gov/projectwild

Expand

This section suggests some things you can use, do, pursue, read, or join to develop as a naturalist.

Journal

EXPERIENCE Make a picture frame with your hands, and hold it up in front of you to frame "pictures" of what you see around you. When you have an image you like, close your eyes and commit the image to memory. Zoom in and out to make all sorts of pictures. Use a real camera to take lots of pictures, if possible, and add the prints to your journal.

REFLECT Think about various natural places that have held special meaning for you throughout your life. What emotions do memories of these places evoke? Years from now, what will you remember about these special spots?

RECORD Using bullet points, make notes about the various special places you've seen in your life — natural places that have influenced you in significant ways. What sensory experiences do you recall about these places? What do these places have in common? Write or draw a few details about this special spot that you want to commit to memory.

Read

Interpretation: Making a Difference on Purpose

Sam H. Ham.
2012. Golden, CO: Fulcrum Publishing. 290 pp.

This book is the long-awaited update to Ham's classic *Environmental Interpretation: A Practical Guide for People With Big Ideas and Small Budgets.* It draws upon recent advances in communication research to lead interpreters to new and insightful pathways for making a difference through their work.

The Interpreter's Guidebook: Techniques for Programs and Presentations

J. Buccholz, B. Lackey, M. Gross, and R. Zimmerman.
2015. Stevens Point, WI: UWSP Foundation Press, Inc. 225 pp.

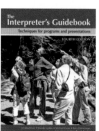

Newly updated, this succinct book is great for all sorts of interpretive programs and presentations — walks, talks, and even puppet shows! It is part of a series written by the faculty at the University of Wisconsin–Stevens Point Schmeeckle Reserve. All of the books in the series are very useful. Find out more at www.interphandbooks.org.

Surf

SEEK – Minnesota's Home of Environmental Education Resources

This website is the portal to environmental education in Minnesota. Use it to find facilities, information, and even advanced training sessions!

www.seek.state.mn.us

National Park Service's Interpretive Development Program

The National Park Service's Interpretive Development Program website is designed to aid all interpreters, no matter who they work for or where they are in their careers, with ongoing professional growth and development. The profession of interpretation is continuously evolving, and this site will help you keep track of the trends and developments in interpretation. Visit it now!

http://idp.eppley.org

Join

The North American Association for Environmental Education

The North American Association for Environmental Education (NAAEE) is an international professional organization for environmental, conservation, and outdoor educators and practitioners. NAAEE supports its members by advocating for the field, facilitating professional development and networking opportunities, providing tools that facilitate communication, and developing quality materials through its "Guidelines for Excellence" series.

www.naaee.net

The National Association for Interpretation

The National Association for Interpretation (NAI) is a nonprofit professional association for interpreters of natural and cultural heritage resources. For more than 50 years, NAI and its parent organizations have encouraged networking, training, and collaboration among members and partners to advance heritage interpretation as a profession. NAI serves 5,000 members in the U.S., Canada, and 30 other countries.

www.interpnet.com

Additional Reading

Tilden, F. (1977). *Interpreting our heritage.* Chapel Hill, NC: University of North Carolina Press.

Trapp, S., Gross, M., and Zimmerman, R. (1994). *Signs, trails, and wayside exhibits.* Stevens Point, WI: UW-SP Foundation Press, Inc.

MASTER
NATURALIST
TOOLBOX

Copyrighted Photographs and Images Used With Permission

Figure 1. Courtesy of Wikimedia Commons

Figure 2. Courtesy of National Park Service

Figure 3. Courtesy of John Loegering, University of Minnesota Extension (Ham photo), University of Wisconsin – Stevens Point (Zimmerman and Gross photos)

Figure 4. Courtesy of Dawn A. Flinn

Figure 5. Courtesy of Dawn A. Flinn

Figure 6. Courtesy of Shawn C. Flinn

Figure 7. Courtesy of Dawn A. Flinn, Minnesota Department of Natural Resources

Figure 8. Courtesy of Dawn A. Flinn, Minnesota Department of Natural Resources

Figure 9. Courtesy of Minnesota Department of Natural Resources

Figure 10. Courtesy of Dawn A. Flinn, Minnesota Department of Natural Resources

Figure 11. Courtesy of Rob Blair, University of Minnesota

Figure 12. Courtesy of Minnesota Department of Natural Resources

Figure 13. Courtesy of Dawn A. Flinn, Minnesota Department of Natural Resources

MASTER
NATURALIST
TOOLBOX

Expand

Chapter 6: Cold, Soggy, and Wet

Bogs and Inland Lakes

Tommy Rodengen and Robert B. Blair

Goal

Understand how physical, chemical, and biological processes combine to create unique ecosystems in bogs and lakes.

Objectives

1. Describe how lakes and bogs form.

2. Explain lake and bog variability through physical, chemical, and biological processes.

3. Relate management practices in lakes and bogs to threats.

4. List at least three unique life forms in lakes and bogs.

Introduction

The interconnected lakes of the North Woods, Great Lakes region were the highways of early *voyageurs* who traded fur amid an area teeming with life and natural splendor. The early voyageurs' heritage is captured in the names of the lakes and canoe routes we still travel on today in Voyageurs National Park and the BWCAW. Often referred to as "Canoe Country," the North Woods, Great Lakes region evokes visions of hills, tall forests of fir and pine, the cry of the loon, the howl of the gray wolf, campfires, cabins, solitude, and, most of all, the lakes.

"My paddle's keen and bright
Flashing with silver
Follow the wild goose flight
Dip, dip, and swing"

— Traditional voyageur folk song sung in a round by passing canoeists in Minnesota's North Woods, Great Lakes region

Lakes (and their landlubber cousins, bogs) are central not only to our image of the north woods, but to the ecosystem itself. And it's not a role we can take for granted. Even though the lakes of this region seem to be relatively pristine, unharmed by human activity, several decades of research have demonstrated that this once-untrammeled ecosystem has been drastically altered by humans. The best known of these impacts are mercury contamination from air pollution, introduction of invasive species, and climate change. But lakes and bogs face other threats as well as humans altering the physical, chemical, and biological processes that make them what they are. Learning about these ecosystems will allow us to more effectively restore damaged ecosystem functions and better manage lakes and bogs in the future.

What Makes Lakes and Bogs?

The precipitation that falls in the North Woods, Great Lakes region travels through wetlands, rivers, and lakes, eventually ending up in the Atlantic Ocean, Arctic Ocean, and Gulf of Mexico. The area that drains into a water body is known as its *watershed*. The waters of the Arctic watershed flow north through the Rainy River, Lake of Woods, and Lake Winnipeg, and finally drain east from the Nelson River into Hudson Bay. The Atlantic watershed drains from Lake Superior to the east through the St. Lawrence River to the Atlantic Ocean. The waters of the Mississippi watershed, which start at the headwaters of the Mississippi River in Itasca State Park, find their drainage course south to the Gulf of Mexico. The city of Hibbing claims that water that falls there could naturally flow into any one of the three watersheds. The juxtaposition of these three watersheds in this region has earned it the title "ridgepole of the continent" (Figure 1).

WATERSHEDS OF THE
NORTH WOODS GREAT LAKES BIOME

Figure 1. Three major watersheds meet in the North Woods, Great Lakes region: the Arctic, the Atlantic, and the Mississippi.

PROGLACIAL LAKES OF THE
NORTH WOODS GREAT LAKES BIOME

Figure 2. Poorly drained deposits left behind by North Woods, Great Lakes proglacial lakes provided ideal conditions for the formation of bogs.

Remember the glacial earth-movers we met in Chapter 1, and the hydrologic cycle we talked about in Chapter 4? Well, here's where they come together. Water collects in low-lying areas of the landscape to form lakes. And most of the low-lying areas in the North Woods, Great Lakes region owe their shape to glacial action. (An exception is the lakes within the Rove Formation in the far northeastern portion of the region, which formed in northeast/southwest valleys cut deep by preglacial erosion.) Some upland area waters drain down from one lake to another, creating a chain of lakes interconnected by small streams.

The most recent glacier also left several shallow, low-lying areas suitable for the initial formation of bogs in the poorly drained deposits of proglacial lakes Agassiz, Upham, and Aikin (Figure 2).

Lakes and bogs form in various ways and various settings. That means each has its own unique set of physical, chemical, and biological characteristics that give it a "personality" all its own.

Bogs are poorly drained wetlands for which precipitation is the main water source. Peat — a rich, spongy organic soil — forms in bogs when the rate

of accumulation of sphagnum moss (which we met in Chapter 2) and other plant and animal matter exceeds the rate of decay in cold, soggy environments. In the North Woods, Great Lakes region, peat can accumulate to form a bog in two ways: *terrestrialization* and *paludification* (Figure 3).

The main physical processes influencing bog development are climate and hydrology. To accumulate peat, a bog must produce peat faster than peat decomposes. In the North Woods, Great Lake region, low temperatures limit decomposition, so peat tends to accumulate. Another critical process in the accumulation of peat is keeping the uppermost layer of undecomposed peat waterlogged. The uppermost layer of peat is generally composed of sphagnum. Below this layer are the decomposing layers of sphagnum mixed with bits of sedges, wood, and other organic material all packed together like ingredients in a granola bar. As a bog builds on itself, the sphagnum will no longer be able to contact the groundwater and will rely on rain and snow for its freshwater source.

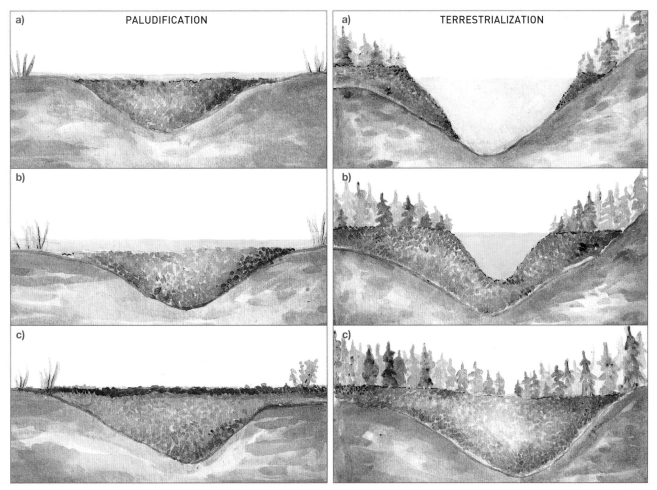

Figure 3. Bogs can form through paludification or terrestrialization. In paludification (left), the top layer of peat (a) is undersaturated with water. Watershed drainage changes and saturates top layer of peat (b), then peat accumulation (c) forms bog. In terrestrialization (right). a small pond or lake begins to be filled with sediments (a). Buildup of sediment provides structure for peat to accumulate (b), then peat accumulation forms the bog (c).

Physics: Setting the Stage

Three main physical processes help make each lake what it is: light penetration, *stratification*, and turnover. Together, these physical processes set the stage for chemical and biological processes that also contribute to the lake's overall characteristics.

How far light can penetrate beneath the surface of a lake depends on what is in the water. Scientists use a tool called a *secchi disk* (Figure 4) to estimate the depth to which light can penetrate. The deeper the light, the deeper photosynthesis can occur. For this reason, changes in light penetration affect biological and chemical processes. Light heats lake water, so deeper light penetration also means more heat.

Heat, in turn, has a fascinating effect on lakes. Density of liquids changes with temperature, with most liquids becoming denser as temperature drops until they finally turn into solids. Water, however, reaches its greatest density at 39 °F, when it is still liquid. That's why ice floats instead of sinking to the bottom of a lake.

Figure 4. A budding scientist helps measure light penetration in a lake using a secchi disk.

The change in density that occurs when water temperature changes leads to seasonal stratification of a lake. After ice melts in the spring (known as "ice out"), the air warms the surface water of a lake to 39 °F—its densest state. This dense water then sinks to the bottom, a phenomenon known as *spring turnover*. This event evenly mixes all the water in the lake. It is especially important for the creatures on the bottom because the surface water carries oxygen with it to the oxygen-deprived depths, making them more hospitable to life.

Spring turnover eventually leads into summer stratification (Figure 5). As the surface water continues to warm, the top layer becomes less dense than the bottom. The lake then stratifies—forms layers. The warmest, most oxygen-rich water forms the top layer, known as the *epilimnion*. Colder water, rich with nutrients released by decomposing matter on the lake bottom, forms the *hypolimnion* layer at the bottom. A transitional *metalimnion* layer forms between the two. Because each species has its own temperature and oxygen preferences, stratification affects where various creatures are found in a lake.

The reverse of spring turnover happens in the fall as the surface waters cool. When the temperature of the top layer drops to 39 °F, that water sinks to the bottom, breaking up the summer stratification. This remixing oxygenates the entire water column, bringing nutrients from the bottom of the lake to the surface and in some cases triggering a fall algal bloom. After the fall mixing, the lake usually does not restratify for the winter. Instead it settles into a pattern where the water temperature gradually drops from a relatively toasty 39 °F at the bottom of the lake to a cool 32 °F below the ice near the surface.

Not all lakes stratify twice per year. Shallow lakes may be mixed all summer by winds that churn the surface, while the bottom of deep lakes may never quite get reached by the spring turnover. In general, lakes greater than 20 feet deep tend to stratify—though this rule may be broken if the lake is very large, very small, or very deep. For example, in a typical year, Pike Lake in St. Louis County, with a maximum depth of 59 feet and 500 acres of surface area, turns over twice. On the other hand, Miner's Pit Lake near Ely (160 feet deep and 138 acres in surface area)

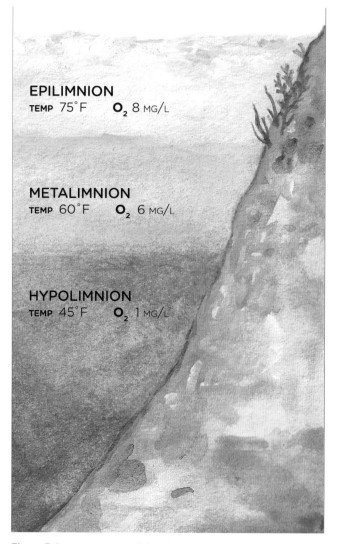

Figure 5. In summer many lakes form three layers with distinct temperatures and available oxygen levels.

EPILIMNION
TEMP 75°F O_2 8 MG/L

METALIMNION
TEMP 60°F O_2 6 MG/L

HYPOLIMNION
TEMP 45°F O_2 1 MG/L

doesn't turnover at all, huge Mille Lacs Lake (43 feet deep and 128,233 acres in surface area) turns over many times, and vast Lake Superior (1,332 feet deep and 31,700 square miles in surface area) turns over twice per year.

Chemistry: Shaping Life

The most important chemical components of lakes and bogs (besides good old H_2O, of course) are phosphorus, nitrogen, oxygen, and hydrogen, largely because of their roles in biological processes.

Phosphorus and nitrogen are limiting nutrients in lake and bog waters: Plants need these elements to grow, and how much nitrogen and phosphorus are found in the water determines the amount of plant

Why Are Lakes Blue?

Lakes appear blue for a couple of reasons. The simplest is that the surface of the water can reflect the color of the sky. Thus, on gray and cloudy days, lakes may not appear as blue as they do on clear days.

Another reason is that when sunlight (white light that contains all colors) hits the water's surface, some light is reflected back, but most of it penetrates the water and interacts with water molecules and whatever is suspended in the water. The longer light waves — those we see as red, orange, and yellow — are more easily absorbed than shorter light waves — those we see as blue and violet — so the light we see reflected is disproportionately blue. Particles such as algae or sediment suspended in the water scatter light and bounce the blue wavelengths back to the surface, strengthening the blue appearance.

growth that can take place. Phosphorus and nitrogen mainly enter a lake when water washes nutrient-rich fallen leaves, other plant parts, or nutrients leached from these materials into a lake — although some enter from the atmosphere as well. When humans enter the picture, often excess nutrients do as well — introduced into the lake from sources such as agricultural runoff, polluted groundwater, inadequate wastewater treatment, and failing septic systems. If these limiting nutrients are supplied to lake waters in excess, phytoplankton — tiny plants that make up the base of the lake's food web — grow unchecked.

Which brings us to number three on the Top Four List of Important Chemicals in lakes and bogs: oxygen. Excessive phytoplankton growth leads to excessive algae death and decomposition, which then leads to a lack of oxygen in the water. And lack of

oxygen, as you know from any time you've tried to hold your breath for more than a minute, is not a good thing for other organisms. In other words, the amount of oxygen in lake water affects what life forms it can support.

The amount of oxygen in the water depends not only on the amount of dead algae, but also on the water temperature and the amount of photosynthesis (related, of course, to the amount of *live* algae). All things being equal, cold water contains more oxygen than warm water. But in a real live lake, all things really aren't equal. As we learned in Chapter 4, more light means more photosynthesis, and more photosynthesis means more oxygen produced. Because light filters into a lake from the surface, there is more oxygen in the epilimnion and less in the hypolimnion.

In fact, the hypolimnion can become entirely devoid of oxygen if cut off from the epilimnion in a condition known as *anoxia*. In North Woods, Great Lakes winters, most (if not all) lakes completely freeze over and heavy snow cover can block the sunlight necessary for photosynthesis, while dying organisms near the bottom of the lake continue to decompose and use the remaining oxygen. This condition can cause high mortality rates in aquatic organisms, which anglers commonly refer to as "winter kill."

The fourth chemical on our Top Four list, hydrogen, is mainly a factor in bogs. Because a mature bog receives most of its water from precipitation, its chemistry is more closely tied to the atmosphere. When sphagnum takes up nutrients from the air, it releases positively charged hydrogen ions. This creates a low pH, or acidic, environment. And that environment supports some very unusual organisms!

Biology: Watery Web

You already know that people with a lot of money are considered rich and those with little money are considered poor. Lakes and bogs can be rich or poor, too — only the currency in their case is not money but the stuff it takes to grow plants. A rich lake — one that has the right stuff to grow lots of plants — is called *eutrophic*. A poor lake is called *oligotrophic*. And an in-between lake is called *mesotrophic* (Figure 6). The typical measures of a lake's wealth (aka trophic

OLIGOTROPHIC

» Low Productivity
» Clear

» Large Population of Predatory Game Fish

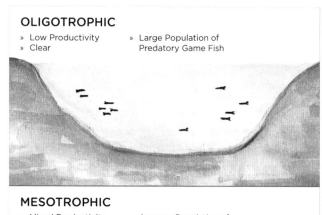

MESOTROPHIC

» Mixed Productivity
» Occasional Algal Bloom

» Average Population of Predatory Game Fish

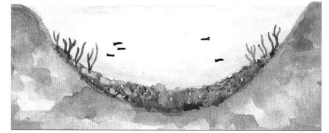

EUTROPHIC

» High Productivity
» Turbid

» Low Population of Predatory Game Fish

Figure 6. The ability of a lake to support plant life is called its trophic status. Oligotrophic lakes support relatively little plant life, while mesotrophic and eutrophic lakes support progressively more.

status) are phosphorus, water clarity, and chlorophyll (Figure 7). Due to a combination of physical and chemical properties, most lakes in the North Woods, Great Lakes region are oligotrophic or mesotrophic.

Remember that food web we met in Chapter 4? It's alive and well in the watery world just as on land. Producers, such as phytoplankton, make up the base of the lake food web. Phytoplankton live a boom-and-bust cycle: Lakes experience phytoplankton "blooms" in early spring as they turn over as well as in mid to late summer if they get excess nutrients from leaky septic systems or fertilizer runoff. Most phytoplankton

are algae. Different species of phytoplankton flourish under different conditions. Over the course of a season, as the temperature, nutrient level, and other traits of a lake change, the mix of phytoplankton changes, too (Figure 8). The presence of lots of phytoplankton is the mark of a eutrophic lake.

The primary consumers in lakes are zooplankton—microscopic organisms that feed on phytoplankton. Zooplankton undergo seasonal population fluctuations that follow the seasonal phytoplankton blooms. Other primary consumers also follow the cycle of life in a lake: For example, *benthic* organisms, which feed off bits of organic material that sink to the bottom of the lake (the *benthos*), thrive during periodic blooms.

Secondary and tertiary consumers, such as fish, prey on other organisms in the lake food web. Different fish thrive with different levels of nutrients, oxygen, and light in different lakes. Trout, for example, favor oligotrophic lakes, while northern pike and largemouth bass thrive in nutrient-rich waters.

Spotlight Species - Diatoms

When you think of life in a lake, you might think of fish or frogs or duckweed. But take a closer look, and an entire universe of life unfolds at the can't-quite-see level. Among the most fascinating of the microscopic organisms you'll find are diatoms (Figure 9).

Found in lakes, streams, ponds and other wet places—even in the feathers of diving birds and on damp tree bark—diatoms are single-celled or colonial algae that encase themselves in see-through shells made of silica, the same mineral that makes up much of beach sand and glass. Minnesota is home to thousands of species of diatoms. Some have shells (known as *frustules*) that look like flat, round boxes. Others look like miniature sausages or grains of rice. Whatever their shape, frustules are riddled with holes that allow nutrients, gases and waste products to pass through.

One of the fascinating things about diatoms is the way they reproduce. Most of the time they reproduce asexually by splitting the top and bottom of their shell apart and growing a new half inside the existing half—the one original diatom becomes two diatoms. The only problem with this process is that one of the resulting diatoms always ends up smaller than the original! (Think about using a shoebox bottom as the top for a new box, and the size of the box bottom you'd have to find to fit it.) After many generations, one of the new diatoms gets so small that it has to reproduce sexually. During sexual reproduction, an expanding, shell-less stage called an *auxospore* forms that restores the offspring to the maximum size and shape for that species of diatom.

Diatoms may be tiny, but they are far from insignificant. An important part of the aquatic food web, they use sunlight captured with chlorophyll to convert carbon dioxide into sugars. Zooplankton, mussels, and other animals might then eat the diatoms, tapping their energy (sugar) for food. This energy might eventually be transferred to insects, fish, bacteria, people, and other organisms. At a global scale, diatoms capture more carbon from the atmosphere than do rain forests and produce 20 percent of the oxygen we breathe.

Because different diatom species prefer different environmental conditions — pH, amount of nutrients, sediment load, and so on — we can learn a lot about the health of a waterway by examining the diatoms living there. Scientists also use diatoms preserved in lake sediments (which get deposited like layers in a cake through time) to help understand the history of a lake and the effects of human activities and environmental change on Minnesota's freshwaters.

BIOME TROPHIC STATUS MEASURMENTS

	North Woods Great Lakes	Prairies and Potholes	Big Woods Big Rivers
Total Phosphorus (mg/L)	0.014–0.027	0.065–0.150	0.023–0.050
Secchi disk (m)	2.4–4.6	0.5–1.0	1.5–3.2
Chlorophyll a (µg/L)	<10	30–80	5–22

Figure 7. Scientists determine the trophic status of lakes by measuring total phosphorus, light penetration, and chlorophyll a.

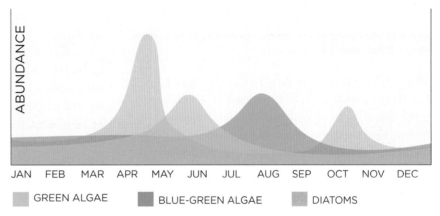

JAN FEB MAR APR MAY JUN JUL AUG SEP OCT NOV DEC

GREEN ALGAE   BLUE-GREEN ALGAE   DIATOMS

Figure 8. Different species of microscopic life flourish as the amount of light and nutrients in a lake changes over the course of a summer. Some blue-green algae, also known as cyanobacteria, produce toxins that can sicken or kill wildlife, pets, and people.

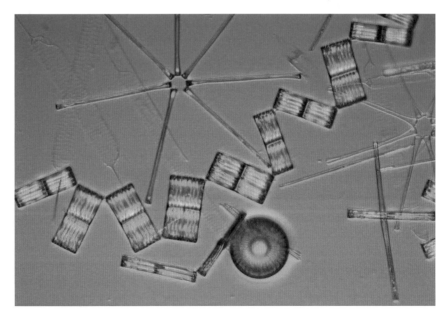

Figure 9. Microscopic algae encased in glasslike boxes, diatoms are found in lakes, rivers, and wetlands throughout Minnesota.

Spotlight Species – Northern pike

If you've ever fished in Minnesota, chances are you've caught a northern pike (Figure 10). This ubiquitous denizen of the deep can thrive in a wide range of temperature and water quality conditions, and is found in nearly every lake and stream in the North Woods, Great Lakes region.

©MN DNR, C. Iverson

Figure 10. Northern pike are common carnivores found in North Woods, Great Lakes waterways.

The northern pike's scientific name, *Esox lucius*—loosely translated as "wolf of the water"—offers a good clue as to what makes it stand out among fish. A voracious predator, it eats mainly fish (including members of its own species), but also occasional ducklings, frogs, and other small animals.

Northern pike are stealth predators. They lurk in vegetation or behind rocks, their muscles tense in preparation, then spring out to snag unsuspecting prey as they swim by. Their sharp, backward-slanted teeth and strong swimming muscles serve them well for this endeavor. Their coloring—olive green to brown on top, white to cream-colored below—is an example of a type of camouflage known as *countershading*, in which an animal is (usually) darker on top and lighter below. Countershading makes it harder for predators and prey to see an animal as a three-dimensional object and in the case of fish, provides a different background-matching color when seen from above and below.

Spotlight Species – Common Loon

If the North Woods, Great Lakes had an official icon, it would probably be the common loon (Figure 11). Minnesota's state bird, this black-and-white charmer is a summertime resident of lakes throughout the region.

Shortly after the ice melts in the spring, it's time to start listening for the call of loons migrating to Minnesota from their wintering grounds in the

Figure 11. The common loon is a beloved icon of the north woods.

southern United States. Many return to the same lake (or at least area) they inhabited the previous year. The males typically arrive first and establish territories. After females arrive, the pairs mate and the females lay one to three eggs. When the chicks hatch about 28 days later, they are already able to swim. Still, they often hitch rides on their parents' backs, which helps keep them warm and protects them from northern pike, eagles, snapping turtles, and other predators.

Loons are a perfect example of adaptation in action. Underwater hunters, they have streamlined bodies, heavy bones, and thick webbed feet located closer to their tail than their bill—all of which help them swim quickly and deftly underwater in pursuit of a fish dinner. They hunt by sight, using their red eyes to spy their prey in Minnesota's sometimes murky or rust-stained waters.

As summer draws to a close, loons shed their bright black-and-white feathers in favor of the more muted gray-and-white plumage they wear in winter. They begin to gather on lakes in preparation for fall migration. The parents leave for the south before the young, which need a little more time to build energy reserves before undertaking the big trip.

Loons are well-known for four common types of calls they make. The tremolo indicates alarm or excitement, and is the call loons make in flight. The wail communicates location information or indicates the presence of a threat or disturbance. The yodel is a territory-marking call. Finally, the birds use a gentle hoot to communicate with young and other loons nearby.

Figure 12. A member of the rhododendron family, Labrador tea grows in bogs and other wetlands.

Figure 13. Small and secretive, the bog lemming is seldom seen in Minnesota.

Spotlight Species – Labrador tea

Hiking through damp North Woods, Great Lakes habitat, you come across a plant that reminds you vaguely of the rhododendrons you see in home landscaping. Introducing Labrador tea — Minnesota's wild version of that familiar plant (Figure 12). The family it belongs to, the heath family (Ericacea), is one of the most common in peatlands.

Growing up to five feet tall, this native evergreen shrub is most at home in the wet, acidic, nutrient-poor soils that characterize northland bogs. In fact, it's often found around black spruce — another plant that doesn't mind wet feet. Labrador tea is easiest to spot in late spring, when it sports bright clusters of white flowers, and in winter, when its leaves are coppery hued and curled under.

Labrador tea reproduces by seed — a single insect-pollinated blossom can produce 50 or more of them. It also can spread by sprouting from underground stems known as *rhizomes*.

Wondering if its moniker means you should brew a beverage from its leaves? Not so fast. Though American Indians made medicines from it and fur traders used it to stretch their supplies of black tea during the long months on trail, it contains harmful chemicals and can cause stomach distress and worse. Unsurprisingly, it's seldom eaten by deer, moose, or other herbivores. Still, it does provide north woods creatures welcome shelter against the elements year round.

Spotlight Species – Bog lemming

The northern bog lemming (Figure 13) is a medium-size rodent found in peatlands, black spruce swamps, and similar wetlands. Or perhaps it would be better to say "not found" — it is only rarely seen in Minnesota, although it is native to the northern part of the state. About five inches long, bog lemmings weigh an ounce or a little more and have short legs, small ears, and a short tail. They travel through trails in the bog vegetation in the summer and in tunnels under snow in the winter, and bear four to eight young, often in underground nests, up to three times per year. Bog lemmings eat grass and sedges and are eaten by weasels, owls, and other raptors.

Figure 14. Bogs may show distinct patterns of interspersed hummocks and hollows, which differ from each other in degree of waterlogging and characteristic vegetation.

As we saw in Chapter 2, bogs come in many flavors, each of which supports its own special mix of plant and animal life. The degree of waterlogging in the top layer of sphagnum controls what plants grow where.

Black spruce and tamarack trees can spring up around the edges of bogs with a little waterlogging, while Labrador tea and leatherleaf can flourish toward the center. In soggier bogs, sedges often take the place of trees. A big bog system may have varying degrees of waterlogging and a corresponding variety of vegetation, creating a unique patterned landscape (Figure 14).

In the patterned bog landscape of Minnesota, some sphagnum grows tightly packed together to form *hummocks*, while some grows loosely matted together to form *hollows* (Figure 15). A number of unusual plants follow suit. The carnivorous pitcher plant, for example, thrives in hollows and lures insects with smelly nectar to the bottom of a pitcher-shaped leaf where the insects cannot escape its downward facing hairs (Figure 16). The carnivorous sundew, which prefers hummocks, secretes a sticky substance near the tips of its leaves to trap insects that fly too close. Why carnivory? The acidic environment of the bog isn't very good at supporting decomposers, so plants need to turn to animals for nutrients they would otherwise find in the soil.

North Woods, Great Lakes region bogs are home to a number of unusual animals as well, including the water shrew, mink frog, and sandhill crane. All told, the bogs harbor more than 300 species of birds, 11 species of small mammals, six species of amphibians, six species of large mammals, and four species of reptiles. For many of these, the bog provides only a seasonal habitat. White-tailed deer, for instance, depend on bogs in the winter for food and shelter, but avoid them in the summer because their pointy legs

Figure 16. Pitcher plants, which thrive in nutrient-poor bogs, use color and nectar to lure insects into a liquid-filled pit formed by a leaf. The insects drown, dissolve, and provide the needed nutrients to the plants.

can become trapped in the loose sphagnum, making them vulnerable to predators such as wolves.

Managing Lakes and Bogs

Fish, swim, snowmobile, ski … people use lakes and bogs in many ways. And when we use them, we change them. That means we need to manage them, too, to make sure they stay healthy.

How an individual lake or bog is managed is determined by what people value most about it, from protecting ecosystem integrity to enhancing recreation. Management practices may include protecting a waterway from pollution, stocking fish, regulating fish harvest, protecting rare species, trying to prevent the introduction of invasive species, and lots more. Let's look at a few case studies of how natural resource managers create plans to protect the integrity of lakes and bogs while also allowing them to meet our needs.

Figure 15. Sphagnum forms hollows and hummocks in patterned bogs.

CASE STUDY 1

VALUE Youth Outdoor Experience

LOCATION Little Boy Lake, Longville, Minnesota

THREAT TO ECOSYSTEM Shoreline Erosion

Camp Olson YMCA in Cass County was founded in 1954 to "preserve a paradise of forest beauty where youth and their leaders will find joy and inspiration for years to come." To date, thousands of campers and staff have experienced the outdoors in this 2,000-acre-plus paradise of forest beauty on the shores of beautiful Little Boy Lake. Campers use the lake for sailing, windsurfing, nature lessons, paddleboarding, kayaking, canoeing, swimming, fishing, and dipping between sauna stints. With so much enjoyment depending on access to the lake, a stable shoreline is essential.

Shoreline erosion occurs at the border between land and lake. This border can become eroded and land can be lost to the lake due to wave action. Causes of shoreline erosion include human activities such as lakeshore development and excessive recreational activity too close to the shore, or natural causes such as ice heaves and windstorms. Stabilization of the land is the most common way to address the threat of shoreline erosion.

The early managers of Camp Olson YMCA recognized the threat of shoreline erosion from recreational activities. In response, they concentrated activities using rock-wall structures to protect the shoreline from excessive erosion (Figure 17). They also worked with the Cass County Soil and Water Conservation District to put 4,160 feet of shoreline on Little Boy Lake into permanent easement — meaning that no commercial or residential development can ever take place on this shoreline. The long-term planning will ensure that this shoreline will be preserved for future generations of campers and staff to enjoy.

CASE STUDY 2

VALUE Economic Development

LOCATION Big Bog State Recreation Area

THREAT TO ECOSYSTEM Peat Mining

When harvested, sphagnum peat decomposes slowly, retains up to 20 times its weight in moisture, and absorbs odors. These qualities make it useful in a variety of applications, most notably horticulture. In Minnesota, peat is most commonly harvested for use as a growing medium supplement for garden soil. The North Woods, Great Lakes region has roughly 7 million acres of peatlands, more than any other state except Alaska. Peat production for horticulture application in Minnesota is a $10-million industry.

To harvest peat, companies drain a bog and allow the top few inches of vegetation to dry before shredding the peat and collecting it in a large vacuum powered by a tractor. Due to the 1991 Minnesota Wetlands Conservation Act, the companies are required to replace or restore the bog when they are done. However, it's impossible to completely restore the original ecosystem functions. Currently, more than 10 peat-mining companies operate in Minnesota on about 3,000 acres of peatland. Balancing economic opportunity with irreversible damage to a fragile

Figure 17. An easement sign and rock wall protect the shoreline around the boathouse at Camp Olson on Little Boy Lake.

ecosystem is a constant challenge in the North Woods, Great Lakes region.

Economic opportunity can be balanced with protection of bogs, however. When Upper Red Lake's walleye population crashed in 1990, many private resorts in the area were forced to close due to lack of tourists. Big Bog State Recreation Area was then established to create a new tourist attraction in the area and protect a 500-square-mile peat bog, the largest in the lower 48 states. The park, which now boasts more than 90,000 visits per year, allows tourists to get an up-close look at the unique flora and fauna on a boardwalk that minimizes ecological impact.

CASE STUDY 3

VALUE Angling

LOCATION Lake of the Woods

THREAT TO ECOSYSTEM Mercury

Most Minnesota lakes contain mercury, a toxic chemical that enters the atmosphere when we burn coal, process taconite, or use mercury-containing paint, then washes into waterways when it rains or snows. Analysis of lake sediments shows that rates at which mercury is deposited into Minnesota lakes have increased threefold since European settlement.

Once in a lake, mercury can be converted into methylmercury. Methylmercury enters the food chain when algae remove it from the water. It passes from one organism to another, becoming more concentrated along the way, until it reaches the largest predators — notably, walleye, northern pike, lake trout, and humans.

Mercury only accumulates in organisms after it has been converted to methylmercury. The more acidic a lake, the faster mercury is converted into methylmercury. That means the low pH waters of the North Woods, Great Lakes region are particularly likely to concentrate mercury up the food chain.

Mercury can cause serious nervous system damage in humans. Of most concern are pregnant women, breastfeeding women, women who may become pregnant in the next several years, and children under age six. The Minnesota Department of Health (MDH) advises these individuals to limit their intake of fish per lake-specific guidelines (Figure 18). You can find the lake-specific consumption guidelines at www.mndnr.gov/lakefind (Figure 19).

Figure 18. According to sample report in Figure 19, this Lake of the Woods angler should limit his consumption of walleye from this lake to one meal per week.

LAKE NAME County, DOWID	Species	General Population				Contaminants
		Meal Advice				
		Unrestricted	1 meal/week	1 meal/month	Do not eat	
LAKE OF THE WOODS Lake of the Woods CO., 39000200	Cisco	All sizes				
	Northern Pike		All Sizes			Mercury
	Sauger		All Sizes			Mercury
	Smallmouth Bass		All Sizes			Mercury
	Walleye		All Sizes			Mercury
	White Sucker	All sizes				
	Yellow Perch	All sizes				

Figure 19. Sample Minnesota Department of Health report. Visit www.health.state.mn.us/divs/eh/fish/index.html for more fish consumption information.

The Minnesota Pollution Control Agency (MPCA) has developed a plan to reduce mercury release from Minnesota sources 76 percent from 2005 levels by 2025. The first step in the plan is to measure existing mercury in watersheds to identify lakes that have mercury concentrations in fish fillets between 0.2 and 0.57 milligrams per kilogram (parts per million). The MPCA will then work with the MDH to understand how mercury gets into and moves through the food chain in different watersheds. The MPCA and MDH will partner with the DNR to reduce mercury in fish and continue to monitor concentrations.

CASE STUDY 4

VALUE Preservation and Enjoyment of Wilderness

LOCATION Boundary Waters Canoe Area Wilderness

THREAT TO ECOSYSTEM Visitor Use

The Boundary Waters Canoe Area Wilderness Act of 1978 created the Boundary Waters Canoe Area Wilderness (BWCAW) to preserve the lakes and forests as wilderness — in the words of the Federal Wilderness Act, "an area where the earth and its community of life are untrammeled by man, where man himself is a visitor who does not remain" — while enhancing public enjoyment (Figure 20).

How can humans both enjoy and preserve something? Even though it's America's most visited wilderness, the BWCAW has done just that using a carefully designed

Figure 20. Fun times in the BWCAW benefit from careful planning on the part of wilderness managers.

visitor distribution system to limit the footprint of visitors.

BWCAW visitor use levels traditionally correlate with negative effects on the ecosystem and other visitors. Negative effects on the ecosystem include disturbance of wildlife, fish, and vegetation; human-started fires; and reduced water quality. Negative effects on other visitors include loss of solitude, noise, poor fishing or hunting, and difficulty viewing wildlife. To reduce these, BWCAW planners decided to limit BWCAW traffic using an entry point quota. Predicted travel behavior of visitors from all available entry points and a target campsite occupancy level of 85 percent per lake determine how many people are allowed to enter from each entry point each day. To mitigate other negative effects, campsites are carefully sited to avoid wildlife hot spots such as eagle nests, minimize erosion at canoe landings, avoid intersite visibility, and have deep enough soil for a pit toilet. Tracking visitor use through surveys, entry point permits, and monitoring of ecological conditions at and around campsites has influenced change in the visitor distribution system. Since its inception, this system has given thousands of visitors the sense of being in the wilderness while mitigating negative environmental impacts. You'll learn even more about the BWCAW in chapter 8.

Conclusion

This chapter explores the various physical, chemical, and biological processes of lakes and bogs in Minnesota's North Woods, Great Lakes region. Interactions among these processes and human influences make each lake or bog unique. Human-induced changes in the natural processes of lakes and bogs and human intervention through management have created a new, human-dominated frontier for modern voyageurs to traverse.

Explore

This section highlights great examples of places to learn about the bogs and lakes of the North Woods. Please check them out online, then head out to discover them in real life!

Savanna Portage State Park – McGregor, Minnesota

WHAT Savanna Portage State Park has many unique habitats for a wide variety of wildlife. You can walk the hiking trails among the oak woods and find bear, deer, skunk, wolf, moose, and coyote. The bogs of the park contain many small animals and birds, such as lemming and certain warblers, which specialize in living there.

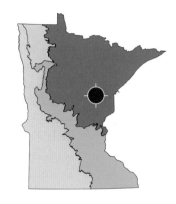

Savanna Portage contains many features that are the remnants of old glaciers that moved through Minnesota. The large bogs are old glacial lakes that once covered many thousands of acres. These old lakes were formed because the glacial ice prevented the water from draining in a natural pattern. At one time an old glacial river flowed through the park to what is now Libby, Minnesota, and the Mississippi River. When the great ice dams melted, the glacial lake water began to seek its natural drainage. These glacial lakes helped form the present-day Savanna River and the St. Louis River. If you stand in the right place in the park, water on one side of you will flow to the Gulf of Mexico via the Mississippi River, water on the other side flows to the Atlantic Ocean via Lake Superior and the St. Lawrence Seaway. The rolling hills and the sandy soil are all remnants of the glaciers that once covered Minnesota.

WHEN Visit in the summer to enjoy the lakes and bogs of the park. Visit in the winter to explore the park on skis.

WHERE The park is 17 miles northeast of McGregor. Take U.S. Highway 65 to County Road 14, then follow County Road 20 ten miles to the park.

WHO Savanna Portage State Park, 55626 Lake Place, McGregor, MN 55760, (218) 426-3271

FOR MORE INFORMATION www.mndnr.gov/state_parks/savanna_portage

Voyageurs National Park – International Falls, Minnesota

WHAT Nearly 200 years ago, voyageurs paddled birch-bark canoes full of animal pelts and trade goods through the area surrounding Voyageurs National Park on their way to Lake Athabasca, Canada. Today people explore the park by houseboat, motorboat, canoe, and kayak. Voyageurs is a water-based park where you must leave your car and take to the water to fully experience the lakes, islands, and shorelines of the park.

WHEN During the warm months of summer the park is a destination for people who enjoy exploring by boat. The interconnected waterways and miles of shoreline offer unparalleled opportunities for water-based activities. During the cold northern winters the park is transformed into a world of white. Frozen lake surfaces provide access to people on snowmobiles, while trails through the forest welcome those exploring on snowshoes or cross-country skis.

WHERE Voyageurs National Park is approximately five hours north of Minneapolis–St. Paul and three hours north of Duluth on U.S. Highway 53. Many visitors enter the park by water. Public boat launch ramps are available at the Rainy Lake, Kabetogama Lake, and Ash River visitor centers. Numerous resorts also offer boat access into the park.

WHO Voyageurs National Park, 3131 Highway 53, International Falls, MN 56649, (218) 283-6600

FOR MORE INFORMATION www.nps.gov/voya

Orr Bog Walk – Orr, Minnesota

WHAT Located in the town of Orr in St. Louis County, a trail and a boardwalk along the Pelican River provide access to a northern peat bog and end with a view of Pelican Lake. The surrounding Kabetogama State Forest is home to many boreal mammals and birds, including yellow-bellied flycatchers, black-backed woodpeckers, boreal chickadees, gray jays, great gray owls, bay-breasted warblers, olive-sided flycatchers, Cape May warblers, northern hawk owls, northern goshawks, and sharp-shinned hawks. Pelican Lake is home to white pelicans, double-crested cormorants, and bald eagles, to name a few. Red-necked grebes live along the Pelican River. Moose and wolves are rare but present.

WHEN Visit late May to June for migrating songbirds; May to September for nesting forest birds, waterbirds, and waterfowl; winter (in years when many northern owls disperse south) for great gray owls, northern hawk owls, and boreal owls.

WHERE Start directly behind the Orr visitor center on U.S. Highway 53 in Orr.

WHO The city of Orr, in cooperation with the National Park Service and the state of Minnesota, 4429 Highway 53, Orr, MN 55771, (218) 757-3932.

FOR MORE INFORMATION www.orrminnesota.com

MASTER
NATURALIST
TOOLBOX

Teach

This section features lesson plans focusing on lakes and bogs in the North Woods, Great Lakes region. You may experience some of these activities as a student in your Master Naturalist class. The lessons are adaptable to a wide range of audiences, ages, and settings. Feel free to use them to teach others what you have learned!

LESSON 1

Hot Water, Cold Water

Objective

Participants will understand stratification of lakes by temperature.

Audience Type

Teen/Adult

Supplies

☐ Clear glasses (half as many as there are participants)
☐ Colored ice cubes (half as many as there are participants)
☐ Pitcher of warm tap water
☐ Paper and pencil per group
☐ Copy of Figure 21

Background

As most compounds change from a liquid to a solid, the molecules become more tightly packed (denser). Water, in contrast, is most dense at 39 °F and becomes less dense at both higher and lower temperatures (Figure 20). Consequently, ice floats while water at temperatures just above freezing sinks. Because of this density–temperature relationship, deeper lakes in the North Woods, Great Lakes region tend to *stratify* — separate into distinct layers based on temperature (Figure 21).

Spring

In lakes that freeze over in the winter, the bulk of the water in the lake will be at 39 °F during the winter, capped by a less-dense ice layer at 32 °F. As the weather warms in spring, the ice melts. The surface water heats up, and when it reaches 41 °F, the water density is uniform from top to bottom. Wind blowing over the lake at this time can easily mix the water from top to bottom. This is called *turnover,* or overturn (Figure 22). After spring turnover, the surface water continues to absorb heat and warms. As the temperature rises, the water becomes less dense than the water below. Eventually the upper water becomes too warm and too buoyant to mix completely with the denser deeper water.

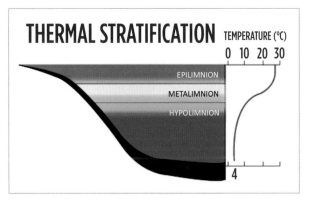

Figure 21. The thermocline is the area of maximum temperature change, and it occurs in the metalimnion. (Note that although "thermocline" is a term often used synonymously with metalimnion, it is the depth at which the change in temperature per unit depth is greatest. Thus, the thermocline is the area of maximum temperature change within the metalimnion.)

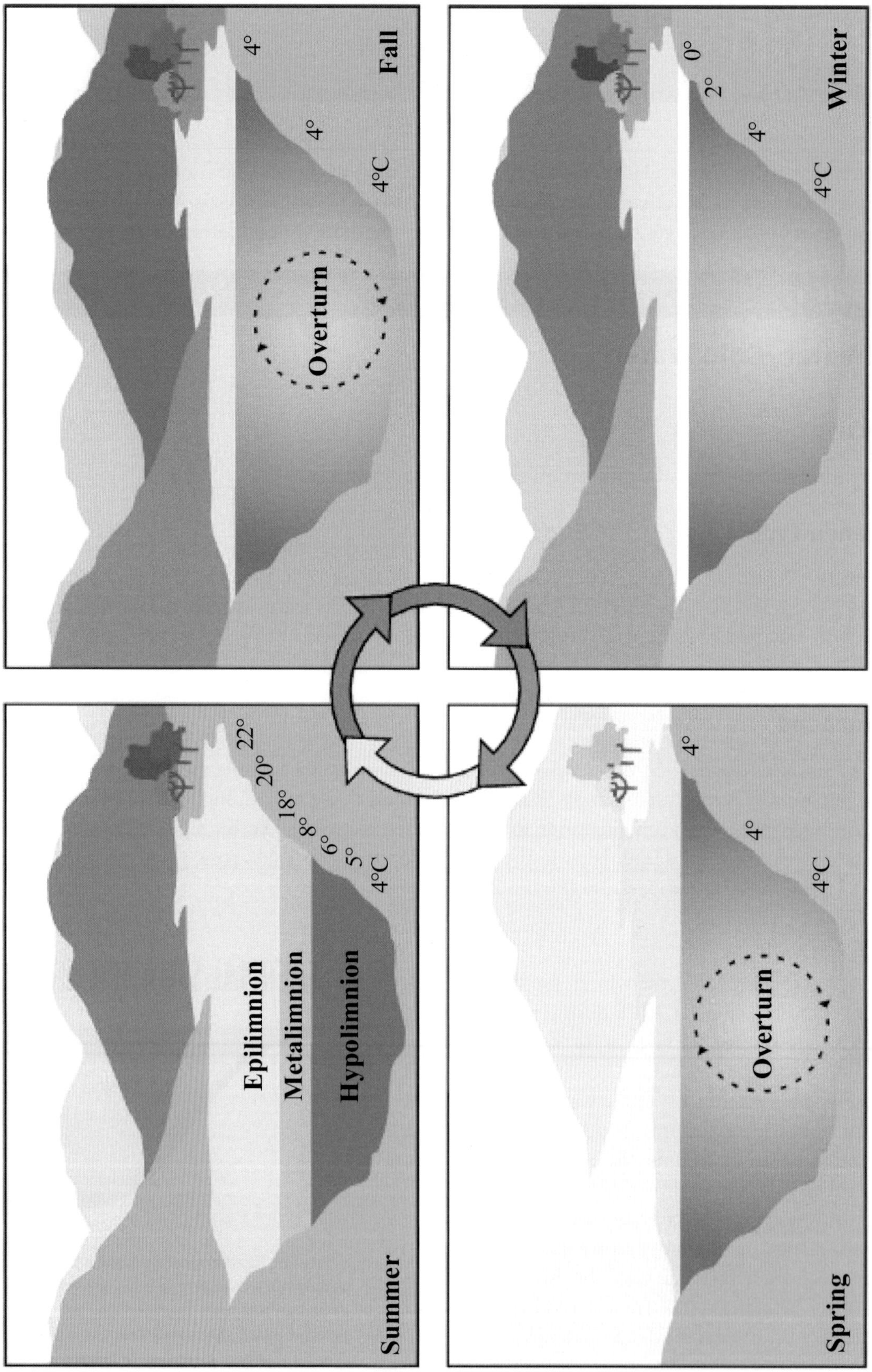

Fall

4°

4°

4°C

Overturn

Winter

0°

2°

4°

4°C

Summer

22°
20°
18°
8°
6°
5°
4°C

Epilimnion

Metalimnion

Hypolimnion

Spring

4°

4°

4°C

Overturn

Figure 22. Most northeastern Minnesota lakes show a regular pattern of mixing and stratification.

Summer

As summer progresses, the temperature and density differences between upper and lower water layers become more distinct. Deep lakes generally become stratified into three identifiable layers, known as the epilimnion, metalimnion, and hypolimnion. The epilimnion is the upper, warm layer, and is typically well-mixed. Below the epilimnion is the metalimnion or thermocline region, a layer of water in which the temperature declines rapidly with depth. The hypolimnion is the bottom layer of colder water. The density change at the metalimnion acts as a barrier that prevents mixing of the epilimnion and hypolimnion for several months during the summer.

The depth of mixing depends in part on the exposure of the lake to wind, but is most closely related to the lake's size. Small to moderate-size lakes (50 to 1,000 acres) reasonably may be expected to stratify and be well-mixed to a depth of ten to 13 feet in north temperate climates. Larger lakes may be well-mixed to a depth of 33 to 49 feet in summer.

Autumn

As the weather cools during autumn, the epilimnion cools, too, reducing the density difference between it and the hypolimnion. As time passes, winds mix the lake to greater depths, and the thermocline gradually deepens. When surface and bottom waters approach the same temperature and density, autumn winds can mix the entire lake; the lake is said to "turn over." The surface water continues to cool until it freezes. A less distinct density stratification than that seen in summer develops under the ice during winter. Most of the water column is at 39 °F, which is denser than the colder, lighter water just below the ice. In this case the stratification is much less stable, because the density difference between 32 °F and 39 °F water is quite small. However, ice isolates the water column from the wind, so the layering persists throughout the winter.

Activity

1. Divide participants into pairs and distribute a clear glass to each pair. Ask groups to predict what will happen when ice cubes made with colored water are placed in a glass of warm water.

2. Have each pair fill a glass halfway with warm water, place a colored ice cube in the glass, and record what happens for three to five minutes. Have pairs take notes on what they see happening and draw pictures of the water in the glass after 30 seconds and two minutes.

3. Facilitate a discussion about what participants observed. Encourage them to talk about why the ice cube floated and the colored cold water sank. Explain that cold water is heavier, or denser, than warm water, but ice is less dense than warm water.

4. Ask participants if they have ideas about how the demonstration might apply to lakes. What time of year is water the coldest in the lake? Is all the water cold? What time of year do you think the water is the warmest in the lake? Is all the water warm? Have you ever gone swimming in a lake and noticed that your arms might be in warm water but your toes are chilly in the deeper water?

5. Introduce lake stratification. Show Figure 22 while you explain the basics of lake stratification: In the summer, the sun heats the top layer of water while the deeper water

MASTER
NATURALIST
TOOLBOX

Teach

remains cold. As the air temperature cools in the fall, so does the surface water of the lake. As the surface water gets colder and denser, it sinks and begins mixing with the water below in a process called turnover or overturn. In winter, the surface water freezes, creating a fairly consistent temperature from top to bottom with the water on the bottom being warmer (more dense) than the water on the top. In the spring, turnover may happen again, facilitated by the sun, wind, tributaries, and groundwater. Turnover is important to help mix nutrients from the hypolimnion and oxygen from the atmosphere throughout the water column.

Lesson above originally titled Phenological Phenomenon and developed for: Science Institute for Educators, 2012–2013 Series. This teacher workshop series located at Great Lakes Aquarium was a partnership among Great Lakes Aquarium, Minnesota DNR's MinnAqua, Minnesota Sea Grant, and Wolf Ridge Environmental Learning. Original lesson can be found at www.glaquarium.org.

MASTER
NATURALIST
TOOLBOX

LESSON 2

Built for a Bog: An Exploration of Minnesota's Bogs

Objective

The participants will understand the physical and biotic factors that make bogs a unique part of the Minnesota landscape.

Audience Type

Teen/Adult

Supplies

☐ All About Bogs cards (one set of six per group)
☐ Whiteboard or large sheet of paper and markers
☐ Bog Organism cards (one set per group)
☐ Paper and pen/pencil per group

Background

Minnesota ranks number one in the United States for meat raffles, bars that you eat, hot dishes, and… peatlands! (That is, if you disqualify the peatlands in Alaska, which are largely underlain by permafrost.) In fact, we have more than 6 million acres of peatlands, including the largest single bog in the lower 48, which covers more than 500 square miles. It is the main feature of Big Bog State Recreation Area and lies directly to the east of Upper Red Lake.

Peatlands are found all over the world in almost any biome. Their main features are that they are wet and that the vegetation in them decomposes more slowly than it grows, which leads to thick mats of dead (but not rotting), wet plant material. In Minnesota, the conditions that create peatlands include stagnant water, cold temperatures, and the presence of sphagnum and sedges. Simplistically, peatlands are divided into two different types: bogs and fens. Fens tend to be connected to groundwater and receive additional water from precipitation and some runoff. Bogs are isolated from groundwater (either perched above it or isolated by a geologic formation) and they receive very little runoff from the surrounding watershed.

The terms *bog*, *marsh*, *swamp*, *peatland*, and *fen* are often used interchangeably and incorrectly. By reading excerpts from a great book on Wisconsin's natural communities (which are also like Minnesota's) called *Wisconsin's Natural Communities: How to Recognize Them, Where to Find Them*, we will begin to understand the differences.

In addition, there are many organisms adapted to life in a bog. They can be categorized as producers (mainly plants), herbivores (eat plants), carnivores (eat animals), omnivores (eat plants and animals), and/or decomposers (help break down plants and animals). A variety of interactions occur among these organisms and their different trophic levels. Some can even be both a producer and a carnivore. The following activity will introduce you to a few of these organisms and their roles.

MASTER
NATURALIST
TOOLBOX

Activity

1. Divide participants into groups of four to six.

2. Have each member of the group take one of the All About Bogs cards until they are all distributed (some participants may need to take two).

3. Have participants silently read their cards.

4. In round-robin fashion, have each person explain to the other members of their group what they learned.

5. When everyone has shared, have each group write down what defines a bog and how it differs from other wetland types.

6. As a large group, list on a white board or large paper the main characteristics of a bog.

7. Tell participants they will now explore some of the organisms found in a bog.

8. Review the terms *producer, herbivore, carnivore, omnivore,* and *decomposer.*

9. Provide each group with a set of bog organism cards and divide them equally among group members.

10. Have individuals in the groups sort their organisms into five groups: producers, herbivores, carnivores, omnivores, and decomposers.

11. After cards are sorted, have the small groups discuss if any organisms should move to a different category. Why or why not?

12. As a group, speculate on (and then write down!) five things that the trophic structure of a bog tells you about life in the bog. How might these affect the plants that grow here? How would these species adapt to these factors? What conclusions can you draw about trophic interactions in a bog?

Text on the All About Bogs cards is taken from:

Hoffman, R. (2002). *Wisconsin's natural communities: How to recognize them, where to find them.* (pp. 60–61). Madison, WI: The University of Wisconsin Press.

Bog Organisms Key

PRODUCERS	HERBIVORES	CARNIVORES	OMNIVORES	DECOMPOSERS
Labrador tea	Lincoln's sparrow	Four-toed salamander	Palm warbler	Round-leaved sundew*
Leatherleaf	Bog lemming	Arctic shrew	Short-ended pea clam	Pitcher plant*
Bog rosemary	Mink frog (juvenile)	Eastern ribbon snake		
Northern blue flag	Cranberry toad bug	Mink frog (adult)		
Round-leaved sundew*		Black-backed woodpecker		
Trailing arbutus		Round-leaved sundew*		
Pitcher plant*		Pitcher plant*		
Rose pogonia		Pitcher plant mosquito		
Calopogon (Tuberous grass-pink)		Four-spotted skimmer		
Tawny cottongrass				
Black spruce				
Tamarack				
Sphagnum (peat) moss (Many species)				

* Appears in more than one category

Cards Instructions

Copy cards from book in black/white or color. Cut cards apart.

MASTER
NATURALIST
TOOLBOX

ALL ABOUT BOGS

Bog, fen, swamp, and marsh are all terms used to describe wetlands. Confusion ensues when the terms are used interchangeably. Belden swamp is actually a fen. Bogus swamp is a bog. Bibon marsh is a swamp. Whether the wetland is a bog, fen, swamp, or marsh depends on the amount of accumulated peat, the water chemistry, and the water flow.

ALL ABOUT BOGS

Short growing seasons and cool temperatures do not permit decomposers such as mites and springtails enough time to keep up with the annual volume of plant growth, and organic material accumulates over the course of time in the form of peat, partially decomposed organic matter (primarily sphagnum moss or sedges). Peat builds faster in acidic conditions because the harsh conditions keep the decomposers at low populations.

Water chemistry refers to the pH of the water — acidity or alkalinity — which helps determine which plant species will grow. *Water flow* refers to the movement and replenishment of waters with minerals absorbed from the soil.

ALL ABOUT BOGS

Bog: Permanently wet land with accumulation of sphagnum peat and water coming from precipitation and runoff. The water is very acidic and can become more acidic as time goes on. Nutrients for plant growth come primarily from rain and snow. Raised bogs are higher in the center and have scattered black spruce growing with sphagnum and leatherleaf. Trees grow slowly on these raised bogs because of the very acidic conditions.

ALL ABOUT BOGS

Fen: An area where peat accumulates and sedges are the primary peat makers. The water is not as acidic as bogs, and nutrients come from the surrounding soil or flowing water. Tamarack is the most numerous tree species in fens, but many trees are absent. Types of fens are poor fen, sedge fen, boreal rich fen, and tamarack fen.

ALL ABOUT BOGS

Swamp: Forested area (primarily white cedar and black ash) that can develop from a fen if calcium-rich water continues to enter. Abundant sphagnum moss can be part of a swamp, but it does not accumulate. Soil dwellers such as nematodes and fungi break down the organic material as rapidly as it accumulates, and the decomposers reach a balance. Types of swamps in Wisconsin (and Minnesota) are white cedar swamps and black ash swamps.

ALL ABOUT BOGS

Marsh: An area where the vegetation contains little or no sphagnum and has abundant grass-like plants. Mineral soil is underwater, and peat does not accumulate. Cattails, bulrush, and pickerelweed are dominant marsh plants.

MASTER
NATURALIST
TOOLBOX

BOG ORGANISMS

Four-toed salamander (*Hemidactylium scutatum*)

BOG ORGANISMS

Lincoln's sparrow (*Melospiza lincolnii*)

BOG ORGANISMS

Arctic shrew (*Sorex arcticus*)

BOG ORGANISMS

Palm warbler (*Setophaga palmarum*)

BOG ORGANISMS

Bog lemming (Synaptomys cooperi)

BOG ORGANISMS

Eastern ribbon snake (*Thamnophis sauritus sauritus*)

MASTER
NATURALIST
TOOLBOX

BOG ORGANISMS

Adult mink frog (*Rana septentrionalis*)

BOG ORGANISMS

Black-backed woodpecker (*Picoides arcticus*)

BOG ORGANISMS

Labrador tea (*Ledum groenlandicum*)

BOG ORGANISMS

Leatherleaf (*Chamaedaphne calyculata*)

BOG ORGANISMS

Bog rosemary (*Andromeda polifolia*)

BOG ORGANISMS

Northern blue flag (*Iris versicolor*)

MASTER
NATURALIST
TOOLBOX

BOG ORGANISMS

Round-leaved sundew (*Drosera rotundifolia*)

BOG ORGANISMS

Trailing arbutus (*Epigaea repens*)

BOG ORGANISMS

Pitcher plant (*Sarracenia purpurea*)

BOG ORGANISMS

Rose pogonia (*Pogonia ophioglossoides*)

BOG ORGANISMS

Calopogon (*Calopogon tuberosus*)

BOG ORGANISMS

Tawny cottongrass (*Eriophorum virginicum*)

MASTER
NATURALIST
TOOLBOX

BOG ORGANISMS

Juvenile mink frog (*Rana septentrionalis*)

BOG ORGANISMS

Tamarack (*Larix laricina*)

BOG ORGANISMS

Black spruce (*Picea mariana*)

BOG ORGANISMS

Sphagnum (peat) moss (Many species)

BOG ORGANISMS

Short-ended pea clam (*Pisidium subtruncatum*)

BOG ORGANISMS

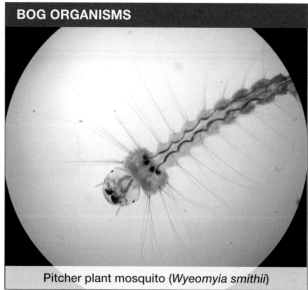

Pitcher plant mosquito (*Wyeomyia smithii*)

BOG ORGANISMS

Four-spotted skimmer (*Libellula quadrimaculata*)

BOG ORGANISMS

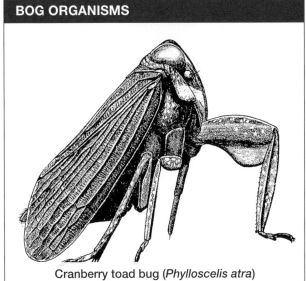

Cranberry toad bug (*Phylloscelis atra*)

PRODUCERS

HERBIVORES

CARNIVORES

OMNIVORES

DECOMPOSERS

MASTER
NATURALIST
TOOLBOX

Conserve

This section highlights organizations that offer opportunities for Minnesota Master Naturalist Volunteers to participate in stewardship and citizen science activities related to lakes and bogs in the North Woods, Great Lakes region. Please visit the websites to learn more.

Citizen Lake Monitoring Program

The Citizen Lake Monitoring Program (CLMP) combines the technical resources of the MPCA with the volunteer efforts of citizens statewide who collect water transparency data using a secchi disk about once a week during the summer. At the end of summer, volunteers send their data sheets to the MPCA to be compiled with other water-quality data.

www.pca.state.mn.us/water/clmp.html

MinnAqua

MinnAqua educates people of all ages and stages about aquatic ecosystems, management, and resource issues; fosters stewardship of natural resources; and helps people acquire skills related to aquatic careers and recreation. MinnAqua education specialists and interns partner with schools, youth groups, and community organizations to hold fishing and aquatic education programs throughout the state. They also have materials online to help environmental educators, teachers, and volunteer naturalists (i.e., you!) introduce kids and others to fishing and aquatic habitats.

www.mndnr.gov/minnaqua

Adopt-a-River Program

Citizens "adopt" a section of river, ravine, pond, lake, or wetland they would like to see cleaned up, then organize volunteers and conduct cleanups. The program is run through the Conservation Corps of Minnesota and Iowa. The Conservation Corps can provide advice, supplies, promotional assistance, review, and recognition.

www.conservationcorps.org/adoptariver/

Expand

This section suggests some things you can use, do, pursue, read, or join to develop as a naturalist.

Journal

EXPERIENCE Consider how your special spot is connected to Minnesota's lakes and bogs through the water cycle (Chapter 4). Can you find evidence of water, such as humidity or damp soil, that may have been in (or is headed to) bigger bodies of water?

REFLECT Consider the other natural cycles taking place right now at your special spot, such as carbon cycles, nutrient cycles, seasonal cycles, and the lunar cycle. How much happens at this site that we don't see? How much happens that we can't see?

RECORD Use natural objects to draw or depict something that is present but can't be seen at your spot. Crush leaves or flower petals onto your paper, make paint out of wet soil or bark, etc.

Read

Beneath the Surface: A Natural History of a Fisherman's Lake

Bruce M. Carlson.
2007. St. Paul: Minnesota Historical Society Press 250 pp.

This book is an in-depth examination of Ten Mile Lake near Hackensack, Minnesota, which Bruce Carlson has been visiting and studying for 50 years. The focus is on the dynamics of a lake from the perspective of the fish that live there and the angler trying to catch them.

The Patterned Peatlands of Minnesota

H. E. Wright, Jr., Barbara A. Coffin, and Norman E. Aaseng, editors.
1992. Minneapolis: University of Minnesota Press. 544 pp.

This illustrated book covers the ecological and political significance of the largest peatland complex in the lower 48 states. The 19 lessons include sections on animals, plants, hydrology, human use, and conservation. It is a bit academic, but is still the best read on Minnesota bogs available.

Surf

Minnesota DNR Lake Finder

This site is a portal to data on more than 4,500 lakes and rivers in Minnesota, including lake surveys, depth maps, water quality data, water clarity data, notes, and fish consumption advice. Check out your favorite lake.

www.mndnr.gov/lakefind

Water on the Web

Water on the Web, based at the University of Minnesota–Duluth, provides everything you ever wanted to know about limnology in one easy-to-access site. Links to data from sampling stations across the United States (including Minnesota) allow you to explore lake and river dynamics on your own.

http://waterontheweb.org

Join

Minnesota Waters

Minnesota Waters engages citizens, policy makers, and others in protecting and restoring Minnesota's lakes and rivers. It supports programs in citizen monitoring, public policy, and watershed stewardship.

www.minnesotawaters.org

Freshwater Society

The Freshwater Society is a Minnesota group dedicated to conserving, restoring, and protecting freshwater resources and their watersheds. It also publishes the fabulous Weatherguide calendars.

www.freshwater.org

MASTER
NATURALIST
TOOLBOX

Copyrighted Photographs and Images Used With Permission

Figure 1: Courtesy of Chris Rodengen of Directional Resources LLC

Figure 2: Courtesy of Chris Rodengen of Directional Resources LLC

Figure 3: Courtesy of Caileigh Speck

Figure 4: Courtesy of Minnesota Pollution Control Agency

Figure 5: Courtesy of Caileigh Speck

Figure 6: Courtesy of Caileigh Speck

Figure 7: Courtesy of the University of Minnesota, adapted from the MPCA.

Figure 8: Courtesy of Caileigh Speck

Figure 9: Courtesy of Mark Edlund, Science Museum of Minnesota

Figure 10: Courtesy of C. Iverson, Minnesota Department of Natural Resources

Figure 11: Courtesy of Benjamin Olson, Professional Photographer, benjamin-olson.com

Figure 12: Courtesy of Dawn A. Flinn, Minnesota Department of Natural Resources

Figure 13: Courtesy of Wikimedia Commons

Figure 14: Courtesy of Dawn A. Flinn, Minnesota Department of Natural Resources

Figure 15: Courtesy of Caileigh Speck

Figure 16: Courtesy of Dawn A. Flinn, Minnesota Department of Natural Resources (left) and Caileigh Speck (right)

Figure 17: Courtesy of Russ Link (left, center, right)

Figure 18: Courtesy of Josh Rutz

Figure 19: Minnesota Department of Health (chart)

Figure 20: Courtesy of Josh Rutz

Figure 21: Courtesy of Great Lakes Aquarium

Figure 22: Courtesy of Great Lakes Aquarium

Bog Organism Photos

Four-toed salamander image courtesy of Wikimedia Commons and Brian Gratwicke https://commons.wikimedia.org/wiki/File:Hemidactylium_scutatum.jpg

Lincoln's sparrow image courtesy of Wikimedia Commons https://commons.wikimedia.org/wiki/File:Lincoln%27s_Sparrow_eating_seeds_in_a_tree_(14051809612).jpg

Arctic shrew image courtesy of Phil Meyers and BioKIDS (Creative Commons) www.biokids.umich.edu/critters/Sorex_arcticus/

Palm warbler image courtesy of Wikimedia Commons https://commons.wikimedia.org/wiki/File:Palm_Warbler,_Indiatlatlantic.jpg

Bog lemming image courtesy of Phil Meyers and BioKIDS (Creative Commons) www.biokids.umich.edu/critters/Synaptomys_cooperi/pictures/resources/contributors/phil_myers/ADW_mammals/Rodentia/synaptomys3416/

Eastern ribbon snake image courtesy of Wikimedia Commons https://commons.wikimedia.org/wiki/File:EasternRibbonSnake.jpg

Mink frog image courtesy of Wikimedia Commons https://commons.wikimedia.org/wiki/File:Mink_Frog.jpg

MASTER
NATURALIST
TOOLBOX

Expand

MASTER
NATURALIST
TOOLBOX

Chapter 7: Lake Superior

A Truly Great Lake

Barb W. Liukkonen and Joan M. Gilmore

Goal

Understand that the Lake Superior environment is the result of unique geographic, geologic, physical, chemical, and biological characteristics, overlain by social and political influences that differ from those influencing other Minnesota lakes

Objective

1. Define the Lake Superior watershed, explaining how the lake, its tributaries, and the surrounding landscape affect each other.

2. Describe the geographic, geologic, physical, chemical, and biological characteristics of Lake Superior and how they are related.

3. Describe non-native organisms that are affecting Lake Superior.

4. Identify unique human uses of and influences on Lake Superior and how these are related to changing physical, chemical, and biological characteristics of the lake.

Introduction

The Inland Ocean. The Sweetwater Sea. Gichigami. The Big Lake. Lake Superior. Each of these is a name for the great lake that dominates northeastern Minnesota, bringing mystery and beauty to the lives of residents and visitors alike. Early French explorers named it Lac Supérieur to indicate that it was the uppermost lake

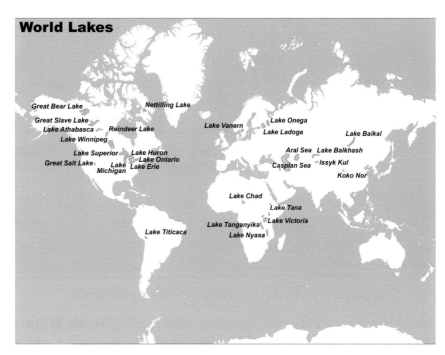

Figure 1. Lake Superior is just one of many great lakes found around the world.

in the Laurentian Great Lakes chain, but it has come to fulfill its name as meaning the most superior, or greatest, of the North American Great Lakes.

Lake Superior is the largest freshwater lake on Earth by surface area and the third largest by volume. It contains about 10 percent of the world's liquid fresh surface water (i.e., not including fresh groundwater or water frozen in glaciers and ice caps). Only Lake Baikal in Siberia and Lake Tanganyika in Tanzania, East Africa, contain more water.

One of Many

While Lake Superior is the largest freshwater lake, it's by no means the only large lake in the world (Figure 1). Every continent, except Australia, has great freshwater lakes, including lakes Baikal and Issyk-kul in Asia; lakes Tanganyika, Victoria, and Malawi in

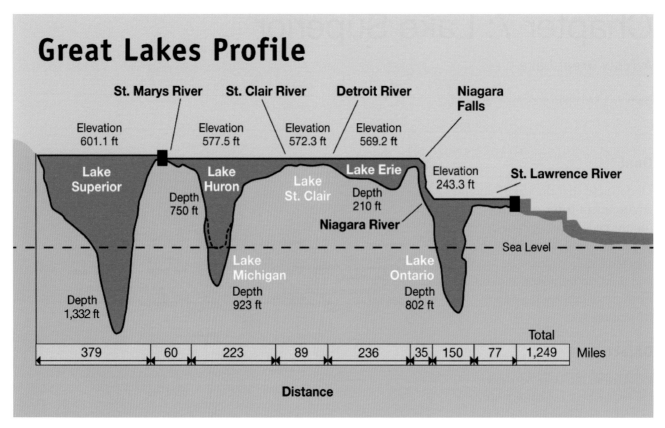

Great Lakes Profile

St. Marys River | St. Clair River | Detroit River | Niagara Falls

Elevation 601.1 ft | Elevation 577.5 ft | Elevation 572.3 ft | Elevation 569.2 ft

Lake Superior | Lake Huron | Lake St. Clair | Lake Erie | Elevation 243.3 ft | St. Lawrence River

Depth 750 ft | Depth 210 ft

Niagara River

Sea Level

Depth 1,332 ft | Lake Michigan Depth 923 ft | Lake Ontario Depth 802 ft

Total

379 | 60 | 223 | 89 | 236 | 35 | 150 | 77 | 1,249 | Miles

Distance

Figure 2. The Laurentian Great Lakes vary greatly in depth and water volume.

Africa; Lake Vostok in Antarctica; Ladoga and Vanern in Europe; and lakes Titicaca and Nicaragua in South America. Great lakes in the Northwest Territory of Canada include Great Slave Lake and Great Bear Lake, and Lake Winnipeg in Manitoba is the 11th largest lake in the world.

Lakes Baikal and Tanganyika are *rift lakes*, formed when continental plates began to split apart, leaving narrow chasms that later filled with fresh water. Baikal is more than a mile (5,371 feet) deep and 395 miles long, while Tanganyika is 4,280 feet in depth and 420 miles long. Although they are very narrow, they are so deep that they hold vast quantities of water. Baikal contains 20 percent of the world's fresh liquid water, twice as much as Lake Superior.

As the French explorers noted, Lake Superior is the top of the chain of the five Laurentian Great Lakes that form part of the border between the U.S. and Canada (Figure 2). Downstream of Superior lie Huron, Michigan, Erie, and Ontario. Lake Michigan is the largest lake contained entirely within a single country. The other four Laurentian Great Lakes are shared by the U.S. and Canada.

Small Watershed, Big Lake

Precipitation that falls on the land may seep in to become groundwater, it may evaporate, or it may run over the surface of the land to a lake or stream. As we learned in Chapter 6, the land area from which water runs into a particular basin is called that basin's *watershed*. Everything that happens on the land within a watershed can affect the quality of the water in the receiving lake or river. Runoff can carry pollutants such as sediment, nutrients, or chemicals, and may be warmer than the body of water receiving it.

Vast areas of land may provide runoff to a lake, and watersheds are often five to ten times as large as the lake they supply. But Lake Superior's watershed, which covers 49,300 square miles, is less than twice the size of the lake (Figure 3). Thus, much of the water that reaches the big lake falls directly onto its surface as rain or snow.

Lake Superior itself is very, very big! It stretches about 350 miles from end to end and about 160 miles from north to south. It covers 31,700 square miles, about one-third the size of Minnesota. If you were to walk

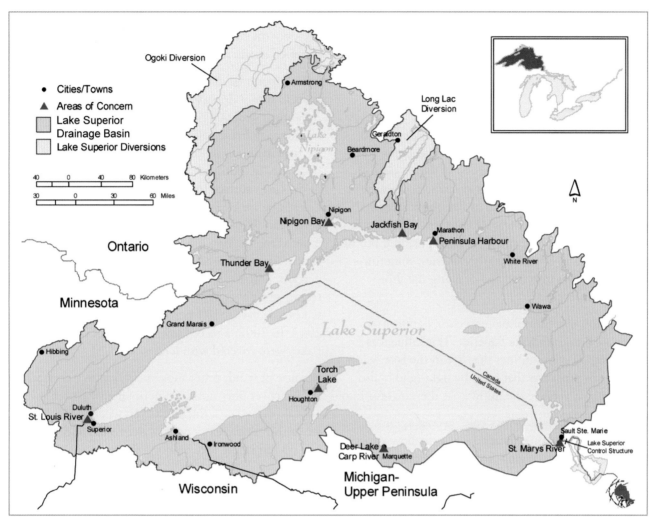

Figure 3. Lake Superior's watershed is small relative to the lake's own surface area.

around the shoreline of Lake Superior, your trip would be 1,826 miles, or about the same as if you walked from Duluth, Minnesota, to Miami, Florida.

In addition to being broad, Lake Superior is deep—482 feet on average. At its deepest point 40 miles off the Upper Peninsula of Michigan, the lake reaches 1,332 feet (Figure 4). If the Trump Tower in Chicago were dropped into Lake Superior's deepest spot, about 50 feet would stick out of the water. Because of its surface area and depth, the big lake contains more than 3 quadrillion (3,000,000,000,000,000) gallons, or 2,900 cubic miles, of water.

Minnesota's "portion" of Lake Superior is relatively small. Of the entire shoreline (1,826 miles) only about 33 percent (608 miles) and 8 percent of the surface area (2,626 square miles) are within Minnesota's

jurisdiction. However, because the lake dips steeply off the North Shore, about 18 percent of the total volume (527 cubic miles) is within Minnesota. The deepest spots within Minnesota's boundary are about

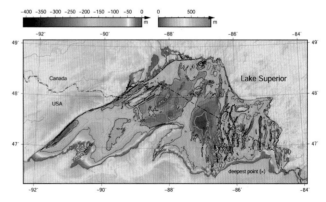

Figure 4. At Lake Superior's deepest point, the lake bottom lies 1,332 feet below the surface.

five miles off Silver Bay and Split Rock Lighthouse where the lake is about 850 feet deep. About 6,200 square miles (12.5 percent) of the lake's watershed is in Minnesota.

Clear and Cold

The water of Lake Superior is extremely clear, with an average underwater visibility of 27 feet and sometimes as much as 75 feet. Near the mouths of rivers and following storms or snowmelt, the water may become *turbid* (cloudy) as fine particles of red clay and other sediments wash into the lake. Plumes of brownish water can often be seen spreading out of the Duluth and Superior harbor entries, sometimes stretching miles into the lake or along the shore where rivers enter.

Because the water is normally so clear, light can penetrate deep into Lake Superior. This influences the biological communities that live in the lake. Clear water helps predators that hunt by sight (and it also helps scuba divers see the shipwrecks they are cruising).

Water in the big lake is very cold, averaging only 40 °F. During warm summer days, in shallow areas with the wind blowing onshore, the temperature of nearshore water may reach into the 70s, but the warm temperatures usually don't last long and swimming in Lake Superior is always a challenge. scuba diving, body and wind surfing, and kayaking have become more popular in recent years, but many people wear dry suits when they are going to be immersed in the lake. Lake Superior's warmest temperatures typically occur in September after a summer of being heated by sunlight and warm air.

Because of the great volume of water in Lake Superior, it takes a lot of energy to change the temperature of the water even a few degrees. As a result, the water that cooled down over winter keeps areas near the lake cooler, even when warm spring air temperatures arrive. And, during the fall and winter, areas near the lake may be warmer than the air "over the hill"—the lake water, warmed during the summer, shares its residual heat.

Lake Superior is different from most inland Minnesota lakes in that it doesn't usually freeze completely over. Areas near shore, in harbors, and around the Apostle Islands may freeze solid enough for vehicular traffic or for opportunities to explore shoreline caves and arches from the ice, but typically only 30 to 40 percent of the lake's surface freezes in most years. In 2014, Lake Superior froze completely across, at least briefly. That year, 91 percent of the Great Lakes' surface was covered by ice. Two other recent years had extensive ice coverage across the Great Lakes: 1979 with 94.7 percent, and 1994 with 90.7 percent. Despite the record-setting ice years of 2014 and 1994, total Great Lakes ice cover fell 71 percent between 1983 and 2012. In 2002, a record low 9.5 percent of the Great Lakes were covered with ice.

Because of wind, water movement, and water depth, the ice cover does not form permanently or achieve great—or equal—thickness everywhere. Wind causes ice to shift and creates open water zones, and ice may pile up out in the lake or along shores.

Surprisingly, ice cover also affects the summer water temperature. Since 1980, Lake Superior summer

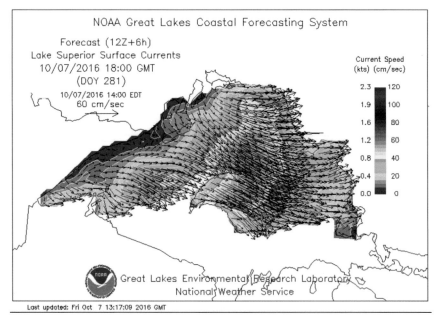

Figure 5. Lake Superior water circulation patterns vary throughout the year. To see today's flow visit www.glerl.noaa.gov/res/glcfs/currents/.

water temperatures have increased about 2 °F while summer temperatures of the air above the lake have increased about 1 °F. The difference is due to the fact that warmer winter temperatures result in less ice formation. Ice reflects the sun's rays, reducing solar heating of the lake. Less winter ice means warmer water in the spring (greater latent heat) and earlier stratification (remember that concept from Chapter 6?). This allows greater warming of surface waters during the summer and leaves the lake with even more latent heat in the fall and winter, which in turn can lead to even less ice cover.

Like the inland lakes we learned about in Chapter 6, Lake Superior stratifies during the summer and winter. It is *dimictic*. Turnover is critically important for mixing nutrients and oxygen throughout the big lake's water.

In recent years, spring turnover has come earlier to Lake Superior by about half a day per year, leading to an earlier summer stratification. The epilimnion is becoming warmer and deeper, which is causing the fall turnover to happen later. The stratified summer season has increased from an average of 145 days to an average of 170 days in the past century.

On the Move

Water mixing, circulation, and temperature determine how much light and nutrients are available to support phytoplankton and other primary producers, and can influence contaminant transport, spread of invasive species, fishing success, and water quality. The circulation patterns in Lake Superior are complex and variable depending upon depth and season (Figure 5). Currents are largely determined by water temperature and wind patterns. Summer nearshore circulation is driven by temperature because shallow water warms faster, and is affected by the *bathymetry* (bottom profile) of the lake. Summer lakewide circulation is controlled mainly by wind, and shows a strong counterclockwise flow around the lake. Lakewide winter circulation is driven largely by wind, with two large cyclonic cells in the eastern and central basins. As surface water temperatures and wind speeds continue to increase, currents are likely to increase as well.

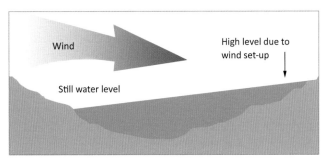

Figure 6. Seiches form when wind, storms, or differences in barometric pressure cause water to pile up on one side of the lake.

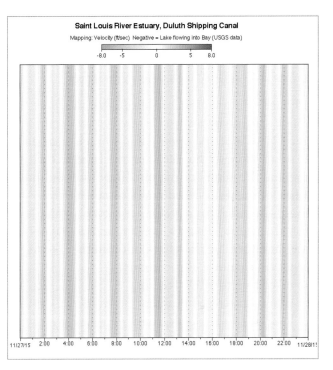

Figure 7. In this diagram showing the pulse of a seiche at the St. Louis River in Duluth, alternating bands of blue and brown indicate a seiche powerful enough to reverse the flow of the St. Louis river at regular intervals.

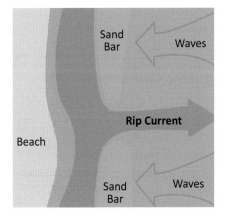

Figure 8. Rip currents are channels of water flowing away from shore. They form after winds force water toward shore for a prolonged period.

Even though it's big, Lake Superior doesn't have tides like the ocean. However, it does experience a phenomenon called a *seiche* (pronounced "saysh"), which is a sloshing motion of water back and forth across the basin (Figure 6). Seiches can occur when water piles up on one side of the lake because of wind, storms, or differences in barometric pressure. When the force causing the pile-up weakens or disappears, the piled-up water flows to the other side of the lake, and then back and forth again with decreasing force and volume (Figure 7). If you're having a hard time imagining that, think of how water moves in a pan full of water that is tipped and then leveled. It takes about eight hours for water to slosh from one side to the other. Seiches may cause water level variations from as little as three inches up to three feet!

Although they are often called riptides, the more properly titled *rip currents* (Figure 8) that occur along Park Point and other shallow beach areas on the south shore of the lake are not related to tidal function, the moon, or the sun. They form on the surface of the water when waves come directly toward the beach for a prolonged period. Water is pushed onshore by waves breaking across shallow areas, and then it rushes back out into the lake in deeper rip channels. Rip currents can extend up to 1,000 feet into the lake and average five miles per hour or two feet per second, creating a hazard for swimmers who risk being swept away from shore.

In and Out

Nearly 850 rivers flow into Lake Superior. There are dramatic differences between tributaries on the North Shore, the south shore, and Canada. The rivers that drain the North Shore (Figure 9) typically rise in glacial lakes or wetlands in the highlands, then flow southeasterly to the lake. The rivers have a low gradient at their upper reaches, but after they drop over the bedrock ridge near the

lake, the gradient is much steeper and waterfalls and cascades are common.

The St. Louis River is the largest U.S. tributary to Lake Superior, and is second in flow volume only to the Nipigon River in Canada. It begins about 13 miles east of Hoyt Lakes and flows 192 miles through a large watershed (3,634 square miles) to an estuary at the western end of the lake, where it forms the boundary between Minnesota and Wisconsin, and Duluth and Superior. In 1987, the International Joint Commission (more about this at the end of the chapter) listed the St. Louis Estuary as one of 43 Areas of Concern (AOCs) in the Great Lakes because of contaminated sediments. Many agency partners and citizens have worked together to address toxic contaminants, manage invasive species, and improve habitat.

The Nipigon River is the largest tributary (by volume) to Lake Superior. Canadian rivers also have many cascades and falls as they approach the Lake. There are no major tributaries on the south shore in Wisconsin or Michigan, and the rivers there tend to have a lower gradient.

Rivers provide runoff that helps recharge the lake's waters and maintain the lake's level. They also can be

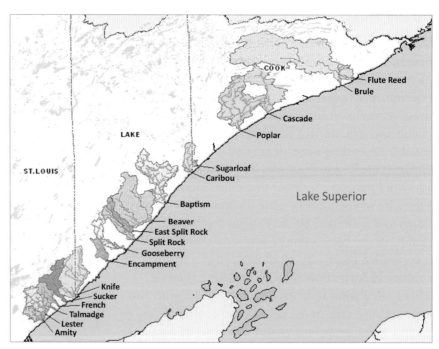

Figure 9. Tributaries that flow from Minnesota into Lake Superior typically arise in inland lakes or wetlands.

a source of pollution from past mining, paper and pulpwood manufacturing, other industrial activity, untreated sewage, or storm-water runoff. Each year, the equivalent of about two feet of precipitation falls onto the watershed and runs off into the lake or seeps in from groundwater. Another two-and-a-half feet or so of rain and snow fall on the surface of Lake Superior. So where does that water go, and why doesn't the lake overflow?

Somewhat more than half the output of Lake Superior (60 percent) flows out to Lake Huron through the St. Marys River, which forms the border between Michigan's Upper Peninsula and Ontario. The average flow from Superior to Huron is 75,000 cubic feet per second (2.4 trillion cubic feet per year). The remainder of output is lost through evaporation from the surface of the lake.

Evaporation is greatest during the winter when air is dry and cold. (Think about how much moisture your skin loses during the winter.) Evaporation is reduced, however, when the water is ice-covered, so a much greater volume of water is lost during winters in which there isn't as much ice.

Lake Superior is about 602 feet above sea level. The long-term (1918–2014) average water level is 602.07 feet. The minimum level recorded was in 1925 when the lake fell to 600.72 feet, and the maximum was reached in 1982 at 603.38 feet. Both extremely high and extremely low levels can affect biological communities, shipping, and natural processes such as shoreline or dune erosion. After very low water levels for years following the mid-1990s, and near-record lows in 2013, Lake Superior (and the other Great Lakes) rebounded in 2014. In October 2015, the lake reached 602.58 feet.

What causes such variation? It's mainly about evaporation. In the 1990s and early 2000s the region experienced very high rates of evaporation and low precipitation, which caused the water levels to drop. In contrast, 2014 was a year with very low evaporation and consistently above-average precipitation, so water levels rebounded.

Residence, or retention, time is the calculated average time that a molecule of water or a substance dissolved in water remains in a lake. It provides an indication of how quickly water quality can change in response to an increase or decrease in contamination. Residence time is based on the time it would take to drain a lake by its outflow if inflow were stopped. Residence time for Lake Superior has been estimated at 191 years and 173 years. Either way, it's a long time for a molecule of water or a contaminant to remain in the lake.

The Lake Effect

Lake Superior is vast enough to create its own weather. It moderates nearby climate, cooling our summers and warming our winters. Winter temperatures near the lake rarely dip below –30 °F, while the rest of northeastern Minnesota may be as cold as –45 °F. The North Shore of Lake Superior receives an average of about 60–70 inches of snow annually, while the rest of Minnesota receives less than 50 inches on average (Figure 10).

The "lake effect" has even more impact along the Lake Superior shorelines of Wisconsin and Michigan, which may receive as much 350 inches of snow in a year. When a cold air mass moves from the west and northwest across the expanse of warmer lake water,

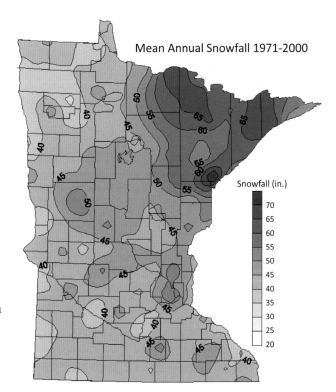

Mean Annual Snowfall 1971-2000

Snowfall (in.)

Figure 10. A map of average annual snowfall in Minnesota shows the effect of Lake Superior, with greater amounts in northeastern Minnesota.

the lower layer of air warms and picks water vapor from the lake. That extra water vapor then freezes and falls as snow on the downwind shore.

During the summer, locals often say, "Bring a jacket. You never know when the wind will come off the lake." Cool air over the lake (remember lake water doesn't reach its warmest temperatures until September) can result in interesting phenomena. Even when air temperatures away from the lake reach the 80s or 90s, air over the lake is cool. This may cause fog over the lake and sunshine over the land, neatly divided along the shoreline. Fog is a common occurrence near Lake Superior; Duluth has an average of 52 foggy days a year, while the Minneapolis/St. Paul area has only about 11 days of fog.

In the fall, Lake Superior frequently experiences northeasterly storms created when low-pressure systems pass over the lake. Winds often reach 50 miles per hour and gusts can reach up to 100 miles per hour. Many ships have sunk during these awe-inspiring storms, including the famous Edmund Fitzgerald that went down in November 1975 near Whitefish Point. At least 240 ships sank near Whitefish Point between 1816 and 1975. A major storm on November 28, 1905, damaged 29 ships, including two that foundered near Stoney Point. In 1907, Congress appropriated $75,000 to build a lighthouse and fog signal at Stoney Point (the current Split Rock Lighthouse) to help prevent future shipwrecks.

Today storms on the big lake continue to threaten large commercial ships, but they also present a major risk for small pleasure boaters and sailors. Because of the highlands along the North Shore, bad weather approaching from the west may be hidden from boaters on the lake. And because of the rugged and undeveloped nature of the North Shore, there are few natural bays or harbors for boaters to dodge into if they are overtaken by a

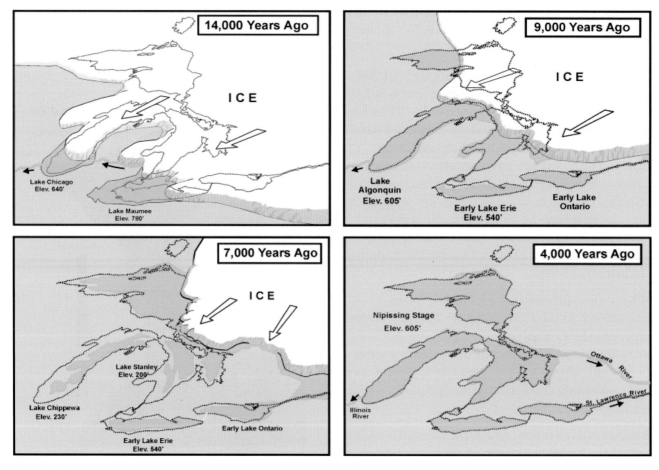

Figure 11. Meltwater trapped between a receding glacier and tall land formations formed Glacial Lake Duluth.

storm. Local communities and state agencies have worked together to develop several safe harbors along the North Shore. They also provide access for launching boats and places for non-boaters to enjoy the lake.

Formation of Lake Superior

The Lake Superior basin has existed for millions of years. It began forming about 1 billion years ago as lava flows poured out of the midcontinent rift we met in Chapter 1, weighing down the surface of the Earth and creating a depression that eventually filled with water. Rifting lasted about 20 million years and produced a blanket of basalt up to thirteen miles thick. You can see evidence of up to seven different lava flows at the Sugarloaf Cove Scientific & Natural Area and along the river cuts and waterfalls of the North Shore state parks. In addition to oozing lava flows (flood basalts), events included some explosive eruptions of pumice and rhyolite (which forms the bluff of Shovel Point and Palisade Head). One recent estimate is that more than 300,000 cubic miles of magma poured out

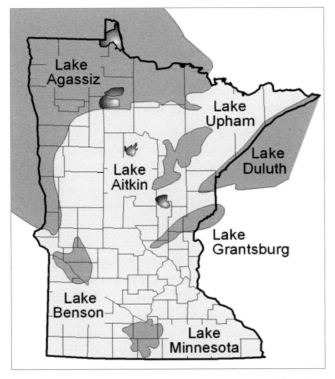

Figure 12. Glacial Lake Duluth is one of several massive lakes that formed in what is now Minnesota in the footprints of the glacier.

through the rift. That's more than 100 times the current volume of Lake Superior!

During the Paleozoic and Mesozoic eras, shallow seas covered much of the interior of North America and deposited the sandstones, shales, and limestones that we see in southern Minnesota. However, there is no evidence these seas encroached as far as northeastern Minnesota. The region probably remained above sea level during this time, slowly weathering and eroding. Ancient rivers carried sand and mud into the basin, forming sedimentary rocks up to five miles thick. Some of these sandstones can be seen at Fond du Lac, Hinckley, and Banning State Park. They also make up the Apostle Islands, Bayfield Peninsula, and Pictured Rocks National Park.

About 2 million years ago, great ice sheets began forming and moving across North America. The continent experienced four major periods of glaciation, and as many as 20 ice sheets covered northeastern Minnesota. Ice lobes moved preferentially through the basin and scoured out the softer sedimentary rocks that had been deposited there. At times the ice was more than a mile thick along the North Shore. As ice melted, the basin filled with water (Figure 11). In between glacial periods rivers carried runoff, sediments, and boulders into the lake.

As the ice started to melt back to the northeast, the meltwater trapped between the face of the ice sheet and high ridges of land around the southern edge of the lake formed Glacial Lake Duluth, the granddaddy of today's Lake Superior (Figure 12). Geologists have identified 28 different levels of Glacial Lake Duluth based on the presence of wave-cut cliffs and beaches. The highest water level was about 450 feet higher than Lake Superior's surface today. If you had stood at Hawk Ridge (a high point in Duluth that rises about 500 feet above the lake's surface) 10,000 years ago, the lake may have lapped at your toes. In cooler times with less melting, the lake level dropped and was once as much as 250 below its present level. The proto-

St. Louis River flowed into the south end of Lake Duluth, cutting a deep channel that included the canyon at Jay Cooke State Park. When the lake level rose to present levels the mouth of the river drowned, forming the current estuary.

When the water level got high enough, it drained out near Brule, Wisconsin, in torrential flows, south through what are now the Namekagen and St. Croix rivers, and ultimately formed the Dalles of the St. Croix River at Taylor's Falls.

Eventually the ice melted back far enough to the northeast that the lake was able to establish an outlet through the St. Marys River, where the land is lower than in the western arm of the lake.

As we learned in Chapter 1, land around the lake is still rebounding from the weight of all that ice. The ice was thicker (and thus heavier) to the north, so the Canadian portion of the watershed is experiencing greater *isostatic rebound* than the south shore. Although the movement is imperceptible to us, the land is actually rising about 18 inches per century.

Lake Superior's unique geologic history makes it a great place to look for remnants of our planet's past. For example, visitors frequently search the North Shore for agates and thomsonite, the stones we met in Chapter 1 that formed as mineral-laden water moved through small pores left by gas bubbles trapped in the cooling lava.

Life in Lake Superior

Of course, a lake is not all about rocks and water. Like other lakes, Superior contains plants and animals, too. But not as many as most other lakes! Lake Superior is oligotrophic — it has very low concentrations of dissolved nutrients. That means that it has less capacity to support biological communities. In fact, its fishery (an area where fish are caught) is only about 10 percent as large as that of Lake Michigan, which has much higher concentrations of nutrients in its water.

Lake Superior's low productivity is the result of several factors. Though the lake has high levels of nitrogen, an essential nutrient (as we learned in Chapter 4), it is extremely low in phosphorus, also an essential nutrient. The watershed is largely composed of igneous rocks covered by very shallow soils that do not release much phosphorus into runoff. Superior's northern latitude means the growing season is short, so aquatic plants and algae don't get a lot of time to grow. And, because the lake is so deep with steep slopes near shore, it lacks shallow zones for extensive plant growth.

Low productivity affects aquatic plants as well as animal populations throughout the food chain, from plankton up to fish.

Fish

Thirty-four species of native fish and another 17 species of non-native fish reproduce in Lake Superior. Two other non-native fish species, the American eel and Atlantic salmon, live but do not reproduce in the lake. Although in 2014 naturally producing Atlantic salmon were discovered very close in St. Mary's River near Sault Ste. Marie, Michigan.

Native fish inhabiting Lake Superior's clear, deep, and cold waters include burbot (aka eelpout or lawyer), deepwater sculpin (mainly nocturnal, lives in the deepest parts of the lake), lake trout, sturgeon, and whitefish. Non-native fish include Chinook salmon, rainbow trout, common carp, sea lamprey, and ruffe.

Other Species

Beyond fish, many species call the Lake Superior watershed home, including bacteria, algae, aquatic plants, macroinvertebrates, aquatic insects, amphibians, reptiles, birds, and mammals.

Bacteria are critical to the aquatic food web, processing carbon-based matter and recycling nutrients through decomposition. Some use sunlight to photosynthesize, and some use sunlight and carbon-based material for energy. Most bacteria in Lake Superior are part of a healthy ecosystem and do not cause disease. Other bacteria can cause illness or indicate the presence of other disease-causing organisms such as viruses and parasites. Beach monitoring in the western end of Lake Superior has detected the presence of these indicator bacteria, particularly after storms that carry runoff from impervious surfaces; areas inhabited by birds, wildlife, livestock, or pets; sources of untreated wastewater; or inadequate septic systems.

The Founding of 3M

Minerals found along the shore of Lake Superior played a role in the founding of one of Minnesota's most famous companies, 3M. In 1902, a group of Two Harbors businessmen formed a company to mine corundum at Crystal Bay, near where U.S. Highway 1 joins U.S. Highway 61. An extremely hard mineral, corundum was used for sandpaper at the time, and the only other source in North American was in Canada. Unfortunately, the mineral the businessmen were mining was not corundum — it was anorthosite, and it was useless for sandpaper. The businessmen ended up finding other funding and sources for abrasive materials and 3M grew into a successful company despite the inauspicious beginning.

Macroinvertebrates are animals that are large enough to see with the naked eye (greater than 0.02 inches, or the size of a pencil dot) and that have no backbone. They include aquatic insects, mites, worms, snails, and crayfish. They spend some part of their life cycle in the benthos, or bottom of the lake.

Diporeia are one kind of macroinvertebrate. They are amphipods and an important food for every fish species in the lake. Although individually they are tiny, they are a very large part of the lake ecosystem. In fact, researchers estimate that they comprise up to 65 percent of the total benthic biomass in some parts of the Great Lakes.

Many other macroinvertebrates, in addition to Diporeia, are important in the Lake Superior food web (Figure 13).

People and Lake Superior

In addition to the natural cycles of change that have faced Lake Superior over millennia, such as the tectonics and lava flows, glaciers, and shifts in vegetation and animal life, human activities have had major impacts on the Lake Superior ecosystem.

Traders used Lake Superior and the other Great Lakes as the equivalent of our highways, traveling across them and using them for transporting furs and trade goods. The first map of Lake Superior was made in 1671 by Jesuit Claude Dablon with his colleague Claude-Jean Allouez. Can you imagine how they mapped the lakeshore, tributaries, islands, and shoals from a canoe?

Fishing

In 1834, the American Fur Company began commercial fishing in Lake Superior to supplement the diminishing fur-trading profits. The company shipped 4,000 to 5,000 barrels of whitefish and lake trout annually during the height of the fishing boom in the mid 1830s. In 1842, the American Fur Company was dissolved, and one by one the old fur trading and fishing posts were abandoned.

After the LaPointe Treaty was signed in 1854 (see Chapter 8), the North Shore was opened up to settlement. Settlers staked many claims and platted small villages. The town of Beaver Bay was platted and registered in St. Louis County in 1856 (before Minnesota was even a state), although there had been cabins built there in 1854 by Thomas Clark, a surveyor and civil engineer. In 1871, the village of Grand Marais was founded and a commercial fishing operation began there.

In 1879, Duluth had 35 commercial fishermen; by 1885, there were 195 fishermen operating out of Duluth and dozens more along the North Shore. Steamers traveled up the shore to deliver supplies and pick up barrels of pickled whitefish and trout. Fish were sold in Minneapolis, St. Paul, Chicago, Kansas City, and St. Louis.

Lake trout supplanted whitefish in the late 1800s. Still, commercial fishing continued to flourish along the North Shore during the early 20th century. The all-time high catch of 10,000 tons was reported in 1915 from Duluth alone. During the 1920s the catch dwindled due to overfishing, and by 1930 it had dropped to less than 4,000 tons annually. In Minnesota there were 300 commercial fishermen in the 1930s. That number dropped to under 100 in the 1970s. As of 2016 the limit is 25.

Lake Superior Food Web

Foodweb based on "Impact of exotic invertebrate invaders on food web structure and function in the Great Lakes: A network analysis approach" by Mason, Krause, and Ulanowicz, 2002 - Modifications for Lake Superior, 2009.

NOAA, Great Lakes Environmental Research Laboratory, 4840 S. State Road, Ann Arbor, MI 734-741-2235 - www.glerl.noaa.gov

Macroinvertebrates

Chironomids/Oligochaetes. Larval insects and worms that live on the lake bottom. Feed on detritus. Species present are a good indicator of water quality.

Amphipods (*Diporeia*). The most common species of amphipod found in fish diets that began declining in the late 1990's.

Opossum shrimp (*Mysis relicta*). An omnivore that feeds on algae and small cladocerans. Migrates into the water column at night.

Mayfly nymphs (*Hexagenia* spp.). A burrowing insect larvae found in warm, shallow water bays and basins, usually in soft sediments. The presence of this sensitive organism indicates good water quality conditions.

Mollusks. A mixture of native and non-native species of snails and clams are eaten by lake whitefish and other bottom feeding fish.

Zebra and quagga mussels (*Dreissena polymorpha* and *Dreissena bugensis*). Established in Lake Superior in 1989 (zebra); 2005 (quagga). Filter-feeders that remove huge quantities of plankton.

Zooplankton (Microscopic animals found in the water column)

Invasive Spiny waterfleas (*Bythotrephes longimanus*). Visual raptorial predator that can depress native waterflea populations.

Native Raptorial waterfleas (*Leptodora kindtii*). Slow moving and patchy distribution of small swarms at relatively low numbers.

Cyclopoid copepods (e.g., *Cyclops bicuspidatus*). Carnivorous copepods that feed on rotifers and other microzooplankton.

Native waterfleas (e.g., *Daphnia galeata*). Filter-feeding waterfleas that can be important for controlling phytoplankton.

Calanoid copepods (e.g., *Diaptomus* spp.). Omnivores that feed on both phytoplankton and microzooplankton.

Rotifers. A diverse group of microzooplankton that, depending on species, feed on phytoplankton, detritus, or other microzooplankton.

Phytoplankton (Algae found in the water column)

Blue-green algae (aka Cyanobacteria). Often inedible and frequently toxic; blooms in late summer and can look like spilled paint on the water surface.

Green algae. Microscopic (single-celled) plants that form the main support of the summer food web. Also includes large nuisance species such as *Cladophora*.

Diatoms. Cold-loving microscopic (single celled) plants encased in silica shells that support the first wave of production in the spring.

Flagellates. Motile, single-celled plants or animals frequently found in high numbers. Most eat bacteria and so may help funnel bacterial products back into the food chain.

Sea Lamprey

Sea lamprey (*Petromyzon marinus*). An aggressive, non-native parasite that fastens onto its prey and rasps out a hole with its rough tongue.

Piscivores (Fish Eaters)

Chinook salmon (*Oncorhynchus tshawytscha*). Pacific salmon species stocked as a trophy fish and to control alewife.

Rainbow trout or Steelhead (*Oncorhynchus mykiss*). A lake strain of non-native rainbow trout, rarely found deeper than 35 feet. Supplemented by stocking.

Brook Trout (*Salvelinus fontinalis*). Native, and is Michigan's state fish. Found in the Great Lakes and throughout the state in many creeks, streams, rivers, and lakes. They require cool, clear, spring-fed streams and pools. Eat zooplankton, crustaceans, worms, fish, terrestrial insects, and aquatic insects.

Lake trout (*Salvelinus namaycush*). Nearly eliminated by sea lampreys during the 1950s and 1960s. Stocking and lamprey control are resulting in its resurgence.

Walleye (*Stizostedion vitreum*). Carnivorous night feeders, eating fishes such as yellow perch and freshwater drum, insects, crayfish, snails, and mudpuppies.

Burbot (*Lota lota*). Elongated, cylindrical, freshwater codfish.

Forage Fish

Lake whitefish (*Coregonus clupeaformis*). Native found in cold waters. Bottom feeder—diets have shifted to include zebra and quagga mussels.

Yellow perch (*Perca flavescens*). Native that schools near shore, usually at depths less than 30 feet.

Bloater (*Coregonus hoyi*). Native deepwater chub feeding on zooplankton and other organisms near the lake bottom. Harvested commercially for smoked fish.

Deepwater sculpin (*Myoxocephalus quadricornis thompsonii*). A native glacial relic that lives at the bottom of cold, deep water feeding on aquatic invertebrates.

Lake herring or Cisco (*Coregonus artedii*). A schooling fish. that prefer deep water. They primarily eat plankton, but also eat insects and small minnows.

Kiyi (*Coregonus kiyi*). A deepwater cisco or chub endemic to the Great Lakes. It is reportedly most abundant at depths greater than 200 feet.

Rainbow Smelt (*Osmerus mordax*). Found in both coastal and offshore habitats. Light-sensitive, so prefer deeper, cooler waters during the warmer seasons.

Ruffe (*Gymnocephalus cernuus*). Native to Eurasia, was introduced to Lake Superior via ballast water. First collected in Lake Superior fish surveys in 1986.

Planktivores/Benthivores

Lake Sturgeon (*Acipenser fulvescens*). Endangered. Eats small clams, snails, crayfish, sideswimmers, and aquatic insect larvae.

82 species of fish, including at least 13 non-natives, make their homes in the waters of Lake Superior. This food web includes only the dominant species.

Figure 13. An example of a Lake Superior food web and its inhabitants.

Sea lamprey and overharvesting decimated the trout populations in the 1950s. Sport anglers lobbied for legislation favoring recreational fishing over commercial fishing. Since 1950, numerous restoration and conservation efforts have helped to stabilize fish population in Lake Superior. Today, anglers along the North Shore enjoy fishing in both the big lake and its tributaries, which have different seasons and catch limits. Popular sportfish include lake trout, salmon (chinook, pink, coho), steelhead (migratory rainbow trout), Kamloops rainbow trout, brook trout and brown trout, as well as walleye and northern pike. In 2011 Minnesota had more than 1.7 million licensed anglers; northeastern Minnesota had more than 253,000 anglers. Retail sales from recreational fishing amounted to over $307 million and 4,458 jobs were directly related to recreational fishing. Local and state tax revenue in 2011 from recreational fishing was over $33 million, while federal tax revenue was nearly $40 million. That same year, an estimated 800 anglers spent over 11,000 days fishing for salmon, steelhead, and lake trout on the Great Lakes.

Logging

Lake Superior was an important source of transportation for Minnesota's early logging industry (which you'll hear a lot more about in Chapter 8). Duluth, Superior City, and Beaver Bay had small sawmills, and in the early 1860s they began shipping lumber to other Lake Superior towns, such as LaPointe, Copper Harbor, and Marquette.

By 1894, 15 mills in Duluth and 17 mills in Superior employed more than 7,700 workers, and at the turn of the century, the Duluth-Superior Harbor was the world's greatest lumber market: A billion feet of lumber was shipped from the North Shore alone in 1902. In 1925, only one lumber mill remained in Duluth, although some timber products continued to be shipped out of the harbor until World War II. Through the 1940s, wood was cut for the pulp and paper industry and rafted to Wisconsin from Gooseberry River, Red Cliff River, Pigeon River, Chicago Bay, and Sugarloaf Landing. You can learn much more about how the pulpwood was hauled, sluiced down to the lake, and rafted over to Ashland if you visit Sugarloaf Cove.

During the white pine logging era, man-made barriers were built along Lake Superior tributaries to hold back water and then sluice logs downstream. Damming tributaries affected fish communities by changing the physical characteristics of river's hydrology (flow, temperature, gradient). Logs careening downstream crashed into stream banks, causing erosion and damaging stream channels. Poor logging techniques, subsequent forest (*slash*) fires, and increased runoff from the loss of vegetation caused excessive sedimentation that clogged tributaries and reached Lake Superior, where the increased turbidity degraded habitat and affected fish populations.

Mining

As with logging, Lake Superior has played an important transportation role for Minnesota's mining industry (which you'll also read a lot about in Chapter 8). Construction of the Duluth & Iron Range Railway began during the summer of 1883 to move iron ore to Agate Bay (present-day Two Harbors), where two 552-foot gravity-feed docks were built to load it onto boats for shipping. During most years from 1892 through 1952, at least a million tons per year came from the Vermilion range. By 1900, the range shipped over 4 million tons of iron ore through Two Harbors.

In 1897, J. D. Rockefeller formed the Bessemer Steamship Company to haul his iron ore from Minnesota's Iron Range to Ohio and return with coal. Andrew Carnegie organized the Pittsburgh Steamship Company in 1898, and another rival, the Minnesota Steamship Company, also built ships to haul ore. By 1900, nearly 100 steamships were hauling ore across the big lake.

High demand during World War I and World War II led to depletion of high-grade iron ore, and the industry switched to extracting iron from lower-grade taconite (iron-bearing sedimentary rock). Reserve Mining Company built a plant at Silver Bay and began shipping taconite pellets in 1955. Taconite processing continues today at this location.

Tourism

Lake Superior is a premier destination for visitors from around the world as well as within Minnesota and the U.S. Visitors take advantage of the great lake's water resources to sail, fish, scuba dive, surf, kayak, skip rocks, and—occasionally—swim. In the Duluth area, tourism has an estimated value of $400 million annually, and it is proportionately valuable for smaller communities along the North Shore. Eight Minnesota state parks along the North Shore give visitors opportunities to participate in both summer and winter activities.

In 2014 visitors spent nearly $800 million in northeastern Minnesota, and tourism was responsible for more than 16,000 private sector jobs in the region. A half million people visited Agate Bay in Two Harbors in 2014 to walk the breakwater, view the lighthouse, skip rocks, or be amazed by the giant ships filling up at the ore docks.

Bringing visitors to the region offers an opportunity to reach and teach new people and increase stewardship of Lake Superior. Engaging residents and visitors in ecotourism opportunities such as birdwatching can further stewardship. On the other hand, tourism poses some challenges for the lake, including increased water use, increased storm-water runoff from impervious surfaces, introduction of non-native species, erosion and damage from off-highway vehicles, and the loss of the intangible "North Shore character."

Modern Shipping

The St. Lawrence Seaway, opened in 1959, made it possible for large commercial ships to travel between Duluth and the Atlantic Ocean, improving our ability to ship raw materials, agricultural commodities, and manufactured products to the East Coast and beyond. If you scan the lake most any day between March and late December, you're likely to see a huge *laker* (a domestic cargo ship) or a *saltie* (an ocean-going vessel) plying the waters of Lake Superior (Figure 14). Duluth/Superior is the largest, farthest-inland freshwater port (Figure 15), the number one volume port in the Great Lakes, and the second largest dry bulk port in the entire U.S. The port receives about 1,000 vessel visits per year, with those vessels carrying a total of some 38 million tons of cargo. In 2010, the port generated $1.5 million in economic impact and provided 11,510 jobs in Minnesota and Wisconsin. The principal outbound cargos are iron ore, coal, and grain. Inbound cargos include limestone, cement, and salt, and, more recently, large shipments of wind turbine components and heavy equipment for energy-related projects (Figure 16).

Taconite is the only commodity shipped from Two Harbors today, with an average of 12.3 million tons shipped annually.

Figure 14. A ship leaves the Duluth-Superior port under the Aerial Lift Bridge.

One way shipping has affected the big lake big time is through introduction of non-native species (more on that later). Another relates to dredging required to ensure that shipping channels remain deep enough for fully loaded ships. Some sediments contain legacy contaminants that can be released with dredging, so care must be taken to ensure the dredged materials are managed properly. Disposing of dredged material can cost up to twice as much as the dredging itself and the Duluth/Superior Harbor dredged material disposal facility is at capacity, so a regional partnership was formed to recycle and reuse dredged materials for purposes such as creating wetlands and sealing contaminated sites so pollutants don't migrate. This effort will allow dredging in the harbor to continue so shipping will not be restricted.

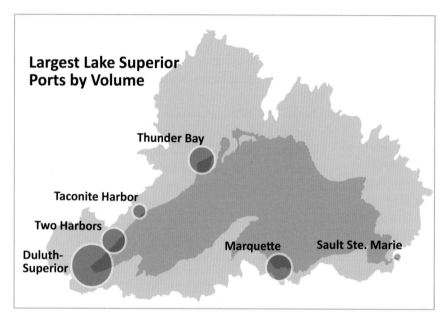

Figure 15. Duluth-Superior is Lake Superior's largest port by volume. Currently there is no shipping out of Taconite Harbor.

Figure 16. Wind turbine components are among the many cargo items that enter Minnesota from overseas via the Port of Duluth.

Withdrawals and Diversions

Duluth, Two Harbors, Beaver Bay, Silver Bay, and Grand Marais all obtain their water supplies from Lake Superior. The cities draw from the lake, chlorinate it, treat it with fluoride, distribute it to homes and businesses, run it through a wastewater treatment facility, and return it to the lake.

The first major diversion of water out of the Great Lakes was in 1887, when the flow of the Chicago River was reversed and water from Lake Michigan was diverted into the river to carry untreated sewage away from Chicago's water intakes and down to the Mississippi River. In Minnesota, in the 1850s, a plan was proposed to create a canal between Lake Superior and the Mississippi River via the St. Croix River to permit shipping via an inland waterway. This proposal even received $10,000 from Congress in 1894 for a feasibility study. Thankfully the project was deemed economically impractical.

In the late 1970s, the Powder River Coal Company proposed a plan to construct a coal slurry pipeline from Wyoming and Montana to Duluth that would use Lake Superior water to suspend the coal. In 1982, on a mandate from Congress, the U.S. Army

Corps of Engineers studied feasibility of diverting water from the Great Lakes to replenish the Ogallala aquifer, which underlies eight states from Texas to South Dakota. In 1998, Canada issued permits to the Nova Group to ship up to 50 tanker vessels of water to unidentified private customers in Asia. None of these proposed projects, however, has proven practical or economically feasible. There are no significant diversions today out of Lake Superior, nor are there likely to be any under our current international agreement.

During the 1940s, two man-made diversions of water into the Lake Superior basin were completed. The Long Lac and Ogoki diversions enabled Canada to increase its electrical generation during World War II. The Ogoki Diversion, completed in 1943, connected the Ogoki River to Lake Nipigon and from there to Lake Superior. The resulting flow averages 5,000 cubic feet per second and slightly increases the net water supply to the Great Lakes basin. The mean water level in Lake Superior was increased by three inches. During times of high water (in 1953, 1973, and 1985), the diversions were temporarily halted.

Pollution

Lake Superior is the clearest and cleanest of the Laurentian Great Lakes. Because of thin soils over igneous bedrock, it naturally has very low concentrations of dissolved or suspended particulates, nutrients, sediment, and organic matter, although following storms or snowmelt, nearshore areas may become reddish brown from runoff delivered by rivers or storm drains.

Wastewater from communities and households along the lake contribute some pollution. Wastewater treatment primarily removes nutrients and pathogens (disease-causing organisms, such as bacteria or viruses), but does not necessarily remove other contaminants, such as chlorinated compounds, endocrine-active chemicals, or microplastics.

Households that aren't hooked up to municipal water and sewer generally use private wells as their source of drinking water and onsite septic systems for treating their wastewater. Constructing and maintaining septic systems can be especially challenging along the North Shore because of fractured bedrock close to the surface or covered with shallow, clay-rich soil. Many systems were installed before current regulations designed to protect public health and water quality in Lake Superior and inland lakes and rivers. Researchers estimate that over 12,000 systems along the North Shore are providing inadequate wastewater treatment and another 1,500 present an imminent threat to public health. Systems that don't properly treat household wastewater may contribute nutrients, pathogens, or other contaminants to Lake Superior and other ground and surface waters in the area.

A recently discovered wastewater-related threat to the Lake Superior ecosystem comes in the form of tiny bits of plastic that come from personal care products such as toothpaste and facial scrub or that form from the breakdown of plastic beach litter. The tiny bits, about 1 micron in diameter (about one-quarter the size of a human red blood cell) can glom onto aquatic pollutants such as PCBs. Researchers are concerned that these so-called "microplastics" may accumulate in and harm fish and other aquatic animals that eat them.

Also a threat are endocrine-active chemicals that get into the water from pharmaceuticals and personal care products. Half or more of medicines consumed pass through the human system into wastewater, and many of those end up in the lake, where they can make it hard for fish and other aquatic animals to reproduce. In other areas of the United States and Europe where these chemicals are present in greater concentrations, they have even been found in drinking water. We don't know how long these chemicals persist in the environment or whether they can accumulate in sediments.

Many pollutants entering Lake Superior come, not from point sources such as wastewater treatment plants, but from the atmosphere. This means it's hard to eliminate the sources. And even though pollutants may be present in very small concentrations, many *bioaccumulate* (build up) in living creatures as one eats another and takes on the toxins it contains (Figure 17). Mercury and polychlorinated byphenols (PCBs) are probably the two best-recognized pollutants in the lake. Plankton, insects, fish, loons, raptors, and even humans can experience developmental or reproductive disorders or other problems as pollutants accumulate in their fat, flesh, or blood.

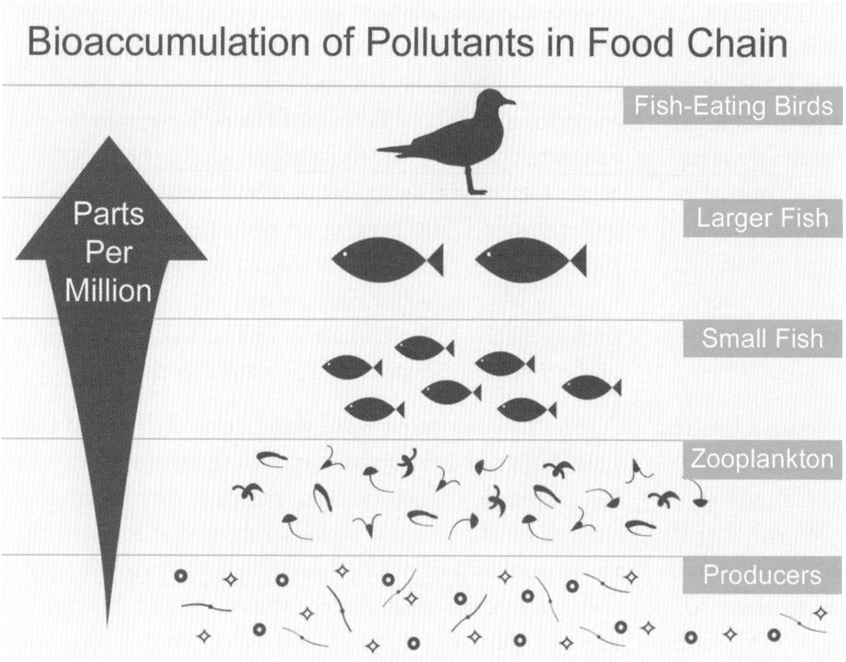

Bioaccumulation of Pollutants in Food Chain

Parts Per Million

Fish-Eating Birds

Larger Fish

Small Fish

Zooplankton

Producers

Figure 17. Pollutants can bioaccumulate (build up) in organisms as they eat other contaminated organisms.

One of the most obvious consequences of bioaccumulation is the issuing of fish consumption advisories. Because pollutants build up in older, larger fish, (as we learned in Chapter 7) the Minnesota Department of Health has developed recommendations regarding how many fish of certain species and sizes and from various locations people should consume to reduce their risk of being harmed by toxics.

Some nearshore areas have become enriched with nutrients from human activities that are carried into the lake as wastewater, storm-water drainage, and increased sediment and nutrient runoff from impervious surfaces. On July 14–15, 2012, observers reported a rare blue-green algae bloom near the Apostle Islands in Wisconsin that was attributed to unusually warm water and a recent flood that had flushed sediment and nutrients into the lake. Severe weather events, floods, pulses of nutrient-rich runoff, and subsequent algae blooms are likely to increase as a changing climate leads to increasingly variable weather and warmer waters.

Non-native Invasive Species

Perhaps one of the greatest impacts humans have had on Lake Superior is introducing non-native plant and animal species. Non-native species can affect human use of the lake by diminishing sport fishing success (e.g., reducing populations of sport fish), making recreation less fun (e.g., beaches littered with sharp shells), damaging equipment and machinery, and clogging water intakes.

Some non-native fish have been intentionally introduced into the lake to provide opportunities for fishing, as food for other fish, or to control other fish populations. These include brown trout (stocked in 1883); rainbow trout (stocked in 1885); common carp (stocked in 1897), and chinook, coho, and pink salmon (stocked in the 1950s and 1960s).

Other non-native fish were accidentally introduced into Lake Superior. The Welland Canal, completed in 1830, connected Lake Superior to the Atlantic Ocean. This led to the introduction of alewife, rainbow smelt, and sea lamprey, among other species, which had a major impact on lake trout populations. Non-native fish that have been accidentally introduced through ballast water (water carried by ships to boost their stability when they're not carrying cargo) include the ruffe, round goby, tubenose goby, and white perch.

As of November 2015, 101 non-native aquatic species have been introduced to Lake Superior through maritime commerce (e.g., ship ballast water and hull fouling), fishing and aquaculture, canals and diversions, the trade of live organisms, tourism and development activities. The exact route of introduction for many of these non-native species is unknown: 28 species may have been introduced through ballast water, while others have come from recreational boating, dumping live bait, or aquaria.

The Coast Guard issued ballast water regulations in 2012 intended to reduce the importation of invasive species into the U.S., pursuant to the National Invasive Species Act passed in 1996. The rule applies to U.S. and foreign ships calling at all U.S. ports (not just the Great Lakes). Previously, ships were required to conduct a ballast water exchange while at sea, but the new rule requires ships to install ballast water management systems onboard.

Recreational boaters almost certainly introduced curly-leaf pondweed and Eurasian watermilfoil, although those nuisance species are not likely to present the same kind of problems in Lake Superior as they have in inland lakes because Lake Superior has limited shallow areas where the plants can thrive.

All introduced species affect the ecosystem in some way by competing for food, disrupting the food web, crowding out or preying on native species, or taking over nesting or other habitats. Some non-native species are very successful in their new ecosystems because they have few predators or other limits on their populations.

Zebra mussels seem to be the poster children for nasty invasive species. They can affect the food web, harm fish, smother native mussels, and litter beaches with their sharp shells. Moreover, they cause billions of dollars of damage annually by clogging water intake valves for power plants and other facilities and attaching to boat motors and other hard surfaces.

The impacts of introduced zooplankton have not been fully identified, but one example provides a worrisome scenario. Spiny water fleas have long spiny tails that make them hard to eat, so fish avoid them. They have seriously altered the food web by feasting on key zooplankton that young fish used to rely on. Thus, their populations increase while the more desirable, edible native zooplankton are in decline. Spiny water fleas also affect recreational fishing, because the gelatinous plankton build up on fishing lines and make them hard to reel in.

The ruffe is a fast-growing, fast-breeding non-native fish that was first found in the Duluth-Superior area in 1986. It can tolerate a wide range of water temperatures and other habitat conditions, so easily thrives in new locations. Because it is so adaptable, it can take up food and space needed by native fish such as walleye and perch and disrupt the balance between predators and prey that is the foundation of a healthy fishery.

Eliminating a non-native species once it has become established is extremely difficult and may not be possible in Lake Superior. Many research efforts aimed at understanding the reproductive and feeding habits of non-native species are underway to find effective methods to control or manage invasive populations.

Leadership for the Lake

Lake Superior's watershed comprises two countries, three states, one province, 16 counties, and innumerable townships and municipalities. As a result, sorting out jurisdictions and responsibilities is a daunting task. Typically federal laws take precedence over state and local regulations, but state and federal laws are generally enforced at the local level and local resources may be inadequate for the task. While everyone agrees that quality water and a healthy ecosystem are very important, not everyone agrees on how to reach those goals.

The U.S. and Canada created the International Joint Commission (IJC) in 1909 because they recognized that each country is affected by the other's action in lake and river systems along the border. The IJC is guided by the Boundary Waters Treaty of 1909, which was enacted to ensure transportation, commerce, and international water rights and provides general principles for preventing and resolving disputes over shared waters. As it regulates shared water uses and investigates transboundary issues, the IJC considers the needs of a range of water issues, including drinking water, commercial shipping, hydroelectric generation, agriculture, industry, fishing, recreational boating, and shoreline property management.

With the help of the IJC, citizens and other organizations, the hope is to manage and maintain the health of this great lake for future generations.

Explore

This section highlights great examples of places you can learn more about Lake Superior. Please check them out online, then head out to discover them in real life!

Iona's Beach SNA

WHAT Iona's Beach Scientific & Natural Area at Iona's Beach is named after an original owner of the Twin Points Resort. The 300-yard-long beach is made up of pink rhyolite cobbles. A mixed coniferous/deciduous forest and alder swamp add ecological diversity to the site.

WHEN The beach is open all year, with free access from the wayside parking area.

WHERE At mile marker 42 on U.S. Highway 61, follow a 1/4-mile trail from the parking area.

WHO DNR SNA Program, Northeast Region, 650 Highway 169, Tower, MN 55790, (218) 753-2580 x244

FOR MORE INFORMATION www.dnr.state.mn.us/snas

Crystal Bay

WHAT Crystal Bay is the location of 3M's original corundum mining site. It's part of Tettegouche State Park, but the site is largely unmarked. There's a turnout on the lake side of U.S. Highway 61, just north of the intersection with U.S. Highway 1. A trail that leads up into the woods or down to the lake. It's steep, but if you go down you'll see the remains of equipment and excavations where 3M mined corundum in the early 1900s. While at Tettegouche State Park also visit Palisade Head, a magnificent ancient lava flow.

WHEN Crystal Bay is open all year, but the trail down to the lake may be slippery due to ice or rain.

WHERE Take U.S. Highway 61 to the intersection with U.S. Highway 1 at Illgen City.

WHO Tettegouche State Park, 5702 Highway 61, Silver Bay, MN 55614, (218) 226-6365.

FOR MORE INFORMATION www.lakesuperior.com/travel/minnesota/242feature-2/

North Shore Commercial Fishing Museum

WHAT The North Shore Commercial Fishing Museum showcases artifacts and stories from historical commercial fishing days to the present through exhibits, talks, presentations, and events.

WHEN 9 a.m.–3 p.m. Sunday–Thursday; 9 a.m.–5 p.m. Friday and Saturday.

WHERE Take U.S. Highway 61 to the junction with Sawbill Trail near Tofte.

WHO 7136 Highway 61, Tofte, Minnesota 55615, (218) 663-7050.

FOR MORE INFORMATION www.commercialfishingmuseum.org

Grand Portage National Monument Heritage Center

WHAT The Grand Portage National Monument Heritage Center provides perspectives on the history and culture of the Grand Portage area. Exhibits and multimedia programs explore Ojibwe culture and the history of Minnesota's fur trade.

WHEN 8:30 a.m.–5 p.m. daily in the summer; 8:30 a.m.–4:30 p.m. Monday–Friday from mid-October until Memorial Day.

WHERE Drive 150 miles northeast of Duluth on U.S. Highway 61 to the community of Grand Portage. Turn right at the sign to Grand Portage National Monument onto Casino Road. Turn left at the stop sign at the intersection of Casino Road and Mile Creek Road. The heritage center is at 170 Mile Creek Road.

WHO Grand Portage National Monument, 170 Mile Creek Rd, Grand Portage, MN 55605, (218) 475-0123.

FOR MORE INFORMATION www.nps.gov/grpo

MASTER
NATURALIST
TOOLBOX

Teach

This section features lesson plans for activities related to Lake Superior. You may experience some of these activities as a student in your Master Naturalist class. The lessons are adaptable to a wide range of audiences, ages, and settings. Feel free to use them to teach others what you have learned!

LESSON 1

Lake Superior Lesson Plans

Objective

Participants will learn about the physical, biological, and cultural aspects of Lake Superior.

Audience Type

Child/Teen

Activity

Developed by the Great Lakes Aquarium, the 178-page *Lake Effects: The Lake Superior Curriculum Guide for Grades K–8* is available online as a PDF at http://glaquarium.org/wp-content/uploads/2015/11/Lake-Effects-BW-copy.pdf. Additional resources and kits related to Lake Superior can also be found at http://glaquarium.org/resourcetype/kits/.

LESSON 2

Lake Superior Game

Objective

Participants will explore differing viewpoints and consider the challenges of preserving and enhancing Lake Superior's ecosystem.

Audience Type

Teen/Adult

Activity

The Lake Superior Game is available online from Minnesota Sea Grant at www.seagrant.umn.edu/publications/S3. It takes about an hour to play.

This section highlights organizations that offer opportunities for Minnesota Master Naturalist Volunteers to participate in stewardship and citizen science activities as field naturalists in the North Woods, Great Lakes region. Please visit the websites to learn more.

Lake Superior Day

Held the third Sunday in July each year, Lake Superior Day provides an opportunity for communities all around the lake to call attention to and celebrate this amazing natural resource. Various communities participate with concerts, family activities, displays, dragon boat races, and other events and activities.

www.superiorforum.org/outreach-2/lake-superior-day

Lake County and Cook County Soil and Water Conservation Districts

The soil and water conservation districts offer activities in which volunteers can get involved, from busting exotic species to planting trees to youth field days.

www.co.lake.mn.us/departments/soil_and_water_conservation_district
http://co.cook.mn.us/2016site/index.php/soil-and-water

Expand

This section suggests some things you can use, do, pursue, read, or join to develop as a naturalist.

Journal

EXPERIENCE Go out in a fishing boat on Lake Superior and experience what it feels like to be in a small boat bobbing about on the world's greatest lake. Or watch fishing vessels and other boats from the shore. What are your strongest feelings? Will it matter if you don't catch any fish?

REFLECT Imagine how it would have felt to have been an early settler living on the shore of Lake Superior, catching fish for your livelihood. What hardships would you have faced? Do you think you would ever have felt warm and dry? What would happen if you didn't catch any fish?

RECORD Write a poem describing your feelings when out on the lake or what you imagined it would be like to be an early subsistence angler.

Read

Geology on Display: Geology and Scenery of Minnesota's North Shore State Parks

John Green.
2005. St. Paul: Minnesota Department of Natural Resources. 70 pp.

Learn all about the grand geological events that shaped Lake Superior and its rugged North Shore—then see their footprints firsthand by checking out state park features showcased in this book.

North Shore: A Natural History of Minnesota's Superior Coast

Chel Anderson and Adelheid Fischer.
2015. University of Minnesota Press. 632 pp.

A wonderfully detailed book on the natural history of the North Shore broken into five sections: Headwaters, Highlands, Nearshore, Lake Superior, and Islands.

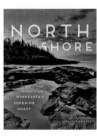

Surf

Minnesota Sea Grant

This information-loaded website includes facts and figures about Lake Superior and its watershed; details on fish, shipping, and invasive species; and updates on recent research about the big lake.

www.seagrant.umn.edu

St. Louis River Estuary Stories and Science

Explore stories of the estuary through the eyes of people that live and work there, and delve into the science of the interplay between humans and ecosystems. Challenge yourself with real-world "GeoQuests," or see how maps capture the beauty and complexity of this special place.

http://StLouisRiverEstuary.org

Lake Superior Streams

The Lake Superior Streams website provides excellent background information on Lake Superior's tributaries and brings together coastal communities, citizens, students, and managers. Maps, data, and recent research results are available along with action suggestions and valuable links.

www.lakesuperiorstreams.org

Join

Save Lake Superior Association

The Two Harbors–based Save Lake Superior Association was founded in 1969. Members work to protect Lake Superior from air pollution, water pollution, invasive species and more.

www.savelakesuperior.org

North Star Chapter of the Sierra Club

Part of America's oldest and largest grassroots environmental group, the North Star Chapter of the Sierra Club invites individuals to join group outings in Minnesota's great outdoors and provides many opportunities for volunteers to contribute to improving environmental quality in the Lake Superior area and around the state.

http://www.sierraclub.org/minnesota

Sugarloaf: The North Shore Stewardship Association

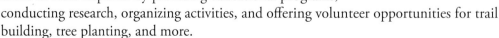

Sugarloaf supports and encourages stewardship of the North Shore of Lake Superior by providing educational programs, conducting research, organizing activities, and offering volunteer opportunities for trail building, tree planting, and more.

www.sugarloafnorthshore.org

MASTER
NATURALIST
TOOLBOX

Copyrighted Photographs and Images Used With Permission

Figure 1: Courtesy of mapsopensource.com

Figure 2: Courtesy of Great Lakes Commission, modified

Figure 3: Courtesy of Environment and Climate Change Canada

Figure 4: Courtesy of Wikimedia Commons

Figure 5: Courtesy of National Oceanic and Atmospheric Administration

Figure 6: Courtesy of University of Minnesota Sea Grant Program

Figure 7: Courtesy of University of Minnesota Sea Grant Program

Figure 8: Courtesy of University of Minnesota Sea Grant Program

Figure 9: Courtesy of Lakesuperiorstreams. 2016. LakeSuperiorStreams: Community Partnerships For UnderstandingWater Quality and Stormwater Impacts at the Head of the Great Lakes (http://lakesuperiorstreams.org). University of Minnesota Duluth, Duluth, MN 55812.

Figure 10: Courtesy of State Climatology Office, Minnesota DNR Division of Ecological and Water Resources

Figure 11: Courtesy of Great Lakes Commission and U.S. Army Corps of Engineers

Figure 12: Courtesy of Minnesota Department of Transportation

Figure 13: Courtesy of National Oceanic and Atmospheric Administration

Figure 14: Courtesy of Joyce L. VanEnkevort, Wikimedia Commons

Figure 15: Courtesy of Pete Markham, Wikimedia Commons, modified

Figure 16: Courtesy of Wikimedia Commons

Figure 17: Courtesy of University of Wisconsin Extension, modified

MASTER NATURALIST TOOLBOX

Expand

Chapter 8: Past, Present, and Future

Human Influence on the North Woods, Great Lakes

Marilyn K. Andersen, Don Elsenheimer, and Stephan P. Carlson

Goal

Understand how past, present, and future human activity shapes the quality and features of the North Woods, Great Lakes region.

Objectives

1. Describe how natural resource use shapes the cultural and natural history of the state.

2. Explain how nature-based recreation affects the landscape.

3. Describe effects of human activities on the ecology of the North Woods, Great Lakes region.

5. Discuss the likely impact of global climate change on the North Woods, Great Lakes region.

Introduction

When you think of northern Minnesota, what comes to mind? Chances are good the mental picture you paint includes forests, lakes, and perhaps wetlands. But this North Woods, Great Lakes landscape we enjoy today is only a quick snapshot in time along a continuum of change that began billions of years ago. As we saw in Chapter 1, volcanoes, collisions of large land masses, erosion, a huge sea, and glaciers all played a role in shaping the land along the way. Plants and animals also have altered the environment. In recent centuries, humans have had a big hand in shaping the woods and waters of this region.

This chapter provides an overview of some of the human influences on the North Woods, Great Lakes region. It begins with an overview of the ways of the Ojibwe, describing a way of living with the land. Then it moves on to explore influences of European immigrants and their descendants — through to the

many ways in which we shape the land and waters of the region today. Although it's impossible to describe every aspect of human impact in such a small space, we've tried to at least give a taste of some of the main areas in which people have made their mark on the North Woods, Great Lakes region over the centuries.

Today we have the power to inflict more damage on our environment than ever before. At the same time, we're also learning to be more aware of our impact and to prevent and mitigate harm. How we balance this give-and-take now and in the future will determine the extent to which nature can continue to meet our needs and the needs of other living things around us.

Living off the Land

People have lived in the Great Lakes Region for thousands of years. There is ample evidence of their lifestyle in the grand mounds left by Laurel Indians at the confluence of the Big Fork and Rainy rivers near International Falls.

Due to lack of archaeological sites, the early history of the North Shore isn't well understood. It is believed that by the 17th century, Ojibwe controlled much of the Lake Superior region.

The Ojibwe traveled the waterways of the north woods with birch-bark canoes and lived in dome-shaped, birch-covered lodges or wigwams. They obtained food, lodging, clothing, and medicines from the plants and animals that lived here. For example, they harvested birch and cedar trees to make canoes and baskets. Branches and greens were used for flooring and for ceremonies. Spruce roots were split and used to sew the birch bark slabs together and the seams were waterproofed with the spruce sap mixed with wood ash from hardwoods. The black ash tree, which grows with its roots in water, was used for

Figure 1. In early spring, the Ojibwe people moved their camps to maple woods, where they collected sap to make sugar.

baskets and snowshoes. The Ojibwe made baskets by pounding the outside of the five-foot ash log to loosen the yearly growth rings. The one-inch strips were then separated from the log, split in half again, and woven into pack baskets for carrying supplies. Animals provided food, and their organs were used to tan hides for clothing.

The lakes and rivers supplied an abundance of fish. The Ojibwe lived close to the water and fished more than they hunted. They wove nets out of the bark of basswood trees and used them year around for fishing. They also hunted woodland game, such as caribou, moose, elk, and deer, along with waterfowl. They offered tobacco to the Great Spirit before and after harvesting plants or animals.

In the spring when sap started to run in the sugar maples, Ojibwe clans moved to their sugar bush camps and collected sap to boil down for sugar to be used in cooking throughout the year (Figure 1). The same trees were tapped year after year with a spile (tubelike funnel) made of sumac wood, tapped into the tree. Sap ran through the spile to birch-bark baskets. Spring also saw the migration of sturgeon,

which swam up streams to spawn before returning to the deep, cold waters of the northern lakes.

Summer was a time to plant and harvest the "Three Sisters Garden," a triad of plants—beans, corn, and squash—that complemented each other. The corn plant provided an important food grain. The bean plant grew up the cornstalk and captured nitrogen from the air, enriching the soil (a process you might remember from Chapter 4!). The squash grew low to the ground, so its leaves kept out the weeds and held in the moisture. Later in the summer families traveled to berry camps, where they harvested and dried blueberries, raspberries, thimbleberries, cranberries, and more. Summer was also a time of celebration with Ojibwe people holding powwows.

In the late summer the Ojibwe traveled to rice camps to harvest manoominike, or wild rice—an annual plant that ripens over a two-week period in the fall. They harvested the plants from canoes using a long pole to push through the rice plants and cedar sticks to pull the rice plant over the gunwale of the canoe and knock the rice off the plant into the bottom of the canoe (Figure 2). This method allowed some of

Figure 2. Traditional methods of harvesting wild rice return some of the seed to the water, where it can give rise to the next year's crop.

reservations. This privatization of the reservations took place on six of the seven reservations in Minnesota, with only the Red Lake band continuing to hold all land as a band.

Today Ojibwe people live throughout the North Woods, Great Lakes region. Many still harvest wild rice, hunt, fish, snare rabbits, and attend berry camps and powwows.

Enter Europeans: The Fur Trade Era

Early French fur traders, the first Europeans to explore the north woods, forged westward through the St. Lawrence Seaway and around the edges of the Great Lakes in the late 1600s, drawn into the waterways and forests beyond. Why? Beaver hats.

European fashion of the time required hats for people in all stations of life, from royal families to business gentlemen to soldiers needing caps. Soft, pliable, resilient, and durable, beaver pelts were the preferred material (Figure 3). Hunger for hats had already depleted Old World beavers, when along came the opening of the New World.

the rice to fall back into the water, seeding the crop for the next year. The harvested seeds were then parched in a pot over an open fire and stomped on or thrashed to separate the husk from the seeds. The seeds were then winnowed by tossing them in the air to separate the shaft or husk from the finished rice. The rice was than stored for the winter.

Winter was the time to tell stories, when the north woods were in the grip of the snow and deep cold. Elders came together to share oral history with the children, teaching them about their tribe's stories, histories, and way of life. It was also trapping time, when the pelts of the beaver, mink, muskrat, martin, weasel, badger, fox, rabbit and other mammals were at their finest for use by the Ojibwe and eventually for trading.

Land cession treaties between the American government and indigenous people in Minnesota Territory began in 1837. Over the next 34 years the Ojibwe people were moved onto reservations. These treaties took away their land but protected the sovereign rights of the tribe and allowed the use and access of all lands for hunting, fishing, and trapping. The 1854 LaPointe Treaty established reservations in the Lake Superior area; under the treaty, bands with reservations have been federally recognized as independent nations. The Davis Act of 1887 allowed Indians to buy, sell, and own private land on

Figure 3. A European taste for beaver-skin hats fed an appetite for beaver pelts that reached deeply into the New World and Midwest.

The Ojibwe played a key role in this business, first as trappers and guides, later as middlemen for the companies seeking the beaver pelts and other furs. Marriages between the fur traders and the daughters of tribal chiefs helped establish

Figure 4. Fur-trading posts were hubs of economic activity for the North Woods, Great Lakes region in the 1700s.

they trotted to the first resting place on the portage, paused for a quick bit of tobacco, then moved on through wet, muddy, insect-infested swampland or rugged, rocky drop-offs paralleling waterfalls. These trips mostly took place in the fall, to port goods and supplies in to the trappers for trade, and in the spring, hauling furs out to the fur company. Relatively few parties overwintered in the backcountry.

Traders set up trading posts and bartered supplies such as hatchets, knives, kettles, and firearms for beaver pelts (Figure 4). The first trading post at Grand Portage was erected soon after 1732. It became the site of a great summer rendezvous, where goods were exchanged and everyone celebrated for two weeks with good food, stories, and music. Voyageurs who spent winters inland brought their pelts. Montreal canoe men from the East brought fresh merchandise. Buildings were set up to accommodate trading, storage of goods, food preparation, and lodging for businessmen unwilling to stay in tents. A summer visit to today's Grand Portage National Monument finds a cast and crew busy reenacting this old trading festival.

French and British traders operated simultaneously through the North Woods, Great Lakes region for years. French domination lasted from around 1680 to 1761. At that point, trade carried on under British domination through the Hudson's Bay Company, the North West Company, and others. North West built a post near modern day Pine City in 1804. The site has been restored and offers reenactors, buildings, and limited operations for tourists to observe.

In 1808, John Jacob Astor founded the American Fur Company, with headquarters at Fond du Lac on the St. Louis River. Its strong connections around

trade routes through Ojibwe territories. The fur trade brought a bartering system that gave the Ojibwe access to traps, guns, metal pots for cooking, cloth, blankets, paints, and beads to sew on their clothing and moccasins. The Ojibwe peoples' knowledge of wild rice, corn, and other native foods, combined with skills in winter survival and use of the birch-bark canoe, were critical success factors for the Europeans. Their knowledge and goods helped the traders survive and succeed in the wilderness.

French Canadian outdoorsmen, or "voyageurs," hauled furs and goods the long distances from their Indian sources, through rivers and rapids, portaging over rugged or swampy country, to trading posts. Pelts were placed in 90-pound packs. On portages, each voyageur carried two packs for up to eight miles per portage. Once loaded with bales on their backs,

George Bonga

Figure 5. Voyageur, trader, and translator George Bonga helped fur traders, voyageurs, and Ojibwe connect across cultures.

George Bonga (Figure 5), a voyageur and fur trader who was active in the area all his life, was born in 1802. Son of a black father and Ojibwe mother, he worked as a fur trader and translator, having learned English, French, and Ojibwe in Montreal, where he had been sent to school.

Bonga's booming voice, sense of humor, towering height, and human decency made him a successful and well-liked crew leader. He participated in both the Ojibwe and the white culture, speaking against white men who treated trappers unfairly, but also writing letters of complaint to the state government about individual Indian agents in the region. He married an Ojibwe woman, Ashwinn, and fathered four children. When the American Fur Company went bankrupt in 1842, the Bonga family became proprietors of a lodge in the Leech Lake area. Bonga's stories and singing entertained travelers there until he died in 1880.

Lake Superior, Lake Vermilion to the north, and the Mississippi to the south dominated the western fur trade, and made it the first million-dollar corporation in American history.

Minnesota's beaver-based fur trade had collapsed by 1840 as a result of diminishing supplies of beaver due to Native American lands being traded limiting trapping areas. In addition, European fashion shifted, reducing demand for beaver hats. By the late 1800s, beavers were nearly extirpated in Minnesota, nudging traders to move westward. While traders dealt with other animals, too, such as egrets for their feathers, the beaver market drove most of the activity. In the late 19th and early 20th centuries, protection by Minnesota's conservation officers enabled populations to rebound, though to only a fraction of the originally estimated 100 to 200 million animals prior to the fur trade.

Aside from thinning the beaver population, Minnesota's landscape saw few changes during the fur trade period. Most transportation was by water, with portages becoming more established. Small villages built up around the traders' compounds, but were accessed primarily by waterway. Native Americans slowly ceded their land to traders in exchange for debt forgiveness, a few supplies, and reservation allotments with off-reservation hunting and gathering rights. Traders turned to land speculation, profiting from real estate trades with industrialists for logging and mining rights. Industry brought rapid and significant changes to the landscape through infrastructure and economy. Roads were built for inland access, development of resources, and commerce. These changes to the land were permanent.

Settling the Wild Country

When the War of 1812 ended British dominance in the new Minnesota territory, several trading centers, army posts, and missions were left for use by American settlers. The war formalized American land ownership, but before lands could be claimed or sold, the U.S. government commissioned a land survey to carve out townships and sections. On the land, section corners were marked by a witness tree or post. The survey recorded the location of each section, natural features and agricultural value, providing reference of what the land was like at that time, forming the basis for the Marschner map we met in Chapter 2. Real estate sales in the wake of the survey brought business investment, settlement, and commerce.

Trails and roads in the territory were few. Rivers froze for four to five months each year, and roads roughly paralleled them. Primitive roads, unless frozen, were hard to travel, particularly with any significant load. Henry Sibley took Minnesota's plight to Washington. D.C., in the late 1840s, and brought home money to begin building a road system. Railroads caught up with this industry in the 1870s and 1880s. Railway companies, such as J. J. Hill's built tracks along the rivers and into the woods to speed transport. As railways slowly reached into the forests, local communities built roads leading to them to expand their own local trade. In this way, rails and roads jointly opened the territory to production and population in leapfrog fashion.

Minnesota became a state in 1858, a time when northern European immigrants began to seek land of their own. Minnesota land was available, and real "roads," as opposed to foot and dogsled trails, were slowly being built. Business grew accordingly, attracting more permanent residents. Some businesses built resorts and cabin rentals, as tourists began to enjoy the North Country. After 1900, tourists began to outnumber year-round residents.

Logging

Loggers entered Minnesota territory around the 1840s from the forests of Michigan and Wisconsin, chasing the endless trail of tall white pines and their closest allies, red and jack pines. White pine made great lumber for building the cities springing up along the Mississippi River, its tributaries, and rail lines (Figure 6). Some trees grew to 200 feet tall, with a three-foot diameter. Loggers used Lake Superior, the St. Croix River, and the Mississippi as main waterways for moving logs to mills that developed downstream. Lumberjacks who lived in logging camps deep in the forest cut the trees, dragged them to the nearest rivers, and cast them down boom sites into the river (Figure 7). The lightweight white pine logs floated downriver with the help of river men to sawmills, such as Ashland, Marine on St. Croix, Stillwater, and St.

Anthony. These logs were made into strong, durable, decay-resistant lumber.

Specialized crews made the trip downriver with the logs (Figure 8). They cleared the river of obstacles, broke up small jams forming at the front, and kept the lumber moving around rocks, rapids, and snags in the river. Other crews rounded up logs that had stalled or floated back into swamps or bogs. As they pried logs apart to break up jams, the stuck logs groaned and creaked, warning the crew to run to the riverbank before the jam gave way, possibly sweeping them to their death.

Logging as Big Business

Numerous logging companies moved their lumber down the same river at the same time. Companies stamped both ends of each log, branding it much as cattlemen branded their cattle in the West, so they could identify and retrieve their own logs at the take-out point downstream. Logging companies faced about 10 percent loss along this river journey. A flood could carry significant portions of logs into backwaters and low timber country. On the other hand, a year of low water levels often grounded logs on rocky bottoms and rapids. Even in good years, some logs sank to the river bottom or became stranded.

Grand Rapids, Bemidji, Park Rapids, Brainerd, Mora, Cloquet, and International Falls were all logging towns, built along the banks of rivers that could float the pine to market.

Water-powered sawmills were built first at Marine on St. Croix, then at Stillwater, which became the sawmill capital for a time. Sawmills needed a supply of water that could power a mill wheel. They often dammed water into a pool or millpond for this purpose. Because millponds froze in the winter, this, too, was seasonal work, until steam engines, running on sawdust and scraps, pumped hot water into the millponds. Sawing then became a year-round business. By the 1860s a new mill at St. Anthony Falls featured band saws that ran on an endless steel belt. As milling moved faster, more and bigger logging camps raced to keep up. Homes, factories, schools, hospitals, and churches were all made of wood and heated by wood, ensuring markets. Railroads required wood for the ties under their tracks and for wooden bridges. Wood built the Midwest, and Minnesota's forests fell to meet the need.

From the time the first lumber was cut at Marine on St. Croix in 1839 to the day the last big log was milled in the Rainy Lake Mill in Virginia in 1929, lumbering in Minnesota was big business. In 1857 alone, some 100 million board feet—a board foot is one foot long by one foot wide by one inch thick—were cut. By 1889, production topped 1 billion board feet, peaking at more than 2 billion board feet annually in 1899.

The white pine boom lasted for about 60 years. As lumber companies cleared white pines from their lands, revenue came to a halt, and they moved their operations to the next site, leaving taxes unpaid. This left a mire of stump lands and tax delinquency. Local governments raised taxes on the surrounding land in the area to pay for basic services, but higher taxes mostly led to more delinquencies. Forfeited lands were advertised as "prime lands cleared for farming." Unfortunately, settlers discovered that forest soils were not suitable for most crops; that growing seasons were too short; and that markets for farm produce were too far away. Supplemental seasonal employment opportunities had also moved on with the logging companies. Some counties zoned outlying areas for forestry and resettled families from depressed areas. A spiral of increasing problems resulted from tax delinquencies.

Figure 6. Lumberjacks cut up a Minnesota pine around 1915.

Figure 7. A load of logs heads to the river to be floated to sawmills downstream.

Figure 8. A drive crew worker tends logs as they float downriver.

A 1914 amendment to the Minnesota Constitution designated accumulating Trust Fund lands for state ownership. For forested lands still under private ownership, the 1927 Forest Law was enacted to allow owners to pay a low annual property tax and pay forest crop taxes only when they harvested trees. Large areas returned to county control and much land became state forests, resulting in the complex public-private ownership pattern of forests we have today.

One percent of the forest remained unlogged. We had changed the face of the land.

The Aftermath

Cut-and-run logging paid no attention to forest regeneration and restoration, and left behind piles up to 15 feet high of tinder-dry brush and stumps, called *slash*. Easily ignited by lightning or a stray spark, slash fueled sweeping forest fires that wiped out trees, habitat, and small communities of northern Minnesota and their residents—Hinckley in 1894, Chisholm in 1908, Baudette in 1910, and Cloquet–Moose Lake in 1918. Known as *holocaust fires*, these blazes claimed hundreds of lives and burned hundreds of thousands of contiguous acres in the North Woods,

Great Lakes region. They also decimated natural seed stocks and small seedlings that could reseed the forests after harvest, further altering the ecosystem.

Before 1920, logging interests regarded the north woods forests simply as a natural resource to be extracted and sold. Awareness dawned at the turn of the 20th century that human activities were destroying the forest. Some Minnesotans called for laws to encourage replanting trees. Others dismissed the challenge, saying that cleared forest would ease the path to farming. Our concepts of long-term land use were as yet uninformed and unorganized. As a result, little can be seen today of the original forest.

Genuine old-growth pine forests are rare and special. A few large remnants persist in Itasca State Park, the BWCAW, and the Lost 40 in the Chippewa National Forest (which we met in Chapter 2). Beginning around 1900, professional modern forestry methods began to be adopted, and with them, early conservation practices. In 1911 the state created the Minnesota Forest Service, a forerunner of the Minnesota DNR. The service began to enforce new laws regarding slash removal, regulate railroads to prevent sparks, require burning permits, and create forest ranger districts throughout the North Woods, Great Lakes region. Chapter 2 provides a useful snapshot of modern forest management.

Transitioning from "rough and ready" logging to forest management took awhile to gain acceptance. Economic and legal struggles naturally occurred along the way. With management, many new preservation developments have taken place. Regional planning across interested industries and agencies has coordinated and minimized land use. Conservation easements pay landowners not to sell their property to developers, for 40 percent of most land values. The Forest Legacy Program and the Land Trust help find funds for these investments. Such laws and practices ensure better use of the forest and other lands, preserving the value of these precious resources.

Mining in the North Woods

If the historical importance of 130 years of North Woods, Great Lakes region mining were better appreciated, Chisholm's famed memorial to Minnesota's iron miners would now be standing on national park land, and the 36-foot-tall statue of a miner at the top would be more often compared to the Statue of Liberty than to the Paul Bunyan statues in Brainerd and Bemidji. Rich red iron ore from the North Woods, Great Lakes region fed the blast furnaces that made the steel that was fashioned into the ships and planes and trucks that helped win two world wars. North Woods, Great Lakes iron went into Chicago's skyscrapers and Detroit's automotive plants. In other words, the products of North Woods, Great Lakes region mines have helped build and shape the world.

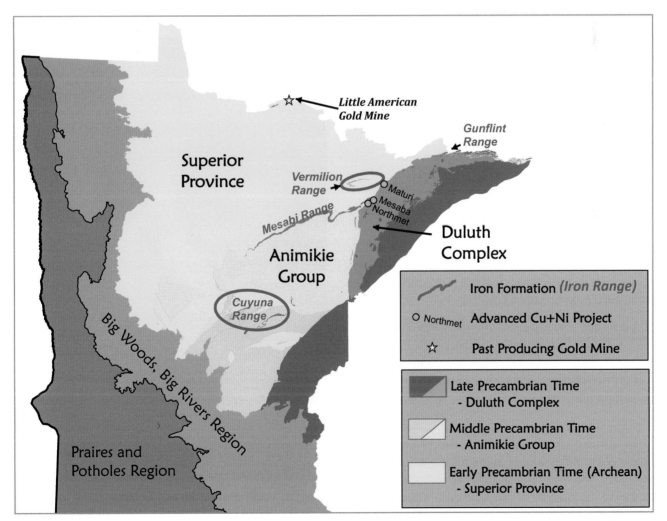

Figure 9. The North Woods, Great Lakes region is home to a variety of minerals of past, present, and future economic interest. These minerals are found within bedrock terrains that were formed during three distinct eras of ancient time.

Many Minerals

The bedrock formations that underlie the thick blanket of glacial sediments covering the North Woods, Great Lakes region are associated with the Archean Superior Province, the Animikie Group (and temporally related Middle Precambrian–aged rocks), and bedrock formed during the great midcontinent rift event (including the Duluth Complex, as described back in Chapter 1). These three great bedrock bodies, formed hundreds of millions of years apart, now stand shoulder to shoulder, like the three different flavors within a carton of Neapolitan ice cream. Each bedrock "flavor" contains different minerals of economic interest (Figure 9).

The best known and most economically and culturally significant economic mineral within the region is iron, which is found in massive ore bodies within the Superior Province (Vermilion Range) and Animikie Group (Gunflint, Cuyuna, and Mesabi ranges).

But iron isn't the only mineral that has drawn attention to the region or provided economic benefit to people living here. In 1865 and 1893, short-lived gold rushes brought prospectors and settlers into the Lake Vermilion and Rainy Lake areas, respectively. While only a single gold mine was opened in Minnesota (the Little American Mine, which operated for two years in Rainy Lake), a good part of the Archean Superior Province within the North Woods, Great Lakes region has high gold potential, and private mineral exploration companies are still actively searching for Minnesota's mother lode. A few companies have even searched for diamonds within these ancient rock formations!

Copper- and nickel-bearing minerals were discovered within the Duluth Complex in the 1940s. Explorers have since identified many ore bodies containing not only copper and nickel, but associated platinum, palladium, and gold.

The glacial sediments that cover all three bedrock types like chocolate syrup over the Neapolitan ice cream contain deposits of sand and gravel (sundae sprinkles, of course) that are known as "industrial minerals." Businesses across the North Woods, Great Lakes region mine this material so it can be used to maintain and construct roads, buildings, and other types of public infrastructure. Another type of industrial mineral found in this region is dimension stone — huge blocks of "granite" rock that are cut in a handful of North Woods, Great Lakes quarries, then polished and used for buildings and countertops all across America.

Iron Mining

Iron mining began in the North Woods, Great Lakes region in the 1880s. Over the following 70 years, some 2.5 billion tons of high-grade (i.e., high iron content) ore was mined from the Vermilion, Cuyuna, and Mesabi ranges. As the high-grade iron ore deposits got closer to being mined out, mining companies developed a process to extract iron from the much larger deposits of low-grade taconite ore and form it into concentrated pellets. This method of iron mining, which started commercially in the 1950s, continues today on the Mesabi Range.

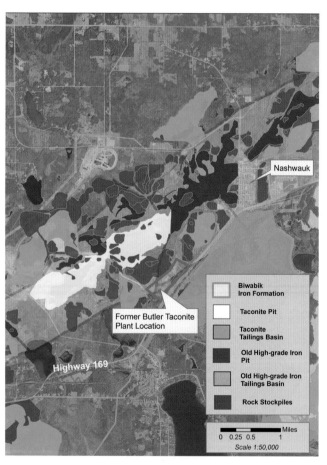

Figure 10. As this small but representative aerial view of a portion of the Mesabi Iron Range shows, iron mining creates intense but localized changes to ecosystems.

At the beginning of 2015, three active taconite companies operated six taconite mines and six pellet plants in the North Woods, Great Lakes region. Two more companies were producing iron ore concentrate from tailings at four old high-grade iron mines. A third company had constructed the world's first commercial pig iron plant and was producing high purity iron (locally called *iron nuggets*) using a new more environmentally friendly process than conventional production.

IRON MINING'S NATURAL LEGACY The largest ecosystem impacts associated with iron mining in the North Woods, Great Lakes region are probably the changes in landforms and the loss of habitat associated with the intense development of surface lands that overlay the ore deposits. It is true that there is nothing halfhearted about this process; Figure 10 shows a representative level of land use associated with old high-grade iron mining and a former taconite mine near Nashwauk.

But it also shows, just a few miles away, the overlying surface is typically undeveloped forest.

The total amount of habitat lost to iron mining is less than 1 percent of the land surface area of the North Woods, Great Lakes region. Much of the acreage associated with historical iron mining has been reclaimed, *revegetated*, and restored to a point where it supports native plants and wildlife (although rock left on the ground at a few old mine sites inhibits revegetation). Figure 11 provides some scenic views of pit lakes, which formed once iron mining stopped and groundwater was allowed to fill the open-pit excavations. These pit lakes are now part of the 5,000-acre Cuyuna Country Recreation Area. Aside from supporting native wildlife (as well as some non-native monster lake trout), this area of intensive historic iron mining now offers some of the best mountain bike trails and scuba diving in the Upper Midwest.

Figure 11. Old iron mines can find new life as recreational areas. The Cuyuna Country Recreation Area, consisting of nearly 5,000 acres of former iron mining areas near Crosby, contains some of Minnesota's best mountain biking trails, as well as 11 pit lakes that were formerly open-pit iron mines. These deep, clear water bodies offer ideal environments for scuba divers and DNR-stocked lake trout.

Perhaps the most commonly cited example of mining-related environmental impact in the North Woods, Great Lakes region is Reserve Mining Company's release of taconite tailings into Lake Superior. The Silver Bay pellet plant had been permitted to deposit tailings in the lake ever since it opened in 1955. In the 1960s, however, fishermen raised concerns about degraded fish habitat. Others worried about water quality and asbestoslike fibers in the unfiltered water supplies of several lake communities (including Duluth) linked to material within the tailings. After a lengthy court battle, the pellet plant shut down temporarily and eventually switched to using an inland disposal basin for tailings in 1980.

Minnesota has a number of laws in place to protect its land, waterways and wildlife from being harmed by mining, including the Minnesota Mineland Reclamation Act of

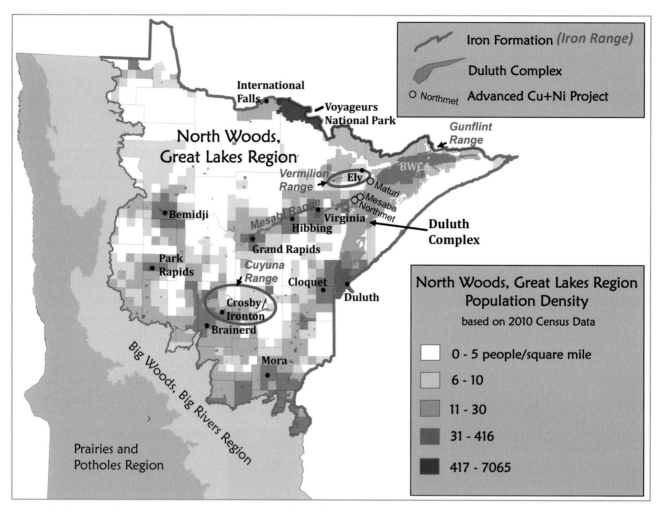

Figure 12. This map of human population density in the North Woods, Great Lakes region shows the influence of iron ranges and the economic opportunities they offer.

1969 and the Minnesota Environmental Rights Act of 1971. State rules establishing how Minnesota iron ore and taconite mining operations could be issued permits to mine were set in 1981.

IRON MINING'S CULTURAL LEGACY Many North Woods, Great Lakes towns and cities have their origins in, and owe their continued economic vitality to, iron mining (Figure 12). On the Vermilion Range, Tower and Ely were built to support iron mining, as were towns such as Ironton on the Cuyuna Range.

The life of a 19-century North Woods, Great Lakes miner was difficult and far too often cut short. The first federal mine safety law, passed in 1891, established bare minimum ventilation requirements for underground mines and prohibited mine operators from hiring children under age 12 (short miners allowed companies to save money by constructing

smaller tunnels). The first significant mine safety regulations were enacted in the 1940s and '50s, after World War II production requirements led to more widespread unionization within the mines.

Today, iron mining is the largest component of the regional economy of northeastern Minnesota, and generates substantial revenues for state and local governments. In 2013 alone, taconite mining operations paid $109 million in production taxes. Three-fourths of the tax revenue is distributed to cities, towns, and schools within the region of historic and active iron mining in the state.

According to a recent economic report by the University of Minnesota Duluth, jobs associated with iron mining account for roughly 30 percent of northeastern Minnesota's gross regional product—three times as much as either timber or tourism. The industry, however, is subjected to both "booms" and "busts" associated with worldwide demand for steel. To lessen the pain when the mines shut down, 25 percent of the taconite production tax goes to the Iron Range Resources and Rehabilitation Board, a state agency, to support job growth in the region outside of the mining industry.

North Woods, Great Lakes mining supports public schools and universities across the entire state. When Minnesota became a state, the federal government designated sections 16 and 36 of every township (or their equivalent) to be used for the benefit of schools. There are currently about 3.5 million acres of trust-held mineral rights in the state. Companies that have leased the right to explore and/or extract minerals from these trust lands have paid hundreds of millions of dollars in royalties to the trust over the years.

Perhaps one of the most enduring—and endearing—cultural impacts of mining in the North Woods, Great Lakes region relates to the people who built the mining communities. The mines drew thousands of European immigrants in the 1800s. Shaped by shared work experience, winters, and geographic isolation, these immigrants formed a fiercely proud and independent collective identity that persists to this day.

Copper-Nickel Mining

A local prospector discovered copper-nickel mineralization in 1948 in a small rock quarry southeast of Ely. The first exploratory drill hole was completed in 1951, and exploration continued through the 1960s. By 1974, metal prices had risen high enough for some of the deposits to be classified as "economic," and two companies proposed opening separate mines. While a mine shaft was sunk at one location in 1976, a comprehensive study on the potential impacts of copper-nickel mining mandated by the Minnesota Legislature pushed any further development off until 1978. By that point, metal prices had fallen enough for the mining companies to lose interest.

In 1985, a DNR geologist examining archived material from the Duluth Complex identified grains associated with platinum and palladium. Subsequent assays revealed high concentrations of these two metals in copper-nickel deposits in the region. Adding the growing value of these two metals (spurred by the 1970 Clean Air Act, which led to their use in catalytic converters) to the value of the previously known copper and nickel made the ore worth pursuing. One copper-nickel mining proposal is currently undergoing environmental review, while two others are in an advanced stage of mineral exploration and project planning.

Looking Ahead

The 36-foot-tall iron miner that looks out over an old high-grade iron mine in Chisholm stands on a stack of huge rust-red steel girders that are placed on top of blocks of high-grade iron ore taken from the Mesabi, Vermilion, and Cuyuna iron ranges. The steel within the girders was made from Minnesota taconite pellets, forming a vertical symbolic transition from the older high-grade mines to today's modern taconite industry. But the statue itself wasn't cast from iron; the internal skeleton structure is welded steel, while the statue's exterior is sheathed in copper, bronze and brass. This copper, of course, didn't come from a north woods mine. But at some point in the future, it may, as the old man is touched up with some local metallic color.

Recreation and Tourism

The striking beauty of the North Woods, Great Lakes region makes it a natural draw for tourists who appreciate fresh air, open space, and the sense of freedom, adventure, and abundance nature offers. Its appeal is widespread. Hunting and fishing, hiking and backpacking, rock climbing, snowmobiling and biking—it seems that everything imaginable has resulted in specialized land use and facilities.

Tourism began in this region in early 1900s. By the 1950s, when the postwar baby boom filled station wagons with eager children, the family vacation had become a tradition. Guided tours, fishing, picnics, camping, and quiet activities were popular early on. Tourists came in summer to live in campsites or rustic lodges and fish in cool, clear waters. In this section, we'll see how this trend has grown into an industry, and what it means to the North Woods, Great Lakes region.

Early 20th century publications and advertising promoted tourism and spending, tacking the north woods onto the American Dream. Over the following decades, naturalists such as Sigurd Olson, Aldo

Leopold, Grace Lee Nute, Florence Jaques, Ernest Oberholtzer, and Francis Lee Jaques gave poetic and artistic voice to the region. New photographic technology helped paint big color pictures in those dreams. Snapshots flew among tourists and their friends and relatives. Together they helped "sell" the north woods while preserving memories and shaping feelings about this wonderful place. People came to regard the north woods as a special sanctuary. The conservation movement grew, along with people's understanding of it. Eventually we were ripe for the next step—wilderness! But that concept grew with difficulty.

Conservation and Wilderness

"Wild country," even in the early 20th century, still implied country not yet developed. Someone would soon find an economic use for it. Rainy Lake, for example, looked like a development opportunity to Edward Backus, timber baron, dam builder, mill owner, financier, developer of the northern reaches of Minnesota, and president of the Ontario & Minnesota Power Company and Minnesota and Ontario Paper Company. In 1925, Backus proposed to turn the Rainy Lake watershed into a hydroelectric power basin by building a series of seven dams across 14,500 square miles, covering what are now the Superior National Forest, Voyageurs National Park, Quetico Provincial Park, and the BWCAW. He would log the area extensively to pay for construction. This plan provided advantages to many builders and developers, who backed Backus.

Ernest Oberholtzer, a writer/naturalist living in the Rainy Lake area, took exception to Backus' plan. In 1928, he helped launch the Quetico-Superior Council, a group of citizens and organizations concerned about preserving the area. It included Sigurd Olson, the iconic naturalist and activist you met in the introduction to this book. That council opposed Backus and his hydro energy development efforts, through courts of law, state legislatures, and the court of public opinion—eventually involving Congress and presidents Franklin D. Roosevelt and Harry Truman. The issue went back and forth between the two factions for five years, with great personal sacrifice by council members and preservationists.

Until then, it had been the job of the USFS to assist lumber companies. Oberholtzer's group sought a new purpose, pitted directly against the Backus plan. One court fight after another slowly attempted to redirect forestry concerns by curbing road building, requiring reforestation, and resolving other development issues. On the last day of its 1929–30 session, the U.S. Congress passed the Shipstead-Nolan Act. This act "withdrew all federal land in the boundary waters region from homesteading or sale, prevented alteration of natural water levels by dams, prohibited logging within 400 feet of shorelines, and preserved the wilderness nature of shorelines." Protection covered 4,000 square miles from Lake Superior on the east to Rainy Lake on the west. Backus' plan had been defeated. A new public awareness of "wilderness" had developed, thanks to the persistent labor of Oberholtzer and the council that had defended it all those years.

Much later, the federal Wilderness Act of 1964, drafted by Howard Zahniser of The Wilderness Society, created a legal definition of wilderness for the entire U.S, protecting 9.1 million acres of federal land: "An area where the earth and its community of life are untrammeled by man, where man himself is a visitor who does not remain."

The BWCAW, a 1.1-million-acre area occupying about a third of the northern portion of Superior National Forest, was among the very earliest federal wilderness areas designated. It extends nearly 150 miles along Canada's Quetico Provincial Park on the north. On the west it adjoins Voyageurs National Park. Set aside in 1926, it was one of the first sites protected by the federal Wilderness Act. In it are 1,200 miles of canoe routes, 11 hiking trails, and 2,000 camping sites. It is revered today by people who salute wilderness, wherever they may be.

The Wilderness Act limits uses of designated lands to protect watersheds and clean-water supplies, as well as habitats supporting diverse wildlife, including endangered species. Logging and drilling for oil and gas are prohibited. People may use wilderness areas for recreation without motorized or mechanical vehicles or equipment—perhaps the most difficult limitation for local opponents to accept. Non-invasive scientific research is permitted in wilderness. The act grandfathers in certain uses that existed before wilderness designation: mining, grazing, and water uses without significant impact on the majority of the area were allowed to remain. Congress considers additional proposals to the law every year, as recommended by federal agencies, grassroots conservationists, or sportsmen's organizations.

Tourism

Minnesotans, even the U.S. Congress, have been quite deliberate about legally protecting Minnesota's North Country, as we just saw with the BWCAW. Tourists who've ventured north to play have popularized it as a great vacation destination. In fact, tourism has become a brisk business in the North Woods, Great Lakes region. Today the BWCAW alone attracts more than 200,000 visitors per year, according to the U.S. Forest Service.

Nearly every Minnesotan has been a tourist "Up North." Activities include fishing, hunting, skiing, camping, escaping to nature, hiking, and taking day trips, canoe trips, and bike trips on mountains or trails all are now part of Minnesota culture. But they have also driven development and infrastructure, including roads, power lines, and sanitation systems. Resorts, lodges, campgrounds, restaurants, and various tourist attractions followed. Each new item adds to the load the land must support, as well as disrupts habitat.

People not only want to visit, they want to stay awhile. Construction of seasonal and year-round homes has grown, driving up the value of forest lands in Minnesota 12 to 15 percent per year since 2000. More than 400,000 acres of private forests have been developed since

1989. As development companies buy tracts of land to subdivide into small acreages or sell large tracts of land for 4,000-square-foot trophy homes, or roads and communities are built to service them all, the land has been fragmented. Seasonal and permanent homes bring new risks of pollution and erosion. Technological advances have supplemented human-powered recreational activities with motorboats, personal watercraft, and off-highway vehicles that allow more and more people to go further and longer into formerly untrammeled places. Engines and petroleum products pollute the area. Cities and

Figure 13. Boreal forests feature special soil, soil organisms, and and trees with roots that succeed in thin soil. Hiking in Minnesota's boreal forests is a major activity for ecotourists.

villages must add utilities for newer, upscale settlers, though adequate budgets may not always follow.

As land use changes, we must balance our impact with protection of our natural resources to ensure sustainability. For example, a recent estimate revealed that up to 75 percent of all rural septic systems along the North Shore are failing or don't meet sanitation codes. Recreational activities that increase erosion, damage waterways, and introduce non-native species can change nature for all time (Figure 13). How can we mitigate their impacts?

All of this attention causes concern for the sustainability of our wilderness. The International Ecotourism Society, an organization dedicated to promoting ecotourism globally, aims to use tourism as a tool for conservation, protection of bio-cultural diversity, and sustainable community development. This society highlights the responsible role of tourists and residents both, as it defines ecotourism as "responsible travel to natural areas that conserves the environment, sustains the well-being of the local people, and involves interpretation and education." This definition implies a vision of the future and our responsibility to it. Their vision requires that sustainable ecotourism must:

- minimize the environmental impacts of tourism

- contribute to a local sustainable economy

- consume minimal amounts of nonrenewable resources

- stress local ownership and the well-being of local people

- support efforts to conserve the environment.

Ecotourism encourages us all to participate in this beloved part of the state, and many Minnesotans "require" at least one trip into the North Country every year, if not more. Sadly, our very presence seems to be loving the region to death. How can we learn to live in harmony with the other organisms with which we share this land?

Non-native Species

Non-native species are living things from other places that have been brought into an ecosystem, usually by people. Some introductions have been deliberate, while others have been accidental. For example, as we saw in Chapter 7, non-native carp, salmon, and steelhead were all stocked in Lake Superior, but zebra mussels were inadvertently introduced to the Great Lakes in ballast water of an ocean-going freighter.

Some non-native species, such as dandelions, are able to fit into their new habitat without causing too much disruption to native species. Others establish themselves and, because they are no longer in the ecosystem in which they evolved, have populations that grow unchecked by natural predators or other limiting factors. Known as *non-native invasive species*, these plants, animals, and other organisms are the party crashers of the natural world. They often spread rapidly, and may eat everything in sight or outcompete native species for food or space. It is usually through competition for food or space that invasive species cause problems. They can change forests and waterways dramatically, disrupting the balance of nature and even threatening the existence of some native species. Examples of non-native

Figure 14. European buckthorn crowds out natural vegetation, decreasing plant and animal diversity. It has been spreading into northern Minnesota.

invasive species in the North Woods, Great Lakes region include purple loosestrife, earthworms, sea lampreys, and spiny waterfleas.

Once non-native invasive species reach an area, it takes a lot of work to contain them to protect the native species that play constructive roles in our ecosystem. If you've ever been involved in a "buckthorn bash" (Figure 14) or other effort to remove non-native plants from an area, you know how tedious such efforts can be—and the frequency with which they need to be repeated to make a difference.

Three factors are increasing the potential for non-native invasive species to threaten the health of North Woods, Great Lakes ecosystems:

- more people entering more places in the region

- increasing interstate and international commerce

- changing climate.

What to do about invasive species? First and best is

Figure 15. The Minnesota DNR's PlayCleanGo campaign reminds Minnesotans to clean their gear to prevent the movement of terrestrial non-native species.

to prevent the problem in the first place. Programs such as the Minnesota DNR's Play, Clean, Go campaign (Figure 15) are working to build awareness of recreationists' role in spreading—and preventing the spread of—non-native invasive species. For example, before leaving your home or a natural area, it's important to remove dirt, plants, and insects from clothing, boots, gear, pets, and vehicles. In addition, laws and regulations, such as those prohibiting the transport of firewood from one part of the state to another, help slow the spread of deadly tree pests such as emerald ash borers.

Climate Change

Minnesota's climate is changing because of atmospheric changes caused largely by combustion of fossil fuels. Computer models predict in the future Minnesota will experience warmer and wetter summers, milder winters, and more extreme weather events such as high-precipitation rainfall or snowfalls and windstorms.

Future Forests

Although there is much uncertainty, changing climate is expected to alter forest composition, tree growth, and populations of plants, mammals, birds, and insects.

Tree species such as oaks and maples are expected to increase in the North Woods, Great Lakes region while others, such as spruce, fir, and white pine, are expected to decrease as climate changes. The trees that are popping up after the recent wind events described in Chapter 2 are not pine and spruce, but red maples, bur oaks, and dogwoods, species that in the recent past typically were not major components of the Boreal Forest biome.

University of Minnesota forest scientist Lee Frelich suggests that if our climate shifts toward warm and dry, Minnesota will look a lot more like Nebraska, with little forest as we know it. Oak savannas could be more successful than boreal forests. On the other hand, if the state becomes warm and wet, it could still be forested, looking more like Ohio. However, new trees take years to arrive, mature, and reproduce. Soils have to adapt. In the meantime, smaller opportunistic plants, such as the invasive species we

St. Lawrence Seaway

The St. Lawrence River, which originally flowed from Lake Ontario to the Atlantic Ocean, has been expanded with locks, canals, and channels that permit ocean-going vessels to travel to the western end of Lake Superior. Canadian and American corporations co-manage the system.

Locks on the St. Lawrence were built as early as 1871. In the 1890s, the U.S. and Canadian governments together proposed deepening the waterway. Trade and hydropower were first seen as sufficient justification. Not immediately successful, the effort continued into the 20th century. During the Cold War, the seaway was seen as a potential military refuge for ships and submarines in case of war with the Soviet Union. The St. Lawrence Seaway finally opened in 1959, connecting the five Great Lakes and the Atlantic Ocean.

Also enjoying greater access were non-native species, including fish, mussels, and protozoa, which enjoyed new travel benefits. Round gobies outcompeted commercial fish and sportfish for food, while zebra and quagga mussels from the Black Sea clogged municipal water and power plants and ate plankton. Viral hemorrhagic septicemia, a disease transported in ballast water, harmed many fish.

By 1993 laws required ships to exchange ballast water from their home ports with Atlantic water before entering the seaway. However, incoming ships full of cargo — and therefore no ballast — were exempt from regulations. Empty ballast tanks nonetheless held tons of mucky water rich with bacteria and marine organisms and their eggs and larvae. Ships with no ballast on board unloaded cargo in Detroit or Cleveland, sucked ballast water into tanks, then headed on to Duluth, Toledo, or Milwaukee, where they dumped all that ballast water and loaded grain to carry back to Europe.

In 2004, the International Maritime Organization drafted a treaty stipulating that dumped ballast water can contain no more than 10 living organisms over 0.002 inches (the diameter of a hair) per meter of water. The U.S. wanted stricter requirements and so did not sign. In 2009 the Coast Guard issued ballast regulations that mimic those of the international agreement.

Environmental groups have called for a moratorium on all St. Lawrence shipping — or simply closing the system. Ocean-going vessels make up only 5 percent of Great Lakes shipping.

described previously, can move in to dominate.

The warming climate will affect other forest species besides trees. Native insects such as forest tent caterpillars, for example, are expected to hatch more than once a season. Forest tent caterpillars typically defoliate a tree during the growing season. While this won't kill the tree, it weakens it and makes it more vulnerable should another insect or disease strike.

Changes Underway

Climate warming is affecting the North Woods, Great Lakes region more rapidly than it is in other parts of the United States. That's because the Boreal Forest biome adjoins both prairie and deciduous forest, creating a *tension zone* where the edges of major weather systems, soil systems, and geology all come together. Turbulence follows. Apparently, so does climate change.

A changing climate affects the North Wood Great Lakes region in a variety of ways, including these:

* Many tree species are migrating north at a rate of six miles per year. The red maple, found as far south as Louisiana, is now sprouting and establishing itself abundantly throughout the BWCAW, including Seagull Lake.

* Some 84 percent of forest bird species have shifted their winter range an average of 75 miles since the 1960s. Birds migrating from distant points are unaware of weather variations in their summer home destinations, and

may arrive a little late. Ideally, bird hatches match insect hatches. Mismatches caused by early spring insect hatches can be devastating for feeding baby birds.

- Warmer winters and earlier springs have increased the odds for the larch beetle, which survives and fits in an extra generation in the early springs we're having, causing greater hardship to tamarack trees. Since the late 1990s, about 65,000 acres of tamaracks have been killed.

- Wildflowers are blooming earlier in the spring. Pollinators may miss their best opportunity for pollen and nectar.

So What?

To some extent, biomes have always shifted their boundaries. Why should coming years be any different?

One reason is growth of other human impacts on the environment that disrupt Earth's balanced and interconnected systems. While humans adapt to many things rapidly, other species have more difficulty. Species extinctions are occurring at increasingly rapid rates. Development has altered how we manage natural areas, such as managing a wooded area with fire, so natural forest reproduction doesn't work as well as it used to. Habitat fragmentation makes it hard for species to migrate in response to changing climate. And invasive species make things even more difficult by competing with native species for resources, sometimes directly attacking and weakening or killing them.

Another issue of particular importance in the North Woods, Great Lakes region is that conditions in the region may not be suitable for more southern species. Thin, moss-covered bedrock of the north woods offer a sufficient "toehold" for the relatively shallow roots of boreal species, but not so much for broadleaf trees. The broadleaf trees have deep tap roots, drop their leaves every fall, and require a high-energy spring start-up every year. This is not a good match for the northern landscape.

How Fast Can Trees Run?

Trees reach reproductive maturity after perhaps 30 or 40 years. In the past 50 years, the climate has moved northward by 70 miles. Climate change is expected to push ecosystems northward another 300 miles in the next 100 years. How will trees fare?

Given that our forests are likely to change, forest managers are working hard to ensure that we have forests — not just scrub land. Three main strategies are being explored to protect forest species, as identified by Susan Galatowitsch, an ecologist at the University of Minnesota: resistance, resilience, and facilitation of forests of the future.

RESISTANCE Resistance attempts to keep the forest boreal. Resistance is unlikely to win the day, but it might buy a few decades, during which other adaptation strategies could mature. Resistance strategies require intensive action. They include performing prescribed burns to increase numbers of fire-dependent species and stimulate genetic diversity; planting seeds rather than saplings so natural selection can help determine which trees survive; reducing deer populations to protect young trees; and eliminating invasive species.

Minnesota DNR forest ecologist John Almendinger has studied area pollen records from 4,000 to 5,000 years ago, when temperatures were warmer than now. He found evidence of balsam firs and black spruce. His findings suggest that at least some of today's species may have the genetic diversity to survive warming.

RESILIENCE Resilience seeks to boost a forest's ability to cope with climate change by diversifying tree species and ages. Diversity would produce more hardwoods but retain a greater variety of species to ensure success despite volatile weather and invasive species.

FACILITATION *Facilitation* attempts to assist migration by planting desirable species where they don't yet grow. For example, the eastern hemlock now grows near Duluth. This native species was never abundant in Minnesota, but Frelich thinks it might be able thrive in more parts of the North Woods, Great Lakes region under new conditions. Facilitation is a controversial strategy since it involves introducing species to an area. It also violates the Wilderness Act, which protects the BWCAW and certain other areas of Minnesota from such "tinkering."

Warm Waters

And what of the waters of the North Woods, Great Lakes region? Groundwater, lakes, streams, and Lake Superior — all are critical to the healthy functioning of ecosystems and as major attractions for tourists. As greenhouse gases increase, scientists expect temperatures to rise, evaporation to increase, and lake levels to fall.

Changes in precipitation and temperature affect waterways, so resident species can lose the habitat they require. Sport fishing species could become limited to smaller and smaller pools or disappear. Stream flow and connectivity, along with groundwater distribution, might become interrupted. Lakes with changing temperatures and water levels will have longer summer stratification, adding to oxygen depletion and formation of dead zones for fish and other aquatic life. In addition, warming may increase human activities that use water, such as irrigation.

Lake Superior's water supply comes as rain or snow (about two-and-a-half feet per year), and from streams and groundwater (about two more feet per year). Years of drought strain that supply. Higher water temperatures and less ice cover suggest that surface water temperatures in the lake may rise by as much as 12.1 °F by 2100, according to Minnesota's Interagency Climate Adaptation Team. This would result in changes in range and distribution of fish species, more toxic algae, and greater risks of invasive species.

Water evaporates fastest on Lake Superior from October to February, when dry, cold northern air absorbs the lake's humidity. A good ice cover limits this loss, but the string of recent warm winters has aggravated it. Loss of winter ice cover would lead to year-round navigation, reduced ranges for cold-water fish species such as whitefish, reduced winter recreation, and even greater lake evaporation.

Lower water levels result in changes in the lakeshore, which in turn lead to changes in erosion, plant, and animal habitat, and perhaps water loss. A study by the National Oceanic and Atmospheric Administration (NOAA) predicts lake levels could drop 2 to 33 feet. A steep drop could close off the connection between lakes Superior and Huron, leaving Lake Superior a closed basin. Salts and dissolved solids entering from rivers would accumulate due to evaporation, and the lake turnover rate would decrease. The lake bottom would become static, or anoxic — devoid of oxygen. Might Lake Superior become a Great Salt Lake?

Modern Resource Management

One of the biggest ways in which humans affect the forests, fish, wildlife, minerals, and other North Woods, Great Lakes natural resources today is through active management.

Before humans had much of an influence on the region, nature took its own course. Then early European settlers saw resources as opportunities for economic exploitation. Today, however, we have created so many changes in — and have so many expectations for — natural resources that we have to actively manage them if we want them to continue to meet our current and future needs and those of other living things. To that end, scientists, resource managers, elected officials, citizens, and others work together to develop and apply practices that allow us to both protect natural resources and meet human needs. To learn more about specific management practices, see Chapter 2 (forests), Chapter 3 (wildlife), Chapter 6 (inland lakes and fisheries), and Chapter 7 (Lake Superior).

The Big Picture

Over the centuries, humans have dramatically altered the North Woods, Great Lakes region. Some changes have made life better for people without irreversibly damaging natural systems. Others have caused harm.

Think about what you can do to help repair past damage and ensure a healthier future for this remarkable region. How can we proceed so that we can benefit from the resources it offers without destroying them? Take on the tasks that you can do. Work out of gratitude and homage to the great work of others. Do you want to say someday, "You should have seen it back when I was a kid! We came, we enjoyed, and we saw it all destroyed!" Better to say: "We did all we could, and we were successful!"

Explore

This section highlights locations of great examples of human impacts on the North Woods, Great Lakes region. Please check them out online, then head out and discover them in real life!

Bois Forte Heritage Center – Tower, Minnesota

WHAT The Bois Forte Heritage Center is dedicated to telling the Bois Forte Ojibwe story. It is an award winning interpretive center with information on the Ojibwe migration, logging, the fur trade, and the Lake Vermilion boarding school. The perspective in all exhibits is that of the Ojibwe. For instance, instead of telling the entire story of logging in the north woods, it focuses on how logging affected the life and environment of the Bois Forte.

WHEN The center is open all year. Allow at least an hour for the inside exhibits and more to visit the tipi, birch-bark dwelling, and remains of an 1856 gold mine.

WHERE The Heritage Center is on the grounds of the Fortune Bay Resort, Casino & Golf Course on Lake Vermilion.

WHO Bois Forte Band of Chippewa, 1610 Farm Road South, Tower, MN 55790, (218) 753-6017

FOR MORE INFORMATION www.boisforte.com/divisions/heritage_center.htm

Forest History Center – Grand Rapids, Minnesota

WHAT The Forest History Center offers a variety of exciting opportunities to explore Minnesota's forests and meet the people who lived and worked in them more than 100 years ago. The center includes an interpretive building where exhibits, films, and displays set the stage for a journey through time and help you understand the story of people and forests. From the interpretive building, you can explore a logging camp, a river wanigan, a USFS station, and nature trails.

WHEN June 1 to Labor Day: Monday–Saturday 10 a.m.–5 p.m.; Sunday, noon–5 p.m. Sept. 2 to May 31: visitor center only, 9 a.m.–4 p.m. Monday–Friday.

WHERE Grand Rapids, southwest of the intersection of U.S. Highway 169 and U.S. Highway 2. Look for signs on U.S. Highway 169 south of town or on U.S. Highway 2 west of town.

WHO Forest History Center, 609 County Road 76, Grand Rapids MN 55744, 218-327-4482

FOR MORE INFORMATION www.mnhs.org/places/sites/fhc and http://events.mnhs.org/calendar

Sugarloaf Cove and Sugarloaf Point SNA – Schroeder, Minnesota

WHAT Home to Consolidated Paper's log rafting operations for 30 years, Sugarloaf Cove was one of the most heavily affected industrial sites on the North Shore. Now it is a one of the most beautiful sites along the North Shore and a valuable place to learn about the natural and human history of the area with a state scientific and natural area at its core. At Sugarloaf Cove, you'll find an easy one-mile interpretive hiking trail that winds through the forest and billion-year-old rocks to breathtaking views of Lake Superior and scenic Sugarloaf Point. You can visit the restoration of a rare Lake Superior coastal wetland, discover the hidden secrets of Sugarloaf Creek and remnants of the logging era as you follow the trail back to the interpretive center, which features extensive information and learning activities.

WHEN To arrange a tour during summer, call (218) 663-7679; during other seasons, call (218) 525-0001.

WHERE Start at the Sugarloaf Cove Interpretive Center, 9096 Highway 61 in Schroeder.

WHO The North Shore Stewardship Association, 6008 London Road, Duluth, MN 55804, (218) 525-0001.

FOR MORE INFORMATION www.sugarloafnorthshore.org

MASTER
NATURALIST
TOOLBOX

Teach

This section features lesson plans focusing on the human impact on the North Woods, Great Lakes region. You may experience some of these activities as a student in your Master Naturalist class. The lessons are adaptable to a wide range of audiences, ages, and settings. Feel free to use them to teach others what you have learned!

LESSON 1

Ripples of Impact

Objective

Participants will be able to identify through group discussion the impact of a given event and suggest how groups or individuals could counter the impact.

Audience Type

Teen/Adult

Supplies

- ☐ Demonstration or depiction of the rings of ripples that result when a stone is thrown into a body of water
- ☐ Paper or whiteboard
- ☐ Markers appropriate to the writing surface
- ☐ Large sheets of paper and markers

Background

Simple events often have consequences we don't immediately foresee. Once begun, consequences continue to occur in a chain, much like the ripples that result when you throw a stone into the water.

An instructive example to discuss in more detail could be the earthworm. A brief overview can be found at http://en.wikipedia.org/wiki/Invasive_earthworms_of_North_America.

Glaciers eliminated native earthworms over much of North America thousands of years ago, so modern ecosystems evolved without them. Asian earthworms hitchhiked to Europe when early explorers inadvertently brought them home with exotic plants to show their patrons what they'd found. Europeans coming to settle in North America brought newly established plants with them. Asian/European earthworms again rode along in the soil and settled in the New World. Earthworms migrated northward in loads of construction soil, in landscaping soils with plants, and as bait for fishing dumped around the shoreline as fishermen headed home. That initiates a cascade of consequences:

- The worms take in organic material from the surface of the forest floor, removing the nutrients new seeds need. Specialized niches disappear, as only the older trees survive. Mycorrhizae associations with roots are often destroyed, starving some established trees.

- Worms digest and excrete the results as they burrow down into the soil, where they establish colonies. Digested nutrients leach into deeper soils, adding bulk.

- Forest diversity diminishes as topsoils are depleted, and new plants fail because their roots do not extend deep enough. Ground cover and canopy are both thinned; remaining vegetation is overbrowsed; survival of remaining organisms becomes much more competitive, and the forest appears thinner.

- As the forest changes, new invasive species such as buckthorn and garlic mustard arrive and thrive, further changing the community.

Activity

1. Introduce the concept of cause and effect using the ripple demonstration or image. Explain this is a very simple model; in ecology, one event often triggers quite a different event, which in turn causes yet another unexpected event. This process is what we want to talk about today.

2. Share the earthworm example above, scaling it to the participants' attention span, or describe another example of the ripple effect. Emphasize how one event launches the next, which in turn causes yet other happenings that we didn't expect but that, once observed and studied, make good sense.

3. Ask participants to describe other ecological events with unexpected consequences. List these on the paper or whiteboard.

4. If time permits, let participants work in groups of three to five, each group choosing a different human impact such as introducing earthworms, fur trading, logging a large area all at once, or allowing polluted water to escape into the watershed. They may describe the subsequent events in a list format, as ripples from a stone in the water, or in some other format that makes sense to them. Give them seven to ten minutes to develop a reasonably robust series of events. Ask reporters from each group to tell about their chosen cause and its effects.

5. When each group has reported, ask questions to stimulate group discussion: How long could this go on? Are all these results negative? What might be some positive results? How could changing the landscape community affect the future? In what ways does climate change further affect the chain of events your small group discussed? In what ways has the North Woods, Great Lakes landscape been changed by human activity?

6. Ask groups to list actions that could be taken to slow or stop the chain of events. What skills, information, and technology would be required? Give them five minutes to suggest two or more controls.

7. Discuss findings, then ask: What future plans of yours could be affected by what we've discussed today? What action could you take to positively impact the causative events? Look for big and little influences.

LESSON 2

Lenses on Environmental Communication

Objective

Participants will choose an environmental issue caused by human activity, then consider it from specific viewpoints so as to challenge their thinking on a problem and to find new possibilities for solutions.

Audience Type

Teen/Adult

Supplies

☐ Hand-drawn and hand-labeled representations of each of the five lenses on 8.5" by 11" paper
☐ Set of Communication Lens cards for each group
☐ Large paper or whiteboard
☐ Markers

Background

When we discuss controversial issues, people tend to engage their most comfortable, familiar habits of thought, and then get no further in their solution. To develop new lines of analysis and problem solving, it is helpful to choose new tools with which to think about issues. This activity asks participants to work in groups using a designated series of "lenses" or viewpoints in working with an issue of their choice. These lenses are:

OBJECTIVE   focus on gathering and analyzing data

EMOTIONAL   focus on personal values and feelings

CRITICAL   focus on caution and worst scenarios

POSITIVE   focus on benefits and best scenarios

CREATIVE   focus on probing possibilities and synthesizing new opportunities

In this activity, participants work in small groups in two rounds of discussion to develop an interpretation of an issue, its factors, and best solutions. In round one, groups work with only one lens. In round two, each group uses all lenses in succession, about five minutes per lens. Afterwards, the large group discusses differences among the interpretations developed, the processes used and how effectively they worked, and how they could be useful when communities communicate about issues.

Activity

1. Ask participants to brainstorm several environmental issues with a variety of contributing factors for each. They are not to resolve the issues at this point, simply identify good topics for further discussion later. Use paper or whiteboard to help capture a variety of ideas, then organize and select the issues to work with. Possibilities might be based on local watershed hazards, management of game populations, forest fragmentation, invasive species, etc.

MASTER
NATURALIST
TOOLBOX

2. Introduce the background material above by asking if participants know people who have set attitudes toward issues that come up. For instance, for some people the sky is always falling — no good can possibly come of a situation. For others, everything is coming up roses, or technology will solve everything. Ask participants to give one or two examples they've experienced.

3. Explain that in science we use a variety of lenses to examine objects. Ever since Anton van Leeuwenhoek invented the microscope in the late 1600s, with many subsequent improvements to better study his "little animalcules," we've been building on his and other, newer concepts. Microscopes and lenses, hand lenses, telescopes, and many kinds of specialized lenses help us examine our world today. The lenses we are talking about in this activity, however, help us examine how we communicate about science. These lenses are really viewpoints — they're how people view a situation. Is someone using "rose-colored glasses"? Or "looking through a glass darkly"? Introduce the five Communication Lenses. Ask participants to give an example of each, and discuss.

4. ROUND ONE Organize participants into five small groups. Ask them to each choose a lens to work with as they discuss the first topic identified in #1, above. Have them write out their lens/description in big letters on a sheet of paper so others can see what their focus is. Ask them to discuss the topic, using only their lens to develop their interpretation of the issue, causes, possible solutions, etc. Give them seven to ten minutes, then ask each group to report their interpretation of the topic. Use these discussion questions:

   To what extent was the lens used apparent to the listeners?

   How did working with a single viewpoint change the working process?

   How does the exclusive use of one lens skew results?

5. ROUND TWO Hand out cards with all five lens images to each group. Instruct groups to use all lenses in turn, working to build a more fair and balanced concept of the issue. Suggest that the group choose each lens to work with for several minutes, then change to another until they've used all five. Give them 15 or 20 minutes to work. Again, ask groups to report their interpretations, along with causes and solutions they might have identified. Use these discussion questions:

   What are your reactions working with different lenses in succession?

   How can the different lenses be used well in group work?

   Which lenses are easiest? Which take more preparation?

   How could a large working group break into specialized functions using these concepts? Which functions might a group need outside help with?

   How are all views useful in developing a good solution?

   Explain that in real life, group work is seldom this disciplined. Being able to "hear" the lenses/viewpoints at work and to point out biases, however, can help achieve breakthroughs in thinking toward new solutions. Awareness of viewpoint in articles about the environment can be an interesting activity, too.

6. Summarize the differences in the groups' work, the process itself, and practices used within communities at large in communicating about issues. Thank participants for their good work.

Resource

de Bono, E. (1985). *Six thinking hats*. USA: Little, Brown and Company. 207 pages.

Communication Lenses

OBJECTIVE
focus on gathering and analyzing data

EMOTIONAL
focus on personal values and feelings

CRITICAL
focus on caution and worst scenarios

POSITIVE
focus on benefits and best scenarios

CREATIVE
focus on probing possibilities and synthesizing new opportunities

Instructions

Copy this page. Make sets for each group. Cut on dotted line. Cut between cards to separate.

MASTER NATURALIST TOOLBOX

Conserve

This section highlights organizations that offer opportunities for Minnesota Master Naturalist Volunteers to participate in stewardship and citizen science activities related to the history of, and resource use in, the North Woods, Great Lakes region. Please visit the websites to learn more.

Minnesota Historical Society

The Minnesota Historical Society is chief caretaker of Minnesota's story — and the History Center is home to the society's vast collections. Through its 26 historic sites and museums, the society offers opportunities for thought-provoking entertainment, learning, and fun. Visitors can discover the power of water at Mill City Museum, enjoy a breathtaking view of Lake Superior at Split Rock Lighthouse, and experience 19th-century frontier living at Historic Fort Snelling. All of the sites have opportunities for volunteers. Visit www.mnhs.org/about/volunteers/contact.html for volunteer opportunities across the state or call (651) 259-3188 to reach the Volunteer Services office.

www.mnhs.org

MINNESOTA
HISTORICAL
SOCIETY

The Trust for Public Land

The Trust for Public Land (TPL) is a national nonprofit land conservation organization that conserves land for people to enjoy as parks, community gardens, historic sites, rural lands, and other natural places, ensuring livable communities for generations to come. It has many ongoing projects in Minnesota, including Minnesota's Working Forest Lands, Healthy Waters for Minnesota, and Parks for People – Twin Cities. Visit the website to learn about how you can contribute to TPL's national efforts.

www.tpl.org

Friends of the Boundary Waters Wilderness

The mission of the Friends of the Boundary Waters Wilderness is to protect, preserve, and restore the wilderness character of the BWCAW and the Quetico-Superior ecosystem. Volunteers may work with USFS staff on campsite and portage maintenance or on monitoring and education efforts that help maintain the BWCAW's wilderness character. Other opportunities are available for presenters, graphic artists, videographers, letters campaign coordinators, events assistants, and grant researchers.

www.friends-bwca.org

Expand

This section suggests some things you can use, do, pursue, read, or join to develop as a naturalist.

Journal

EXPERIENCE Using local or Internet resources, learn about how the land at your spot was used in the past. Look carefully at the area to find evidence of this use that remains.

REFLECT What decisions in the past about using the land affected decisions made later? How have your visits here changed the spot? What potential for improvement does it have for the future? What can you do?

RECORD Record your findings and what you did to improve your spot. Identify some item or feature of your spot that has symbolic significance or similarity with your own life. Describe the meanings this history and potential have for the spot and possible parallels with your own life.

Read

The Forest for the Trees: How Humans Shaped the North Woods

Jeff Forester.
2004. St. Paul: Minnesota Historical Society. 215 pp.

This book presents the ecological history of a watershed that is now part of the Boundary Waters Canoe Area Wilderness. It explores all phases of the human use of this land, from Native Americans through the early pioneers to industrial loggers and finally to preservationists and recreationists.

The Boundary Waters: The Grace of the Wild

Paul Gruchow.
1997. Minneapolis: Milkweed Editions. 202 pp.

This highly personal, sometimes humorous, and nearly poetic book is an account of the author's camping experience and thoughts in the BWCAW. As a nature writer, Gruchow is intent on species, habitat, life ways, and this thing called wilderness. A wolf howling at midnight will startle you into adrenaline-charged pitch blackness no matter how bright the light wherever you read this book. If your experience of the BWCAW is less than you'd wish, let Gruchow share his with you.

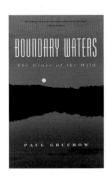

Earthworms of the Great Lakes

Cindy Hale.
2007. Duluth, Minnesota: Kollath-Stensaas Publishing. 36 pp.

This little book presents more information about earthworms than you thought you'd want to know. But it turns out that you do want to know! The gardener's, farmer's, and fisherman's friend is simply death to forests. After explaining the earthworm invasion and its significance, the book goes on to function as a field guide and key to 15 species. It also presents practical ways to collect and preserve earthworms for further study.

Surf

Minnesota Historical Society Maps

A fabulous collection of almost 19,000 maps and 2,000 volumes of atlases from 1849 to present.

http://collections.mnhs.org/maps

Iron Range Resources & Rehabilitation Board

The Iron Range Resources & Rehabilitation Board is a Minnesota state agency located in Eveleth that provides funding to build northeastern Minnesota economies and communities. The website offers valuable information on the region's minerals and forest products industries as well as links to other resources.

http://mn.gov/irrrb

Join

Your Local Historical Society

Minnesota is home to dozens of historical societies. Discover your local one now. It probably needs your help!

www.mnhs.org/localhistory/mho/chsclo.html

Listening Point Foundation

Sigurd Olson created Listening Point, a rugged retreat on Burntside Lake near Ely, in 1956. The Listening Point Foundation, Inc., owns and cares for the property at Listening Point and conducts public tours. It also publishes wilderness education materials and sponsors educational programs. Membership, with two annual newsletters, is free, though donations are encouraged.

http://listeningpointfoundation.org

MASTER
NATURALIST
TOOLBOX

Additional Reading

Alanen, A.R. (1989). "Years of Change on the Iron Range." In (Clark Jr., CE ed.) *Minnesota in a century of change*. St. Paul: Minnesota Historical Society Press. www.mnhum.org/Resources/MN%20in%20a%20Century%20of%20Change%20-%20years%20 of%20change%20on%20the%20iron%20range.pdf

Treuer, A. (2010). *Ojibwe in Minnesota: The people of Minnesota.* St. Paul: Minnesota Historical Society Press.

Copyrighted Photographs and Images Used With Permission

Figure 1. Courtesy of Minnesota Historical Society

Figure 2. Courtesy of Minnesota Historical Society

Figure 3. Courtesy of Wikimedia Commons

Figure 4. Courtesy of Minnesota Historical Society

Figure 5. Courtesy of Minnesota Historical Society

Figure 6. Courtesy of Minnesota Historical Society

Figure 7. Courtesy of Minnesota Historical Society

Figure 8. Courtesy of Minnesota Historical Society

Figure 9. Courtesy of Don Elsenheimer, Minnesota Department of Natural Resources

Figure 10. Courtesy of Don Elsenheimer, Minnesota Department of Natural Resources

Figure 11. Courtesy of Don Elsenheimer, Minnesota Department of Natural Resources

Figure 12. Courtesy of Don Elsenheimer, Minnesota Department of Natural Resources

Figure 13. Courtesy of Marilyn K. Andersen

Figure 14. Courtesy of Dawn A. Flinn, Minnesota Department of Natural Resources

Figure 15. Courtesy of Minnesota Department of Natural Resources

Expand

MASTER NATURALIST TOOLBOX

Chapter 9: Leaving the Nest

Becoming a Full-Fledged Minnesota Master Naturalist Volunteer

Amy R. B. Rager and Nathan J. Meyer

Goal

Understand your role as a Minnesota Master Naturalist Volunteer.

Objectives

1. Practice identifying services, knowledge, ideas, and resources that can serve as the basis of your volunteer work.

2. Explore linking personal volunteering preferences with organizations and people that can use them.

3. Discuss strategies for managing various challenges to volunteer involvement.

4. Practice entering service hours on the Minnesota Master Naturalist website.

Introduction

Your Minnesota Master Naturalist Volunteer training is nearly complete, and you will be ready to fledge soon. In this chapter you will find basic information you need to be successful in your volunteering endeavors, including how to use the Minnesota Master Naturalist website, what counts as volunteer service, and where to find answers to questions.

Capstone Project

First, let's explore the capstone project, a requirement for graduation from your Minnesota Master Naturalist course. Capstones serve as a transition from training to volunteer service under the mentorship of a sponsoring agency or organization. A capstone should be something that can be completed in a relatively short period, such as preparing a program, developing an interpretive brochure for a trail, or planning native landscape restoration. For more

ideas, you might want to visit examples of previously completed capstones at the Minnesota Master Naturalist website. You will present your project to your class at graduation (Figure 1).

Figure 1. Minnesota Master Naturalist Volunteers do a variety of projects, such as worm surveys, to help manage natural resources.

We want your capstone project to reflect your newly acquired knowledge and skills, offer an opportunity to practice new ways of volunteering, and help stimulate connection with organizations that need your help. Therefore, your capstone should be something new to you, not a continuation of a project you've been working on.

It may be possible to use an existing project, however, if you add a new component as your capstone project. For example, if you have been involved in a Buckthorn Bust, you are probably comfortable with the mechanics of ripping out buckthorn and making sure the remnants don't sprout. However, you could expand your skills by adding an educational component and developing a presentation on the natural (and unnatural) history of buckthorn and the reasons buckthorn is aggressively managed in natural areas. The idea is to push you ever so slightly beyond what you are already comfortable doing.

Your instructor will provide a list of useful projects that can be completed for nearby groups and agencies and guide you through the process of selecting a capstone project. Project sponsors may include your local nature center, a school, a state park, a city park system, your town hall — basically any group or agency that would appreciate help from naturalist volunteers. The capstone offers exposure to potential sponsors for your project, introduces you to people and organizations that need volunteers, and showcases available volunteer opportunities.

Another feature of capstone projects is that they are group endeavors. Work with several of your classmates to select and refine a project that uses all of your skills. One of you may be good at writing and editing, another may be great at backbreaking work, and another may be a whiz at developing presentations. The combination is always stronger than the individual effort in capstones. In the past, some Minnesota Master Naturalist Volunteers have attempted to complete a capstone on their own. Most of the individual projects were not as successful as those achieved by a group — and some were downright embarrassing. Consequently, we require that capstone projects involve at least two people.

To help your instructor guide you to a great project, please discuss your interests with your classmates and your instructor. Examine the list of suggested projects prepared by your instructor, and look into other possibilities that tickle your fancy. Once you have narrowed your choices, please complete the capstone proposal form available from your instructor. It will require that you consider the following:

- Who are the members of your group?

- What category of volunteer service (stewardship, interpretation, citizen science, program support) does your project fulfill?

- How does the project use the skills of a naturalist?

- Who are the intended audience members for the project, and what benefits will they receive?

- What is the sponsoring agency or organization for the project, and what are the benefits to that sponsor?

- What resources are needed to complete the project?

- What is the project, and how do you plan to complete it by the end of the class?

You will present your capstone project on the last day of the course. If your capstone involves a management project, you may have to develop a short presentation on what you did and why. If it is an educational project, you may want to introduce your classmates to the material so they can use it in their own teaching. You may record the time spent on your capstone project as part of the 40 hours of volunteer service expected in your first year (Figure 2).

Figure 2. Bud capping and plant surveys are just a few of the capstone projects that Minnesota Master Naturalist Volunteer candidates have carried out.

Volunteer Service

Volunteer service is a vital part of being a Minnesota Master Naturalist Volunteer. Each year, Minnesota Master Naturalist Volunteers across the state devote tens of thousands of hours of their personal time to improving the natural resources of our state with projects such as removing invasive species, leading outdoor activities for youth, and monitoring water quality. These projects not only provide the volunteers with great personal satisfaction, but also make a valuable contribution to the agencies and organizations for which they volunteer. When you complete your Minnesota Master Naturalist training, you join the ranks of this important, dedicated group of volunteers.

> "Never doubt that a small group of thoughtful, committed citizens can change the world. Indeed, it is the only thing that ever has."
>
> — Margaret Mead

Reporting

Each year you will be asked to report your total volunteer service hours online. This information is critical to show the value volunteers have in their communities, which in turn, helps us document program success to our funders and sponsoring agencies. Hours spent on preparation, travel, and the activity itself all count toward your yearly totals. We aggregate all the service hours and projects conducted by Minnesota Master Naturalist Volunteers and prepare a report for various individuals and agencies on the combined impact of our efforts. One way we illustrate the economic impact of the program's volunteer activity is by calculating the service hours at a rate equivalent to the average hourly earnings of all production and nonsupervisory workers on private, nonfarm payrolls in the U.S. as determined by the Bureau of Labor Statistics. Independent Sector (http://independentsector.org) recommends increasing this dollar amount by 12 percent to account for fringe benefits. Using this standard, the estimated value of Minnesota Master Naturalist Volunteer service was well over $1 million in just the first few years of the program. And the impact grows every year!

To maintain your active status in the Minnesota Master Naturalist Volunteer Program you are required to complete 40 hours of volunteer service each year after completing your initial training, starting with the year after the one in which you take the course. You will receive an award pin for every year in which you volunteer 40 hours of service. You will also receive special milestone pins at 100, 250, 500, 1,000, 2,000, 5,000, 10,000, and 25,000 hours.

Categories

The goal of Minnesota Master Naturalist Volunteer service is to enhance local communities by improving natural areas and educating people about Minnesota's natural environment. We want you to decide if your volunteer service qualifies. The activity needs to:

- relate to Minnesota's natural or environmental cultural history

- occur in Minnesota

- be hosted or sponsored by an organization

- be unpaid.

If all of these are the case, then you have found an appropriate volunteer opportunity. If any are not, you should probably pursue another volunteer activity to achieve your 40 hours. If you're not sure, contact info@minnesotamasternaturalist.org or (888) 241-4532 for help making a decision.

Volunteer opportunities should fit into one of four categories: **Citizen Science**, **Education and Interpretation**, **Program Support**, or **Stewardship**. Learn more on the following page.

Advanced Training

To help you continue learning and building your understanding of Minnesota's ecosystems, each year you are required to participate in at least eight hours of advanced training. We have developed some advanced training opportunities, such as the annual Minnesota Master Naturalist conference, but you can also learn a great deal about Minnesota from any number of groups and organizations. You know best where you need to focus your advanced training and learning. Use your best judgment to determine if a class is truly "advanced" for you.

If you pursue advanced training that is not part of the Minnesota Master Naturalist Program, great! Let us know about it, especially if you would recommend it to other Minnesota Master Naturalist Volunteers. You might also want to let us know about less effective training sessions so we can steer volunteers away from them.

Minnesota Master Naturalist Volunteer Categories

Minnesota Master Naturalist volunteer opportunities should fit into one of these four categories:

Citizen Science

Citizen Science involves helping with scientific research. These projects usually consist of gathering data and sharing it with researchers. Examples include:

- participating in the Audubon Christmas Bird Count
- collecting data on monarch larvae
- monitoring water quality
- collecting data on frog calling in the spring.

Education and Interpretation

Education and Interpretation involves developing or delivering educational programs or materials. Examples include:

- helping teach visitors about wildflowers at a nature center
- leading or assisting with a natural history hike
- creating a brochure or sign for a natural area
- assisting with an environmental education program for a school or organized group
- writing an article on bird migration for a park newsletter.

Program Support

Program Support involves helping keep programs running efficiently. Examples include:

- helping plan the statewide Master Naturalist Volunteer Annual Conference
- preparing mailings for a local nature center
- working in the store at a nature center
- scanning lake data for the Minnesota DNR database
- staffing a booth at an event promoting the Minnesota Master Naturalist Program.

Stewardship

Stewardship involves natural resource management activities. Examples include:

- leading an invasive species removal project
- helping develop a school forest management plan
- assisting with restoration: collecting native seeds, planting native species
- improving trails to prevent erosion.

Examples that would not qualify as Minnesota Master Naturalist Volunteer service include:

- counting turtle eggs in Costa Rica
- cleaning cat cages at the animal shelter
- working at a private plant nursery
- collecting phenology data at your cabin that are not reported to an organized group.

Minnesota Master Naturalist advanced training needs to focus on an aspect of Minnesota's natural or environmental cultural history and be a formal training or class. Most advanced training opportunities will occur in Minnesota and have an outdoor component. Examples include:

- Project WET, Project WILD, Project Learning Tree training

- a class on plant or animal identification

- water quality monitoring training

- a class on Minnesota's geology or climate

- volunteer orientation for a nature center

- a class on forest management

- a webinar about an appropriate topic

- a lecture about environmental sustainability.

Examples of things that don't qualify as Minnesota Master Naturalist advanced training include:

- watching television (Even if it is Minnesota nature-related show, we want you to get outside!)

- birding with friends

- identifying trees at your cabin with family

- reading a Minnesota natural history book (except if you do it as part of a reading group associated with a Minnesota Master Naturalist Volunteer chapter!)

You are not expected to pursue advanced training in the same year you complete your initial Minnesota Master Naturalist course — the course covers your learning needs for the year. This requirement will begin the following year.

Reporting Your Hours

Now that you know what to do, let's figure out how to report it! The Minnesota Master Naturalist website is designed to let you track your service and advanced training hours by category and see your total hours. If you do not have access to the Internet, you can send us a paper copy of your hours and we will enter them online for you. You can download the form to use for this from the Minnesota Master Naturalist website or contact our office at (888) 241-4532 and we'll send a paper copy to you.

To track your hours using the Minnesota Master Naturalist website:

1. **Find the site**

   First, go to www.MinnesotaMasterNaturalist.org. Next, bookmark the page, because you will come back here often!

2. **Create an account**

   If you are currently in a class or have taken Minnesota Master Naturalist training in the past, you already have an account with a user name and password. If you know your user name but have forgotten your password see "Resurrect a Forgotten Password" on the next page. Please do not create a new account if you forget your information.

   If you don't have an account, click on "My Account" at the top of the page and follow the "Create an Account" prompt. Fill out all the boxes that appear on the page and click "Create Account."

3. **Log in**

   You can now log in and access parts of the website that are only available to registered users. Click on the My Account tab and fill in your user name and password in the boxes that appear in the box. Once these have been correctly entered, click "Log In." You should see a headline that says [Your Name]'s Master Naturalist Dashboard.

Other Ways to Use the Website

Change Your Personal Information

In this section, you can click on "My Account" to update your personal information, such as your name, address, email address, and phone number. If you move, let us know! You can also change your password here.

Complete an Interest Survey

This survey is designed to help us to know more about you. We use this information to see what topics people want to learn more about, for more detailed demographic information, and to see what skills and knowledge you may have to offer the program. You can update the survey at any time, as your interests, skills, and knowledge change.

Resurrect a Forgotten Password

If you have forgotten your password, click on the "Lost/Forgotten Password?" link. You will be directed to enter your email address and a temporary password will be send to your email account. You can enter the temporary password, and then reset your new password. For password information contact our administrator at (888) 241-4532, or email info@minnesotamasternaturalist.org. Please do not create a new account if you forget your information.

Use My Dashboard

Clicking on "My Account" on the top will open up a screen where you can not only enter volunteer hours, but also find volunteer opportunities, locate advanced training, keep track of your past classes, see if you are registered for any upcoming Minnesota Master Naturalist Program offerings, see what awards you have earned, link to available resources, and link to social networks (Facebook, Ning, Flickr, and Master Naturalist Blog). Your cumulative service totals will also appear her with a dollar value for your service. A gauge in the upper left of screen will give an indication of where you are as you work toward your 40-hour annual service requirement.

4. **Enter service and advanced training hours**

   Click on "Enter Service Hours." The program always defaults to the current calendar year. To see other years, click on the year pull-down box and change to the year you wish to see.

   You will see a record of the hours you have entered, organized by volunteer service category. If you want to submit additional hours, click on "+Add Citizen Science Record" (or "+Add Interpretive Project Record" or "+Add Program Support Record" or "+Add Stewardship Record"). Enter the date of service; the name of the person/organization for whom you volunteered; the ZIP code for the location where the service was performed; the number of hours you spent on preparation, travel, and doing the project (if a fraction enter a "0" for the whole number); the name of the sponsor (which may be in the pull down list, or you can add a new sponsor in the box provided); and a short description of what you did. Remember to give enough information, while being brief: Who, what, when, and where are the important things to include.

   If everyone conscientiously completes all data fields, we are able to generate some impressive reports. For example, if you want to brag to your city council about the Minnesota Master Naturalist Program and what volunteers are doing in your community, we can punch a few buttons and give you a customized list of all of the projects and the amount of time spent in your ZIP code. Just ask—we are always willing to help.

Recording your service and training hours is essential to the success of the Minnesota Master Naturalist Program. The entire program is based on the idea that participants will take the training we provide and use it for good. The total number of volunteer service hours is a key benchmark we watch to measure involvement in and dedication to our program. These totals are reported to University of Minnesota Extension and the Minnesota DNR to justify staff time spent developing and managing the program and to judge whether the partnership is worth continuing. Total service hours are also reported to funders and used in funding requests to demonstrate the value and impact of the program. Even though your hours may not seem like much, every little bit helps!

If entering data on the Internet makes you want to throw your computer out the window, we will enter the data for you—it is that important. Please make a copy of the Volunteer Hour Record Sheet, fill it out, and send it to the Minnesota Master Naturalist Program administrative office.

Volunteering

Volunteering is the core activity of being a Minnesota Master Naturalist Volunteer. We want it to be fun, fulfilling, useful, and educational. With volunteering, however, comes responsibility.

The Minnesota Master Naturalist Program is sponsored jointly by University of Minnesota Extension and the Minnesota DNR. As a Master Naturalist Volunteer, you represent both entities, and you are expected to provide an excellent example of outreach on behalf of both. In addition, you probably represent yet another group—the sponsor of your activity. We have designed the program so that you are rarely volunteering for the Minnesota Master Naturalist Program itself, but rather are a Minnesota Master Naturalist Volunteer who is volunteering for a local nature center, school, refuge, state park, etc. Consequently, you should make sure that you understand the expectations of volunteers from your sponsoring organization.

In general, the following pointers will work in most situations:

- Remember to introduce yourself as a Minnesota Master Naturalist Volunteer.

- Always wear your name tag.

- Be reliable, be on time (early), and be prepared.

- Be professional.

- If you don't know the answer, say you'll find out—don't guess!

- Have fun.

To guide you in your role as a Master Naturalist Volunteer, we have developed a code of ethics (see following page). (Actually, truth be told, we modified this code of ethics with permission from the West Virginia Master Naturalist Program. It would not be very ethical to claim a code of ethics as our own unless we actually had created it from scratch.) If you are uncertain about how to respond in a situation, this code may offer you some guidance.

Logo and Photograph Use

Use the Minnesota Master Naturalist logo on any materials you develop as a Master Naturalist Volunteer. It is available on our website for download in various formats, or by emailing info@minnesotamasternaturalist.org (Figure 3).

Figure 3. The Minnesota Master Naturalist logo is available for use on any materials you develop. Please visit the website to download high-resolution versions.

Remember to properly credit sources for information and photographs. In addition, you may need to seek formal permission to use resources you find on the Internet. It is your job to cite any resources correctly. If you need help wading through the morass of copyright permission, visit the University of Minnesota Libraries' website on copyrights (www.lib.umn.edu/copyright). It has several resources explaining copyright and fair use. Just because you're using a piece of text or an image for an educational endeavor doesn't mean you're exempt from copyright laws!

Collecting Natural Items

As a Minnesota Master Naturalist Volunteer you might wish to collect natural items for use in your volunteer service. Picking plants or gathering rocks in your yard is fine but collecting many types of feathers is not. Make sure you know the laws or you could end up with a misdemeanor or a large fine! Nature centers and many educational facilities have feathers, bones, furs, and other natural items they use for education. They also have state or federal permits to keep them. As a Minnesota Master Naturalist Volunteer, you may use these items. Laws are in place to protect the animals. Play it safe — do not collect items from the wild, and work with a facility if you need something specific, including live animals, for a program you're doing (Figure 4).

Master Naturalist Chapters

The last piece in supporting you as a volunteer is your local Minnesota Master Naturalist Program chapter. We realize that some people view being a naturalist as a solitary experience involved in communing with nature. (Think of Henry David Thoreau at Walden Pond.) We also realize that humans are social animals

Figure 4. Many facilities have permits that cover volunteers using their live animals and natural items for education.

who enjoy interacting with one another (think of Thoreau's cabin being a ten-minute walk from town so he could have dinner with his friend Amos Bronson Alcott to discuss writing *Walden*). By having active, local chapters we support Master Naturalist Volunteers who want to meet one another and volunteer on projects together.

Chapters are a way for Minnesota Master Naturalist Program graduates and instructors to share their experiences with others in the program, enrich relationships with natural resource experts, cooperate in identifying local stewardship needs, and become more involved in environmental events and projects in their communities. They include groups of volunteers in an area who agree to abide by program standards and structures for meeting, fundraising, and operating.

Chapters consist of at least eight Minnesota Master Naturalist Volunteers who meet periodically for networking; sharing service projects, training, and volunteer opportunities; discussing group service projects; and planning field trips. Chapters typically meet at a naturalist-oriented host organization such as a nature center or state park. Chapter members may also meet to take field trips, perform volunteer service, listen to a guest speaker, or tour exhibits.

If you'd like to find out more about chapters in your area, sign in to the Minnesota Master Naturalist Program website and look under "About Us." You can have a casual affiliation with a chapter — for example, simply showing up for interesting events — or you may choose to be even more involved and become a leader in your region. If no chapter exists near you, you can start your own! We will be happy to connect you with other Master Naturalist Volunteers near you who might want to meet and find local sponsors.

Conclusion

The Minnesota Master Naturalist Program welcomes you. We hope this course has been interesting, useful, and fun. We encourage you to pursue volunteer opportunities, attend the annual conference, take advantage of advanced training, and join a chapter. If we can help you become a better volunteer, let us know how, and we will!

Minnesota Master Naturalist Volunteer Code of Ethics

The mission of the Minnesota Master Naturalist Program is to promote awareness, understanding, and stewardship of Minnesota's natural environment by developing a corps of well-informed citizens dedicated to conservation education and service within their communities.

Certified Minnesota Master Naturalist Volunteers promote responsible stewardship of Minnesota's natural resources. They look for opportunities to educate Minnesotans in an appreciation of how natural systems work and how we all depend on these natural systems. They recognize that one person cannot be an expert in every field. Master Naturalist Volunteers are resource people. If they do not have answers, they know where to find them.

When deciding whether an action is right or wrong, they should follow the guidance offered by Aldo Leopold in *A Sand County Almanac*:

> **"A thing is right when it tends to preserve the integrity, stability, and beauty of the biotic community. It is wrong when it tends otherwise."**

Minnesota Master Naturalist Volunteers will subscribe to the following standards when representing the program:

- Maintain high standards of integrity, conduct, service, and performance.
- Know and follow established program guidelines and policies. Be courteous and respectful of others and their views. Promote a spirit of cooperation in all activities.
- Act as trustworthy and ethical stewards of the environment.
- Encourage the use of current and sound scientific information in education and in management decisions.
- Do not use the Minnesota Master Naturalist Volunteer title or logo for personal profit.
- Promote and support the Minnesota Master Naturalist Program.

The University of Minnesota Board of Regents has a Code of Conduct that volunteers are required to adhere to. Please reference the code at http://regents.umn.edu/sites/default/files/policies/Code_of_Conduct.pdf.

If you have questions or concerns about how to represent the program, or to report violations of this code, please contact the program director at (888) 241-4532 or info@minnesotamasternaturalist.org.

Special thanks to the West Virginia Master Naturalist Program for permission to draw from its Standards of Conduct and Ethics.

Volunteer Hour Record Sheet

Use this form only if you are unable to enter your hours online yourself. Photocopy this page to record your additional hours. Please record your volunteer service hours on this sheet for the year and mail it to the Minnesota Master Naturalist Program Office by December 15. The staff will enter it into the database and you will receive a copy of your total hours for the year. Forty hours of service is required in a year to earn the pin for that year. All information must be entered into the database to determine the total number of hours.

NAME	
ADDRESS	
CITY STATE ZIP	
PHONE	EMAIL

1. VOLUNTEER SERVICE CATEGORY (CITIZEN SCIENCE, INTERPRETIVE, PROGRAM SUPPORT, STEWARDSHIP)
2. DATE OF SERVICE
3. CONTACT PERSON
4. SPONSORING ORGANIZATION AND ZIP CODE
5. PROJECT THEME AND DESCRIPTION
6. TOTAL ATTENDEES
7. AUDIENCE TYPE (YOUTH, ADULT, SENIOR, MIXED AGES)
8. PREP HOURS
9. TRAVEL HOURS
10. MILES TRAVELED
11. SERVICE HOURS
12. ZIP CODE OF LOCATION WHERE PROJECT CONDUCTED

ALL FORMS ARE DUE TO THE STATE PROGRAM OFFICE BY DECEMBER 15 OF EACH YEAR.
Send completed form to:
Minnesota Master Naturalist Program
University of Minnesota Extension Regional Office, Morris
46352 State Highway 329
Morris, MN 56267-0471

Explore

This section highlights groups and organizations dedicated to volunteering. Because volunteering is something you do, and not a place you go, this set of suggested explorations is offered just to get you thinking about volunteerism.

RSVP – Your Community, Minnesota

WHAT RSVP connects volunteers age 55 and over with service opportunities in their communities that match their skills and availability. More than 500,000 volunteers act as mentors, coaches, or companions to people in need or contribute their skills and expertise to community projects and organizations. They may build houses, immunize children, or help nonprofit organizations improve and protect the environment. RSVP is a part of Senior Corps, a program of the Corporation for National and Community Service.

WHEN Volunteer opportunities are available throughout the year.

WHERE Volunteer opportunities are available throughout Minnesota.

WHO The Corporation for National and Community Service, 1201 New York Avenue NW, Washington, DC 20525, (202) 606-5000

FOR MORE INFORMATION www.seniorcorps.gov/about/programs/rsvp.asp

Points of Light Institute – Anywhere, USA

WHAT The Points of Light Institute uses four dynamic enterprises to help people transform our world. The HandsOn Network mobilizes millions of people to take action, GenerationOn gives young people the opportunity to make change through service, AmeriCorps Alums works to support the next generation of service leaders, and Points of Light Corporate Institute works with companies to engage employees in volunteer service sector.

POINTS
OF LIGHT

WHEN Volunteer opportunities are available throughout the year.

WHERE Volunteer opportunities are available throughout the world.

WHO Points of Light Institute, 600 Means Street, Suite 210, Atlanta, GA 30318, (800) 865-8683

FOR MORE INFORMATION www.pointsoflight.org

Teach

MASTER NATURALIST TOOLBOX

This section features a lesson to help you determine what you would be good at doing as a volunteer, as well as what you would enjoy doing as a volunteer.

LESSON 1

Imagine the Perfect Volunteer Opportunity

Objectives

Participants will practice identifying services, knowledge, ideas, and resources they are willing to share as a volunteer.

Participants will explore a process for linking their personal volunteering preferences with organizations and people that can use them.

Participants will discuss strategies for managing various challenges to volunteer involvement.

Audience Type

Adult

Supplies

☐ 6 to 8 small sticky notes per participant
☐ Copy of "Identify Your Perfect Volunteer Opportunity" worksheet for each participant
☐ Copy of "Managing Challenges to Volunteering" worksheet for each participant
☐ Pen or pencil for each participant

Background

This activity will help you identify volunteer opportunities that excite you. It will also introduce you to ways to manage the challenges of sustained volunteering that you may encounter over time.

We will begin by assuming that your ideal volunteer opportunities spring from your own passions and motivations—the things you would happily give away simply for the personal joy of giving. To find your perfect volunteer opportunities, you simply need to find situations where your passions, motivations, and things you would happily give away will be most helpful to others. Volunteerism expert Ivan Scheier calls this the Mini-Max Principle: Make the minimum difference in what you want to do to have the maximum positive effect on other people. Uncovering these Mini-Max opportunities involves a process of considering your desires, abilities, needs, and who can help you get started.

Getting started and happily sustaining your volunteer activity can present a variety of challenges. Through our years of experience with volunteers, we have developed a volunteer service model. The model consists of three basic phases: recruiting, volunteering, and assessing. Each phase has multiple parts involving both the Minnesota Master Naturalist Volunteer and the Minnesota Master Naturalist Program (or the organization for which you volunteer).

The process of volunteering will be unique from one opportunity to the next and from one person to another. In some cases, it will evolve from your own searching or from prompts received from the Minnesota Master Naturalist Program via the weekly blog, Web postings, or emails notifying you of opportunities. As you grow in your involvement with the Minnesota Master Naturalist Program and its partners, you will move through the three phases and make adjustments as needed — maybe deciding to continue in a role you really enjoy, or stepping back and assessing to discover that you need to make a change to stay engaged. Regardless, it will be helpful to revisit the processes and strategies you develop in these activities to make sure you are feeling satisfied with your volunteer service choice.

Activity 1 - Introduction

1. Hand out pens/pencils and sticky notes and ask participants to divide their paper into two equal piles — one to record Glad Gives (things they would gladly give away) and the other to record Needs/Wants.

2. Instruct participants to mull over their personal experience, possessions, homes, jobs, etc. On the Glad Gives paper, they should write three or four services, ideas, information, resources, etc. — things they would be willing to give happily to another person (child care, mending, teaching sign language, car repair, etc.). On the Needs/Wants set of paper, they should write three or four resources, services, information, etc., that they would love someone to provide them to improve their lives (apples, a new stove, gardening information, etc.)

3. Ask participants to stick their Glad Gives on one wall, and their Needs/Wants on another.

    Provide time for participants to peruse the items taped on each wall. Ask if any are interested in accepting a Glad Give. Are any interested in fulfilling a Need/Want? Do any Glad Gives seem to fulfill something on the Needs/Wants wall? Match them up, share a few more and discuss. The goal of this activity is to spark a free-flowing exchange of Glad Gives and Needs/Wants. Therefore, it is fine if participants toss in a few Needs/Wants when you are sharing Glad Gives, and vice-versa. Challenge them to match seemingly obscure Glad Gives and Needs/Wants. For instance, a person in a class might be willing to give her teenage child (jokingly — sort of) and someone else might want housework done. This could be a great match!

4. Ask participants to describe the process they just went through. What worked well? Were their Needs/Wants unmet? Glad Gives? Who or what could meet the Needs/Wants or take the Glad Gives? Then ask them how their observations apply to identifying/getting involved in volunteering. What can we learn about volunteering from this experience?

5. Share Scheier's Mini-Max principle — "Make the minimum difference in what a person wants to do and can do which has the maximum positive impact on other people." How to identify the perfect volunteer opportunity? There is always someone out there who needs what you are gladly willing to give.

6. Use group discussion following the activity to process the results and then develop and apply broad conclusions.

MASTER
NATURALIST
TOOLBOX

Activity 2 - Identifying Volunteer Opportunities

1. Introduce the goal of the activity—working through the process of finding the perfect volunteer opportunity.

2. Hand out copies of the "Identify Your Perfect Volunteer Opportunity" worksheet. Briefly review each section of the chart with participants:

   When thinking through the perfect volunteer opportunity, you will need to think through your motivation for volunteering. Adult volunteers are motivated by three kinds of things: achievement, affiliation, and power/influence. Knowing which motivates you will help you to get connected to the best volunteer opportunity for you.

   ACHIEVEMENT can be defined as the desire to learn more, improve one's self, or help people or the environment. An example would be taking the initial Minnesota Master Naturalist Volunteer training to learn more about the biome in which you live or helping a child learn to appreciate nature.

   AFFILIATION is the connection between you and a program, agency, organization, or group. One example would be wishing to become an active nature center volunteer or wanting the credibility of saying you are a Minnesota Master Naturalist Volunteer.

   POWER/INFLUENCE involves putting yourself in a place where you are able to provide input that leads to change. Examples include contacting your elected official to offer information about an environmental issue, running for a seat on the park board, and using your knowledge/skills to make policy at your place of work more environmentally friendly.

3. Ask participants for a good example of a Glad Give or use one from the introduction. Use this example to work through the chart as a group. In large groups, it may be helpful to split into groups of three to five participants to work through the chart.

4. Discuss what works well or might be improved in this chart. It may be helpful to log improvements as a group using a PowerPoint slide or large printout. Hopefully, the brainstorming will result in a person to call to identify some opportunities.

Activity 3 – Managing Challenges to Volunteering

1. Introduce the goal of the activity — identifying strategies to overcome some of the challenges that can make volunteering seem difficult.

2. Hand out copies of the "Managing Challenges to Volunteering" worksheet. Briefly review each section of the chart with participants and have them summarize the following on the inside sectors of the chart:

   SATISFACTION THAT I SEEK To get the most out of volunteering, participants need to identify their passions and motivation, and consider how they expect the volunteer experience to satisfy them. In *The Call of Service: A Witness to Idealism*, Robert Coles describes a variety of satisfactions, including a social/physical impact, achieving a moral purpose, gaining personal affirmation, maintaining stoic endurance, and boosting success. Research on master gardeners has documented connectivity with like-minded individuals, status, and education. We have learned that Master Naturalist Volunteers gain from learning about, benefiting, and teaching others about nature. In addition, volunteering helps them stay connected to nature. We might add mitigating environmental concerns to the list. Satisfaction in volunteering can also come from personal growth, success in career, new friendships, etc. And we may look for different satisfactions from different volunteer opportunities. Surveys have shown that Master Naturalist Volunteer students come to a class with the primary motivation of gaining new knowledge, but find they enjoy the social aspect of the class as much as the actual content learning.

Volunteers may have a predetermined idea of what or where they will be volunteering, or they may come with no clue what they can or should do. The Minnesota Master Naturalist Program works to create connections between volunteers and those seeking volunteers. Ask yourself which of these options will work well for you.

Feedback is vital to any successful volunteer program. It allows volunteers to reflect on the work they're doing and to think about how it aligns with their motivations and personal goals. It also allows the host to assess the volunteer. Remember, every match is not made in heaven!! Sometimes the thing you think you wanted to do will turn out to be your worst nightmare. Volunteer feedback is the time and place for you to decide if you will continue in the role, find a new role, take a break, or exit the program entirely. No program will serve everyone's needs forever. If you are feeling like things are no longer a good fit for you, it is fine to move on to something else that better meets your needs.

A FOOT IN THE DOOR A county volunteer coordinator provided an example of this challenge when describing how hard it is for some Master Gardeners to stand up in front of a class the first time, or take the initiative to call a community education director even though they want to volunteer as an educator. It is tough to take the steps necessary to create opportunities and overcome our own trepidations. But, we will never get anywhere if we don't get a foot in the door.

GROWING WEARY After some time in a volunteering role, Cole contends we can grow weary or resigned. The role gets boring, or it seems like our goals will never be achieved.

GROWING CYNICAL Like weariness and resignation, Cole describes how volunteers can become cynical when working with disinterested or even opposing publics. This was clear in his affiliations with gender and cultural-rights activists. However, it seems to apply well in many natural resource conservation and education projects as well.

ARROGANCE AND BITTERNESS Again, Cole notes instances where experienced volunteers develop arrogance about their roles or bitterness toward those they serve or the people with whom they work. Imagine the volunteer who thinks the project or event could never succeed without her/him. No one else ever lives up to his or her expectations.

BATTLING BURNOUT Cole describes how those who get over-involved in volunteering or who let weariness/cynicism/bitterness fester can burnout.

3. Using the chart on the following pages, ask participants to describe some of the satisfactions they have gained from previous volunteering. Discuss why understanding these personal motivators are important. For instance, a person looking for connection

MASTER
NATURALIST
TOOLBOX

with like-minded individuals is unlikely to be satisfied in a volunteer opportunity that involves sitting alone and stuffing envelopes in a nonprofit office. Ideally, we want to find the opportunity that matches our preferences.

4. Focus on the "foot in the door" and "weariness" sectors. Brainstorm with participants some strategies for managing each. Discuss things that have worked for them in the past. (It may also be helpful to seed the audience with an experienced volunteer or two upon whom you can call to discuss these issues.) They can write strategies/resources/etc., in the areas outside of the sectors.

5. Discuss things that work well or might be improved in this chart. For instance, discuss ways the cycle reflects all of the things we tackle in life. Participants might be challenged to describe how the various sectors are interrelated. Does one really feed the next? Can burnout happen before weariness? Or without bitterness? It seems the cycle presents a holistic vision of volunteer challenges rather than a systematic list of challenges. Likewise, they will likely discover that many of the strategies to overcome these challenges are overlapping. Perhaps there is an essential set of strategies for maintaining energy as a volunteer? It may be helpful to log improvements as a group using a PowerPoint slide or large printout.

Activity 4 – Conclusion

1. Provide participants a few minutes to reflect on the experience and apply it to their future volunteering activities. What are the big lessons learned? How will this change the way participants look for and get involved in volunteer opportunities?

2. It is important to point out the singular direction of the activities; they help participants identify their passions and link them to worthwhile volunteer opportunities. However, there are also instances when we are asked to volunteer in pre-existing roles that may not fit exactly with our passions. What then? Ask if there is something satisfying there; is the focus of the event worthwhile, is the organization worth supporting, does this get a foot in the door? Understanding our motivations and satisfactions clearly prepares us to more easily answer this question.

Resources

Coles, R. (1993). *The call of service: A witness to idealism.* New York: Houghton Mifflin Company. Chapters 2, 3, and 4 describe kinds of volunteer service, different types of satisfaction for volunteers, and hazards of volunteering. Cole's hazards form the basis of the volunteer challenge cycle and inform the process of identifying preferences.

Laughlin, S. (1990). *The challenge of working with extenders.* Journal of Extension, 28(3). www.joe.org/joe/1990fall/f1.html.

Rohs, F. R., Stribling, J. H., Westerfield, R. R. 2002. *What Personally Attracts Master Volunteers to the Master Gardener Program?* Journal of Extension, 40(4). www.joe. org/joe/2002august/rb5.shtml.

Scheier, I. (1981). *The new people approach handbook.* Boulder, CO: Yellowfire Press. Available online at academic.regis.edu/volunteer/ivan/. Chapters 3 and 4 of this book inform the process of identifying personal passions and linking adapted for the introduction to this presentation.

Wolford, M., Cox, K., and Kulp, K.. 2001. *Effective motivators for Master Volunteer Program Development.* Journal of Extension, 39(2). www.joe.org/joe/2001april/rb4. html

Identify Your Perfect Volunteer Opportunity Worksheet

Based on Ivan Scheier's *The New People Approach Handbook*.
Available online at http://academic.regis.edu/volunteer/ivan/

DESIRE	ABILITY	NEED	LINKING	CONTACTS
What I enjoy doing	What I know that helps me do what I like doing well (information, ideas, skills, resources)	What I need to learn in order to do what I like doing well	How what I like doing can help others	Who can help me get started doing what I enjoy

Managing Challenges to Volunteering Worksheet

Based on Robert Coles' *The Call to Service: A Witness to Idealism*. New York: Houghton Mifflin Co. 1994

VOLUNTEER PHASE	STRATEGIES TO MANAGE CHALLENGES
Satisfaction That I Seek	
Getting a Foot in the Door	
Growing Weary	
Growing Cynical	
Arrogance and Bitterness	
Battling Burnout	

Conserve

This section highlights organizations that offer opportunities and training for Minnesota Master Naturalist Volunteers to volunteer (think: your Minnesota Master Naturalist Chapter!) Please visit the websites to learn more.

Volunteer.gov

This site coordinates volunteer opportunities for many of the agencies that manage federal lands, including the U.S. Army Corps of Engineers, USFS, Bureau of Land Management, U.S. Geological Survey, U.S. Fish and Wildlife Service, National Park Service, U.S. Bureau of Reclamation, and Natural Resources Conservation Service. You can find a list of volunteer program managers for the various agencies at www.volunteer. gov/gov/contactList.cfm. Opportunities in Minnesota include conducting living history at the Grand Portage National Monument and being a campground host at the Cross Lake Recreation Area.

www.volunteer.gov/gov

Minnesota DNR Volunteer Programs

The DNR sponsors dozens of volunteer programs and has thousands of volunteering opportunities ranging from working in scientific and natural areas to instructing enforcement education programs. Sign up at www.mndnr.gov/volunteering to receive notification about volunteer opportunities.

www.mndnr.gov/volunteering

Expand

This section suggests some things you can use, do, pursue, read, or join to develop as a naturalist.

Journal

EXPERIENCE Invite a friend to join you in a visit to your special spot. Give your friend a tour of the observations you've made.

REFLECT How does it feel to condense your experience of your special spot into a brief "show and tell" for another person? How is your experience of your spot different when another person is present? What did/can you do to help the person understand what the special spot means to you?

RECORD Write a few questions an interviewer visiting your spot should ask you — questions whose answers will reveal the most important insights you've made about your site. Answer your questions.

Read

Principles and Practices for Nonprofit Excellence

2014. St. Paul: Minnesota Council of Nonprofits. 38 pp.

This publication, available for download at www.minnesotanonprofits.org, provides tools and rules to help nonprofit staff and board members work efficiently and effectively.

Surf

The Free Management Library

This site has a large selection of materials for developing and managing volunteer programs. Go here if you are thinking of starting a Minnesota Master Naturalist Program Chapter!

www.managementhelp.org

Energize: Especially for Leaders of Volunteers

Energize is a consulting firm that helps organizations work with volunteers. It also has a fabulous inventory of free online publications covering topics such as volunteer recruitment, training, and evaluation.

www.energizeinc.com

Expand

Join

Alliance of Natural Resource Outreach and Service Programs

The Alliance of Natural Resource Outreach and Service Programs (ANROSP) is the national organization that supports the development of master naturalist programs. Although ANROSP's membership consists mainly of statewide programs and their managers (including the Minnesota Master Naturalist Program), individuals can also join.

ANROSP
Alliance of Natural Resource Outreach and Service Programs

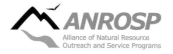

anrosp.org

Amherst H. Wilder Foundation

The Amherst H. Wilder Foundation is a nonprofit health and human services organization that has served the greater St. Paul area since 1906. It operates dozens of programs that help children succeed in school, older adults remain independent, troubled youth create healthy futures, and individuals and families maintain long-term housing. Although not directly related to natural resources and conservation, its catalog of publications and often-free workshops are dedicated to the good management and operation of all nonprofits.

AMHERST H. WILDER FOUNDATION
Here for good.

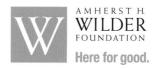

www.wilder.org

Copyrighted Photographs and Images Used With Permission

Figure 1. Courtesy of James Pointer, Minnesota Department of Natural Resources

Figure 2. Courtesy of John Loegering, University of Minnesota

Figure 3. Courtesy of the Minnesota Master Naturalist Program

Figure 4. Courtesy of Dawn A. Flinn, Minnesota Department of Natural Resources

MASTER NATURALIST TOOLBOX

Appendix

Minnesota Maps

BIOMES

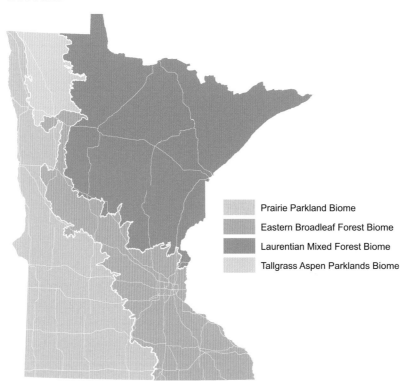

Prairie Parkland Biome

Eastern Broadleaf Forest Biome

Laurentian Mixed Forest Biome

Tallgrass Aspen Parklands Biome

MAJOR LAKES

Lake of
the Woods

Rainy Lake

Kabetogama Lake

Upper Red Lake

Lower Red Lake

Lake
Vermilion

Cass
Lake

Lake
Winnibigoshish

Lake Superior

Leech
Lake

Mille Lacs
Lake

CITIES

Hallock

Roseau

Baudette

International Falls

Warren

Thief River Falls

Red Lake Falls

Crookston

Grand Marais

Bagley

Bemidji

Ada

Mahnomen

Grand Rapids

Moorhead

Walker

Two Harbors

Park Rapids

Duluth

Detroit Lakes

Carlton

Breckenridge

Wadena

Aitkin

Fergus Falls

Brainerd

Elbow Lake

Long Prairie

Little Falls

Mora

Wheaton

Alexandria

Pine City

Milaca

Glenwood

Foley

Cambridge

Morris

Benson

St. Cloud

Center City

Ortonville

Elk River

Buffalo

Willmar

Litchfield

Anoka

Madison

Minneapolis

Stillwater

Montevideo

Glencoe

St. Paul

Granite Falls

Olivia

Chaska

Hastings

Redwood Falls

Shakopee

Ivanhoe

Gaylord

Red Wing

Marshall

St. Peter

Wabasha

New Ulm

Le Center

Faribault

Pipestone

Mankato

Waseca

Owatonna

Winona

Slayton

St. James

Dodge Center

Rochester

Luverne

Windom

Albert Lea

Austin

Preston

Caledonia

Worthington

Jackson

Fairmont

Blue Earth

NATIONAL FORESTS

Chippewa National Forest

Superior National Forest

Superior National Forest

RIVERS

Red Lake

Vermilion

Big Fork

Little Fork

Mississippi

Cloquet

Lake Superior Water Trail

Crow Wing

Kettle

Ottertail

Snake

Long Prairie

Rum

Pomme de Terre

Sauk

Chippewa

St. Croix

Redwood

Minnesota

Cannon

Cottonwood

Zumbro

Whitewater

Watonwan

Straight

Des Moines

Root

STATE FORESTS

Northwest Angle

Lost River

Lake of the Woods

Smokey Bear

Beltrami Island

Pine Island

Kabetogama

Red Lake

Koochiching

Burntside

Insula Lake

Grand Portage

Big Fork

Bear Island

Pat Bayle

Lake Isabella

Buena Vista

Blackduck

Sturgeon River

Finland

Mississippi Headwaters

Bowstring

White Earth

Welsh Lake

Cloquet Valley

Smoky Hills

Two Inlets

Battleground

Whiteface River

Badoura

Remer

Savanna

Huntersville

Foot Hills

Emily

Fond Du Lac

Lyons

Waukenabo

Pillsbury

Solana

Nemadji

Wealthwood

D.A.R.

St. Croix

Rum River

Chengwatana

Birch Lakes

Sand Dunes

R J D Memorial Hardwood

STATE PARKS

- Garden Island
- Zippel Bay
- Lake Bronson
- Hayes Lake
- Franz Jevne
- Old Mill
- Big Bog
- Red River
- Grand Portage
- Judge C.R. Magney
- Soudan Underground Mine
- Bear Head Lake
- Scenic
- McCarthy Beach
- Cascade River
- Lake Bemidji
- Temperance River
- George Crosby Manitou
- Hill Annex Mine
- Tettegouche
- Itasca
- Schoolcraft
- Split Rock Lighthouse
- Gooseberry Falls
- Buffalo River
- Savanna Portage
- Maplewood
- Jay Cooke
- Cuyuna Country
- Glendalough
- Moose Lake
- Crow Wing
- Father Hennepin
- Lake Carlos
- Mille Lacs Kathio
- Banning
- Charles A. Lindbergh
- St. Croix
- Big Stone Lake
- Glacial Lakes
- Wild River
- Monson Lake
- Sibley
- Lake Maria
- Interstate
- William O'Brien
- Lac qui Parle
- Greenleaf Lake
- St. Croix Islands
- Fort Snelling
- Upper Sioux Agency
- Afton
- Minnesota Valley
- Camden
- Fort Ridgely
- Frontenac
- Flandrau
- Nerstrand Big Woods
- Lake Shetek
- Sakatah Lake
- John A. Latsch
- Minneopa
- Carley
- Whitewater
- Split Rock Creek
- Rice Lake
- Great River Bluffs
- Blue Mounds
- Kilen Woods
- Myre Big Island
- Beaver Creek Valley
- Lake Louise
- Forestville/Mystery Cave

SCIENTIFIC AND NATIONAL AREAS

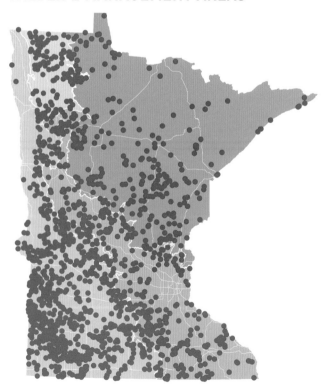

WILDLIFE MANAGEMENT AREAS

Glossary

abiotic: those aspects of a system pertaining to non-living features

acclimate: the process of an individual organism adjusting to environmental changes within its lifetime

adaptation: a trait favored by the process of natural selection because it improves an organism's chances of surviving and reproducing in its habitat

amygdule: the mineral-filled holes of igneous extrusive rocks

anoxia: the absence of oxygen from an environment

archaea: organisms with no cell nucleus

assemblage: a group of associated organism populations that exist in the same region at the same time

ATP (adenosine triphosphate): a molecule that captures, holds, and then releases energy to power cells

auxospore: a shellless stage in diatom sexual reproduction that restores the offspring to the maximum size and shape for that species of diatom

bag limits: a regulation regarding the maximum number of animals an individual may catch, kill, and keep within a specified time period

basalt: a gray to bluish igneous extrusive rock made up of crystals undetectable to the human eye that may have holes and amygdules

bathymetry: the bottom profile of a body of water

bedrock: the rock that we see at the surface of the Earth or that lies immediately beneath the soil

benthic: organisms that feed off bits of organic material that sink to the bottom of a lake

benthos: the organic material that sinks to the bottom of a lake

bioaccumulate: the accumulation of pollutants in living creatures as one organism eats another and takes in its contaminants.

biological diversity: the variety of species within a specified geographic region, the variability among living organisms on earth

biomass: organic plant or animal material

bryophytes: land plants that do not have true vascular tissue

camouflage: a way animals or plants blend into their environment

canopy: the combined cover from the top layers of trees in a forested area

carnivore: animals that eat other animals to gain energy

carrion: the decomposing remains of an animal

carrying capacity: the maximum population level that can be supported by available resources

cellulose: an important component of plant cell walls; only animals with special enzymes may digest it

chemical defense: toxins or poisons used by plants to defend themselves from predation; sometimes these chemicals are called plant secondary compounds

chlorophyll: a molecule that can trap the sun's energy and then use it in a chemical reaction, usually found in chloroplasts

chloroplasts: cell structures composed of chlorophyll that trap and transform the sun's energy into a form organisms can use

clear-cutting: a harvest method used to regenerate tree species that need full sunlight—typically species that regenerate after a catastrophic fire

climax community: a stable state in an ecosystem reached after the ecosystem has passed through a series of successional states; this stable state is often an area of mature growth, as in a "climax forest."

competition: the struggle between organisms for resources, mates, and niches

consumer: an organism that relies on other organisms for sustenance and energy (e.g., animals and fungi). In a classic food chain, primary consumers eat plants (producers), secondary consumers eat primary consumers, and tertiary consumers eat secondary consumers

corvid: a family of birds (which includes jays, crows, and ravens) known for their intelligence, problem-solving ability, and propensity to eat many kinds of food

craton: a stable piece of the Earth's crust

cyanobacteria: blue-green colored bacteria that derive their energy from photosynthesis

decomposer: organisms that eat dead things and break down organic material

desiccate: to dry up

dikes: igneous rock formations that develop in cracks in rock layers

disturbance: a short-term change of environmental conditions that can alter succession in an ecosystem's plant community (e.g., fire, flood, wind, human activity).

duff: a layer of fallen needles found in forested regions, sometimes several inches thick

ecology: the study of the abundance and distribution of organisms and their interactions with each other and with their environment

ecosystem: a unit consisting of all living things in an area, the non-living physical and chemical factors in their environment, and the processes and flows that connect them

enzyme: catalysts for complex biochemical reactions

epilimnion: the top layer of a thermally stratified lake, with the warmest, most oxygen-rich water

erosion: the wearing away of a surface—rock, soil, or other—by wind, rain, sun, gravity, or ice

eutrophic: highly productive nutrient-enriched lakes that have high levels of nitrogen, phosphorus, and other nutrients. Eutrophic conditions can cause algae

blooms that deplete oxygen levels in the water, causing die-off of lake organisms and poor water quality

evapotranspiration: the combined effect of moisture lost from the soil due to evaporation and that lost through plant transpiration

extrusive: igneous rocks that have risen to the surface of the Earth and cooled quickly

facilitation: a method of forest climate adaption in which desirable species are planted where they do not yet grow

fen: a type of peatland with boglike characteristics, although, unlike bogs, it is fed by water flowing in from the surrounding watershed

food web: a depiction of the network of energy flows among organisms at various trophic levels within an ecosystem

forbs: nonwoody flowering plants other than sedges, grasses, and rushes

forest floor: the lowest layer of the forest, below the herb layer, often composed of decomposers and duff

frustules: diatom shells that are riddled with holes that allow nutrients, gases, and waste products to pass through

gneiss: a metamorphic rock with visible bands shaped from the high pressure present during its formation.

group selection: a forest management technique in which small groups of trees, rather than individual trees, are harvested

habitat: the natural or "home" environment where an organism lives or grows

herb layer: a layer of the forest composed of seedlings, grasses, and forbs that provide food and habitat for mice, chipmunks, insects, frogs, and more

herbaceous: a type of plant that lacks a continuous woody stem above ground

herbivore: organisms that gain energy by eating plants

horticultural: the field of study related to the growing of plants

hummock: a mound of earth that rises above a bog or marsh

hydrologic cycle: the cycle of water through bodies of water, organisms, and the atmosphere via evaporation, condensation, and precipitation

hypolimnion: the bottom layer of a thermally stratified lake, with colder water and nutrients released by decomposing matter on the lake bottom.

igneous rock: a type of rock formed when magma cools

interglacial: a warmer time within periods of glaciation.

interspecific: a form of competition where members of a species compete with individuals from other species

intraspecific: a form of competition where members of the same species compete between one another

intrusive: igneous rocks that remain under the surface of the Earth and cool slowly

invasive: a non-native species that is transported to a new area and may cause economic or environmental harm

isostatic rebound: the process of reestablishing a previous state after an extended depression, usually caused by the weight of a glacier

laker: a domestic cargo ship

legume: a plant in the pea family

lenticel: the dark spots on trees such as birch that allow an exchange of air between layers of the tree through the relatively impermeable skin

lignin: a structural support material for plants

limiting nutrients: nutrients that determine the amount of plant growth that can take place

lycophytes: a plant group including quillworts, spike mosses, and clubmosses

macroinvertebrates: animals that are large enough to be seen with the naked eye, have no backbone, and spend part of their life cycle at the bottom of a lake; includes aquatic insects, mites, worms, snails, and crayfish

management plan: a formal collection of goals with the associated steps necessary to actualize them

mantle: the fluid layer between the Earth's core and the outer crust.

marsh: a wetland with standing or slow-flowing water

mechanical defense: structures on the exterior of a plant that protect against consumption by other organisms

mélange: a mixture of rock fragments formed from tectonic forces

mesic: a habitat with a balanced amount of moisture

mesotrophic: lakes that contain moderate quantities of nutrients and are moderately productive in terms of aquatic, animal, and plant life; falls between oligotrophic and eutrophic

metalimnion: the transitional middle layer of a thermally stratified lake, where temperature decreases rapidly as water depth increases

metamorphic rock: rocks formed by the pressure and heat below the Earth's surface

metamorphosis: the transformation of the form of an organism

mid-story: the middle layer of the forest, often filled with understory trees

migration: the movement of animals to areas where food and other resources are available

minerals: naturally occurring substances made up of inorganic matter (not derived from living things) with a specific chemical composition, such as quartz

mutualism: a relationship between two organisms in which both benefit, a +/+ interaction

neascus: a parasite that makes some fish fillets look like they've been sprinkled with pepper

nitrogenases: enzymes that allow some microorganisms to take nitrogen from the atmosphere and convert it to a form that is usable by other organisms

nutrients: the components of food necessary for the survival and growth of an organism

oligotrophic: clear, nutrient-poor, less-productive lakes that are free of aquatic plants and algal blooms, yet rich in dissolved oxygen

omnivore: an organism that can derive energy and nutrients from both plants and animals

orogeny: a deformation of the Earth's crust by tectonic forces that may result in mountain formation

paludification: the transformation of a forested area into a bog

parasitism: a relationship between two organisms in which only the parasite benefits, a +/- interaction; the interaction differs from predation in that parasites usually don't kill their host in one fell swoop

peatland: wet areas composed mainly of sphagnum moss in which the vegetation decomposes more slowly than it grows

photosynthesis: the process by which plants, algae, and cyanobacteria transform the sun's energy into a form that is useful for themselves and other living things

phytoplankton: tiny plants that make up the base of the lake's food web

piscivore: a creature that specializes in eating fish; e.g., game fish, birds, and animals outside the aquatic environment

plate tectonics: the scientific theory describing the convergence, divergence, and transformation of large parts of the Earth's crust

population: the total amount of a certain type of organism in a specific area

population monitoring: estimating the overall size of a species' population by counting individual animals or locating scats, tracks, nests, and so on, to provide data for management decisions

precipitate: solidify from a solution

predator: an organism that consumes other organisms for energy

prey: an organism hunted and eaten by predators

producer: an organism that captures the sun's energy and converts it into energy for its own biological functions; usually this process occurs through photosynthesis

radiometric dating: a process that uses the abundance of radioactive isotopes to determine the age of various materials

regolith: a collection of loose rock and other matter that is on top of bedrock

residence time: in hydrology, the amount of time that a molecule of water stays in a specific state

resilience: a method of forest protection that boosts a forest's ability to cope with climate change by diversifying tree species and ages

revegetate: the process of recovering an area in vegetation

rhizomes: modified underground stems from which more plants may sprout

rift lake: a lake formed from the sinking of the Earth's surface caused by tectonic forces

secchi disk: a black and white circular disk used to measure water transparency

sedimentary rock: rocks formed from compacted sediment, plants, shells, or minerals through the processes of pressure or evaporation

seiche: the sloshing motion of water back and forth across a basin

serotinous: a type of plant species that has seeds or cones that lie dormant for long periods and require exposure to fire to open; forests that rely on fire as part of their reproductive cycle

shelterwood cut: a forest management technique in which a forester marks specific trees for removal over a period of years to increase the vigor and seed production of the remaining trees and establish an even-aged stand over time

shrub layer: a forest layer composed of saplings and smaller woody plants and inhabited by insects and browsers

sills: igneous rock formations that form in cracks running parallel to the rock layers

size limits (slot limit): the setting of a maximum or minimum weight or length of a species, usually fish, that may be caught and kept in order to protect smaller or larger individuals; a slot limit defines a range of sizes of fish that are protected (i.e., fish that are within the length range must be immediately returned to the water) or unprotected and thus may be harvested

slash: piles of dry brush and stumps left behind by logging

sphagnum: a moisture-loving moss, often found in bogs

stratification: the process through which water layers of different densities form in lakes, often seasonally by the effects of temperature

stromatolite: structures that form in shallow water when cyanobacteria or other microorganisms trap sedimentary grains and cement them together.

subduct: the process by which a tectonic plate moves underneath another plate on contact

succession: one community of plants replacing another as an ecosystem matures

symbiosis: a mutually beneficial relationship between organisms

tension zone: an area where the edges of major weather systems, soil systems, and geology all come together

terrestrialization: the process by which a body of water fills with sediments

thermocline: the temperature gradient in the metalimnion

till: a mixture of rock and other material left over after glacial movement through a region

torpor: a brief state of lowered body temperature and heart, respiration, and metabolic rates in winter, experienced by small mammals

trophic levels: the different nutritive layers of a food chain or food web

turbid: the cloudiness of water

vermin: animal or insect species that are considered a nuisance

voyageur: trader who used the interconnected lakes of the North Woods, Great Lakes region as a means of transportation

watershed: the land area that drains into a body of water

wildlife management: the application of scientific knowledge and technical skills to influence animals' habitat, behavior, and abundance

zooplankton: tiny aquatic herbivores (such as daphnia, copepods, or larval fish) that are primary consumers in the aquatic food web

Acronyms

ADDIE– Analyze, Design, Develop, Implement, Evaluate

ANROSP – Alliance of Natural Resource Outreach and Service Programs

AOCs – Areas of Concern

BWCAW – Boundary Waters Canoe Area Wilderness

CLMP – Citizen Lake Monitoring Program

D.C. - District of Columbia

DNA – Deoxyribonucleic Acid

DNR – Department of Natural Resources

ECS – Ecological Classification System

EPA – Environmental Protection Agency

GPS – Global Positioning System

IJC – International Joint Commission

MAEE – Minnesota Association for Environmental Education

MDH – Minnesota Department of Health

MN – Minnesota

MNA – Minnesota Naturalists' Association

MNgage – Minnesota Volunteer Precipitation Observing Program

MPCA – Minnesota Pollution Control Agency

NAAEE – North American Association for Environmental Education

NAI – National Association for Interpretation

NOAA – National Oceanic and Atmospheric Administration

NRCS – Natural Resources Conservation Service

SNA – Scientific & Natural Areas

TCA – Tree Care Advocate

TNC – The Nature Conservancy

TPL – Trust for Public Land

USDA – United States Department of Agriculture

USFS – United States Forest Service

WET – Water Education for Teachers

YMCA - Young Men's Christian Association

ZIP – Zone Improvement Plan

Index

Symbols

A

B

Minnesota Loon Monitoring Program (MLMP) 110
Minnesota Master Naturalist logo 283
Minnesota Master Naturalist Program 8, 25
Minnesota Master Naturalist Volunteer 7, 8
Minnesota Master Naturalist Volunteer Code of Ethics 285
Minnesota Mineland Reclamation Act of 1969 255
Minnesota Naturalists' Association 23
Minnesota Pollution Control Agency (MPCA) 195, 212
Minnesota Steamship Company 230
Minnesota Tree Care Advocate 82
Minnesota Volunteer Precipitation Observing Program (MNgage) 46
Mississippi River 71, 120, 132, 135, 183, 197, 232, 250
Mississippi watershed 183
Molts 90
Moonworts 54
Moose 5, 11, 40, 55, 58, 65, 85, 88, 91, 99, 101, 110, 112, 126, 130, 131, 157, 173, 191, 197, 198, 246, 252
Moose Lake 252
Moose Lake Agate and Geological Interpretive Center 40
Moosewatch Expedition 110
Moraine 35
Mosquitoes 64, 87, 93
Mosses 53, 54, 55, 64, 67, 68, 82, 96, 305
Mountain maple 64
Muir, John 7
Muskrat 94
Mutualism 131, 132, 305
Mycorrhizae associations 267
Mycorrhizal fungi 57, 59, 66, 131

N

Namekagen River 226
Nashville warbler 95, 96
National Association for Interpretation (NAI) 181
National Map Corps 46
National Oceanic and Atmospheric Administration (NOAA) 264
Native earthworms 267
Natural history 8
Naturalist 7, 15
Natural Resources Conservation Service 46
Nature Conservancy 82
Neascus 126, 305
Needs/Wants 289
Nerstrand State Park 51
Nested grid 138
Niche 99, 121, 127
Nipigon River 222
Nitrogen 58, 59, 66, 115, 119, 122, 123, 125, 134, 142, 186, 187, 226, 246, 304, 305
nitrogenases 123, 305
Nitrogen Cycle 123
Non-native species 106, 231, 232, 234, 235, 260, 261, 262, 305

North American Association for Environmental Education (NAAEE) 181
Northern blue flag 205, 208, 216
Northern bog lemming 95
Northern leopard frog 94
Northern pike 142, 143, 145, 146, 188, 190, 194, 230
Northern red oak 52, 64, 94
Northern rough-winged swallow 96
Northern waterthrush 96
Northern white cedar 56, 88, 95, 96
Northland Arboretum 136
North Shore Commercial Fishing Museum 238
North West Company 248
Nova Group 233
Nute, Grace Lee 258
Nutrients 53, 54, 55, 59, 62, 63, 64, 66, 67, 89, 117, 119, 123, 125, 126, 130, 131, 134, 141, 142, 144, 145, 186, 187, 188, 189, 192, 202, 206, 218, 221, 226, 233, 234, 267, 304, 305, 306
Nymph 87

O

Oak savannas 261
Oberhauser, Karen S. 3, 5, 115
Oberholtzer, Ernest 258
Ogallala aquifer 233
Ogoki Diversion 233
Ogoki River 233
Ojibwe 238, 245, 246, 247, 248, 249, 265, 275
Oligotrophic 187, 188, 226, 305
Olive-sided flycatcher 95, 96
Olson, Sigurd F. 7, 16, 17, 18, 22, 156, 257, 258, 274
Omnivore 89, 99, 117, 129, 203, 204, 205, 306
Orchids 54, 57, 66
Orogeny 30, 31, 32, 42, 306
Orr Bog Walk 198
Ovenbird 94, 95, 96
Overturn. *See* Turnover
Ox-eye daisy 57

P

Paleozoic Era 34
Palisade Head 39, 42, 225, 237
Palladium 254, 257
Palm warbler 205, 207, 215
Paludification 184, 185, 306
Pangaea 34
Paper birch 53, 58, 62, 94
Parasites 91, 93, 130, 131, 226, 306
Parasitism 128, 129, 130, 306
Pathogens 233
Peat 55, 184, 193
Peatland 36, 66, 67, 95, 306
    Acid Peatland 66
    Forested Rich Peatland 66
    Open Rich Peatland 67

Peatland Shrubs
    red-osier dogwood 64
    willow 57, 71, 89, 118
Peat moss 54
Permian period 34
Pharmaceuticals 233
Phenology 13, 155
Phosphorus 66, 119, 142, 186, 187, 188, 189, 226, 304
Photosynthesis 31, 116, 117, 123, 124, 142, 185, 187, 304, 306
Phycobilisomes 116
Phytoplankton 56, 117, 126, 142, 144, 145, 187, 188, 221, 306
Pickerelweed 58, 206
Pictured Rocks National Park 225
Pileated woodpecker 94, 96
Pillbugs 64
Pincushion moss 54
Pine 9, 12, 19, 51, 53, 54, 55, 56, 62, 63, 64, 65, 68, 71, 88, 90, 92, 95, 101, 102, 128, 129, 130, 132, 136, 175, 176, 183, 230, 250, 251, 252, 261
Pine marten 12, 90, 101, 102
Pine siskin 95, 96
piscivore 126, 306
Pitcher plant 54, 57, 192
Pitcher plant mosquito 205, 210, 216
Pittsburgh Steamship Company 230
Plant Community 66
plate tectonics 30, 32, 34, 306
Platinum 254, 257
Points of Light Institute 287
Pollinators 57, 132, 134, 263
Pollutants 218, 232, 233, 234, 303
Pollution 195, 233
Polychlorinated byphenols (PCBs) 233
Polypody. *See* Herbaceous plants
Polytrichum mosses 54
Pondweeds 58
Population 64, 65, 88, 91, 97, 101, 106, 121, 128, 129, 131, 133, 206, 226, 230, 234, 235, 249, 260, 261, 263, 269, 303, 306
Porcupine 95
Powder River Coal Company 232
Powwows 246, 247
Prairie Parkland 10
precipitate 306
Predation 65, 128, 129, 130, 143, 303, 306
Predator 306
Predators 61, 65, 89, 90, 106, 127, 129, 130, 142, 143, 144, 145, 146, 177, 190, 192, 194, 220, 235, 260, 306
Prey 306
Primary consumers 117
Principles of Interpretation 160
Producer 117, 118, 119, 126, 141, 142, 188, 203, 204, 205, 221, 304, 306
Proglacial lakes 36
Program Support 279, 282, 286
Project Learning Tree (PLT) 179, 281
Project WET 179, 281
Project WILD 179, 281
Proterozoic Eon 31